New York Convention
To Know Itself in China

主编◎张玉林　周立新

纽约公约
在中国见证成长

上册 Book I

新华出版社

图书在版编目（CIP）数据

纽约公约：在中国见证成长．上册／张玉林，周立新主编．

北京：新华出版社，2024.6.

ISBN 978-7-5166-7439-0

Ⅰ．D997.4

中国国家版本馆 CIP 数据核字第 202466W6R3 号

纽约公约：在中国见证成长．上册

主编： 张玉林　周立新

出版发行： 新华出版社有限责任公司

（北京市石景山区京原路 8 号　邮编：100040）

印刷： 三河市君旺印务有限公司

成品尺寸： 170mm×240mm 1/16	**印张：** 11.25　**字数：** 160 千字
版次： 2024 年 7 月第 1 版	**印次：** 2024 年 7 月第 1 次印刷
书号： ISBN 978-7-5166-7439-0	**定价：** 58.00 元（上下册）

微店　　视频号小店　　抖店　　京东旗舰店　　请加我的企业微信

微信公众号　　喜马拉雅　　小红书　　淘宝旗舰店　　扫码添加专属客服

编者按

2022 年 7 月，全世界都在经历欧洲俄乌战争的至暗时刻，北京大学暑期学校开设了一门独特的法律英语暑期课程。该课程的重点是平实的法律英语写作，学生们学习如何在国际商事仲裁领域使用通俗易懂的英语进行法律写作。

课程结束后，一群热爱法律英语写作的学生在指导老师 Dr. Zhang 的提议下，在纽约公约项目中继续进行写作。

本书主要由该暑期课程的学生写作作品汇编而成，他们来自北京大学、上海交通大学、华南师范大学、复旦大学等。各章节作者除暑期课程的学生外，还包括非诉纠纷解决程序领域的法律英语践行者，包括来自中国当地的律师事务所、仲裁法学会、仲裁委员会和学界的朋友。

本书的基本主题是：1987 年，《联合国承认及执行外国仲裁裁决公约》（《纽约公约》）通过中国加入该公约的方式来到中华大地，并从此逐渐被认为是中国国际仲裁制度的顶梁柱之一。至出版之日，中国加入《纽约公约》已有 36 年。这 36 年里，中国经济改革和发展的超越性增长同步腾飞，亦见证了《纽约公约》所载明的国际仲裁理念在中国的植入和成长。

本书通过考察特定的法律领域和法律英语写作的发展，旨在传播关于国际商事仲裁概念的通识性知识，以及对于某一领域内法律发展的成功取决于该特定领域对诸如《纽约公约》等国际公约规则的相互承认和执行的认知。

本书各章的起草是以简洁英文写作方式首先完成，所以"脚注"都在英文版中注明。有关中文版的相应脚注，除特别标明的外，读者可从英文版中查找并阅读。

我们感谢暑期课程的所有参与者，以及所有通过艰苦的研究与写作实践支持这一纽约公约写作项目的非诉纠纷解决程序领域的朋友们。特别感谢联合编辑和协助编辑，是他们的帮助将这本书从项目变成现实。

感谢的话也要送给我们的战友们，包括贸仲、中国仲裁法学研究会和法律英语教学与测试研究会的同人们，是你们的持之以恒造就了一大批对国际仲裁和英语实践孜孜不倦的学子们！真诚地感谢你们的坚持和执着！

张玉林　博　士

周立新　大律师

Editor's Note

In July 2022, while the world was experiencing hard times , a unique legal English summer course (the "Summer Course") was offered to students across the region at Peking University. The course focused on legal writing in plain English. Students were taught how to do legal writing in plain English in the field of international commercial arbitration.

After the course was completed, some students who love legal writing kept on the momentum of the New York Convention Writing Project as proposed by the instructor Dr. Jerry Zhang.

This book is primarily the compendium of the writing work of the summer students of that course. Students are from Peking University, Shanghai Jiaotong University, South China Normal University and Fudan University, etc. In addition to the student chapters there are also chapters from legal English writing practitioners from the ADR field including friends from Chinese law firms, Chinese arbitration law academy, Chinese arbitration commissions, and university teachers.

The essential theme of this book is that the 1958 United Nations Convention on the Recognition and Enforcement of Foreign Arbitral Awards (the "New York Convention") came to China by way of China's accession to the Convention in 1987 and has gradually been acknowledged as one of the backbones of China's international arbitration system ever since. At the time of publication, 36 years have passed since China became a member state of the New York Convention. This thirty—six year paralleled the spectacular growth of China's economic reform and development in China and we witnessed the implantation and growth of the concept of international arbitration in China enshrined under the New York Convention.

Through looking at a specific area of law and development in legal English writing, this book aims to enhance public knowledge about the concept of international commercial arbitration and the appreciation that success of the development of law in a certain area depends on mutuality of recognition and enforcement of the rules of the international convention such as the New York Convention in international arbitration.

The chapters were first drafted in simple legal English. All footnotes were inserted into the English texts. Except otherwise noted, readers may look for the corresponding footnotes of the Chinese version from the

English version and read the footnotes from there.

We are thankful to all participants of the Summer Course, and all friends from the ADR field who supported this New York Convention Writing Project through the diligent and meticulous practice of research and writing. Special thanks go to the co−editors and assistant editors who helped transform this book from project into reality.

Words of great gratitude will also go to our colleagues and friends and leaders from Peking university, China International Econmic and Trade Arbitration Commission(CIETAC), China Academy of Arbitration Law(CALL) and CAAL' s Legal English Teaching and Testing Commission. It is your years of persistence and tenacity that teaches and cultivates groups of legal English users and international arbitration practitioners who are fluent in legal English and Chinese. For this, we extend our sincere gratitude!

List of Contributors

Preface (Part 1):   Yuan Yifan 袁一凡 (PKU SFL)

Preamble (Part 1):   Tan Jian 谭剑 (CAAL)

Preface (Part 2):   Wang Chengjie 王承杰 (CIETAC)

Forward (Part 2):   Frank Falian Zhang 张法连 (CUPL)

Editor-in-Chief: Jerry Yulin Zhang 张玉林 (Linli Law)

Co-Editor: Thomas Manson KC BFSU, Foreign Expert

                     Edward Chow 周立新 (Gary Soo's Chambers)

Main Writers:

Chen Sirui 陈思瑞 (UCASS)

Gao Liang 高梁 (Gaopeng & Partners)

Gao Yafei 高雅菲 (PKU Yuanpei College)

Jin Xin 金鑫 (South China Normal University)

Liu Wing Sze, Daisy 廖咏诗 (PKU Law School)

Liu Leyang 刘乐阳 (CIETAC Hubei Sub-Commission)

Liu Xinyi 刘心仪 (Fudan University)

Lu Kexin 陆可欣 (Shanghai Jiao Tong University)

Ma Chen 马琛 (CAAL)

Ma Ruijing 马瑞璟 (Minzhu University Law School)

Myo Su Thant (Sydney University Law School)

Peng Zhu 彭竹 (Fangda Partners)

Adam Zeguang Peng 彭泽光 (PKU Law School)

Wang Wenqian 王文倩 (Shandong University of Political Science and Law)

Xu Yixin 徐怡欣 (PKU Law School)

Gustav Kunhao Yang 杨昆灏 (EUI)

Yuan Yifan 袁一凡 (PKU SFL)

Zhao Yizhi 赵逸之 (PKU SFL)

序 言

2022年7月，我在北京大学校园里参加了北大暑期法律英语课程。为期一个月的课程描绘了一幅涉外商事仲裁中适用法律的宏伟图景，令人印象深刻，受益匪浅，且极具实践意义。张玉林老师在授课中的旁征博引，展现了作为一个资深的法律从业者和优秀教师的严谨治学精神，整个课程的内容翔实充分。也正是因为这门课程，我能够很荣幸地参与这个课后关于《联合国承认及执行外国仲裁裁决公约》（《纽约公约》）的写作项目。

随着全球化之风逐渐吹遍全球，涉外商业活动和涉外贸易纠纷也更为常见。然而，与这些商业活动密切相关的涉外商事仲裁领域，在中国尚未成为一个被充分深耕和广为人知的学科。自1987年中国适用《纽约公约》以来，中国国际经济贸易仲裁委员会等相关仲裁机构和仲裁委员会一直在推动本地仲裁法与《纽约公约》在涉外商事仲裁实践中的适用和发展。近年来，越来越多的法院的涉外商事仲裁判决中援引了《纽约公约》的规定，越发彰显《纽约公约》在中国的重要性。为此，我们精心编写了本书，希望能对《纽约公约》在中国的传播和理解作出贡献。本书包含了来自不同阶层和社会群体的作品，讨论了《纽约公约》的基本精神和公约中的详细条款，并在不同的现实情况下通过具体案例进行了生动的说明。

我怀着极大的荣幸和热情，作为学生代表写下这篇前言。2022年夏日里那段微风拂面的日子，稍纵即逝，难以忘怀，它为我打开了一个涉外商事仲裁的广阔世界和它的核心原则所构成的公约——《纽约公约》。俗话说，功夫不负有心人。在此成书之际，感谢所有参与者的努力和付出，尤其感谢各位知名编辑的无私帮助和奉献。回顾那些字斟句酌、案例研究的日日夜夜，我相信这本凝聚各方共同努力的书，在克服了无数困难之后，会在不远的将来为读者展现其价值。

袁一凡

北京大学外国语学院学生

2023 年 2 月 19 日

Preface

In July 2022, I was taking PKU's Summer Legal English course on the campus of Peking University. The one-month course depicted a grand picture of the application of laws in international commercial arbitration which was impressive, beneficial and practically significant. Prof. Zhang demonstrated rigorous scholarship as an experienced legal professional and outstanding instructor by quoting substantially from many authoritative sources and citing well documented stories. It is also because of this course that I am honored to be involved in the subsequent writing project on the United Nations Convention on the Recognition and Enforcement of Foreign Arbitral Awards ("NYC").

As the wind of globalization gradually blows over the world, it is much more common to see international commercial activities and trade disputes in China. However, the field of international commercial arbitration, which is closely related to those commercial activities, has not become a well−developed and widely known subject in China yet. Ever since China' s accession to of the New York Convention in 1987, relative arbitration institutions and commissions such as CIETAC have been promoting the application and development of local arbitration laws and the NYC in the practice of foreign commercial arbitration. In recent years, the importance of NYC in China has been demonstrated by the increasing number of the foreign−commercial related decisions of the court which often refer to the provisions of NYC. In response to these, this book is elaborately prepared to hopefully contribute to the spread and comprehension of the New York Convention in China. The book contains works from various legal segments representing different walks of life, and discusses the basic spirit of NYC and the detailed articles in the convention which are vividly illustrative through case studies in different realistic situations.

With great honor and passion, I am writing this preface as a student representative. The breezy summer days in 2022 are behind, but are unforgettable. They opened a world of international commercial arbitration and its core and backbone treaty, NYC, for me. As it goes, things come in favor of those who are prepared. On the occasion of the publication of this book, thanks to all the participants' works and efforts and especially thanks to the Editors' selfless help and devotion. Looking back to those days and nights choosing words, sentences and cases with great care, I believe this book of joint efforts, after overcoming uncountable difficulties, will demonstrate its value for the readers in the future.

Yuan Yifan

Student of Peking University, the School of Foreign Language

February 19, 2023

目录
Contents

Book I 上册

前言 / 1

Preamble / 3

第一章　简介——以邻为友 / 5

Chapter 1

Introduction — Treating Neighbors as Friends / 11

第二章　跨境国际商事仲裁中的"国际"意涵 / 18

　　一、基本概念 / 18

　　二、中国的法律实践 / 19

　　三、国际层面上的法律实践 / 21

　　结语 / 24

Chapter 2　What is "International" in International Commercial Arbitration

　　　　　　Crossing Borders / 26

　　1.Basic Concepts / 26

　　2. Legal Practice in China / 28

　　3. Legal Practice at the International Level / 31

　　Conclusion / 35

第三章　当合同关系出现问题时，如何处理争议？ / 37

　　一、争议解决的司法方式 / 38

　　二、替代性争议解决 / 38

　　三、仲裁 / 40

　　结语 / 43

Chapter 3　When a Contractual Relationship Broke up, How to Deal with the Disputes? / 44

　　1. Judicial Dispute Resolution / 45

　　2. Alternative Dispute Resolution / 46

　　3. Arbitration / 48

　　Conclusion / 51

第四章　商事仲裁为何优于法院管辖 / 53

　　一、当事人意思自治是仲裁的基石 / 53

　　二、与民事诉讼法对比 / 54

　　三、仲裁的一裁终局性 / 55

　　四、仲裁程序中当事人的自主性 / 56

　　五、案例分析 / 56

　　结语 / 59

Chapter 4　Why Commercial Arbitration Prevails over Court Jurisdiction / 60

　　1. Party Autonomy is the Cornerstone of Arbitration / 60

　　2. Contrast with the Civil Procedure Law / 61

　　3. Finality of Arbitration / 63

　　4. Party Autonomy in Arbitration Proceedings / 63

　　5. Case Study / 64

　　Conclusion / 67

第五章　仲裁员不能超出合同当事人约定的范围 / 69

　　一、仲裁权力来源的混合学说 / 69

二、国际公约和各国法律规定 / 71

三、案例分析 / 72

四、挑战性问题 / 74

结语 / 75

Chapter 5 Arbitrators Cannot Go beyond What the Contracting Parties Have Agreed / 76

1. Hybrid Sources of the Power of Arbitration / 77

2. International Convention and National Laws / 78

3. Case Studies / 79

4. Challenges / 81

Conclusion / 83

第六章 仲裁员的公正和效率义务 / 84

一、什么是"公正义务"？ / 84

二、如何保障仲裁员的公正性？ / 86

三、什么是"效率义务"？ / 87

四、如何保障仲裁员遵循效率义务？ / 88

结语 / 89

Chapter 6 Arbitrator's Impartial Role and Efficiency Duty / 90

1. What is "Impartial Role"? / 90

2. How to Ensure Arbitrator's Impartiality? / 92

3. What Is "Efficiency Duty"? / 94

4. How to Ensure Arbitrator's Efficiency? / 94

Conclusion / 96

第七章 临时仲裁在中国有它的生命力 / 97

一、什么是临时仲裁？ / 97

二、临时仲裁为何在中国具有生命力？ / 98

三、临时仲裁在中国的生命力如何体现？ / 99

结语 / 101

Chapter 7　Ad Hoc Arbitration Has its Life in China / 103

　　1. What is Ad Hoc Arbitration? / 104

　　2. Why Ad Hoc Arbitration Has its Life in China? / 105

　　3. How Ad Hoc Arbitration Has its Life in China? / 106

　　Conclusion / 108

第八章　败诉方针对裁决书的救济 / 109

　　一、一般理论 / 109

　　二、在中国大陆撤销仲裁裁决的途径 / 111

　　三、案例分析 / 114

　　结语 / 116

Chapter 8　The Losing Party's Recourse against the Arbitral Award / 117

　　1. A General Legal Theory / 117

　　2. Setting Aside Arbitral Awards in Chinese Mainland / 119

　　3. Case Study / 123

　　Conclusion / 126

第九章　胜诉方的执行路线 / 127

　　一、《纽约公约》和强制执行 / 127

　　二、拒绝承认和执行裁决的理由 / 128

　　结论和展望 / 133

Chapter 9　The Winning Party's Route towards Enforcement / 135

　　1.The New York Convention and Enforcement / 135

　　2. Grounds for Refusal to Recognize and Enforce the Award / 136

　　Conclusion and Outlook for the future / 142

附件一　Convention on the Recognition and Enforcement of Foreign Arbitral Awards / 143

附件二　承认及执行外国公断裁决公约 / 150

Book Ⅱ 下册

序　言 / 158

Preface / 160

前　言 / 162

Forward / 164

第十章　某些案件中仲裁与调解相结合的实践 / 166

　　一、什么是调解？ / 166

　　二、调解能否适用于仲裁？ / 167

　　三、贸仲委与香港调解实践之比较 / 170

　　四、我国法院诉讼中的调解结合 / 171

　　五、《新加坡调解公约》与调解的未来运用 / 171

Chapter 10　In Some Cases, Arb-Med May Well Work in Practice / 174

　　1. What is Mediation? / 174

　　2. Can Mediation Be Used in Arbitration? / 176

　　3. CIETAC Practice and Comparison with HK Practice / 178

　　4. Mediation Combined in Court Proceedings in China / 179

　　5. Singapore Mediation Convention and the Use of Mediation in the Future / 180

第十一章　仲裁员是否在法律上免责？ / 183

　　一、仲裁员责任制度总体性介绍 / 183

　　二、中国仲裁员责任制度 / 186

　　结语 / 188

Chapter 11　Are Arbitrators Legally Exempt From Liability? / 189

　　1. Arbitrators' Liability System in General / 189

　　2. Arbitrators' Liability System in China / 192

Concluding Remarks / 194

第十二章　元宇宙业务中的仲裁 / 196

　　一、元宇宙中的仲裁协议 / 196

　　二、仲裁程序中的元宇宙技术 / 198

　　三、仲裁裁决的执行 / 200

　　结语 / 203

Chapter 12　Arbitration in Metaverse Business / 205

　　1. Arbitration Agreements in the Metaverse / 205

　　2. Metaverse Technology in Arbitration Proceedings / 207

　　3. Enforcement of Arbitral Awards / 209

　　Concluding remarks / 213

第十三章　条约必须履行——近年来根据《纽约公约》在中国及其他地区
　　　　　（涉及中国）的执行案例 / 216

　　一、《纽约公约》关于承认和执行的相关条款 / 216

　　二、近期《纽约公约》在中国的执行案例分析 / 218

　　三、根据《纽约公约》在其他地区执行中国仲裁裁决 / 220

　　四、外国仲裁裁决的执行展望 / 223

**Chapter 13　Treaty Must Be Performed — Recent Enforcement Cases under the
　　　　　New York Convention in China and Beyond (Involving China) / 227**

　　1. Relevant Provisions of the New York Convention on Recognition and Enforcement
　　　　of Foreign Arbitral Awards / 228

　　2. Analysis of Recent Enforcement Cases of the New York Convention in China / 229

　　3. Enforcement of Chinese Arbitration Awards in Other Regions under the New York
　　　　Convention / 231

　　4. Prospects for the Enforcement of Foreign Arbitral Awards / 236

第十四章　香港地区适用《纽约公约》仲裁裁决的执行现况 / 240

　　一、《纽约公约》适用于香港特别行政区的理据 / 241

二、香港法院支持执行仲裁的立场 / 242

三、援引《纽约公约》的实际案例 / 245

四、承认和执行内地裁决 / 248

结语 / 249

Chapter 14　Enforcement of Convention Awards in the HKSAR / 250

　　1. Applicability of the NYC to the HKSAR / 251

　　2. The Hong Kong Court's Pro-Enforcement Approach / 252

　　3. Practical Cases Invoking the Provision of the NYC / 255

　　4. Recognition and Enforcement of Mainland Awards / 259

　　Conclusion / 260

第十五章　新加坡涉上海合同关系的最新案例 / 262

一、仲裁地 / 263

二、仲裁协议的适用法律 / 264

三、仲裁协议的有效性 / 266

四、仲裁裁决的执行 / 268

结语 / 269

Chapter 15　Recent Cases from Singapore in Contractual Relationships Involving Shanghai / 270

　　1. Seat of Arbitration / 271

　　2. Proper Law of the Arbitration Agreement / 272

　　3. Validity of the Arbitration Agreement / 274

　　4. Enforcement of the Arbitral Award / 276

　　Conclusion / 278

第十六章　《示范法》在哪里与《纽约公约》相吻合？ / 279

一、目的与原则 / 279

二、《示范法》需要的改进 / 280

三、两文件的关键异同 / 281

四、《示范法》与中国《仲裁法》 / 284

结语 —— 未来的中国仲裁 / 285

Chapter 16　Where Does the Model Law Meet the New York Convention? / 286

　　1. Purpose and Principles / 286

　　2. Improvements Needed for the Model Law / 287

　　3. Analysis of Key Commonalities / 289

　　4. Model Law and Chinese Arbitration Law / 292

　　Conclusion — Future Chinese Arbitration / 293

第十七章　谁说《纽约公约》不适用于台湾呢？ / 295

　　一、台湾仲裁立法与纽约公约 / 295

　　二、外国仲裁裁决在台湾的有关案例 / 298

Chapter 17　Who Says New York Convention Does Not Apply to Taiwan? / 301

　　1. Taiwan Arbitration Legislation and the New York Convention / 301

　　2. Recent Cases concerning Foreign Arbitral Awards in Taiwan / 305

第十八章　跨国法视角下《纽约公约》在中国的理解与适用 / 308

　　一、概览：当代中国的仲裁法 / 308

　　二、中国法院的视角下《纽约公约》在中国的适用 / 311

　　三、司法实践中中国法院对《纽约公约》的解释 / 314

　　结语：中国仲裁法的未来 / 316

Chapter 18　The New York Convention in China: From A Transnational Law Aspect / 318

　　1. An Overview: Arbitration Law in Contemporary China / 318

　　2. The Application of the New York Convention in China: From the Chinese Court's Perspective / 321

　　3. Interpretation of New York Convention in China / 325

　　Conclusion: The Future of Chinese Arbitration Law / 327

第十九章　结语——山洪冲不走的，雨后观澜坚如磐石 / 330

　　一、仲裁合意及和谐精神 / 330

二、当事人意思自治和自强不息的理念 / 331

三、各方陈述案情的机会和兼听则明思维 / 332

四、法院有限干预和仲裁自治性意识 / 333

五、爱邻如己与天助自助者精神 / 334

Chapter 19 Concluding Remarks—What Stays in the Mountain Torrents Becomes Rock Solid after the Rain / 336

1. Consensus and Harmony / 337

2. Party Autonomy and Self–Improvement / 337

3. Opportunity to Present its Case and Hearing Both Sides / 339

4. Limited Court Intervention and Arbitral Autonomy / 339

5. Loving One's Neighbor Like Loving Oneself v. He Who Helps Others Helps. / 341

附件三 生产销售协议（中文） / 343

附件四 授权书 / 354

Index / 356

前　言

联合国《承认及执行外国仲裁裁决公约》(《纽约公约》)被公认为全球执行最有效的国际公约，截至 2023 年 7 月末，已在 172 个国家生效，涵盖了全球主要经济体和绝大多数国家。《纽约公约》解决的核心问题是跨境仲裁裁决的承认与执行问题，生效 60 多年来，国际经贸环境发生了翻天覆地的变化，尽管其确立的基本原则、规定的基本内容对国际商事活动仍然适用，但围绕《纽约公约》相关条款如何适应变化了的世界经济活动的研讨，始终是国际仲裁界密切关注和积极参与的重要话题。

仲裁是一门理论与实践结合极为紧密的学科，仲裁从业人员的能力养成，要注重遵循人们认识世界、改造世界的基本规律，即通过实践 – 认识、再实践 – 再认识，不断提高理论认知水平，不断拓展实践的广度和深度。而若想成为好的涉外仲裁从业人员，一是要精研细磨《纽约公约》，这是仲裁业界的启蒙课程。二是要熟练掌握国际仲裁最为通用的语言——英语，这是涉外工作的看家本领。三是要勇于参与涉外仲裁实践，这是快速成长的不二法门。

我们欣喜地看到，在统筹国内法治和涉外法治的大背景下，一批理论功底深厚、实践经验丰富、英语水平高超的资深仲裁专家，指导一批风华正茂、奋发上进的仲裁青年，围绕《纽约公约》的基本精神和具体条文，通过理论探讨、实证分析、案例解剖等方式，对《纽约公约》进行沉浸式学习，这种方式，对于涉外仲裁人才培养而言，不失为一种非常有益的探索。他们的学习成果，就构成了本书的主要内容。

中国仲裁法学研究会作为全国唯一的仲裁法学领域的学术社团，坚持以推动我国仲裁行业高质量发展为己任，愿意将本书推荐给国内外的仲裁从业人员，同时也期待本书的出版，能够起到良好的示范作用，让更多市场主体关注仲裁、选择仲裁，让更多青年法律人才学习仲裁、参与仲裁，共同推动仲裁事业的繁荣发展。

谭剑

中国仲裁法学研究会秘书长

2023 年 8 月 15 日

Preamble

The United Nations Convention on the Recognition and Enforcement of Foreign Arbitral Awards (the New York Convention) is recognized as the most effectively implemented international convention in the world. As at the end of July 2023, the Convention had entered into force in 172 countries, covering the major economies and the vast majority of countries worldwide. The core issues addressed by *the New York Convention* surrounds the recognition and enforcement of cross-border arbitral awards. Over the past more than 60 years since its entry into force, the international economic and trade environment has undergone radical changes. Although the basic principles established and the basic contents of its provisions are still applicable to international commercial activities, how the relevant provisions of the New York Convention can be adapted to ever changing world economic activities has always been an important topic of concern and calls for active participation in the international arbitration community. *The New York Convention* is an important topic to which the international arbitration community pays close attention.

Arbitration is the subject that combines theory and practice very closely. Arbitration practitioners should follow the basic laws of the people to understand and transform the world. Through practice-knowledge and practice-knowledge again, it is to continuously improve the level of theoretical cognition and to continuously expand the breadth and depth of the practice. To become a good practitioner of foreign-related arbitration, firstly, one should study the text of *the New York Convention*, which is an introductory course for the arbitration industry. Secondly, he/she should master the most common language of international arbitration — English, which is the most widely used language in foreign-related work. Thirdly, he/she should have the courage to participate in the practice of foreign-related arbitration, which is the only way to grow rapidly.

We are very pleased to see that, in the context of integrating the domestic rule of law and foreign-related rule of law, a group of senior arbitration experts with profound theoretical background, rich practical experience and high English proficiency are guiding a group of young arbitration practitioners who are in the prime of their lives and are striving for advancement by way of immersive learning of the New York Convention through theoretical discussions, empirical analyses and case study, focusing on the basic spirit of the New York Convention and its specific provisions. This approach is a very useful exploration for the cultivation of talents in foreign-related arbitration. The results of their learning constitute the main content of this book.

As the sole academic society in the field of arbitration law in China, China Academy of Arbitration Law (CAAL) insists on promoting the high-quality development of China's arbitration industry as its own responsibility, and is willing to recommend this book to all the arbitration practitioners. While looking forward to the publication of this book, we expect that the book will play a good role as a model, so as to guide more market entities to pay attention to arbitration and choose arbitration, and to call more young legal talents to learn about arbitration and participate in arbitration, and to jointly promote the prosperous development of arbitration.

Tan Jian

Secretary General of China Academy of Arbitration Law

15 August, 2023

第一章
简介——以邻为友

张玉林 周立新

国际贸易与商务活动通过国际条约和公约得以维持。本书将 1958 年完成的《联合国承认及执行外国仲裁裁决公约》（《纽约公约》）作为主要的国际条约，从争端解决的角度看其如何支持国际贸易和商业体系。

国际贸易通常涉及来自不同国家的当事人之间的合同。销售商品或提供服务的合同是跨国界各方之间处理其贸易关系的法律文件。虽然单个人可能通过口头方式与外方建立销售或工作关系，但这种销售或工作关系随着时间的推移可能会被打破——销售订单可能不被支付，交付货物标的时未获得相应的价金给付，企业权益可能会受到侵害。

我们以一份生产销售协议（"MSA"）为例。（本书附件三为一份简化了的中文协议示例。）

正如你所见，MSA 的双方是作为制造商和销售商（中方）的 [泰平公司]，以及作为买方（外方）的 MERINGE。观察这份 MSA 示例，你可以在双方的销售合同中看到什么使其成为"国际"，正是双方所处的地理位置使这一定义变得清晰。对于其他同样影响到中国语境下"国际"定义的事项，你可以在上册第二章中找到。如果从国家边境以内的角度考察，"国际"的概念更多会被称为"涉外"。该章中的 Siemens v Golden Landmark 案例告诉我们，还有哪些因素可以使某合同关系成为"涉外"合同关系。MSA 示例体现出，这是一位中国当事人和新加坡当事人之间的涉外合同，新加坡一方许可其 MERGINGE 商标，并指定其关联公司为中国境内的货物接收方。

在具有类似性质的仅有两方当事人的销售合同中，在出口项目中，通常卖方是中方当事人，而买方则为外方当事人。在相反的合同关系中，即在进口项目中，卖方是外国当事人，而买方（进口商）则为中国当事人。这两种类型的合同通常被称为"出口合同"和"进口合同"。这些合同所处理的是货物的跨境流动，货物的跨境流动使中国的对外贸易额在过去 40 年的开放政策下逐年增加。

合同在充分履行时，为各方创造价值。正是这些商品和服务贸易中的合同，成为与全世界进行国际贸易往来的中坚力量。监管者和市场经营者在现实生活中很容易看到合同的价值，而普通公民看到经济的增长与市场的繁盛，其实是由越来越多的跨境合同所支撑的。

然而，当合同没有得到履行，那么纠纷自然会产生，必须通过各种纠纷解决程序来解决。本书第 3 章对中国和跨国界的各种现代纠纷解决方法进行了介绍。你会发现为什么法院在现代社会中得以存在，以及替代性争端解决方式包括哪些？什么是仲裁和调解？它们又有什么区别？当事人意思自治原则对一个新兴市场来说意味着什么？作者在第三章中对这些问题提供了自己的答案和评论。

MSA 示例包含一个仲裁条款。这是一个普通的合同条款，只有两到三个英文句子，但是它具有巨大的力量来基础性地支撑着现代国际商事仲裁制度。该条款如果是有效的，将回答为什么当事人在解决争端时不选择法院，以及当事人为何采用仲裁作为争议解决的首选方法等问题。

本书第四章讨论了一份合同如何具有排除法院管辖权的作用，以实现合同纠纷以民间方式予以有效解决。在中国经济改革和发展的背景下，市场的变化反映出，在跨境合同中，市场在中国的仲裁地选择方面发挥了重要作用。这一章讨论的近期涉外仲裁领域的案例值得读者关注。中国是一个不断变化的市场,这种变化对世界其他地区的争议解决实践和从业人员的业务具有长期且深远的影响。市场整合仍在继续,而这种发端于本土变化的影响也将持续下去。

仲裁员是一群具有相对资深的仲裁和商业纠纷解决知识与经验的专业人士。他们是《中华人民共和国仲裁法》规定的"公道正派的人员"[①]。当事人必须从仲裁机构保存的仲裁员名单中选择这些公道正派的人。虽然仲裁员在国际商业界似乎拥有十分光鲜的工作,但他们受《纽约公约》所制定的规则约束。国际仲裁体系基于规则的秩序,要求所有仲裁员自我警醒并意识到他们仲裁权力的来源,在尊重当事人意思自治的同时遵守法律。在第五章中,你会发现关于仲裁员权力来源的各种理论,并了解各个国家在实践中如何处理对仲裁员权力的限制。如果一方不是仲裁协议的当事人,有关该方的诉求很可能不会在仲裁中被受理,也不会在随后的裁决执行过程中获得支持。

仲裁是由"公道正派的人"进行裁决的。但并非所有公道正派的人都能进行仲裁。《仲裁法》规定了法律资格:仲裁员必须从事仲裁工作8年以上;或从事律师工作8年以上;或担任法官8年以上;或从事法律研究或法律教育工作,具有高级职称;或掌握法律知识,从事经济贸易等领域的专业工作,具有高级职称或同等专业水平。[②]

除此之外,并非所有公道正派的合格人士都可以进行仲裁。仲裁员必须由争议双方当事人选定,或由争议双方当事人约定的仲裁机构或专业团体指定。因此,仲裁员是那些具有法律资格并且被任命为涉及当事人争议案件的仲裁员的人担任。

---

① 《中华人民共和国仲裁法》第13条。
② 同上。

发生争议的各方都希望争议能够得到高效且有效的解决。仲裁员的选择是以解决争端为整体目标导向的。仲裁员如何适当地采取行动以实现争议解决的目的，这涉及仲裁员在处理仲裁程序直至程序结束的过程中应当以何种方式行事。本书第六章讨论了仲裁员在处理仲裁程序中的公正和高效义务。

第七章探讨了一个作为自然人的中国仲裁员任职的有趣话题。《纽约公约》第一条第二款为临时仲裁奠定了基础，其中规定："公断裁决"一词不仅指专案选派之公断员所做裁决，亦指当事人提请裁断之常设公断机构所做裁决。在这一条款中，临时仲裁被接受为国际社会中的一类仲裁。[①]然而，根据中国法律规定，临时仲裁在《中华人民共和国仲裁法》中受到了限制。第七章告诉我们，这种限制对于中国仲裁实践的发展是不合适的。相反，临时仲裁在中国拥有自己的生命力，更能体现当事人意思自治的基本原则，新修订的《中华人民共和国仲裁法》将促进临时仲裁在中国的稳步发展。

第八章和第九章是关于《纽约公约》项下撤销和执行仲裁裁决的姊妹章。第八章论及败诉方希望撤销裁决的情况，而第九章则讨论胜诉方希望执行裁决的情况。仲裁涉及一个对抗性的过程，在其中每一方都有机会对另一方的案情进行论证，而仲裁员作出决定，宣布谁有权依法可以获得何种赔偿或法律救济。因此，仲裁程序结束之时往往会分出一个赢家和一个输家。赢家希望执行仲裁裁决，而输家则可能希望撤销裁决。中国法律根据《纽约公约》的规定，同样清晰列明了法院可以拒绝执行裁决的理由。

下册探讨在双循环经济政策中，纽约公约在有关国家或领域执行的实务案例。第十章谈及仲裁程序中的调解。第十一章讨论国际仲裁中仲裁员责任的问题。世界上存在不同的法律制度，以保护仲裁员免受当事人的民事诉讼。一些国家给予仲裁员责任豁免权，就像给予法官豁免权一样，因

---

① 在当时的联合国中文用语中，"公断"一词即"仲裁"，"公断员"即"仲裁员"。

此使其在作出仲裁裁决时，不必担心民事责任。其他国家对仲裁员的责任则具有更加严格的规定。在以仲裁方式处理跨国界争端时，仲裁员必须谨慎考虑在不同法律体系中担任仲裁员的任职机会（及风险）。

从第十二章到第十七章，你会发现不同国家和地区之间相互影响的一些有趣话题。仲裁员在元宇宙世界中是做什么的（第十二章）？在中国国际经济贸易仲裁委员会的仲裁裁决中，《纽约公约》为何以及如何被贯彻执行（第十三章）？什么原因可能导致仲裁裁决没有根据《纽约公约》执行？仲裁协议是否有效？仲裁通知是否适当？仲裁庭是否根据各方协议对仲裁庭成员的组成进行适当地任命？你还可以在第十三章中找到非常生动的实务案例。

第十四章和第十五章是本书的另一组姊妹章，其中包括来自香港特别行政区和新加坡仲裁领域的最新精彩案例。一些案例在法律的选择、法律对合同和仲裁协议的适用、仲裁地点的选择等问题上具有法律先例的价值。另外一些来自香港特别行政区的案例表明，在将香港建设成为一个具有友善支持国际仲裁环境的现代争议解决中心方面，香港的司法机构和特别行政区政府展现了强劲的实力。

第十六章是关于对《纽约公约》和《联合国国际贸易法委员会国际商事仲裁示范法》的共同之处和差异的比较研究。第十七章试图从法律实施的角度探讨，为什么《纽约公约》应当适用于台湾，以及如果不适用，为什么其在当前环境下还不适用。第十八章从条约解释的角度并以跨国法律的视角来透视《纽约公约》。

在本书的最后，本着求同存异的精神，我们用一个关于法律文化共性问题的自由篇章来总结，为什么《纽约公约》下的各种概念实际上可以在中国的文化肌理中寻觅到它们相似的根基。一些从法律文化视角的有趣观察，体现了人类作为"社会动物"生活和共存于世界的人性中的人性，以及贯穿地域差异的原则。

我们需要和谐与和平作为支持，正如世界上的自然人和法人通过当事人意思自治获得相互支持那样。当事人在跨境贸易和投资中做交易时，自己进行合同的拟定。其对于合同条款施加的注意，便于当事人根据自己的意愿为合同履行和争议解决提前定下基调。当事人可以直接根据一套仲裁规则选择仲裁员，正如本书所附的 MSA 示例中表征的那样，授权中国仲裁法学研究会（CAAL）[①] 来指定仲裁员，这种临时性的仲裁程序可以更直接地由当事人自己管理。

我们与邻居、与邻国相处时，不论国境远近，首先需要友谊及真诚来帮助别人，以爱及以礼相待。我们内心所含的人类之爱在心脏的两瓣心房之间穿梭，并不时反思作为自然人的仲裁员和作为自然人或法人的纠纷当事人的局限性。对正义和人类幸福生活的追求促进了我们出于理性和恻隐之心的行为，不仅把别人与别国当作邻居，还应在适当的法律权利支持以及对他人的责任关系中处理自己的事务。虽然可能存在语言和文化上的差异，但是我们相信自己的信念和倚重当事人意思自治的共同人性是共通的。自然人的自由不仅在各个国家的宪法框架下受到法律保护，而且还受到跨境商业法和国际仲裁制度的保护。

国际贸易的蓬勃发展与旅游业的兴旺，不单为商贩带来生意及商机，通过人与人的交往，也减少了战争及冲突的诱因，因为透过国际贸易，已经足以使人各取所需，疏通有无。

---

① 在当事人的仲裁条款中，指定机构可以是新成立的中国仲裁协会。

Chapter 1

Introduction — Treating Neighbors as Friends

Jerry Zhang   Edward Chou

International trade and commerce is **maintained** through international treaties and conventions. This book takes *the United Nations Convention on the Recognition and Enforcement of Foreign Arbitral Awards* done in 1958 (the *"New York Convention"*) as the principal international treaty that has supported the system of international trade and commerce from a dispute resolution perspective.

International trade typically involves a contract between parties from different countries. Contracts for sale of goods or provision of services are the legal documents between the cross-border parties to deal with their trade relationship. While one may have a sales or working relationship with a foreign party based on word of mouth, such sales or working relationship may be broken in times of change. Sales orders may go unpaid, and your business may get hurt when deliveries are not appropriately honored in terms of payment.

We take an example of a manufacturing and sales agreement ("MSA"). (A sample extract of agreement in Chinese is Attachment 3 of the book.)

As you can see, the two parties to the MSA are [Taiping] being the manufacturer and seller (the Chinese Party), and MERINGE/ being the buyer (the Foreign Party). Looking at the sample MSA, you can see what makes it "international" in a sales contract between the two parties. It is the location of the parties that makes the definition clear. For other matters that also affect the definition of "international" in Chinese context, you can find them in **Chapter 2, Book** Ⅰ. The concept of "international", when examined from within the border of the country, is more often termed as "foreign-related". The case *Siemens v Golden Landmark* in the chapter tells us what other elements may render a contractual relationship a "foreign-related" contractual relationship. The sample MSA shows it is foreign-related contract between a Chinese party and a Singapore party who licensed its trademark, and designated its affiliated company as the receiver of the goods within China.

In a sales contract of similar nature in an export project where there are only two parties, usually the seller is the Chinese party and the buyer is the foreign party. In a reverse contractual relationship such as in an import project, the seller will be the foreign party and the buyer (the importer) will be the Chinese party. These two types of contract are ordinarily called export contracts and import contracts. These contracts deal with the flow of goods across the border, and such flow of goods across borders makes China's foreign trade volume increase year by year in the past four decades under the Open Door Policy.

Contracts create value for the parties when they are fully performed. It is these contracts in the trade in goods and services that serve as the backbone of the foreign trade with the world. Regulators and market operators well see the value of the contracts in real life. Ordinary citizens see the growth of the economy and the flourishing of the market that is supported by the increasing number of cross-border contracts.

When contracts are not performed, then disputes will naturally arise and must be resolved through the various dispute resolution processes. **Chapter 3** of the book provides a glimpse of the various modern methods of dispute resolution in China and across borders. You will find why the courts exist in a modern society, and what are the meanings of alternative dispute resolution. What is arbitration and mediation, what are their differences? What does the principle of party autonomy mean to an emerging market? These are some of the questions to which the author provides her answers and comments in Chapter 3.

The sample MSA contains an arbitration clause. It is an ordinary contract clause having only two or three English sentences. It has tremendous power to cushion support a modern system of international commercial arbitration. The provision, if it is effective, will answer the question why the courts are not selected by the parties in dispute resolution, and how arbitration may be adopted by the parties as a preferred dispute resolution method.

Chapter 4 of the book discusses the methodology of how a contract may have the effect of excluding the court jurisdiction in order to achieve private and efficient resolution of contractual disputes. In the context of economic reform and development in China, market changes reflect the force of the market in shaping the choices of the place of arbitration in China in a cross-border contract. Recent cases in foreign-related arbitration field discussed in this chapter are worthy of the reader's attention. China is a changing marketplace with such changes that have a long and far-reaching impact on the dispute resolution practice and the business of practitioners in other parts of the world. The market integration continues, such impact from the local changes will continue.

Arbitrators are a group of relatively senior persons who have expertise in arbitration and commercial dispute resolution. They are "righteous and upright" persons under the Arbitration Law of the PRC[1]. Parties must choose these righteous and upright persons from a list of arbitrators maintained by the arbitration institutions. While arbitrators may seem to work in glorious positions in the international commerce community, they are bound by the rules created under the New York Convention. The rule-based order of the international arbitration system requires all arbitrators to be self-conscious and aware of their source of the power to arbitrate and comply with the law while respecting party autonomy. In **Chapter 5**, you will find the various theories on the source of the power of the arbitrators, and see how various countries deal with the limitation of the arbitrator's powers in practice. If a party is not party to the arbitration agreement, the claims regarding that party will not likely be entertained in arbitration, or in the subsequent enforcement process.

Arbitrations are conducted by "righteous and upright" persons. But not all righteous and upright" person can conduct arbitrations. There are legal qualifications

---

[1] Article 13 of the PRC Arbitration Law.

under the Arbitration Law. Arbitrators must have been engaged in arbitration work for at least eight years; or have worked as a lawyer for at least eight years; or have served as a judge for at least eight years; or have been engaged in legal research or legal education, possessing a senior professional title; or have acquired the knowledge of law, engaged in the professional work in the field of economy and trade, etc., possessing a senior professional title or having an equivalent professional level.[1]

Further, not all qualified persons who are righteous and upright may conduct arbitration. Arbitrators must be appointed by the parties in dispute or by arbitration institutions or professional bodies agreed upon by the parties in dispute. Therefore, arbitrators are those persons who are legally qualified and are appointed to act as arbitrators in cases involving disputes of the parties.

Parties who are in dispute want to have the dispute resolved efficiently and effectively. The choice of arbitrators is made for the whole purpose of dispute resolution. How can arbitrators act appropriately to achieve the purpose of dispute resolution. This touches on the ways in which the arbitrator must act in processing the arbitration procedures towards the end of the dispute resolution. **Chapter 6** discusses the impartiality and efficiency duty of the arbitrators in conducting the arbitration proceedings.

Chapter 7 explores an interesting subject on the individual Chinese arbitrators as natural persons. The New York Convention laid out the foundation for *ad hoc* arbitration in Article I 2 where it states that arbitral awards include not only awards made by arbitrators appointed by the parties but also awards made by permanent institutions chosen by the parties. In this provision, *ad hoc* arbitration is accepted as one category of arbitration in the international community. However, through the local legal provisions, *ad hoc* arbitration was restricted under the Arbitration Law of the PRC. The chapter tells us that such restrictions are inappropriate for the growth of the Chinese arbitration practice. Instead, *ad hoc* arbitration has its own life in China , and the amended PRC Arbitration Law will promote *ad hoc* arbitration stably in China.

Chapters 8 and 9 are sister chapters regarding the setting aside and enforcement

---

[1] Article 13 of the PRC Arbitration Law.

of arbitral awards under the New York Convention. **Chapter 8** deals with the situations where the losing party wants to set aside an award and **Chapter 9** deals with situations where the winning party wants to enforce the award. Arbitration involves an adversarial process where each party argues their case against the other, and the arbitrators make a decision to declare who is entitled to what compensation or legal remedies under the law. Therefore, there is often a winner or a loser at the end of the proceedings. While the winner wants to enforce the arbitral awards, the loser may wish to set aside the award. Chinese law also clearly provides the reasons where enforcement of the award may be refused according to the provisions of the New York Convention.

Book Ⅱ of the book covered various practical aspects from the implementation of the New York Convention in the relevant countries in the background of dual economic circulation policy in China. **Chapter 10** deals with mediation conducted in the process of arbitration. **Chapter 11** addresses the subject of the liability of arbitrators in international arbitration. There are different legal systems in the world that protect arbitrators from civil suit from the parties. Some countries grant immunity of liability just like immunity to judges so the judicial decisions are made free from fear of civil liability. Other countries have stricter rules on arbitrator's liability. One has to be careful to consider the opportunity (and risks) of acting as arbitrator under different systems of law in dealing with cross-border disputes by way of arbitration.

From **Chapter 12** to **Chapter 17**, you will find an interesting cluster of topics with interplay between different countries and regions. What do arbitrators do in the metaverse world (**Chapter 12**)? Why and how the New York Convention has been performed in the case of CIETAC arbitration awards (**Chapter 13**)? What may have caused the arbitral awards not been enforced under the New York Convention? Is the arbitration agreement valid? Is the notice of arbitration appropriate? Are the tribunal composed of persons appropriately appointed according to parties' agreement? You can find vivid and interesting cases in the Chapter 13.

Recent cases from Hong Kong SAR and from Singapore in **Chapters 14 and 15**, another set of sister chapters to read in the book, include fascinating cases in the field of arbitration in Hong Kong SAR and Singapore. Some cases are of legal precedent values in relation to the questions of choice of law, law applicable to the contract and to the arbitration agreement, choice of seat of arbitration etc. Some other cases from Hong Kong SAR show how Hong Kong remains strong from both the judiciary and the SAR Government on building Hong Kong as a modern dispute resolution hub with a pro-arbitration environment.

Chapter 16 deals with a comparative study of commonalities and differences under the New York Convention and the UNCITRAL Model Law. **Chapter 17** attempts to address why the New York Convention should be applied to Taiwan, as a matter of law, and if not, why it does not apply in the current environment. **Chapter 18** looks at the New York Convention from treaty interpretation perspective and from the stand point of transnational law aspect.

In the spirit of seeking commonality while reserving differences, we conclude the book by a liberal chapter on the question of commonality in legal culture to sum up why the various concepts under the New York Convention actually can find their roots similarly grown in Chinese cultural texture. Some interesting observations from the cultural aspects enshrine the principles that cut through the geological differences and land in the humanity of the humanity as "a social animal" living and co-existing in the world.

We need harmony and peace as supported by the natural and legal persons in mutual relationship in the world with party autonomy in mind. The parties write their own contract when they do transactions in cross-border trade and investment. Attention may be paid to the terms of the contract so that the parties may set the tone for the performance of the contract and the dispute resolution of their own will. Parties may choose arbitrators directly according to a set of arbitration rules, as suggested in the MSA attached to the book, which authorizes the China Academy of Arbitration Law (CAAL)[①] to appoint arbitrators, an *ad hoc* arbitration process that is more directly managed by the parties themselves.

We need friendship and sincerity to help others first, to treat others with respect and to do so when we live with our neighbors, regardless whether it is a neighboring

---

① The appointing authority could be the newly established China Arbitration Association, in parties' arbitration clause.

friend or a neighboring country, far or near. We have the human love in the heart that travels between the two auricles of the heart and reflect from time to time on our limitations as natural person arbitrators and as natural or legal person parties to disputes. The seeking of justice and human happiness in life promotes our merciful and rational act of not only treating others as our neighbors but also treating our own affairs under appropriate legal authority and our duty to others. While there might be language and culture differences, our common humanity of believing in ourselves and leaning on party autonomy remains the same. The freedom of natural persons is legally protected under not only the constitutional framework of individual states but also cross-border commercial law and the international arbitration regime.

The growth of international trade, coupled with the flourishing of international travel industry, not only bring business and commercial opportunities to citizens and international traders, but also reduces the causes to war or conflict through people-people interaction, as it suffices for people to get what they need, and exchange what they have, through international trade.

第二章

跨境国际商事仲裁中的"国际"意涵

彭泽光

国际商事仲裁是国际司法中重要的概念，当中所谓"国际"一词应为合意，需要得到进一步的理清和阐明。本章首先会梳理目前学界中存在的学说，然后介绍我国在实务中是如何辨析"国际"这一模糊含义的。最后，本章以比较法为视角分析其他域外发达国家的实务操作。通过上述三个分析角度，笔者希望本章可以给予读者以一览无余的全面认知，了解"国际"在国际商事仲裁中的意涵。

一、基本概念

事实上，学界对"国际商事仲裁的国际性"的讨论并不多。但需要指出的是，"国际商事仲裁的国际性"是理解什么是国际商事仲裁的前提。以下是目前学术界比较主流的一些观点。

（一）地理标准

国际商事仲裁处理的是来自不同国家的当事人之间的纠纷。首先要考虑当事人的所在地或仲裁地点。通常而言，仲裁地、当事人的国籍、住所或居所、法人注册地、公司管理中心所在地等联结点之一具有国际因素的，该商事仲裁为视为国际商事仲裁。英国、瑞典、瑞士等欧洲国家，以及埃及、叙利亚等阿拉伯国家，在判断仲裁的国际性时，均采用此标准。

（二）根据争议性质确定仲裁归属

以争议的性质为标准来确定仲裁的归属。本标准根据争议的性质考虑仲裁。如果争议涉及国际商事利益，解决该商事争议的仲裁为国际商事仲裁。法国、美国、加拿大等国家均采用该标准。

（三）混合标准

使用一组混合标准来确定仲裁是否为国际商事仲裁。在这组混合标准下，人们考虑了以下要素：第一，对营业地位于不同国家的当事人之间的争议进行仲裁；第二，仲裁地与当事人当时营业地不在同一国家的仲裁；第三，主要义务履行地及当事人的商业仲裁所在地不同；第四，与争议标的关系最密切的地点与当事人营业地不在同一国家的仲裁；第五，当事人明确同意争议标的涉及一个以上国家的仲裁。

二、中国的法律实践

中国采用混合标准。根据中国国际私法理论和司法实践，民事法律关系的涉外或国际性质应当从广义上进行解释，即只要主体、客体或内容中至少有一项与中国大陆地区以外的司法管辖区有关，则相当于具有国际性。具体而言：

民事关系具有下列情形之一的，人民法院可以认定其为涉外民事关系：（1）当事人一方或双方是外国公民、外国法人或者其他组织、无国籍人；（2）当事人一方或双方的经常居所地在中华人民共和国领域外；（3）标的物在中华人民共和国领域外；（4）产生、变更或者消灭民事关系的法律事实发生在中华人民共和国领域外；（5）可以认定为涉外民事关系的其他情形。

在此，我们可以通过几个典型案例，进一步了解国际商事仲裁中的"国际"概念是如何在中国实践中得到"认定"的。

在"江苏航天万源风电设备制造有限公司与艾尔姆风能叶片制品（天津）有限公司申请确认仲裁协议效力纠纷案"中，双方订立仲裁条款：双方签订的《贸易协议》，约定相关争议可提交北京国际商会仲裁。对此，最高法院在答复中表示："订立《贸易协议》的双方当事人均为中国法人，标的物在中国，协议也在中国订立和履行，无涉外民事关系的构成要素，该协议不属于涉外合同。由于仲裁管辖权系法律授予的权力，而我国法律没有规定当事人可以将不具有涉外因素的争议交由境外仲裁机构或者在我国境外临时仲裁，故本案当事人约定将有关争议提交国际商会仲裁没有法律依据。"

同样，在"六盘水恒鼎实业有限公司与张洪星矿业权转让纠纷案"中[①]，最高人民法院也指出：非涉外民事案件当事人约定，争议由中国大陆以外的仲裁机构裁决。该协议应被视为无效，因为它违反了"司法主权原则"。

司法解释的规定实际上是根据传统法律关系的三个要素，即法律关系的主体、客体和内容来界定涉外因素。然而，随着自贸区的发展和"一带一路"影响的深入，传统的三要素法律认定方法已经难以涵盖许多新型跨境经贸合作。司法解释第一条第五款是一个典型的兜底条款。该兜底条款的表述是："可以认定为涉外民事关系的其他情形。"

据此，西门子案件的具体裁判理由：

● 仲裁协议有效：涉外合同虽不具有典型的涉外因素，但与国内普通

---

① 2019年度仲裁司法审查实践观察报告——主题四：承认（认可）和/或执行域外仲裁裁决制度实践观察，http://www.tiantonglaw.com/Content/2020/08-20/1123290941.html.

合同有显著区别，可认定为涉外民事法律关系；

● 该案中的仲裁条款约定："合同纠纷必须提交新加坡国际仲裁中心"，涉案合同的仲裁条款系明确表示同意，含义是明确的。

因此，判断仲裁条款效力的关键在于所涉合同是否具有涉外因素。

本案当事人均为在中国注册的法人，标的物的交付地和现所在地均在中国境内，表面上不符合"司法解释"第一条前四款规定。但是：

（a.）本案主体具有一定的涉外因素：其注册地在自贸区内，均为外商独资企业，其资金来源、权益归属、经营决策都与外国投资者密切关系；

（b.）涉案合同的履行特征具有涉外因素。

综上所述，本案所涉合同明显不同于一般意义上的内销合同，符合司法解释第一条第五款"兜底"的规定即所谓"其他情形"。可以认定为涉外民事关系"；故具有涉外因素，仲裁条款有效。

最高人民法院根据西门子案的实际情况所采取的分析方法，应归功于近期以最高人民法院为首的中国法院在实践中倾向于向仲裁条款提供司法支持的友善趋势。

三、国际层面上的法律实践

根据《联合国国际货物销售合同公约》（CISG），国际货物销售合同在条约层面受到法律规制。我们研究了《销售公约》下的"国际"概念，以了解 20 世纪 80 年代联合国国际贸易法委员会（UNCITRAL）考虑了哪些国际货物销售合同。

（一）《联合国国际货物销售合同公约》

《销售公约》是联合国国际贸易法委员会为调整国际货物买卖合同关系而制定的最重要的国际条约。1986 年 11 月 12 日，中国正式成为 CISG 缔约国。CISG 于 1988 年 1 月 1 日生效。

截至目前，CISG 缔约国数量已达 97 个，"一带一路"沿线重要国家，如俄罗斯、白俄罗斯、蒙古、吉尔吉斯斯坦、乌克兰、乌兹别克斯坦、巴基斯坦、立陶宛、老挝、越南、柬埔寨、新加坡、丹麦、捷克、埃及、法国、德国、波兰、荷兰、塞尔维亚、伊拉克、意大利等均为 CISG 缔约国。

"国际"的定义在公约的开篇就已经给出。可参照本条约第一条关于"适用范围"的规定。根据第一条的规定，简言之，CISG 仅需满足两个条件即可适用：第一，涉案合同当事人的营业地在不同国家；其次，这些国家是 CISG 的缔约方，国际私法规则导致适用缔约国的法律。换言之，合同双方均有营业场所的国家为 CISG 缔约国；且双方均未在适用法律方面明确排除 CISG 的适用。

CISG 并未直接界定什么是"国际"，而是通过当事人的营业地间接回应了国际货物买卖合同的国际性。"国际"的概念是通过双方的营业地来理解的。位于不同缔约国的当事人之间的货物买卖合同将被视为国际货物买卖合同。由此类合同引起的争议的商事仲裁属于国际商事仲裁。

通过解释《公约》适用于何种情况，间接规定了《公约》第一条中"国际"的定义，具体如下：

第一条 （1）本公约适用于营业地在不同国家的当事人之间所订立的货物销售合同：a.如果这些国家是缔约国；或 b.如果国际私法规则导致适用某一缔约国的法律。（2）当事人营业地在不同国家的事实，如果从合同或从订立合同前任何时候或订立合同时，当事人之间的任何交易或当事人透露的情报均看不出，应不予考虑。（3）在确定本公约的适用时，当事人的国籍和当事人或合同的民事或商业性质，应不予考虑。

在最近一起涉及中国一线城市卖方向当地农户销售养猪设备的合同纠纷案件中，争议的焦点是农户未能向城市卖方公司付款。当事人在合同中约定，CISG 适用于合同及合同纠纷的争议解决。但是，由于《销售公约》

的上述规定，《销售公约》适用于营业地位于不同缔约国的当事人之间的货物销售合同，仲裁庭最终裁定合同纠纷应由当事人协商解决。双方合同应适用中国法律，而不是 CISG 的规定，因为买卖合同的双方都是中国人，其营业场所在中国。

（二）《纽约公约》

"国际"与"国内"的区别在于，国际仲裁与国内仲裁一般受不同的法律制度管辖。有关国际商事仲裁的公约和规则，主要是为适应国际贸易成熟发展的需要而制定，是专门为国际商事仲裁构建的一套日趋完善的法律制度。《纽约公约》仅适用于具有"外国"和"非内国"的"国际"成分的仲裁裁决。"国际"的概念应该从仲裁裁决是否来自外国或是否为申请执行地法律项下"非内国"裁决的角度来理解。

对于"国际"仲裁裁决，《纽约公约》第一条第一款的表述如下：

第 1 条　一、仲裁裁决，因自然人或法人间之争议而产生且在声请承认及执行地所在国以外之国家领土内作成者，其承认及执行适用本公约。本公约对于仲裁裁决经声请承认及执行地所在国认为非内国裁决者，亦适用之。

简而言之，外国裁决可在《纽约公约》的签署国得以承认和执行。该裁决受《纽约公约》保护，前提是该裁决必须在该国被视为 (i) 在国外作出（"外国"裁决），或 (ii) 被视为在非国内作出（"非国内"裁决）。"外国"裁决更易判断：裁决在仲裁地作出，而"仲裁地"可在当事人的仲裁协议中约定，如无协议，则由仲裁庭或仲裁机构确定，在请求承认和执行裁决的国家以外的国家所作的裁决是"外国"裁决。"仲裁地国"和"申请承认和执行裁决所在地的国家"不是同一个国家，仲裁地国的裁决可以认定为外国裁决。一般而言，"非国内"裁决，是指即使裁决本身不是"外国裁决"，在寻求承认和执行裁决的国家被视为"非国内"的裁决。

（三）案例学习

案例学习：Vitiello v. Home Buyers Resale Warranty Corp

2017 年 2 月，原告和 LNAA 签订了一份在萨拉托加斯普林斯建造房屋的合同，该合同受 LNAA 购买的有限保修合同的约束，该合同拒绝任何明示或暗示的保证，支持 HBWC 管理的保修。质保合同第四条载有仲裁条款，规定原告与 LNAA、HBWC 之间发生质保纠纷，应通过仲裁解决。仲裁条款还阐明，它"包括并涉及州际贸易"和"应受美国联邦仲裁法管辖，不包括任何不同或不一致的州或地方法律、法规或司法规则"。根据仲裁条款，仲裁费用由仲裁员自行决定在各方之间分配。房屋最终出现各种缺陷，原告对 LNAA 提起仲裁，并声称所有维修都在保修合同范围内。此案后来争诉至纽约法院。

问题是美国联邦仲裁法（FAA）是否适用于本案的争议。原告争辩说，FAA 不适用于本案的争议，因为与 LNAA 的合同完全是本地（本州内）的。

上诉法院认为，虽然原告与 LNAA 之间的建筑合同可能仅涉及在纽约州的活动，但原告与被告之间的争议涉及保修合同的条款及其管理。作为管理者的 HBWC 是保修合同的一方，任何有关 FAA 适用性的决定都必须考虑到 HBWC 的经济活动及其是否"影响州际贸易"。HBWC 总部位于科罗拉多州，但在美国各地开展业务，为 48 个州的建筑商和房主提供保修服务。因此，很明显，HBWC 在保修方面的商业活动对州际贸易具有重大影响，因此导致适用 FAA。

结语

本文概述了国际商事仲裁中"国际"的具体概念。笔者首先简要介绍了学术界的一些基本分类。其次，本章梳理了我国法律实践的情况，并通过几个典型案例介绍了具体含义。最后，本章运用比较法的方法，对重要的、流行的国际法律规范和一些国家的地方法律规范进行比较阐述。希望读者通过本章的阅读，对中外法学中有关国际商事仲裁中的"国际"的概念有更清晰的认识。

Chapter 2

What is "International" in International Commercial Arbitration Crossing Borders

Adam Pang

International commercial arbitration is an important concept in private international law, and the meaning of "international" needs to be further clarified. This chapter sorts out the current theories in legal academia, and then introduces how China recognizes the vague meaning of "international" in practice. Finally, this chapter analyzes the practice of other developed countries from a comparative law perspective. Through the above three perspectives, this chapter hopes to give readers a comprehensive introduction to what is "international" in international commercial arbitration.

1.Basic Concepts[①]

In fact, there are not many discussions on the "internationality of international commercial arbitration" in academic circles. It should be pointed out that, the "internationality of international commercial arbitration" is a prerequisite for understanding what international commercial arbitration is. The following are some of

---

① See A. Redfern and M. Hunter, *Law and Practice of International Commercial Arbitration*, 2nd ed., London: Sweet & Maxwell, 1991, pp. 15-16.

the relatively mainstream views in the current academic circle:

(1) Geographical criteria

International commercial arbitration deals with disputes of the parties from different countries. Location of the parties or of the place of arbitration is first to be considered. If one of the connecting factors, such as the place of arbitration, the nationality of the parties, domicile or residence, the place of registration of the legal person and the location of the company management center, has an international factor, such commercial arbitration is regarded as international commercial arbitration. European countries such as the United Kingdom, Sweden, and Switzerland, as well as Arab countries such as Egypt and Syria, all adopt this standard when determining the internationality of arbitration.

(2) Determine the attribution of arbitration according to the nature of the dispute

The standard of the nature of the dispute is used to determine the attribution of arbitration. This standard considers the arbitration according to the nature of the dispute. If the dispute involves international commercial interests, the arbitration to resolve this commercial dispute is an international commercial arbitration. Countries such as France[1], the United States[2] and Canada[3] have adopted this standard.

(3) Mixed standards

A cluster of mixed standards is used to determine whether the arbitration is an international commercial arbitration. The following elements are considered under this cluster of mixed standards: First, arbitration of disputes between parties whose places of business are in different countries; Second, arbitration in which the place of

---

[1] See A. Redfern and M. Hunter, *Law and Practice of International Commercial Arbitration*, 2nd ed., London: Sweet&Maxwell, 1991, pp. 15-16.

[2] 参见韩健：《现代国际商事仲裁法的理论与实践》（第 2 版），法律出版社 2000 年版，第 4 页。

[3] 参见韩德培主编：《国际私法》，北京大学出版社、高等教育出版社 2014 年版，第 530 页。

arbitration and the parties' places of business are located in different countries at that time; Third, the place of performance of main obligations and the parties' business arbitrations located in different countries; Fourth, arbitration in which the place most closely related to the subject of the dispute and the parties' places of business are located in different countries; Fifth, the parties expressly agree to arbitration in which the subject of the dispute is related to more than one country.

2. Legal Practice in China

China adopts the mixed standards approach. According to Chinese private international law theory and judicial practice, the foreign-related or international nature of civil legal relations should be interpreted in a broad sense, that is, as long as at least one of the subject, object or content is related to a jurisdiction other than mainland China, it is equivalent to having an international character. In particular:

First, the nationality of one or both parties is not Chinese; Second, the domicile of one or both parties is not in China; Third, the subject matter of the dispute is not within the territory of China; Fourth, the legal facts of the establishment, modification or termination of civil and commercial legal relations occur outside China; Fifth, if the domicile of the parties, the subject matter of the dispute or the legal facts occur in Hong Kong, Macao and Taiwan regions, it may also be regarded as an international or foreign-related arbitration.[1]

Here, we can learn more about how the "international" concept in international commercial arbitration is recognized in Chinese practice through several typical cases.

In the dispute over the application of Jiangsu Aerospace Wanyuan Wind Power Equipment Manufacturing Co., Ltd. and Elm Wind Energy Blade Products (Tianjin) Co., Ltd. to confirm the validity of the arbitration agreement[2], the parties entered into

---

[1] 《最高人民法院关于适用〈中华人民共和国涉外民事关系法律适用法〉若干问题的解释(一)》(《涉外法律适用法司法解释》) 第一条。

[2] 江苏航天万源风电设备制造有限公司与艾尔姆风能叶片制品(天津)有限公司申请确认仲裁协议效力纠纷案。

an arbitration clause in the "Trade Agreement" between the two parties, stipulating that the relevant disputes can be submitted to the International Chamber of Commerce for arbitration in Beijing. In this regard, the Supreme Court stated in its reply: "The parties to the Trade Agreement are both Chinese legal persons, the subject matter is in China, and the agreement is also concluded and performed in China. There are no elements of foreign-related civil relations, and the agreement does not belong to foreign-related contracts. Since the jurisdiction of arbitration is the power conferred by the law, and Chinese law does not stipulate that the parties can submit disputes that do not have foreign-related elements to an overseas arbitration institution or ad hoc arbitration outside China. To sum up, the agreement of the parties in this case has no legal basis."

Similarly, in the case of Liupanshui Hengding Industrial Co., Ltd. and Zhang Hongxing's dispute over the dispute over the transfer of mining rights the Supreme People's Court also pointed out that "the parties to a non-foreign-related civil case agreed that the dispute shall be decided by an arbitration institution outside Mainland China. This agreement should be deemed invalid because it violates the "principle of judicial sovereignty."

The provisions of judicial interpretation are actually based on the three elements of traditional legal relationship, namely the subject, object and content of legal relationship, to define foreign-related factors. However, with the development of the free trade zone and the deepening of the influence of the "Belt and Road", the traditional three-element legal identification method has been difficult to cover many new types of cross-border economic and trade cooperation. Paragraph 5 of Article 1 of the Judicial Interpretation[1] is a typical "catch-all clause".[2] It includes the "catch-all clause" in the words — "and other circumstances that may be considered as foreign related elements".

Accordingly, in the recent case[3], Siemens v. Golden Landmark's application[4]

---

[1] 《最高人民法院关于适用〈中华人民共和国涉外民事关系法律适用法〉若干问题的解释（一）》（《涉外法律适用法司法解释》）第一条。
[2] （五）可以认定为涉外民事关系的其他情形。
[3] "西门子 v. 黄金置地"申请承认和执行外国仲裁裁决一案。
[4] https://www.allbrightlaw.com/SH/CN/10475/45f49dc0260f7f4d.aspx.

for recognition and enforcement of foreign arbitral awards, the catch-all clause gave the judge an opportunity to expand the interpretation of "foreign-related factors"; The Supreme People's Court not only subsequently endorsed the judgment, but also took the opportunity to issue an express opinion, giving a more expanded explanation of the "foreign-related factors" related to the free trade zone.

Reasons for judgment in this Siemens case:

● The arbitration agreement is valid: although the contract involved does not have typical foreign-related factors, yet it is significantly different from ordinary domestic contracts, it can be identified as a foreign-related civil legal relationship;

● The arbitration clause of the contract involved in the case "contract disputes must be submitted to the Singapore International Arbitration Centre for arbitration" is clearly agreed and the meaning is clear.

Therefore, the key to judging the validity of the arbitration clause is whether the contract involved has foreign elements.

The parties to this case are all legal persons registered in China, the place of delivery and the current location of the subject matter are both within the territory of China, which on the surface does not meet the first four paragraphs of Article 1 of the Judicial Interpretation. But:

(a) The subject of this case has certain foreign-related factors: the places of registration are in the free trade zone, all are wholly foreign-owned enterprises, and the source of capital, ownership of interests, and business decisions of the company are closely related to foreign investors;

(b) The performance characteristics of the contract involved in the case have foreign-related factors.

Based on the above circumstances, the contract involved in the case is obviously different from the domestic sales contract in the ordinary meaning, which conforms to the "catch-all clause" of Article 1, Paragraph 5 of the Judicial Interpretation: "other circumstances that can be identified as foreign-related civil relations"; therefore it has foreign-related factors, and the arbitration clause is valid .

The analytical approach adopted by the Supreme People's Court based on the factual circumstances of the Siemens case should be accredited to the recent trend of the PRC courts led by the Supreme People's Court in extending practical judicial support in favor of arbitration clauses in China.

3. Legal Practice at the International Level

International sale of goods is regulated at the treaty level under the United Nations Convention on Contracts for the International Sale of Goods (CISG). We examine the concept of "international" under the CISG to understand what contracts of international sale of goods were considered at the level of the United Nations Commission on International Trade Law (UNCITRAL) in the 1980s.

(1) The CISG

"CISG" is the most important international treaty formulated by UNCITRAL to adjust the contractual relationship of the international sale of goods. CISG came into effect on January 1, 1988. On December 11, 1986, China officially became a party to the CISG.

As of January 2022, there were 94 contracting states[①] to the CISG in total, representing over two thirds of the global economy, and important countries along the "Belt and Road", such as Russia, Belarus, Mongolia, Kyrgyzstan, Ukraine, Uzbekistan, Pakistan, Lithuania, Laos, Vietnam, Cambodia, Singapore, Denmark, Czech Republic, Egypt, France, Germany, Poland, the Netherlands, Serbia, Iraq, Italy, etc. are all CISG contracting states.

The definition of "international" is set out in the beginning of the Convention. One can refer to the provisions of Article 1 of this treaty on "sphere of application". According to Article 1, the CISG only needs to meet two conditions for application: firstly, the parties to the contract in issue have their places of business in different states; secondly, these states are Contracting Parties to the CISG, and the rules of private international law lead to the application of the law of the Contracting State.

---

① Adopting the CISG – Hong Kong enhances its openness to international trade Talking Point Asia – November 2022, https://www.jdsupra.com/legalnews/adopting-the-cisg-hong-kong-enhances-4461681/.

In other words, the countries where both parties to the contract have their places of business are CISG Contracting States; and both parties did not expressly exclude the application of CISG in terms of applicable law.[①]

CISG does not directly define what is "international", but indirectly responds to the international nature of international sale of goods contract through the place of business of the parties. The concept of "international" is understood through the place of business of the parties. A sale of goods contract between parties located in different Contracting States will be considered as an international sale of goods contract. Commercial arbitration of disputes arising from such a contract would be an international commercial arbitration.

By explaining to what circumstances the Convention applies, it indirectly prescribed the definition of "international" under the Convention in Article 1, as follows:

Article 1

(1) This Convention applies to contracts of sale of goods between parties whose places of business are in different States:

(a) when the States are Contracting States; or

(b) when the rules of private international law lead to the application of the law of a Contracting State.

(2) The fact that the parties have their places of business in different States is to be disregarded whenever this fact does not appear either from the contract or from any dealings between, or from information disclosed by, the parties at any time before or at the conclusion of the contract.

(3) Neither the nationality of the parties nor the civil or commercial character of the parties or of the contract is to be taken into consideration in determining the application of this Convention.

In a recent case involving a contract of sales of equipment for raising pigs to the local farmers from a seller in first tier city in China, the dispute centers on the failure of the payment by the farmer to the urban seller company. The parties agreed

---

① Article 6, CISG.

in the contract that the CISG applies to the contract and dispute resolution of the contractual disputes. However, due to the above-mentioned provision of the CISG that CISG applies to contracts of sale of goods between parties whose places of business are located in different Contracting States, the Tribunal finally determines that the contractual disputes are to be resolved by agreement of the parties according to Chinese law, instead of the provisions of CISG, because the two parties to the sales contract are both Chinese persons with their places of business in China.

(2) The New York Convention

The difference between "international" and "domestic" is that international arbitration and domestic arbitration generally are regulated under different legal systems. The conventions and rules applicable to international commercial arbitration are mainly to meet the needs of the mature development of international trade, and they are also a set of increasingly perfect legal systems specially constructed for international commercial arbitration. The New York Convention applies only to arbitral awards with an "international" element to the extent involving "foreign" or "non-domestic". The concept of "international" is to be understood from the vantage point of whether the awards come from a foreign state or considered as "non-domestic" under the law of the enforcing state.

For "international" arbitral awards, the New York Convention's expression in Article 1, paragraph 1 is as follows:

Article I

1. This Convention shall apply to the recognition and enforcement of arbitral awards made in the territory of a State other than the State where the recognition and enforcement of such awards are sought, and arising out of differences between persons, whether physical or legal. It shall also apply to arbitral awards not considered as domestic awards in the State where their recognition and enforcement are sought.

To put it simply, an award goes to a signatory country to the New York Convention for the purpose of recognition and enforcement. The award is protected by the New York Convention on the premise that the award must be considered in that country as (i) it is made abroad (i.e. a "foreign" award), or (ii) it is deemed to have been made non-domestic (i.e. a "non-domestic" award). A "foreign" award is easier to judge: the award is made at the place of arbitration, which may be stipulated in the parties' arbitration agreement, or determined by the arbitral tribunal or arbitration institution in the absence of such agreement, in the territory of the state other than the state where the recognition and enforcement of the award is sought. The "country of the seat of arbitration" and "the country where the recognition and enforcement of the award is applied for" are not the same country, so they can be recognized as foreign awards. In general, a "non-domestic" award means that even if the award itself is not a "foreign award", it is considered a "non-domestic" award in the country where recognition and enforcement of the award is sought.

(3) Case Study

Case study: Vitiello v. Home Buyers Resale Warranty Corp[①]

In February 2017, plaintiffs and LNAA entered into a contract for the construction of a home in Saratoga Springs, which was covered by a limited warranty contract purchased by LNAA, which denied any express or implied warranty in favor of the warranty administered by HBWC. Article 4 of the warranty contract contains an arbitration clause, which stipulates that any disputes involving warranty between the plaintiff, LNAA and HBWC shall be resolved through arbitration. The arbitration clause also clarifies that it "includes and involves interstate commerce" and "shall be governed by the Federal Arbitration Act (FAA), excluding any different or inconsistent state or local laws, regulations, or rules of justice." Under the arbitration clause, the costs of the arbitration are distributed among the parties at the discretion of the arbitrator. The home ended up with various defects, and the plaintiffs brought arbitration against the LNAA and claimed that all repairs were covered by the warranty contract. The case subsequently went to court in New York State.

The issue is whether FAA applies to the dispute in the case. The plaintiffs contend that the FAA does not apply to the dispute in this case because the contract with the

---

① https://iidps.bit.edu.cn/gatsw/4627f69635d14b128114833209de5fbd.htm.

LNAA is entirely local.

The Court of Appeals held that, while the construction contract between the plaintiff and the LNAA may have concerned only activities in the state of New York, the dispute between the plaintiff and the defendant concerned both the terms of the warranty contract and its administration. HBWC, as administrator, is a party to the warranty contract, and any decision regarding FAA applicability must take into account HBWC's economic activity and whether it "affects interstate commerce." HBWC is headquartered in Colorado, but operates across the United States, offering warranties to builders and homeowners in 48 states. Thus, it is clear that HBWC's commercial activities with respect to warranties have a material effect on interstate commerce and thus lead to the application of the FAA.

Conclusion

This chapter summarizes the specific concept of "international" in international commercial arbitration. The author first briefly introduces some basic classifications in the academic world; secondly, the chapter sorts out the situation of China's legal practice, and introduces the specific meanings through several typical cases. Finally, using the method of comparative law, the chapter makes an exposition of important and popular international legal norms and some local legal norms. It is hoped that readers have a clearer understanding of what international commercial arbitration is in Chinese and foreign law.

References:

参考文献

[1] See A. Redfern and M. Hunter, *Law and Practice of International Commercial Arbitration*, 2nd ed., London: Sweet & Maxwell, 1991, pp. 15-16.

[2] See A. Redfern and M. Hunter, *Law and Practice of International Commercial Arbitration*, 2nd ed., London: Sweet & Maxwell, 1991, pp. 15-16.

[3] 参见韩健：《现代国际商事仲裁法的理论与实践》（第2版），法律出版社2000年版，第4页。

[4] 参见韩德培主编：《国际私法》，北京大学出版社、高等教育出版社2014年版，第530页。

[5] 《最高人民法院关于适用〈中华人民共和国涉外民事关系法律适用法〉若干问题的解释（一）》（《涉外法律适用法司法解释》）第一条。

[6] 江苏航天万源风电设备制造有限公司与艾尔姆风能叶片制品（天津）有限公司申请确认仲裁协议效力纠纷案。

[7] 盘水恒鼎实业有限公司与张洪兴采矿权转让合同争议管辖权异议案。

[8] 《最高人民法院关于适用〈中华人民共和国涉外民事关系法律适用法〉若干问题的解释（一）》（《涉外法律适用法司法解释》）第一条。

[9] "西门子 v. 黄金置地"申请承认和执行外国仲裁裁决一案。

[10] Article 6, CISG.

[11] If Chinese translation is needed, please go to: http://www.bjac.org.cn/news/view.asp?id=1071,

[12] Shimabukuro, J.O. , "The Federal Arbitrational Act: Background and Recent Developments", 2003.

[13] https://mp.weixin.qq.com/s/0w1QvWkZDoPwUPtk3wvlhg.

[14] https://iidps.bit.edu.cn/gatsw/4627f69635d14b128114833209de5fbd.htm.

第三章

当合同关系出现问题时，如何处理争议？

王文倩

　　从谈判到签署再到履行，合同各方都期望整个过程一帆风顺，没有错误发生，没人背信弃义。然而，事与愿违是家常便饭，合同时常发生纠纷。如果合同在胁迫或不当影响下订立，可能会被撤销。合同各方对条款的解释可能意见不一。当合同走向终点，结局并不总会让各方都满意。可能会发生违约行为，使无过错方处于不利地位。目的实现可能受阻，尽管各方均无过错，履约依然无法实现。

　　无过错方会要求过错方承担赔偿责任，乃至终止合同。当目的实现受阻时，损失将不得不在各方之间分配。争议难免发生，需要争议解决机制介入。争议解决方式都有哪些？应该继续由合同各方自行解决，还是应该找第三方介入？幸运的是，法律已经提供了一套具有不同程度的自主性、保密性和可执行性的解决方案供当事方选择。发生合同纠纷时，可以诉诸法院。但在许多情况下，各方不必对簿公堂。为了保持交易的稳定性，如果合同关系尚未破裂，合同方可能希望自行或在第三方介入的情况下于庭外解决争议。争议解决方式总体上可分为诉讼和替代性争议解决（ADR）。

一、 争议解决的司法方式

通过诉讼解决争议，寻求司法机关支持，结果具有终局性和可执行性。司法是"最后一道防线"，如果其他争议解决方式失败，法院会主持正义，保护当事人的合法权益不受损失。然而，诉讼程序漫长且昂贵，通过诉讼解决争议变得越来越不受欢迎。

跨国诉讼则更为复杂。通常情况下，不同国家的多个法院均拥有跨国合同纠纷的管辖权。各方都有权将同一争端诉诸其所选择的法院，法院可以根据法院地的程序法来审理案件。因此，当事人有可能就同一标的提起多起诉讼，承担更高昂的成本，产生平行诉讼问题。平行诉讼会将当事人拖入旷日持久的法律纠纷，带来巨大的不确定性，不同法院可能从不同角度解释事实和适用的法律，得出相互矛盾的判决。为解决这一问题，当事人可以在合同中选择管辖法院。

除《关于承认和执行外国民事和商事判决的公约》（海牙判决公约）外，目前未有法律机制使某国判决在他国得以执行。因此，外国判决的执行只有通过各国之间缔结有关承认和执行外国判决的条约或通过国际礼让实现。

二、 替代性争议解决

替代性争议解决（ADR）包括一系列帮助争议各方找到满意解决方案的方法。争议的性质及严重程度、争议各方的特点以及涉及的金额不同，替代性争议解决的最佳方式也不同。传统、正式的争议解决方法需要耗费大量时间和成本。当事人利用不同类型的替代性争议解决方法，可以更大程度掌控案件，降低成本，实现保密性。

替代性争议解决虽基于争议各方的合意，但难以具备约束力。大量替代性争议解决活动中达成的协议，只能依赖当事人自愿履行。如果一方食言，前期的努力便付之东流。由于替代性争议解决旨在解决诉讼无法满足的需求，当事人不仅可以采用既有的替代性争议解决方式，还可以量身定制新的方式。在实践中，从建筑工程项目到劳动就业保护，不同的情形适用不同的替代性争议解决方式。替代性争议解决本身具有丰富多样性，本章仅就最常见的方式展开论述。

（一）协商

合同关系建立在合同各方的相互信任之上，需历经深思熟虑、漫长的协商与谈判，绝非一时之功。如果双方决定不再合作，将带来大量沉没成本。如果还有和平磋商的空间，双方往往都希望在相互理解和礼让的基础上解决争议。合同关系是协商的产物，其发展与维系也有赖于贯穿于合同履行始终的协商过程。因此，国际商事合同往往会规定如下条款："由本协议引起的任何争议必须由双方通过友好协商解决。"

因此，协商是国际商事交易中解决争议的首要手段。然而，由于协商仅基于各方维持合同关系的真实意图，通过协商达成的协议并不具有高于合同的法律约束力。协商解决的问题仍是合同层面的问题，有被推翻的可能性。

（二）调解（Mediation and Conciliation）

当我们无法与他人就某个问题达成一致意见，会邀请一名第三人给出公正的看法。国际商事活动中亦是如此。当谈判无法继续，公正和独立的第三方可以介入，推进争议解决过程，这种争议解决的方式称为调解。调解的过程在各方推动的友好气氛下进行，最终解决争议的方案可由当事人提出，也可由协助双方当事人的调解员提出。

长期以来，中国人珍视和谐。无论是在日常生活中还是在商业交易中，我们坚持和谐相处，避免紧张的关系阻碍本可实现的合作成果。这种精神亦体现在解决争议、维护和谐的协商和调解活动中。

替代性争议解决还有许多形式，如微型审判，指邀请一名受人尊敬的律师或法官作为第三方与来自争议双方的代表共同处理纠纷，以及早期中立评估，即第三方就案件可能的处理结果进行评估预测。这些方式为解决争议提供了友好的环境，但是最后的结果往往不具有约束力，会带来很大的不确定性。仲裁便是解决这一问题的良方。仲裁在最大程度上尊重当事人的自由意愿，同时又能够形成具有约束力、终局性且可强制执行的决定。仲裁结合了诉讼程序的确定性和其他替代性争议解决方式的灵活性，是国际商事纠纷中最常见的争议解决方法，将在下部分详细阐述。

三、仲裁

仲裁能够在司法系统之外解决争议，是现代商业世界无法取代的争议解决方式。本节将重点讨论仲裁的性质、特征及其应用。

（一）仲裁简介

仲裁是一种历史悠久的争议解决方法。国际商事仲裁在国际商事活动蓬勃发展后，成为一种不可或缺的跨境争议解决形式，其历史可以追溯到1794年。1794年，美国与英国之间签署条约，同意通过仲裁解决双方争端。1899年，常设仲裁法院于海牙和平会议上成立。1958年，《承认及执行外国仲裁裁决公约》于纽约通过，现有170多个签署国，已成为现代仲裁制度的基础。1985年，博采世界各国法律专家意见的《联合国国际贸易法委员会国际商事仲裁示范法》问世，它作为国际仲裁活动统一的示范性法律，被许多国家参考或直接采用。

中国的仲裁历史起源于1956年。《纽约公约》问世前的两年，中国国际经济贸易仲裁委员会成立。仲裁成为当时解决纠纷的推荐方式。改革开放以来，仲裁变得越发重要。中国于1986年加入《纽约公约》，于1991年将"涉外仲裁"规则作为独立章节写入《民事诉讼法》，并于1994年通过《中华人民共和国仲裁法》。该法标志着完整的仲裁体系在中国建立。然而，这部法律已无法适应当今不断变化的商业环境，因此正在进行全面修订。2021年，现行仲裁法的修订草案正式公开征求意见。

（二）优势一：当事人意思自治

当事人意思自治是指争议当事人在仲裁活动中享有灵活的选择权，其决定始终受到尊重。一旦仲裁协议生效，仲裁庭或仲裁员的管辖权就基于当事人将争议诉诸仲裁的合意产生。当事人可以通过仲裁协议来满足自身需求，决定仲裁地点、仲裁规则、仲裁程序，以及各方选定的适合审理该争议的仲裁员。在仲裁过程中，当事人可以决定使用何种语言，是否有必要开庭，是否想通过调解或和解来解决争议。如果能够达成和解或调解协议，视为与仲裁裁决具有同等效力。当事人意思自治是民事活动的原则，贯穿仲裁过程始终。在仲裁的支持下，国际贸易活动的参与者可以拥有高效、便捷和充满活力的商业环境。

（三）优势2：司法对仲裁的有限干预

法院支持并尊重仲裁员对争议的独立判断，这是国际商事仲裁的显著特点。

案例研究：FCA Canada Inc. v. Reid-Lamontagne, 2019 ONSC 364

事实：在汽车制造商FCA加拿大公司（"FCA"）与消费者Christine Reid-Lamontagne之间的仲裁活动中，仲裁员命令FCA拆除并更换导致Lamontagne汽车故障的车辆启动器。该裁决的依据是一份旨在解决消费者与主要汽车制造商之间小型纠纷的仲裁协议。FCA申请撤销该裁决，其中一个理由是，该裁决认定存在当前缺陷。FCA认为该裁决不合理，应该予以撤销。法院认为，FCA该主张实质上是对事实调查的质疑，而非对仲裁协议范围的质疑，故法院无权干涉。

本案判决中，法官强调，"对仲裁的司法干预必须控制在极小的限度内"。法官反复表明，法院只审查程序性问题，事实认定等实质性问题超出了法院的干预范围。只要裁决是由仲裁员在合法程序下合理做出的，法院就必须支持，即使法官如在仲裁员的位置上可能不会得出相同的结论。本撤销申请的适用法律是加拿大阿尔伯塔省 1991 年的《仲裁法》。法律规定："任何法院不得干预本法所辖事项，但本法规定的以下目的除外：（a）协助仲裁程序开展；（b）确保仲裁按照仲裁协议进行；（c）防止仲裁协议一方受到明显不公平或不平等的对待；以及（d）执行仲裁裁决。"值得注意的是，该法并未采用《示范法》，但是却呼应了《示范法》的基本精神，这些原则已被国际仲裁界普遍接受。同样，《示范法》第 5 条规定："在本法所辖事项中，除非本法另有规定，否则法院不得干预。"在国际商事仲裁中，普遍认为法院介入仲裁程序的权力十分有限，即使介入，也仅是出于协助和监督的目的。这为争议各方带来了极大的确定性和效率。一旦适当的仲裁程序结束，各方便可获得具有约束力的争议解决方案。

（四）优势 3：承认和执行得到保障

跨国诉讼面临的一个主要问题是，判决在另一个司法辖区内可能不被承认或执行。该问题可以通过商事仲裁来弥补，尤其是在《纽约公约》签署国进行的仲裁。如上文所述，世界上许多国家的法院在承认或执行仲裁裁决之前，仅审查仲裁裁决的程序性事项。《纽约公约》规定，"除非另有规定，任何仲裁裁决都应在签署国得到承认和执行"，这让仲裁裁决的承认和执行变得更加便利。公约在第五条第一款中列出了法院可能拒绝承认和执行的五种情形。除此以外，签署国不应对任何外国裁决设置不合理的障碍。《纽约公约》是国际仲裁领域的一个成功的多边条约，它确保仲裁裁决具有约束力，可在世界上大多数地区执行，增强了商业活动主体选择仲裁作为其首要争议解决方式的信心。

结语

本章围绕"合同关系出现问题时如何处理争议"展开探讨。总体上，当事人可以选择司法和非司法方法解决争议。前者受主权国家的司法体系保护，后者也被称为"替代性争议解决"，旨在帮助争议各方以更灵活、友好的方式解决问题。然而，除了仲裁之外，大多数替代性争议解决方式都未能产生具有约束力的结果。因此，仲裁已成为备受欢迎的争议解决方法，特别是在国际商事活动中。来自不同国家的当事人之间产生争议时，司法措施会降低效率，造成许多不确定性。然而，得益于《纽约公约》和《示范法》，世界范围内的仲裁实践越来越具统一性，仲裁裁决的承认与执行几乎不受阻碍。

Chapter 3

When a Contractual Relationship Broke up, How to Deal with the Disputes?

Wenqian Wang

In a contract, every party expects smooth sailing throughout the entire process, from preliminary negotiation, to execution and all the way to performance. No mistake occurs; no one breaks his promise. However, things do not always go the way one wishes. It is commonplace that problems arise with a contract from time to time. A contract might get vitiated if the agreement is found to have reached under duress or undue influence. The parties to the contract may not be on the same page when it comes to the interpretation of the terms. And when the contract comes to an end, it does not always end with performance satisfactory to each party. There might be a breach which puts the innocent party at a disadvantage, or a frustration, making performance impossible, though neither party has a fault.

In most cases, the innocent party will hold the party at fault accountable, either claiming damages or seeking to end the contract. When frustration occurs, loss will have to be distributed among the parties. Such a situation may inevitably lead to disputes and that's when dispute resolution fits in. In what ways can these disputes be settled? Should such disagreement remain at the sole helm of the contracting parties or should a third-party step in to help? Luckily, the law has offered a set of resolutions to choose, with varied levels of autonomy, confidentiality and enforceability. When contractual disputes arise, the parties may resort to a court. But in many cases, they do not have to end up being plaintiff and defendant. To maintain the stability of business transactions, if there is no rupture between the parties, they may want to settle the disputes out of court, either by themselves or with the involvement of a third party. Dispute resolution can be roughly divided into litigation, a judicial method, and alternative dispute resolution (ADR), a non-judicial vehicle.

1. Judicial Dispute Resolution

Dispute resolution through litigation provides contractual parties with finality and enforceability, endorsed by the authority of a judicial body. Litigation is the last resort. If other dispute resolution methods fail, the court is ready to administer justice and protect the legitimate rights and interests of the parties at loss. However, given the long and costly process involved during litigation, it has become less and less popular.

The discussion of litigation in international transactions brings about new complications. Usually, the jurisdiction of an international dispute may fall on multiple courts in different countries. Each party is entitled to resort to the court it selects for the same dispute and the selected court may hear the case in accordance with legal procedures under the *lex fori*, or the law of the court. Thus, it is possible that the parties initiate more than one lawsuit regarding the same subject. They may end up with higher costs and judgements with inconsistent opinions, which brings to the paradox of parallel litigation. It is no doubt that parallel litigation will drag the parties into a long-drawn-out legal wrangle with immense uncertainty since different courts may interpret the facts and laws from different perspectives and inevitably come up with conflicting judgements or decisions. One solution to this issue is that the parties choose a certain court in their contract prior to the dispute.

Except for the *Convention on the Recognition and Enforcement of Foreign Judgments in Civil or Commercial Matters* (the "Hague Judgments Convention"), there is currently no legal mechanism that makes judgements, decisions and verdicts made in one country automatically enforced in another country. Thus, enforcement can only be enabled in one country through treaties concluded with others regarding the recognition and enforcement of foreign judgements. Otherwise, such enforcement could only be made possible via international comity.

2. Alternative Dispute Resolution

Alternative dispute resolution (ADR) consists of a variety of approaches which aim at helping the parties to a dispute find a satisfactory solution. It varies regarding the nature and severity of the dispute, the characteristics of the parties to the dispute, or the amount of money involved. Due to the time-consuming and costly procedures required in traditional and formal dispute settlement methods, different types of alternative dispute resolution are capitalized on to help parties gain more control over their cases, reduce costs or ensure confidentiality.

Though ADR arises from mutual consent from the parties in dispute, it is worth noting that few ADR approaches produce a binding decision. Agreements reached during a large number of ADR activities can only be enforced by the performance of the parties' duties. If one side breaks his words, the previous efforts will be in vain. In theory, since ADR is invented to address the needs of which litigation falls short, the parties not only can use settled ADR forms but create their own approaches. In practice, different ADRs are applied in different scenarios, ranging from construction projects to employment rights protection. Given the diversity of ADR itself, this chapter will only be able to introduce methods that are most commonly seen in our daily life in China.

(1) Negotiation

Contractual relationship is not created with the snap of a finger. It is built on mutual trust between each party after a long process of deliberation, consultation and negotiation. Those would become the sunken cost if the parties decide that they are no longer partners. Generally, the parties want to settle the dispute based on mutual understanding and comity if there is still room for peaceful talks. Contractual relationships, the child of long-term negotiation, can also grow and sustain with negotiation during the performance of the contract. That is why an international commercial contract provides such terms as follows:

"Any dispute arising from this Agreement must be settled by the Parties through amicable negotiation."

Negotiation is thus the first resort to disputes in international business transactions. And since it is based on the sincere intention of the parties to keep their contracts in continual performance, agreements reached between them carry no better binding force than a contract. Everything settled during the negotiation can be reversed or taken back as a matter of contract negotiation.

(2) Mediation and Conciliation

When a person cannot reach an agreement with his/her friend on an issue, it is natural for him/her to invite another third person to give some fair opinions. The same may happen in international business. When negotiations cannot move forward, an unbiased and independent third party can be introduced to facilitate the dispute settlement process. Such a way of settling disputes is mediation and conciliation. Though the two words are often used as synonyms, there are subtle differences. Under mediation, the third-party mediator helps the parties to reach an agreement through amicable discussion. Whether the parties will find a way out of the conflict or not still depends on the parties themselves. The mediator may not direct them to a specific solution. While under conciliation, the conciliator may play an advisory role and guide the parties to the solution of the disputes. But be it mediation or conciliation, the process of dispute settlement is still fueled by the parties' goodwill in a friendly atmosphere.

Chinese people have long taken harmony as the most precious thing, both in their daily life and in business transactions. We cherish harmony because tensions can only make things worse, deteriorating what people could have achieved together. This spirit is reflected in negotiation, mediation and conciliation, as they all seek to settle disputes while maintaining harmony at the same time.

There are many other types of ADRs, such as Mini Trial, in which a respected lawyer or judge is invited as a third party, handling the dispute with representatives from both parties and Early Neutral Evaluation where a third party gives an evaluation of how the dispute might be resolved. All of these methods provide a less hostile environment for dispute settlement, though the outcome in the end often carries no binding force, creating a great deal of uncertainty. That is when arbitration sets in. It respects the parties' free will to the largest extent and at the same time, leads to a binding, final and enforceable decision. Arbitration combines the certainty litigation provides and the flexibility other ADRs can offer, which makes it the most common ADR method in dealing with international commercial disputes. To this end, arbitration will be specifically introduced below.

3. Arbitration

Arbitration, a platform which enables dispute settlement out of the judicial system, has become irreplaceable in the modern commercial world. This section will focus on the ABC of arbitration, its distinctive features, and its application.

(1) Arbitration in General

Arbitration is a time-honored method of dispute resolution. Even international arbitration, a form of settling cross-border disputes which becomes indispensable after international commerce started to boom, can be traced back to 1794, when the United States of America and Great Britain signed a treaty and agreed to resolve disputes through arbitration. Later in 1899, the Permanent Court of Arbitration (PCA) was founded at the Hague Peace Conferences. In 1958, the New York Convention on the Recognition and Enforcement of Foreign Arbitral Awards was established. It has become the foundation of the modern arbitration system, with more than 170 signatories. In 1985, the UNCITRAL Model Law was ratified after adopting opinions of legal experts from countries worldwide. It serves as a unified and demonstrative law for international arbitration practice, thus directly applied or referenced by a large number of countries.

China's history of arbitration originated in 1956, when the China International Economic and Trade Arbitration Commission was founded two years prior to the birth of the New York Convention. Arbitration became one of the recommended ways to settle disputes back then. Since the reform and opening up launched, arbitration has become more and more important. China joined the New York Convention in 1986, prescribed rules on "foreign-related arbitration" as a separate chapter in the Civil Procedure Law in 1991, and passed the Arbitration Law of the PRC in 1994. The Law marks the establishment of a complete arbitration system in China. However, since it can no longer adapt to the ever-changing commercial landscape nowadays, extensive changes are being made. In 2021, the draft of the amendment to the existing arbitration law was officially publicized for opinions.

(2) Advantage 1: Party Autonomy

Party autonomy means that the parties to a dispute enjoy the flexibility to choose what they want in arbitration activities and such decisions will always be respected. Once the arbitration agreement takes effect, the jurisdiction of an arbitral tribunal or an arbitrator is thus created based on the consent of the parties to resort their disputes to arbitration. Arbitration agreements serve as a medium through which the parties can tailor their needs, including the seat of the arbitration, the arbitral rules and procedures, and the arbitrators who they deem have the knowledge of the subject matter of the dispute. During the arbitration process, the parties can decide on which language(s) to be used, whether hearings are necessary or whether they want to resolve their disputes through mediation or conciliation. If such an agreement can be reached, they will be deemed as having the same effect as an arbitral award. Party autonomy, a guiding principle for handling civil affairs, is followed through the entire arbitration process. Thus, with the support of arbitration, entities involved in international trade can enjoy an enabling commercial environment which is efficient, convenient and dynamic.

(3) Advantage 2: Limited Judicial Intervention in Arbitration

One distinctive feature of international commercial arbitration is that the court supports and respects arbitrators' independent judgement on a certain dispute.

Case study: FCA Canada Inc. v. Reid-Lamontagne, 2019 ONSC 364

Facts: In an arbitration between FCA Canada Inc. ("FCA"), a car manufacturer and Christine Reid-Lamontagne, a consumer who bought

FCA's vehicle, the arbitrator ordered that FCA remove and replace the Vehicle's Starter which causes failure of Lamontagne's car. The award was made in accordance with an arbitration agreement designed to resolve small disputes between consumers and major automotive vehicle manufacturers. FCA brings an application to set aside the award. One alternative argument is that the award finds that there was a current defect, which FCA thought was unreasonable and ought to be set aside. The court held that this argument was in essence questioning fact-finding instead of the scope of the Arbitration Agreement, which cannot be handled by the court.

In this case, the judge stressed that "judicial intervention in arbitrations must be very narrow". He repeatedly said that the court only reviews procedural issues and substantive questions such as facts finding are beyond the scope of the court's intervention. As long as the decision is reasonably made by the arbitrator under legitimate procedures, the court has to support it even though the judge may not come to the same conclusion if he/she were the arbitrator. The governing law of this application is *the Arbitration Act*, 1991 of Alberta, Canada. It provides that "no court may intervene in matters governed by this Act, except for the following purposes as provided by this Act: (a) to assist the arbitration process; (b) to ensure that an arbitration is carried on in accordance with the arbitration agreement; (c) to prevent manifestly unfair or unequal treatment of a party to an arbitration agreement; and (d) to enforce awards". It is worth noting that this act is not prescribed under the UNCITRAL Model Law, but even so this act echoes some basic guiding spirits of the model law, which are generally accepted by the international arbitration community. In the UNCITRAL Model Law, similarly, Article 5 provides that "in matters governed by this Law, no court shall intervene except where so provided in this Law." Thus, it is widely recognized that in international commercial arbitration, the court only has limited power to step in the arbitration process and if it does, the intervention is purely for assistance and supervision. This ensures tremendous certainty and efficiency for the parties to a dispute, since they can expect that a binding solution may take shape once a proper arbitration process comes to an end.

(4) Advantage 3: Guaranteed Recognition and Enforcement

A major concern of cross-border litigation is that the final decision might not be recognized or enforced in another jurisdiction. Such a disadvantage can be compensated by commercial arbitration, especially for those carried out in signatories of the New York Convention. As we've discussed above, courts in many countries in the world only review the procedures of the arbitration awards before they recognize or enforce them. *The New York Convention* has made recognition and enforcement even more accessible by providing that any arbitration award should be recognized and enforced in signatories unless otherwise specified. The Convention listed five conditions in Paragraph 1, Article V under which the court might refuse the recognition and enforcement. Except for that, no unreasonable barriers should the signatories pose to any foreign awards. *The New York Convention* is a successful multi-lateral treaty in the realm of international arbitration. It shores up commercial entities' confidence in choosing arbitration as their top dispute resolution method by ensuring that their awards are not only binding, but enforceable in most parts of the world.

Conclusion

This chapter discusses how to deal with disputes when a contractual relationship goes wrong. Basically, the parties may either choose litigation and non-judicial methods. The former is backed by the judicial system of a sovereign state and the latter, which is also called "alternative dispute resolution", helps the parties to a dispute get things settled in more flexible and amicable ways. However, most of the ADRs cannot lead to a binding outcome, except for arbitration. It has thus become a highly welcomed dispute resolution method, especially in international commerce. When it comes to disputes among parties from different nations, judicial measures create a lot of uncertainty and reduce efficiency. Thanks to *the New York Convention* and *the UNCITRAL Model Law*, arbitration practice in the world is increasingly unified and the recognition and enforcement of arbitral awards enjoys few barriers.

Reference:

参考文献

[1] 郭寿康、赵秀文：《国际经济法》，中国人民大学出版社 2015 年版，第 337—372 页。

[2] 张法连、姜芳：《英美法律文化教程》，北京大学出版社 2018 年版，第 55 页。

[3] *A Brief History of Arbitration* (no date) *Americanbar.org*, Available at: https://www.americanbar.org/groups/tort_trial_insurance_practice/publications/the_brief/2018-19/summer/a-brief-history-arbitration/ (Accessed: December 2, 2022).

[4] Charman, M. *Contract law*, Cullompton, Devon: Willan Publishing, 2016.

[5] Ian Carson *et al. , Contract dispute resolution: How to resolve a contract dispute, Harper James*, Available at: https://harperjames.co.uk/article/how-to-resolve-a-contract-dispute-step-by-step/ (Accessed: December 2, 2022).

[6] Moses, M.L. and Caenegem, W.V. , *The principles and practice of International Commercial Arbitration*, New York: Cambridge University Press, 2008.

第四章
商事仲裁为何优于法院管辖

陆可欣

国际商事仲裁是指国际经济贸易活动中的当事人双方根据事先或事后的仲裁协议，将其争议提交给特设仲裁庭或常设仲裁机构进行审理，并作出有约束力的仲裁裁决的制度。与法院管辖权相比，国际商事仲裁因当事人的自治原则、仲裁的公正性和效率而备受国内外各方的推崇。

一、当事人意思自治是仲裁的基石

商事仲裁是当事人选择的产物，是当事人合意的结果。意思自治奠定了国际商事仲裁制度的合理性与合法性的基础，当事人的仲裁协议构成仲裁的"基本法"，因此其重要性是不言而喻的。

仲裁会在最大限度上尊重当事人的意思自治，当事人在不违反强行法规定的前提下有权合意选择仲裁机构、仲裁地、仲裁员资格和数量、仲裁程序、适用法律、仲裁语言等各类要素，并且诉讼原则上是公开的而仲裁原则上是保密的。

国际商事仲裁当事人意思自治的作用主要有三点：

首先，与诉讼程序相比，意思自治增强了当事人对仲裁制度的信任。

意思自治与程序正义、实体正义联系密切，从而使得当事人有权影响源自于当事人之间商业交易的仲裁程序。

其次，当事人意思自治是仲裁思维的基础。由于仲裁思维本质上是商事思维，而商事思维的基础是意思自治，以当事人自主性为底层逻辑的商事仲裁之所以历久不衰、蓬勃发展，相较于法院而言，仲裁机构和仲裁庭更加有效率，能够更加快速地对争议做出裁决，促进了商业纠纷公正、有效地解决，提高了商务事项的经办效率，节约当事人的时间成本、经济成本、人力成本。

最后，当事人意思自治深刻影响了仲裁制度的发展。当事人、仲裁机构、司法机关三方共同促进仲裁发展，包括当事人意思自治与司法机关监督权、仲裁机构管理权的协调。

二、与民事诉讼法对比

《中华人民共和国民事诉讼法》第十条规定了两审终审制度，即如当事人对一审判决不服，应当在法定期限内提起上诉，通过二审程序寻求权利救济；再审审查程序是民事诉讼法在特定情形下赋予当事人的特殊救济措施，是当事人在穷尽常规救济途径后的特殊救济程序。但是其中存在以下几个问题：

第一，由于法律规定的上诉条件过于宽松，造成民事案件的上诉率非常高，其直接影响是中级法院的案件数量过多，导致审判效率降低，与商事领域对于效率的追求相悖。

第二，依照目前的规定，我国一个民事案件经过两级法院的审判后最终产生法律效力，当事人取得最终裁决遥遥无期，当事人需要花费大量时间、金钱成本。而不同于《中华人民共和国民事诉讼法》，以2022年修订的《上海仲裁委员会仲裁规则》（《上仲规则2022》）为例，国内各仲裁机构的仲裁规则对于裁决期限有一定的限制。《上仲规则 2022》第五十条前三项规定"（一）本规则第二条第二项第 1 目所涉争议案件（中国内地仲裁案件），应当在受理之日起 5 个月内作出裁决。（二）本规则第二条第二项第 2 目、第 3 目所涉争议案件（涉及中国香港特别行政区、澳门特别行政区或者台湾地区的仲裁案件、国际和涉外仲裁案件），应当在受理之日起 7 个月内作出裁决。（三）本规则第二条第二项第 1 目所涉争议案件（中国内地仲裁案件）适用第九章快速程序的，应当在受理之日起 3 个月内作出裁决"。但该等限制并非强制性的，《上仲规则 2022》第五十条第四项规定："（四）确有特殊情况和正当理由需要延长裁决期限的，经仲裁委主任审核后，可以适当延长。"

第三，由于我国民事诉讼法中存在再审制度，造成两审终审制不是真正意义上的最终终审，降低了商事活动以及争议解决的可预期性，从而给当事人造成法律关系的不稳定。

三、仲裁的一裁终局性

相比之下，仲裁的一裁终局性极大地节省作出裁决的时间、提高争议解决的效率。即仲裁裁决一经作出后，除非法定的极少数情况可被撤销或不予执行外，即发生法律效力，当事人就同一纠纷再申请仲裁或者向人民法院起诉的，仲裁委员会或者人民法院不予受理。

一裁终局性的高效性优势不言而喻，此外，仲裁的一裁终局制度还维护了当事人之间的仲裁协议的契约性质。依据仲裁意定性的原理，当事人就争议解决方式达成了协议，也即自愿接受了一裁终局的审理模式，无论其结果是否符合公平正义，双方都甘愿接受，即便一方或者双方都认为结果不公正，也都甘愿以放弃追求实体正义为代价而追求程序高效带来的最终结果，是一种保障双方仲裁协议之契约性质的可信承诺。

四、仲裁程序中当事人的自主性

仲裁协议是国际商事仲裁的基础与原点，当事人对仲裁协议的内容具有广泛的自由选择权与自主决定权。仲裁规则是当事人的行动指南，也是仲裁庭与仲裁机构的权力宪章。仲裁规则内容对当事人意思自治的保障体现在：当事人可以选择并修改仲裁规则、约定案件审理以及约定适用特殊程序。同时，当事人有权选择仲裁员、约定仲裁庭的人数甚至影响仲裁庭的权力都是意思自治的重要组成部分。特别地，在当今社会分工趋向于精细化的背景之下，对于一些专业领域的仲裁，如海商、医疗、知识产权等领域，当事人可以通过对仲裁员的经验、过往经历等不同角度的考察，对仲裁员的资格进行具体而明确的约定。广泛而灵活的选择自由与决定自由使当事人可以在争议解决中充分考虑自身情况，从而创造出一种自生的自我维持的争议解决秩序。

相比之下，若当事人将争议诉诸法院，并不会被赋予选择法官的权利，需自行承担被分配的法官具有不同的种族、地域、学历甚至性别的偏好等许多不确定因素的风险。并且，诉讼的管辖需要依照国家法律对于管辖问题的规定，比如在我国就需要遵照《中华人民共和国民事诉讼法》及相关规定，按相应的级别管辖和地域管辖分配案件。而仲裁的管辖主要取决于当事人对于仲裁机构的自主选定。

仲裁程序中当事人被赋予的极大的自主性，也即当事人的意思自治不仅构成了国际商事仲裁制度的合法性与合理性基础，而且赋予了其生机勃勃的发展动力。

五、案例分析

2013 年以来，通过人民法院的司法实践活动，围绕人们优先选择商事仲裁而非诉诸法院这一问题的迷思逐步明朗，司法机关的实践渐趋一致，境外仲裁机构在内地仲裁已经可以破冰起航，即将迎来新的发展机遇。由此，本文简要回顾过去几年中具有里程碑意义的三个司法案例，说明国际商事仲裁受到广泛欢迎趋势背后的法律逻辑——尊重当事人的协议选择。

（一）2013 年 3 月的"龙利得案"

2013 年，最高人民法院在《关于申请人安徽省龙利得包装印刷有限公司与被申请人 BP Agnati S.R.L 申请确认仲裁协议效力案的请示的复函》中首次明确表示国际商会仲裁院是当事人选定的"明确具体的仲裁机构"，符合《仲裁法》第十六条关于"选定的仲裁委员会"的规定，满足了中国法关于仲裁协议须选择机构仲裁的要求。这是一个有突破意义的标志性案例，它终结了此前一直存在的争论。正如诺顿罗氏公司所言，尽管"龙利得案"的判决对其他中国法院没有约束力，然而，该决定标志着最高人民法院采取了比以前在中国看到的更支持仲裁的立场的另一个谨慎步骤。它让很多人放心，在未来的几年里，中国法院可能会像亚洲和全球的主要仲裁管辖区一样，允许各种外国和国内仲裁机构在其管辖范围内运作。

但是由于请示范围所限，最高人民法院在本案的答复中并不涉及国际商会仲裁院在上海仲裁后其作出的仲裁裁决属于什么性质的裁决（是外国裁决、非内国裁决还是中国裁决），以及在内地是否有执行的法律依据问题。这些问题只能留待在之后合适的个案中解决。

（二）2018 年 6 月的"大成产业案"

2016 年 3 月，大成株式会社、大成广州公司作为共同申请人向新加坡国际仲裁中心（SIAC）提出仲裁申请。在仲裁过程中，针对仲裁庭多数成员作出的仲裁地为新加坡的管辖权决定，当事人在新加坡高等法院和新加坡最高法院上诉庭兴讼，案件名称简称 BNA v BNB。（关于此案的更多信息，请参考本书第十五章。）

最高法院在"龙利得案"的司法意见应当坚持，顺应国际潮流的做法亦应当允许。本案这一裁定再次向世人展示了中国法院支持当事人选择境外仲裁机构来华仲裁的积极态度。因而，通过制度配套、司法支持，境外仲裁机构在华仲裁鸣笛起航。

（三）2020 年 8 月的"布兰特伍德案"

相较于"龙利得案"和"大成产业案"，"布兰特伍德案"案在处理境外仲裁机构在内地仲裁问题上又前进了一大步。广州中院不仅在之前的民事裁定书中确认国际商会仲裁院的仲裁协议有效，而且在仲裁裁决的执行阶段还进一步明确了这类裁决的国籍属性和执行裁决的法律依据。

关于裁决的籍属，申请执行人布兰特伍德公司原本希望法院采取"仲裁机构所在地标准"，走捷径认定本案裁决为法国裁决或者香港裁决，因为本案仲裁机构总部或者受理案件的分支机构所在地分别为法国和中国香港。若如是，则本案裁决可以视为法国裁决或香港裁决，从而《纽约公约》或者内地和香港相互执行裁决安排得以适用。被申请执行人则提出本案裁决不属于《纽约公约》第一条第（1）款项下的"非内国裁决"。广州中院在本案中没有回避裁决的籍属问题，既没有按照"仲裁机构所在地标准"认定本案裁决为法国裁决或香港裁决，也没有认定本案裁决为"非内国裁决"，而是认为外国仲裁机构在中国内地作出的涉外性质的仲裁裁决，可以视为中国涉外仲裁裁决。广州中院的这一认定值得称赞，首先，这是中国法院首次明确境外仲裁机构在中国内地作出裁决的性质，具有标杆意义；其次，摒弃"仲裁机构所在地标准"，以"仲裁地标准"确定仲裁裁决具有仲裁地所在国国籍，符合国际仲裁的主流观点；再次，若将境外仲裁机构在中国内地作出的仲裁裁决视为"非内国裁决"，将有可能无法逾越我国加入《纽约公约》时所作出的"互惠保留"，于执行无助益；最后，即使不考虑"互惠保留"而依据《纽约公约》解决裁决的执行问题，《纽约公约》也会因其本身的局限不能解决裁决的其他司法监督问题，因此"非内国裁决"的解决方案并不周延，容易顾此失彼。

结语

幸而，上述三个案例为解决外国仲裁机构在中国大陆进行仲裁的相关问题开辟了快速通道。"龙利得案"解决了外国仲裁机构在中国大陆进行仲裁的仲裁协议的有效性问题，"大成产业案"澄清了外国仲裁机构在中国大陆进行的仲裁不涉及仲裁市场的开放，"布兰特伍德案"则为按照仲裁地标准确定此类仲裁裁决的来源和执行依据提供了指导。它们都完成了同样的任务，即面对《仲裁法》的空白和当事人愿意通过境外仲裁机构在内地进行仲裁的现实需要，创造性地解决《仲裁法》颁布时不明确的问题。

商事仲裁的核心目标是构建自我维持的争议解决秩序，其价值内涵是自由权利本身及其保障方式。对国际商业缺陷仲裁条款的有效性和中国仲裁有效性的发展进行回顾，可以发现商业仲裁相对于法院管辖的优越性，它可以通过更快速与恰当的争端解决和更便捷与公平的裁决执行，大大促进国际金融和跨境交易的流动。因此，相较于法院的诉讼程序，商事仲裁以当事人意思自治原则为基石，成为兼具契约性、自治性的一种重要纠纷化解方式，越来越多的当事人选择将争议提交仲裁解决。

Chapter 4

Why Commercial Arbitration Prevails over Court Jurisdiction

Kexin Lu

Commercial arbitration is a system whereby parties in economic and trade activities submit their disputes to an *ad hoc* arbitral tribunal or a permanent arbitral institution for hearing and rendering a binding arbitral award, pursuant to a prior or subsequent arbitration agreement. Compared with court jurisdiction, commercial arbitration is highly valued by domestic and international parties for its principle of party autonomy, impartiality and efficiency.

1. Party Autonomy is the Cornerstone of Arbitration

Commercial arbitration is the outgrowth of the parties' choice and the result of their consent. The importance of the parties' arbitration agreement, which constitutes the "basic law" of arbitration, cannot be overstated as the principle of party autonomy lays the foundation for the rationality and legitimacy of the international commercial arbitration system.

Arbitration will respect the parties' autonomy to the greatest extent possible, and the parties will have the right to choose consensually, subject to the provisions of *jus cogens*, various elements such as the arbitral institution, the place of arbitration, the qualifications and number of arbitrators, the arbitration procedure, the applicable law, the language of the arbitration, etc. Litigation will be public while arbitration will be confidential in principle.

There are three main effects of party autonomy in international commercial arbitration.

At first, in contrast to litigation proceedings, the principle of party autonomy enhances the parties' trust in the arbitration system. Party autonomy is closely linked to procedural and substantive justice, which gives the parties the right to influence the arbitration process arising out of their own commercial transaction.

In addition, party autonomy is the basis of the arbitral mindset. As arbitration mindset is essentially business sense, it is an outgrowth of the natural choice of the parties in a free and competitive commercial market. It is precisely because business sense is based on party autonomy, the reason why commercial arbitration, with party autonomy as its underlying logic, has endured and flourished is that arbitral institutions and arbitral tribunals are more efficient than courts and can decide disputes more quickly, facilitating the fair and effective resolution of commercial disputes, improving the efficiency of handling commercial matters and saving parties' time, economic and human costs.

Eventually, the principle of party autonomy has profoundly influenced the development of the arbitration system. The parties, the arbitral institution and the judiciary jointly propelled the development of arbitration, including the coordination of party autonomy with the supervisory power of the judiciary and the administrative power of the arbitral institution.

2. Contrast with the Civil Procedure Law

Article 10 of the *Civil Procedure Law of the People's Republic of China* provides for a system of final adjudication in two trials, i.e. if the parties are not satisfied with the first instance judgment, they should appeal within the statutory period and seek relief of their rights through the second instance procedure; the retrial review procedure is a special relief measure granted to the parties under specific circumstances by the

Civil Procedure Law, and is a special relief procedure for the parties after they have exhausted the conventional relief channels. However, there are several problems with it as follows.

Firstly, the overly lenient conditions for appeal under the law have resulted in a very high rate of appeals in civil cases, the direct effect of which is an excessive number of cases in the intermediate courts, leading to inefficient trials, contrary to the pursuit of efficiency in the commercial field.

Secondly, in accordance with the current regulations, in China a civil case eventually takes legal effect after a trial by two levels of courts, and the parties are unable to obtain a final award for a long time, which may cost them a huge amount of time and money. Unlike *the Civil Procedure Law of the People's Republic of China*, the arbitration rules of the various domestic arbitration institutions have certain limitations on the duration of an award, as exemplified by *the Shanghai Arbitration Commission Arbitration Rules as amended in 2022*. The first three items of Article 50 *of the Shanghai Arbitration Rules 2022* provide that "(1) In cases of disputes especially in arbitration cases in Mainland China covered by Article II-2-(a) of these Rules, an award shall be made within five months from the date of acceptance. (2) In the case of disputes covered by Article II-2-(b) and II-2-(c) of these Rules (arbitration cases involving the Hong Kong Special Administrative Region of China, the Macao Special Administrative Region or Taiwan, and international and foreign-related arbitration cases), the award shall be rendered within seven months from the date of acceptance. (3) In cases of disputes covered by Article II-2-(a) of these Rules to which Chapter IX expedited procedures apply, the award shall be rendered within three months from the date of acceptance". However, such restrictions are not mandatory, as Article L-4 of *the Shanghai Arbitration Rules 2022* provides that "(4) Where there are special circumstances and justifiable reasons for extending the period for making an award, the period may be appropriately extended after examination by the Director of the Arbitration Commission."

Thirdly, the existence of the retrial system in China's Civil Procedure Law has resulted in a two-trial final adjudication system that is not truly final, reducing the predictability of commercial activities as well as dispute resolution, thus creating instability in legal relationships for the parties.

3. Finality of Arbitration

In contrast, the finality of arbitration greatly reduces the time required to render an award and increases the efficiency of dispute resolution. In other words, once an arbitral award has been made, it becomes legally effective, except in the rare cases where it is set aside or unenforceable by law, and if the parties apply for arbitration or file a lawsuit with the People's Court in respect of the same dispute, the arbitration committee or the People's Court will not accept it.

The efficiency of arbitration is self-evident. Furthermore, the finality of arbitration preserves the contractual nature of the arbitration agreement between the parties. By agreeing on a method of dispute resolution, the parties have voluntarily accepted the finality of the arbitration, whether or not the outcome is fair and just, and even if one or both parties believe that the outcome is unjust, they are willing to forego the pursuit of substantive justice in favour of the efficiency of the process. It is a credible commitment that guarantees the contractual nature of the parties' arbitration agreement.

4. Party Autonomy in Arbitration Proceedings

The arbitration agreement is the basis and origin of international commercial arbitration, and the parties have broad freedom of choice and autonomy over the content of the arbitration agreement. The arbitration rules are the parties' guide to action and the charter of authority of the arbitral tribunal and the arbitral institution. The content of the arbitration rules guarantees the parties' autonomy in that they can choose and amend the arbitration rules, agree on the hearing of the case and the application of special procedures. Simultaneously, the right of the parties to choose the arbitrators, to agree on the number of arbitral tribunal members and even to influence the power of the arbitral tribunal are all indispensable components of party autonomy. Particularly, in the context of increasingly refined division of labour nowadays, in some specialized areas of arbitration, such as maritime, medical and intellectual property, the parties can make specific and clear agreements on the qualifications of the arbitrators by examining their résumé and past experience from different perspectives. The broad and flexible freedom of choice and decision allows the parties to take full account of their own circumstances in dispute resolution, thus creating a self-generating and self-sustaining dispute resolution order.

In comparison, if a party brings a dispute to court, it is not given the right to choose a judge and has to bear the risk of being assigned a judge with different ethnic, geographical, educational or even gender preferences, among many other uncertainties. Moreover, the jurisdiction of litigation is subject to the provisions of national law on jurisdictional issues, such as *the Civil Procedure Law of the People's Republic of China* and related regulations, which allocate cases according to the appropriate level of jurisdiction and territorial jurisdiction while jurisdiction in arbitration depends on the parties' choice of arbitration institution.

The great autonomy granted to the parties in arbitration proceedings, i.e. the autonomy of the parties, not only forms the basis of the legitimacy and rationality of the international commercial arbitration system, but also gives it the impetus to flourish.

5. Case Study

Since 2013, through the judicial practice activities of the People's Courts, the maze surrounding the issue of why people prefer commercial arbitration to court jurisdiction has gradually become clearer, and the practice of the judiciary has become more consistent, with foreign arbitral institutions being able to break the ice and set sail in mainland arbitration, which is about to embrace new opportunities for development. This chapter thus briefly reviews three landmark judicial cases from the past few years to illustrate the legal logic behind the trend of international commercial arbitration which has enjoyed wide popularity — the respect for the parties' choice of agreement.

(1) The "Longlide" case, March 2013

In 2013, the Supreme People's Court, in its "Reply Letter on the Application for Confirmation of the Validity of the Arbitration Agreement between the Claimant

Anhui Longlide Packaging and Printing Co. and the Respondent BP Agnati S.R.L"[1], in line with Article 16 of the *Arbitration Law*, which provides for a "chosen arbitration committee" and satisfies the requirement of Chinese law that arbitration agreements must be arbitrated by a chosen institution. This is a landmark case which puts an end to ongoing debates. According to Norton Rose, even though "the Longlide decision has no binding force upon other Chinese courts, it marks another cautious step by the SPC to take a more pro-arbitration stance than has previously been seen in China. It reassures many that, in years to come, Chinese courts may allow for the operation of a variety of foreign and domestic arbitration institutions in their jurisdiction, as do the leading arbitration jurisdictions in Asia and worldwide." [2]

However, due to the scope of the request, the Supreme People's Court's response did not address the essence of the arbitral award rendered by the ICC Court of Arbitration in Shanghai (whether it was a foreign award, a non-domestic award or a Chinese award) and whether it had a legal basis for enforcement in the Mainland. These questions can only be left to be resolved later in appropriate individual cases.

(2) The BNA v BNB case, June 2018

In March 2016, Taisei Corporation and Taisei Guangzhou Corporation filed an application for arbitration as co-appellants before Singapore International Arbitration Centre (SIAC). In the course of the arbitration, the parties litigated in the High Court of Singapore[3] and the Court of Appeal of the Supreme Court of Singapore[4] against the decision of the majority of the arbitral tribunal that the place of arbitration should be Singapore. (For more information of this case, please refer to Chapter 15 of the Book.)

The Supreme People's Court's judicial opinion in the Longlide case must be adhered to, and the practice of adapting to international trends should be allowed. This decision once again demonstrates the positive attitude of the Chinese courts in

---

[1] *Anhui Longlide Packing and Printing Co, Ltd v. BP Agnati S.R.L (2013), Supreme People's Court of People's Republic of China.*

[2] *The Longlide decision | Global law firm | Norton Rose Fulbright.*

[3] *BNA v BNB and Anor* [2019] SGHC 142.

[4] *BNA v BNB and Anor* [2019] SGCA 84.

supporting the parties' choice of overseas arbitral institutions to arbitrate in China. Therefore, through institutional support and judicial support, overseas arbitral institutions have set sail in China.

(3) The "Brentwood" case, August 2020

Compared to the Longlide case and the BNA v BNB cases, the Brentwood case[①] has made a huge stride forward in dealing with the issue of arbitration by foreign arbitral institutions in the Mainland. In its previous civil ruling, the Guangzhou Intermediate Court not only confirmed the validity of the arbitration agreement referring to the ICC arbitration rules, but also further clarified the nationality attributes of such awards and the legal basis for enforcement of the awards at the enforcement stage.

With regard to the nationality attributes of the award, the applicant Brentwood had hoped that the court would adopt the "criteria for the seat of the arbitration institution" and take the shortcut of finding that the award was a French award or a Hong Kong award, since the seat of the arbitral institution or the branch that received the case was in France and Hong Kong respectively. If so, the award could be considered a French award or a Hong Kong award and the New York Convention or the arrangement for reciprocal enforcement of awards between the Mainland and Hong Kong would apply. The respondent enforcer argued that *the award was not a "non-domestic award" under Article I (1) of the New York Convention*. The Guangzhou Intermediate Court did not avoid the question of the nationality attributes of the award in this case, but it neither held the view that the award was a French award or a Hong Kong award in accordance with the "criteria for the seat of the arbitration institution", nor that the award was a "non-domestic award", but disserted that an arbitral award of a foreign arbitral institution made in mainland China which is foreign in nature could be regarded as a foreign arbitral award in China. The Guangzhou Intermediate Court is to be commended for this determination. First, it is the first time that a Chinese court has clarified the

---

① *Brentwood Industries v Guangdong Valve An Long Machinery Complete Equipment Engineering Co Ltd (2015) Sui Zhong Fa Min Si Chu Zi No.* 62 [Brentwood Industries v 广东阀安龙机械成套设备工程有限公司 (2015) 穗中法民四初字第 62 号]。

nature of an award made by an overseas arbitral institution in Mainland China, which is of benchmark significance. Second, it conforms to the mainstream view of international arbitration to abandon the "criteria for the seat of the arbitration institution" and use the "criteria for the place of arbitration" to determine that the arbitral award has the nationality of the country where the arbitration takes place. Third, if arbitral awards made by foreign arbitral institutions in Mainland China are regarded as "non-domestic awards", it may not be possible to go beyond the "reciprocal reservation" made when China acceded to *the New York Conventionand* and will not contribute to its implementation. Finally, even if the "reciprocity reservation" is not taken into account and *the New York Convention* is relied upon to resolve the enforcement of the award, the Convention would not be able to address other issues of judicial supervision of the award due to its own limitations, so the solution of "non-domestic awards" is not comprehensive and may easily neglect one side and lose the other.

Conclusion

Fortunately, the above three cases have opened the fast lane for resolving issues relating to arbitration by foreign arbitral institutions in Mainland China. The Longlide Case resolved the issue of the validity of arbitration agreements for arbitrations conducted by foreign arbitral institutions in Mainland China; the BNA v BNB Case clarified that arbitrations conducted by foreign arbitral institutions in Mainland China do not involve the opening of the arbitration market; and the Brentwood Case provided guidance on the determination of the nationality attributes and enforcement basis of such arbitral awards in accordance with the criteria for the place of arbitration. They all accomplish the same task, which is to creatively address issues that were not clear when the Arbitration Law was enacted, in the face of the gaps in *the Arbitration Law* and the real need for parties to be willing to arbitrate in the Mainland through offshore arbitration institutions.

The core objective of commercial arbitration is to build a self-sustaining dispute resolution order, the value of which is embedded in the right to freedom itself and the way it is safeguarded. A review of the validity of international commercial defective arbitration clauses and the development of the efficacy of arbitration in China reveals the superiority of commercial arbitration over court jurisdiction, which can greatly facilitate the flow of international financial and cross-border transactions through more rapid & proper dispute resolution and more convenient & fair enforcement of awards. Thus, in contrast to court jurisdiction proceedings, commercial arbitration, based on the principle of party autonomy as the cornerstone of court proceedings, has become a crucial form of dispute resolution that is both contractual and autonomous, with more and more parties choosing to submit their disputes to arbitration.

References:

[1] 李玉泉：《国际民事诉讼与国际商事仲裁》，武汉大学出版社1994年版，第254页。

[2] 加里·B.博恩著：《国际仲裁：法律与实践》，白麟、陈福勇、李汀洁、魏奎楠、许如清、赵航、赵梦伊译.商务印书馆2020年版，第148—152页。

[3] Born, G. (2021). International Arbitration: Law and Practice (Second Edition), 2nd edition. Alphen aan den Rijn, The Netherlands: (© Kluwer Law International; Kluwer Law International 2015) pp. 92-93.

[4] Berger, Klaus Peter. Private Dispute Resolution in International Business: Negotiation, Mediation, Arbitration, Vol. II Handbook, Ed. 3. Wolters Kluwer Law & Business, 2015.

[5] 王生长：《从"龙利得案"到"布兰特伍德案"：境外仲裁机构在中国内地仲裁的突破》，https://mp.weixin.qq.com/s?src=11&timestamp=1669600797&ver=4193&signature=dkZ7oQNMatVYCoMudReBU9JRLvuI5zHU6XlIEPUPrx5IapwMK9tc1iYy3k1u7pn7tGggfrbZ445XQF8q0lQS-iip6F0l*jglmKCLpVgDxQkuqr6ygukABRZxl-XQ86X6&new=1/2020-10-23.

[6] 何隽铭：《商事仲裁实务问答（一）：商事仲裁是什么 | 威科先行》，https://mp.weixin.qq.com/s/yfffLp88ZeCxvv_aUgHhYQ.

[7] 黄艳娜：《论商事仲裁一裁终局制度的利弊及救济困境》，https://mp.weixin.qq.com/s/jNZ-LXUczBS4yn2pGpu1SA.

[8] 李贤森：《国际商事仲裁当事人意思自治保障与限制问题研究》，法律出版社2022年版。

第五章

仲裁员不能超出合同当事人约定的范围

马　琛

　　仲裁员不能超出合同当事人约定的范围是一种普遍共识，它从深层反映了仲裁的意思自治精神。仲裁与诉讼的重要区别就在于仲裁遵循当事人的合法约定：当事人可以选择仲裁机构、仲裁规则、仲裁员、仲裁地和仲裁适用的法律、仲裁语言、仲裁程序以及需要提请仲裁员决定的事项。

　　作为一种受欢迎的争议解决方式，仲裁的目的是通过仲裁裁决解决当事人间的争议，仲裁员会尽其所能确保仲裁裁决的有效，而超出当事人约定是最常见的一种撤销仲裁裁决的理由。

　　本章将讨论仲裁权力来源的混合学说从而加强对意思自治原则重要性的理解，同时，介绍国际公约和各国法律中的禁止超出当事人约定范围的相关规定，展示实践发展中的典型案例，以及该话题下具有挑战性和争议性的问题。

一、仲裁权力来源的混合学说

　　学者们对仲裁权力的来源有着不同观点。仲裁权力来源是仲裁的基本问题，因为仲裁的体系、实践和发展都建立在这个基本问题之上。同时，它也有助于我们理解为什么仲裁员不能超出合同当事人约定的范围。在此，介绍三个主要的理论学说。

（一）契约理论

契约理论认为仲裁来源于当事人的仲裁协议，不需要国家授权。仲裁权力来源于仲裁协议，而不是法律，也不是公权力。仲裁最重要的特点是意思自治。缺少当事人的仲裁协议，仲裁将不会发生。

（二）司法权理论

司法权理论认为仲裁来源于法律和公权力的授权。虽然仲裁始于仲裁协议，但如果没有国家授权，仲裁员则不得受理案件或作出裁决。因此，仲裁权力受制于司法权，国家也可以在其管辖范围内监督仲裁。

（三）混合理论

混合理论认为契约和司法权理论都只体现了仲裁权力来源的一个方面，仲裁来源于仲裁协议，但同样需要法律的授权和监督。当事人需要在法律允许和保护的范围内达成协议。混合理论结合了契约理论和司法权理论的优点，被现代学者广泛采纳。

当事人意思自治被认为是仲裁的最大优势和仲裁的本质特征，是仲裁的灵魂。毫无疑问，仲裁只能在存在有效仲裁协议时启动。仲裁协议是一种程序契约，受私法保护，仲裁是一种给予当事人选择程序的自由且排除诉讼管辖的争议解决体系。

二、国际公约和各国法律规定

第一，在《中国仲裁法》中，超出当事人约定是撤销仲裁裁决的理由之一。《中国仲裁法》第58条规定：没有仲裁协议，或者裁决的事项不属于仲裁协议的范围或者仲裁委员会无权仲裁，或者仲裁庭的组成或者仲裁程序违反法定程序的，当事人可以起诉法院撤销仲裁裁决。

对于"裁决事项不属于仲裁协议范围或者仲裁委员会无权仲裁"的情形，2018年最高人民法院出台的司法解释第13条进行了阐释："裁决的事项超出仲裁协议约定的范围，或者裁决的事项属于依照法律规定或者当事人选择的仲裁规则规定不可仲裁的事项，或者裁决内容超出当事人仲裁请求的范围，或者裁决的仲裁机构非仲裁协议所约定的。"

第二，《纽约公约》奠定了承认和执行国际仲裁裁决的基石。根据《纽约公约》第5条第1款（c）（d）项的规定，无论程序上还是实体上，超出当事人约定将导致仲裁裁决的不予承认和执行：仲裁机构的组成或仲裁程序与当事人间的协议不符，或裁决所处理的争议不是提交仲裁的标的或不在仲裁条款之列，或裁决决定的事项超出了提交仲裁的事项范围，则不予承认和执行仲裁裁决，但裁决中提交仲裁的事项可与超出部分划分时，仲裁范围内的裁决部分应予承认和执行。

第三，联合国国际贸易法委员会示范法已经被多个法域采纳，如加拿大和香港特别行政区。《示范法》第34条第（iii）(iv)款的规定与《纽约公约》基本一致："裁决处理的争议不是提交仲裁意图裁定的事项或不在提交仲裁的范围之列，或者裁决书中内含对提交仲裁的范围以外事项的决定""仲裁庭的组成或仲裁程序与当事人的约定不一致，除非此种约定与当事人不得背离的本法规定相抵触"，则会导致仲裁裁决的撤销。同时，示范法也体现了部分裁决独立于超裁部分的原则。

第四，我们必须提及，有着悠久仲裁传统的英国法律采取支持仲裁的态度。根据英国1996年仲裁法第68条，只有当存在影响仲裁庭、仲裁程序或裁决的严重不当行为时，当事人才可以向法院提出异议。严重不规范行为指法院认为对申请方已造成或将造成实质性的不公正，包括仲裁庭超越其权限（除超出实体管辖权外，见第67条）；仲裁庭未根据当事人约定的程序进行仲裁；仲裁庭未处理当事人请求的所有事项；由当事人授予有关仲裁程序或裁决权力的仲裁机构、其他机构或个人超越其授权范围。

三、案例分析

基于上述法律规定，我们介绍两个典型案例帮助加深理解。一是关于三个不同国家对"超出"一词做出的认定；二是关于当事人不明确的国际仲裁裁决在中国的执行问题。

（一）Sonera 与 Cukurova 仲裁案

2005年，Sonera与Cukurova达成书面协议（同意后续签署最终购买协议）和Sonera意向购买土耳其最大移动电话运营商Turkcell所持有的52.91%的Cukurova股权的购买协议草案。两份协议中，双方当事人均约定"因本协议引起的或与本协议有关的任何争议或索赔……应最终根据巴黎国际商会仲裁规则（"ICC规则"）……进行解决"。

然而，在达成最终购买协议前，Cukurova公开宣称拒绝将股权售与Sonera。因此，Sonera根据书面协议的仲裁条款向Cukurova提起仲裁程序，但Cukurova主张"书面协议"和"最终购买协议"是两个独立的合同，仲裁庭没有管辖权。

仲裁庭认为其具有管辖权，并裁决Cukurova向Sonera支付损害赔偿金9.32亿美元。随后，Sonera向英国、美国和荷兰申请执行裁决，各国法院均支持了Sonera的仲裁裁决执行申请。

三国法院认为，案件关键是当事人已经达成的仲裁协议是否覆盖了仲裁庭的管辖权。美国法院和荷兰法院认为，法院应当进行实质审查并全面考虑和尊重仲裁庭的理由和决定。本案中，当事人宽泛地约定"因本协议引起的或与本协议有关的任何争议或索赔应最终根据 ICC 规则解决"。这一仲裁条款当然包括了因是否达成购买协议而引发的争议。

同时，英国法院审查案件后，认为初步协议和正式购买协议是基于同一交易。当事人是有意打包解决相关争议，而非将两个合同割裂开。因此，三国法院均认为本案未违反《纽约公约》第 5 条第（1）款。

三国法院的决定体现了不同法域对《纽约公约》的相似解读和实践。当判断本案是否超出当事人的仲裁协议时，三国法院均遵循当事人意思自治原则，强调了当事人的真实意愿和仲裁庭的授权范围。

（二）GMI 和芜湖冶炼厂仲裁案

美国 GMI 公司和中国的芜湖冶炼厂签署带有仲裁条款的销售协议。2001 年，GMI 以未完成交付为由向伦敦金属交易所申请仲裁，起诉芜湖冶炼厂和芜湖恒鑫铜业集团有限公司两个被申请人。仲裁庭裁决芜湖冶炼厂向 GMI 公司赔偿损失并裁决由两个被申请人支付仲裁费和押金。根据仲裁裁决，GIM 公司向中国法院申请执行两个被申请人。

最高人民法院认为，本案中仲裁庭应当只裁决 GMI 公司和芜湖冶炼厂之间的争议，仲裁裁决约束三个当事人则超出了仲裁协议的范围。同时，根据《纽约公约》第 5 条第 (1) 款的规定，最高人民法院认为本案的仲裁裁决是可分的，芜湖冶炼厂独立承担责任的部分显然应当被执行，但涉及其他被申请人的部分不予执行。

四、挑战性问题

（一）仲裁员是否有权决定当事人没有在合同中约定的事项？

仲裁是意思自治的产物，当当事人没有在合同中约定某个事项，但必须对该事项作出决定时，一个明智的仲裁员应当首先询问当事人双方的意见。平等阐述事实与观点是当事人的基本权利。当当事人双方向仲裁庭表达观点时，他们的权利就得到了尊重和保护。而后，仲裁员可以在充分考虑双方意见的情况下作出决定。

毕竟仲裁员就是被选任来对当事人无法达成共识的事项作出决定的。然而，如果一些决定并不必要，如无关当事人的诉求或不影响案件进程和最终裁决，仲裁员应当避免作出不必要的决定。

（二）仲裁员是否有权调解案件或担任调解员？

仲裁中的调解是一种传统的中国智慧。中国有着悠久的调解传统，并将调解带进了仲裁。仲裁过程中，在达成仲裁裁决前，仲裁员可以转变为调解员对案件进行调解。我们称这种方式为调解与仲裁相结合（Arb-Med）。

仲裁过程中的信息可以在调解中使用，但如果调解失败，当事人在调解中的陈述不能用于仲裁，也不能影响仲裁结果。仲裁员将仅根据仲裁程序中展示的事实和法律制作仲裁裁决。如果调解成功，仲裁员可以根据调解结果制作仲裁裁决。

很多仲裁机构如贸仲、北仲，允许仲裁中的调解。虽然在中国调解经常以这种方式得以实践，但仲裁与调解相结合的方式在其他法域并不常见。

与此同时，还有另一种争议解决方式被称为先调解后仲裁。在先调解后仲裁的案件中，当事人同意在仲裁前将案件先提交调解，如果当事人没能在调解中解决争端，仲裁程序将被启动。如果当事人同意，调解员可以担任后面的仲裁员，如果当事人不同意，可以选择其他仲裁员，这样就避免了仲裁员被调解中的信息所影响的风险，当事人也能更加信任、对仲裁裁决更有信心。

结语

本章我们首先介绍了仲裁权力的混合来源和当事人意思自治原则，从而深挖仲裁员不能超出当事人合同约定的真正内涵；而后，通过中国法、纽约公约、联合国贸易法委员会示范法、英国法以及典型案例展示了超裁导致裁决撤销的原则；最后，我们讨论了挑战性问题，丰富了本章内容和情形。作为仲裁的一种基本原则和国际上的普遍共识，仲裁员不可以超出合同当事人约定，当事人在法律框架下的真实意愿才是仲裁的真正准则。

参考文献

[1] 侯登华：《当事人合意对司法管辖权的效力问题——以仲裁协议为研究对象》，《河北学刊》2014 年第 34 卷第 6 期，第 157—161 页。

[2] 谢菁菁：《国际商事仲裁中的当事人意思自治与司法审查》，《河北法学》2009 年第 27 卷第 7 期，第 23—27 页。

[3] 谢雄青、胡彦涛：《论仲裁的性质及其权威的来源》，《湖南科技学院学报》2014 年第 35 卷第 4 期，第 131—134 页。

[4] 刘璐：《欧美法院对国际商事仲裁中"超裁"问题的认定标准及启示——以索尼拉案为例》，《法律适用》2018 年第 12 期，第 117—121 页。

[5] Cukurova Holding AS v Sonera Holding BV (British Virgin Islands) [2014] UKPC 15 (13 May 2014).

[6] 《最高人民法院关于美国 GMI 公司申请承认英国伦敦金属交易所仲裁裁决案的复函》，（2003）民四他字第 12 号。

Chapter 5

Arbitrators Cannot Go beyond What the Contracting Parties Have Agreed

Chen Ma

There is a general consensus that arbitrators cannot go beyond what the contracting parties have agreed, which stems from the spirit of party autonomy in arbitration. Arbitration is different from litigation in that arbitration follows parties' legitimate agreement: parties can choose the arbitral institution, arbitral rules, arbitrators, the seat and place of arbitration, and the applicable law in arbitration, the language of arbitration, the procedure of arbitration, the issues which require decision from the arbitrators.

As a popular option for dispute resolution, arbitration aims at making an award to solve the disputes between parties, and arbitrators will try their best to ensure that the arbitral award is valid. Exceeding the agreement of parties is one of the most common grounds which result in the award being set aside.

In this chapter, we discuss the hybrid sources of the power to arbitrate to stress the significance of party autonomy, and international conventions and national laws that relate to the prohibition of going beyond parties' agreement. We also discuss the typical cases which show the development in practice, and the challenges and controversial issues under this topic.

1. Hybrid Sources of the Power of Arbitration

Scholars have different opinions on the source of the power of arbitration. The source of the power of arbitration is a basic issue of arbitration as the system, practice and development of arbitration are built on this basic issue, and it's also helpful to understand why arbitrators cannot go beyond what the contracting parties have agreed. Hence, we present three main theories:

(1) Contract Theory

Contract theory states that arbitration stems from parties' arbitration agreement, with no need for authorization from the state. The arbitrators' power stems from the arbitration agreement, not the law, nor the public authority. The most essential feature of arbitration is party autonomy. Absent the parties' arbitration agreement, arbitration cannot take place. (Xie and Hu, 2014, p.131)

(2) Jurisdictional Theory

Jurisdictional theory states that arbitration stems from the law and public authority's authorization. Although arbitration starts from the arbitration agreement, if the state does not provide the authorization, arbitrators cannot accept cases or render awards. Therefore, the power of arbitration is limited by judicial power, and the state can also supervise arbitration within its jurisdiction. (Xie and Hu, 2014, p.131)

(3) Hybrid Theory

Hybrid theory states that both contract theory and jurisdictional theory show one-side of the source of power of arbitration. Arbitration comes from arbitration agreement, but it also requires the supervision and authorization of law. Parties have to come to an agreement under the permission and protection of the law. Combining the advantages of contract theory and jurisdictional theory, hybrid theory is generally accepted by modern scholars. (Xie and Hu, 2014, p.131)

Party autonomy, the biggest advantage and the nature of arbitration, is the soul of arbitration. There is no doubt that arbitration can start only when there is a valid arbitration agreement. Arbitration agreement is a contract of procedure, and is protected by the private law. Arbitration is a dispute system that gives parties the freedom to choose procedure and exclude litigation. (Hou, 2014, p.160)

2. International Convention and National Laws

Firstly, exceeding the parties' agreement is a ground for setting aside arbitral awards in *Chinese Arbitration Law*. Article 58 of *China's Arbitration Law* provides that if there is no arbitral agreement, or the issues decided in the award do not fall within the scope of the arbitral agreement, or the arbitration commission has no power to arbitrate, or the formation of the arbitral tribunal or the arbitral procedure violates the legal procedure, a party can appeal to the court to set aside the arbitral award.

The Supreme Court has issued judicial interpretations in 2018 to clarify the circumstances of "the issues decided in the award do not fall within the scope of the arbitral agreement or arbitration commission has no power to arbitrate" in article 13, which include the following: "the issues decided in the award go beyond the scope agreed in the arbitral agreement, or are non-arbitrable in accordance with the law or the arbitration rule chosen by the parties, or the content of the award is beyond the scope of the parties' arbitration claims, or the arbitral institution is not the one agreed in arbitral agreement."

Secondly, *the New York Convention* lays the foundation for the recognition and enforcement of an international arbitral award. According to article V 1 (c) (d) of *New York Convention*, no matter procedurally or substantially, exceeding the parties' agreement can result in the refusal of recognition and enforcement of the arbitral award: if the composition of the arbitral authority or the arbitral procedure was not in accordance with the agreement of the parties, or the award deals with a difference not contemplated by or not falling within the terms of the submission to arbitration, or it contains decisions on matters beyond the scope of the submission to arbitration, recognition and enforcement of the award may be refused, but if the decisions on matters submitted to arbitration can be separated from those not so submitted, that part of the award which contains decisions on matters submitted to arbitration may be recognized and enforced.

Thirdly, the UNCITRAL Model Law has been adopted by many jurisdictions, such as Canada and Hong Kong SAR. Article 34(iii) (iv)of the *Model Law is basically* consistent with *the New York Convention*: "the award deals with a dispute not contemplated by or not falling within the terms of the submission to arbitration, or contains decisions on matters beyond the scope of the submission to arbitration" "the composition of the arbitral tribunal or the arbitral procedure was not in accordance with the agreement of the parties, unless such agreement was in conflict with a provision of this Law from which the parties cannot derogate". These may lead to setting aside. Meanwhile, the Model Law also shows the principle that a partial award can be separated from the part exceeding the terms of submission to arbitration.

Finally, we must mention that, with strong tradition of arbitration, UK law takes a pro-arbitration attitude. According to section 68 of Arbitration Act 1996, only if there is serious irregularity affecting the tribunal, the proceedings or the award, a party may apply to the court challenging an award. Serious irregularity means an irregularity which the court considers has caused or will cause substantial injustice to the applicant, including the tribunal exceeding its powers (otherwise than by exceeding its substantive jurisdiction: see section 67), failure by the tribunal to conduct the proceedings in accordance with the procedure agreed by the parties, failure by the tribunal to deal with all the issues that were put to it, any arbitral or other institution or person vested by the parties with powers in relation to the proceedings or the award exceeding its powers.

3. Case Studies

Based on the above provisions, we come to two typical cases to strengthen the understanding of our topic. One is about the identification of "beyond" in three different countries; the other is about the enforcement of an international arbitral award in China on the issue of uncertain parties.

(1) Sonera v. Cukurova[①]

In 2005, Sonera and Cukurova entered into a letter agreement (agreed to sign a final purchase agreement later) and a draft purchase agreement regarding the potential purchase by Sonera of the Cukurova group's entire 52.91% shareholding in Turkcell Holding, which was the largest mobile phone operator in Turkey. In both agreements, parties agreed "[a]ny dispute, controversy or claim arising out of or in connection with this Agreement...shall be finally settled under the Rules of Arbitration of the International Chamber of Commerce in Paris (the 'ICC Rules') ..."

However, before entering into the final purchase agreement, Cukurova publicly announced that it would not sell the shares to Sonera. Thus, Sonera commenced arbitration proceedings against Cukurova pursuant to the arbitration clause in the Letter Agreement, while Cukurova claimed the arbitral tribunal had no jurisdiction because the "letter agreement" and "final purchase agreement" should be two separate contracts.

The arbitral tribunal upheld its jurisdiction and Cukurova was ordered to pay $932 million in damages to Sonera. Then, Sonera applied for the enforcement of the award in the UK, USA, and Netherlands and all three national courts supported Sonera on the enforcement of the arbitral award.

The three courts took the view that the key issue was whether the tribunal's jurisdiction was under the arbitral agreement the parties had agreed. The US court and the court in the Netherlands stated that the court should control substantive review and fully consider and respect the arbitral tribunal's reasons and decisions. In the case, parties broadly agreed "[a]ny dispute, controversy or claim arising out of or in connection with this Agreement shall be finally settled under ICC Rules". The arbitration clause certainly included the dispute caused by whether the purchase agreement had been reached.

Moreover, the UK court reviewed the case and stated that the preliminary contract and the formal contract of purchase are under one same trade. Parties tended to deal with the relevant disputes together, not to cut the two contracts separately. Therefore, all three courts took the same view that the case did not breach article 5(1) of *the New*

---

① Cukurova Holding AS v Sonera Holding BV (British Virgin Islands) [2014] UKPC 15 (13 May 2014).

York Convention.

The three courts showed the similar understanding and practice of *New York Convention* in different jurisdictions. When decided whether it exceeded parties' arbitration agreement, the three courts followed the principle of party autonomy, and stressed on the parties' true intention and the scope of authorization to the arbitral tribunal.

(2) GMI v. Wuhu Smelter[①]

GMI, a US company, and China's Wuhu Smelter signed a sale contract with an arbitration clause. In 2001, GMI applied for arbitration to the arbitral tribunal of the London Metal Exchange on the ground of incomplete delivery by suing two respondents, Wuhu Smelter and Wuhu Hengxin Copper Industry Group Co. Ltd.. The arbitral tribunal ordered Wuhu Smelter to pay damages to GMI and ordered the respondents to pay the arbitration fee and deposit. In accordance with the arbitral award, GMI applied for enforcement to the Chinese court and joined the two respondents together.

However, the Supreme Court stated, in this case, arbitral tribunal should only arbitrate the dispute between GMI and Wuhu Smelter. The arbitral award binding upon three parties was beyond the scope of the arbitral agreement. According to Article 5(1) of *New York Convention*, the Supreme Court stated, the arbitral award in this case was separable. The part of Wuhu Smelter's independent liability clearly should be enforced, but the part of the other respondent should not be enforced.

4. Challenges

(1) Do arbitrators have the power to decide what the parties have not agreed in their contract?

As arbitration is the product of party autonomy, when there is something not agreed by the parties in their contract but necessary enough to make a decision, a wise

---

① GMI v. Wuhu Smelter, 2003, the forth civil court of the Supreme People's Court, No.12.

arbitrator should ask both parties for their opinions first. The right to present the cases by both parties is the basic entitlement of the parties. When both parties express their opinions to the tribunal, their rights are respected and protected. Then, arbitrators can make the decisions which sufficiently considers both parties' opinions.

After all, arbitrators are appointed to make decisions on what the parties cannot come to an agreement. However, when some decisions are not necessary, such as irrelevancy to the parties' claims, or not affecting the progress of the case or final award, arbitrators must refrain from making an unnecessary decision.

(2) Do arbitrators have the power to mediate case or act as mediators?

Mediation during arbitration is traditional Chinese wisdom. China has a long tradition of mediation and brings mediation into arbitration, which means, during the arbitration, before coming to an the arbitral award, arbitrators can turn themselves into mediators and mediate the case. Here, we call this arbitration combined with mediation (Arb-Med).

The background information in the arbitration process can be used in mediation, but if the mediation fails, parties' statements in mediation cannot be used in arbitration, nor affecting the result in arbitration. Arbitrators will make the arbitral award according to the fact and law as presented in arbitration process only. If the mediation succeeds, arbitrators can make an arbitral award accordings to the mediation result.

Many arbitral institutions, like CIETAC and Beijing Arbitration Commission (BAC), allow mediation during arbitration. Although mediation is often-practiced in China in this way, Arb-Med in the combined way is not common in other jurisdictions.

Meanwhile, there is another dispute resolution option called Med-Arb. In Med-Arb case, parties agree to submit the case to mediation before arbitration, and if parties fail to make a settlement in mediation, arbitration will be started. If parties agree, mediators can be the arbitrators later, but if parties disagree, they can choose other arbitrators, which avoids the risk that arbitrators being poisoned by the information presented in mediation, and parties can have more trust and confidence in the arbitral award.

Conclusion

In this chapter, we firstly introduce hybrid sources of the power of arbitration and party autonomy to explore the true meaning of arbitrators not to exceed what the contract parties agreed. Then, Chinese Law, New York Convention, UNCITRAL Model Law, UK law, and typical cases show the principle of setting aside an arbitral award when exceeding parties' agreement. Finally, we discuss challenging questions to enrich the concept and situations. As a basic principle in arbitration and a generally accepted principle in international arbitration, arbitrators cannot exceed what the contracting parties have agreed. Parties' intention under the law is the true criterion in arbitration.

List of References:

[1] Hou, D. (2014) 'The effect of parties' agreement to jurisdiction--with the object of arbitration agreement', *Hebei Academic Journal*, 34(6), pp.157-161.

[2] Xie, J. (2009) 'Party's autonomy and judicial review in international commercial arbitration', *Hebei Law Science*, 27(7), pp.23-27.

[3] Xie, Q. and Hu, Y. (2014) 'On the nature of arbitration and the source of its authority', *Journal of Hunan University of Science and Engineering*, 35(4), pp.131-134.

[4] Liu, L. (2018) 'The Judging Standard and Enlightenment of European and American Courts on the Issue of "Excess of Authority" in International Commercial Arbitration -- A Case study of Sonera', *Journal of Law Application*, (12), pp.117-121.

[5] Cukurova Holding AS v Sonera Holding BV (British Virgin Islands) [2014] UKPC 15 (13 May 2014).

[6] GMI v. Wuhu Smelter, 2003, the forth civil court of the Supreme People's Court, No.12.

第六章

仲裁员的公正和效率义务

徐怡欣

1996 年英国仲裁法第 33 条规定了两项仲裁员最基本的义务——公正和效率义务："（1）仲裁庭应：(a) 公平及公正地对待当事人，给予各方当事人合理的机会陈述案件并抗辩对方当事人的陈述，并 (b) 根据特定案件的具体情况采取合适的程序，避免不必要的延误或开支，以对待决事项提供公平的解决方式……"本章将依次介绍上述两项义务的定义、特点以及制度保证。

一、什么是"公正义务"？

首先，我们应当区分仲裁员的"公正性"和"独立性"。学者 Redfern 和 Hunter 指出，"独立性"着眼于仲裁员和当事人的利益关系，是一种较为客观的检验；而"公正性"着眼于仲裁员实际上表现出来的偏见，它是较为主观和抽象的。[①]

然而，"公正性"和"独立性"也并非总是泾渭分明。例如，1987 年

[①] *See* Nigel Blackaby, Constantine Partasides, Alan Redfern & Martin Hunter, *Redfern and Hunter on International Arbitration (Sixth Edition)*, Oxford University Press, 2015, p.255.

瑞士国际私法法典只对"独立性"提出了要求，但实践中通常被当事人援引以质疑仲裁员的"公正性"。又如，1999 年瑞典仲裁法第八条列举了仲裁员"不公正"的几种表现，但其中前两种在另一些国家被视为"不独立"。也有学者认为"公正性"和"独立性"没有实质区别——如果事实相同，那么基于公正性和基于独立性的质疑结果也将相同。①

其次，我们应当区分"公正义务"和"按照法律办事的义务"。"依法办事的义务"顾名思义，其审查标准是法律，因此比"独立义务"的审查更加具体——例如，每一方当事人都应当受到平等对待，都应当在听证中享有公平的阐述观点的机会；又如，仲裁庭或仲裁员不得在一方当事人缺席的情况下与另一方当事人进行讨论，除非讨论的问题是仲裁庭庭长的提名问题，或缺席当事人已经得到适当的通知但仍不出席。②

仲裁员即使履行了"公正义务"和"独立义务"，也仍然可能违反"依法办事的义务"。例如，一名仲裁员与各方当事人不存在任何亲属关系、经济关系或任何类似关系，但他 / 她仍然可能在申请人（或其代理人）缺席的情况下，与被申请人的代理人讨论案件，从而违反上文所举例的"不得在一方当事人缺席的情况下与另一方当事人进行讨论"的法律规定，也即违反了"依法办事的义务"。

需要注意的是，仲裁员的指定方式以及自身偏好会影响他们的公正性。绝大多数的仲裁员是当事人指定的——一方面，在不同的候选人之间进行选择时，各方当事人很可能指定那些既有观点有利于本方立场的人；另一方面，有些法律从业者的经济来源主要是仲裁业务，因此，他们可能从自身利益出发，

---

① *See* Christopher Koch, *Standards and Procedures for Disqualifying Arbitrators*, 20 Journal of International Arbitration 325, 332 (2003).

② *See* Nigel Blackaby, Constantine Partasides, Alan Redfern and Martin Hunter, *Redfern and Hunter on International Arbitration (Sixth Edition)*, Oxford University Press, 2015, pp.330-331.

不去违背指定人的意愿。事实上，对于当事人指定的仲裁员在仲裁中的确切作用以及该作用与"公正义务"的兼容性，仲裁界存在争议。在这种情况中，仲裁庭主席被认为在确保仲裁庭公平公正行事方面具有特殊作用，无论该主席是由当事人提名的仲裁员共同指定的，还是由指定机构或法院指定的。[①]

在自身偏好方面，仲裁员难免会对社会主要问题存在一些既有的意见。"（法官）一定会被自己的经历塑造，并从这些经历中获得启示；我们不能期望他们在被任命为法官时突然摆脱这些经历。"[②] 仲裁员也是同理。

二、如何保障仲裁员的公正性?

要求仲裁员披露可能影响其公正性的因素，是保障仲裁员公正性的重要手段。实践中的过程通常是这样：首先，仲裁员候选人将相关因素披露给本方当事人；其次，如果本方当事人认为该候选人的公正性以及其他方面没有任何问题，那么该候选人就接受该方当事人的委任，并将自己的情况（包括需要披露的内容）正式通知给对方当事人；最后，根据正式通知中的内容，对方当事人可能对该仲裁员提出质疑。

从另一个角度看，"披露"也是仲裁员免受质疑的重要手段。如果仲裁员曾经披露了所有可能导致其仲裁员资格被质疑的理由和事实，但并没有在规定的异议期限内被质疑，那么期限过后，当事人就不能再质疑该仲裁员。然而，需要注意的是，即使披露和异议期限已经过去，仲裁员也依然应当遵循公正义务；在接下来的整个程序过程中，一旦可能影响其公正性的情况出现，仲裁员就应当尽快通知当事人和其他仲裁员。

一个问题是，一项因素是否会影响仲裁员的公正性，并不总是客观、

---

① *Halliburton Company v Chubb Bermuda Insurance Ltd*, 2020 UKSC 48, at para 59-66.
② *R. v. S. (R.D.)*, 1997 CanLII 324 (SCC), [1997] 3 SCR 484, at para. 38

明确的。因此，仲裁员和各方律师往往无法确定应当披露的范围。同时，国际商业的发展（例如，大型集团公司以及国际律师事务所的发展）导致了更多的披露，产生了对披露和利益冲突问题的更加复杂的分析。因此，当事人有更多的机会通过申请回避来拖延仲裁程序或拒绝对方选择的仲裁员。披露出任何轻微或严重的关系，都可能导致无根据或无意义的回避申请。

可见，国际仲裁机构有必要保护国际仲裁程序免受策略性的无根据回避申请的打扰，并保护程序的合法性免受缺乏确定且统一适用的披露、质疑和回避要求的标准的影响。

在上述背景下，国际律师协会于 2004 年制定了《国际律师协会国际仲裁利益冲突指引》。该指引吸取了来自不同司法管辖区的 19 位经验丰富的从业人员的综合经验，建立了一套处理具体情形的统一原则，从而避免来自不同文化背景的仲裁员适用截然不同的披露标准。[1] 指引的最新标准于 2014 年通过。修订后的指引指出："尽管 2004 年'指引'的基本方法不应改变，但 2004 年'指引'未考虑到的披露情形在某些情况下仍需要披露。还有必要重申，要求披露的事实——或仲裁员作出披露的事实——并不意味着对仲裁员的公正性或独立性存在怀疑。事实上，披露标准与申请回避标准不同。"[2]

三、什么是"效率义务"？

正如一句法律格言所说，"迟到的正义不是正义"。在国际商事仲裁领域，不适当的拖延可能导致交易受阻、错失商业机会，从而对当事人造成损害。此外，保持基本的效率、在合理的时间期限内结束仲裁，也是节约成本、保持仲裁机构竞争力的要求。

---

[1] *See* Scherer, *The IBA Guidelines on Conflicts of Interest in International Arbitration: The first five years 2004-2009*, 4 Disp Res Intl 15 (2010).
[2] 请参阅国际律师协会：《国际律师协会国际仲裁利益冲突指引》（2014），第 iii 页。

因此，法律要求仲裁员行动迅速。例如，1985 年《联合国国际贸易法委员会国际商事仲裁示范法》第 14 条第 1 款规定："仲裁员无履行职责的法律行为能力或事实行为能力或者由于其他原因未能不过分迟延地行事的，其若辞职或者当事人约定其委任终止的，其委任即告终止……"

具体而言，我们很容易在仲裁规则中找到时间限制。例如，2021 年《国际商会仲裁规则》第 31 条规定："（1）仲裁庭必须作出终局裁决的期限为六个月……（2）仲裁院可依仲裁庭说明理由的请求延长该期限，或在其认为必要时自行决定延长该期限。"

四、如何保障仲裁员遵循效率义务？

（一）时间限制

为仲裁程序的每个阶段设定时间限制，是确保效率的常用方法。例如，2015 年《中国国际经济贸易仲裁委员会仲裁规则》第 66 条第 1 款规定："收到仲裁申请书后，仲裁委员会仲裁院认为仲裁申请符合本规则第十二条规定的受理条件的，应当在 5 天内通知当事人。"

（二）仲裁员资格要求

在每个具体的仲裁中，仲裁员都应具备相应的素质。仲裁员应当具有相关领域的经验，应当是具有组织性的和高效的，应当具有和他人合作并建立共识的能力。上述品质都应当在选择仲裁员时予以考虑。同样重要的是确保仲裁员有足够的时间和精力投入到本次仲裁中。例如，《国际商会仲裁规则》第 11 条第 2 款规定，"在获得任命或确认前，仲裁员候选人应签署一份有关接受任命、有时间处理案件、具有中立性和独立性的声明"。2014 年《伦敦国际仲裁院规则》第 5 条第 4 款也要求仲裁员候选人确认他们"准备、愿意并能够投入足够的时间、勤奋和稳定性的努力，以确保仲裁迅速和有效进行"。

（三）简易程序

简易程序对程序事项的要求比普通程序低、因此速度更快。在适当情况下，将适用简易程序。

例如，2018 年《香港国际仲裁中心机构仲裁规则》第 42 条第 1 款规定了三种可以适用简易程序的情况："(a) 争议金额，即所有请求和反请求（或任何抵销答辩或交叉请求）金额之和，不超过由 HKIAC 设定并于仲裁通知提交之日公布于其网站上的金额；或 (b) 各方当事人同意；或 (c) 出现极为紧急的情况。"

（四）案件管理

一些主要的仲裁机构修订了其仲裁规则，以提高仲裁效率。例如，《国际商会仲裁规则》要求开设强制性的案件管理会议，并在会议中拟订程序时间表："1. 在拟订审理范围书时，或在拟订后尽可能短的时间内，仲裁庭应召开案件管理会议，与当事人协商可以根据第 22 条第（2）款采取的程序措施。2. 仲裁庭应在上述会议期间或会议之后尽快制定一份其打算遵循的旨在高效进行仲裁的程序时间表。该程序时间表及其任何修改内容均应通知仲裁院和各方当事人。"

结语

公正义务致力于使仲裁员不受偏见影响，效率义务则至力于在合理时间内结束仲裁。一方面，它们互相补充，从而保证仲裁的质量并限制其成本；另一方面，它们存在一定对立，有必要维持公正和高效之间的平衡。

Chapter 6

Arbitrator's Impartial Role and Efficiency Duty

Yixin Xu

Article 33 of the Arbitration Act 1996 in England imposes two of the primary duties of an arbitrator, impartiality and efficiency: "(1) The tribunal shall — (a) act fairly and impartially as between the parties, giving each party a reasonable opportunity of putting his case and dealing with that of his opponent, and (b) adopt procedures suitable to the circumstances of the particular case, avoiding unnecessary delay or expense, so as to provide a fair means for the resolution of the matters falling to be determined..." In this chapter, we will learn the basic definition, some features and essential rules of these duties in turn.

1. What is "Impartial Role"?

It may be necessary to clarify the relationship between "impartiality" and "independence". According to Redfern and Hunter, "independence" is concerned with the relationship between an arbitrator and one of the parties, which is an "objective" test of avoiding conflict of interest, while "impartiality" is connected with actual or apparent bias of an arbitrator, which is a "subjective" and more abstract concept.[1]

However, some phenomena seem to show that independence and impartiality are

---

[1] *See* Nigel Blackaby, Constantine Partasides, Alan Redfern & Martin Hunter, *Redfern and Hunter on International Arbitration (Sixth Edition)*, Oxford University Press, 2015, p.255.

not distinguished clearly in some occasions. For example, the Swiss Code of Private International Law of 1987 only made a request of arbitrator's independence, while it was usually cited by parties to doubt the impartiality of arbitrator. Another example is Article 8 of Swedish 1999 Arbitration Act. This Act required the impartiality of arbitrator and listed some kinds of situation of partiality, the first and second of which were considered as dependence in some other countries. Therefore, some scholars hold the opinion that there are no substantial differences between the meanings of impartiality and independence, and "with the same facts, the outcome of a challenge based on independence and one based on impartiality will be identical".[1]

Moreover, the duty to be impartial is different from the duty to act judicially. The latter duty, as its name suggests, is reviewed against the law and is therefore even more concrete than the duty of independence. For example, each party must be accorded equality of treatment and given a fair opportunity to present their case at the hearing. Another example is that neither the arbitral tribunal as a whole nor any of its individual members should discuss the case with one party in the absence of the other, unless in connection with the nomination of the president of the arbitral tribunal, and each absent party having failed to attend a meeting or hearing must have been giving proper notice to do so.[2]

It is not hard to understand that even if the arbitrator is impartial, he or she may still violate the duty to act judicially. For example, an arbitrator having no domestic, economic or other kinds of relationship with both parties may still talk with the agent of respondent without the attendance of applicant or his agent, thus violating the duty to act judicially and treat both parties equally.

Further, the appointment of arbitrator and issue preferences may be relevant to impartiality. Most of arbitrators are party-appointed. On the one hand, a party is

---

[1] *See* Christopher Koch, *Standards and Procedures for Disqualifying Arbitrators*, 20 Journal of International Arbitration 325, 332 (2003).

[2] *See* Nigel Blackaby, Constantine Partasides, Alan Redfern and Martin Hunter, *Redfern and Hunter on International Arbitration (Sixth Edition)*, Oxford University Press, 2015, pp.330-331.

likely to choose one whose opinions favor the appointing party. On the other hand, for those practitioners "whose livelihood depends to a significant degree on acting as arbitrators"[1], it may be in their interest not to go against the wishes of the party who has appointed them. Actually, "there is a debate within the arbitration community as to the precise role of the party-appointed arbitrator and the compatibility of that role with the requirement of impartiality"[2]. In this context, "it is perceived that the person chairing the tribunal, whether appointed by the party-nominated arbitrators jointly or by an appointing institution or the court, has a particular role in making sure that the tribunal acts fairly and impartially".[3]

In respect of issue preferences, an arbitrator unavoidably has some formed opinions on leading issues of society. "(Judges) will certainly have been shaped by, and have gained insight from, their different experiences, and cannot be expected to divorce themselves from those experiences on the occasion of their appointment to the bench."[4] Similarly, the same phenomenon applies to arbitrators.

2. How to Ensure Arbitrator's Impartiality?

An important way to ensure the impartiality of an arbitrator is to disclose relevant elements of arbitrator that may affect their impartiality. In practice, a person who will be nominated as arbitrator by one party usually discloses his relevant facts to that party. And if there is no doubt about the impartiality and other matters of that person, he will accept the nomination then send formal letter to both parties, in which relevant facts shall be listed. The other party may challenge the arbitrator according to those facts if necessary.

Meanwhile, disclosure also serves as an important way for arbitrators to avoid being challenged. If one arbitrator has disclosed all reasons and facts that may be

---

[1] *Halliburton Company v Chubb Bermuda Insurance Ltd*, 2020 UKSC 48, at para 59.
[2] Ibid, at para 66.
[3] 8Ibid, at para 62.
[4] *R. v. S. (R.D.)*, 1997 CanLII 324 (SCC), [1997] 3 SCR 484, at para. 38

cited to challenge his qualification as an arbitrator and there is no objection about his qualification within the time limit, then parties cannot successfully doubt his qualification during the procedure that follows. However, it should be noticed that after disclosure and dissenting period, the duty of impartiality still exists within the whole procedure, during which the arbitrator should disclose to parties and the other arbitrators as soon as possible any new-arising circumstances that may cause doubt to his impartiality.

However, whether a fact will affect impartiality is not always objectively clear. Therefore, arbitrators and counsel representing the parties are often unable to determine the scope of disclosure. Meanwhile, the growth of international business, including large group companies as well as international law firms, has led to more disclosure, generating more complex analysis of disclosure and conflict of interest issues. Parties have more opportunities to use recusal applications against arbitrators to delay the arbitration process or to deny the opposing party's choice of arbitrator. Disclosure of any relationship, whether minor or serious, will likely lead to unfounded or frivolous recusal claims.

To summarize, it is in the interest of the international arbitration community to protect international arbitration proceedings from the straitjacket of unfounded recusal claims against arbitrators, as well as to protect the legitimacy of the proceedings from being compromised by uncertainty and the lack of uniformly applied standards for disclosure, challenge and recusal claims.

The IBA Guidelines on Conflicts of Interest in International Arbitration were created in 2004 under the above background. Drawn on the combined experience of nineteen experienced practitioners from different jurisdictions, the 2004 Guidelines establish a common set of principles addressing concrete situations and thus avoid the risk of arbitrators from different cultures applying radically different standards of disclosure.[1] A more recent version of the IBA Guidelines was adopted in 2014. The revised guidelines note "... while the basic approach of the 2004 Guidelines should

---

[1] *See* Scherer, *The IBA Guidelines on Conflicts of Interest in International Arbitration: The first five years 2004-2009*, 4 Disp Res Intl 15 (2010).

not be altered, disclosure should be required in certain circumstances not contemplated in the 2004 Guidelines. It is also essential to reaffirm that the fact of requiring disclosure— or of an arbitrator making a disclosure — does not imply the existence of doubts as to the impartiality or independence of the arbitrator. Indeed, the standard for disclosure differs from the standard for challenge."[①]

3. What Is "Efficiency Duty"?

As a legal maxim says, "justice delayed is justice denied". In the field of international commercial arbitration, undue delay may lead to the blocking of transaction and missing of commercial opportunity, thus causing damage to the parties. In addition, maintaining basic efficiency and ending the arbitration within a reasonable time limit are also a way to save costs and keep arbitration institutions in contention.

Therefore, arbitrators are required by law to act promptly. For example, Article 14 (1) of *UNCITRAL Model Law* says, "If an arbitrator becomes *de jure* or *de facto* unable to perform his functions or for other reasons fails to act without undue delay, his mandate terminates if he withdraws from his office or if the parties agree on the termination..."

Moreover, we can easily find similar kinds of time limits in the arbitration rules. For example, Article 31 of *ICC Arbitration Rules* says, "(1) The time limit within which the arbitral tribunal must render its final award is six months ... (2) The Court may extend the time limit pursuant to a reasoned request from the arbitral tribunal or on its own initiative if it decides it is necessary to do so."

4. How to Ensure Arbitrator's Efficiency?

(1) Time Limits

One of the common methods to ensure efficiency is to set time limits for each stage of arbitration procedure. Take CIETAC Arbitration for example: "Article 66 (1) Upon

---

① See IBA, *The IBA Guidelines on Conflicts of Interest in International Arbitration* (2014) at page III.

receipt of a Request for Arbitration, where the Arbitration Court finds the Request to meet the requirements specified in Article 12 of these Rules, the Arbitration Court shall notify the parties accordingly within five (5) days from its receipt of the Request."

(2) Qualities Required

In each specific arbitration, arbitrators are required to have the appropriate qualities. The arbitrator should have experience in relevant fields, should be organized and efficient, and should have the ability to work with others and build a consensus. These shall all be considered when choosing an arbitrator. It is equally important to ensure that the arbitrators have enough time and energy. For example, Article 11 (2) of *ICC Arbitration Rules* says, "Before appointment or confirmation, a prospective arbitrator shall sign a statement of acceptance, availability, impartiality and independence." Article 5 (4) of *LCIA 2014 Rules* requires arbitrator candidates to confirm that they are "ready, willing and able to devote sufficient time, diligence and industry to ensure the expeditious and efficient conduct of the arbitration".

(3) Expedited Procedure

Where appropriate, expedited procedure will be conducted, which is less demanding on procedural matters than ordinary procedure and is therefore faster.

For example, article 42 (1) of *2018 HKIAC Administered Arbitration Rules* sets out three circumstances where expedited procedure may apply: "(a) the amount in dispute representing the aggregate of any claim and counterclaim (or any set-off defence or cross-claim) does not exceed the amount set by HKIAC, as stated on HKIAC's website on the date the Notice of Arbitration is submitted; or (b) the parties so agree; or (c) in cases of exceptional urgency."

(4) Case Management

A few major institutions have revised their rules to improve the efficiency of arbitrations. For example, the *ICC Rules* requires a compulsory case management conference, where a procedural timetable shall be drawn up: "Article 24 Case Management Conference and Procedural Timetable: 1. When drawing up the Terms of Reference or as soon as possible thereafter, the arbitral tribunal shall hold a case management conference to consult the parties on procedural measures that may be adopted pursuant to Article 22(2). 2. During such conference, or as soon as possible thereafter, the arbitral tribunal shall establish the procedural timetable that it intends to follow for the efficient conduct of the arbitration. The procedural timetable and any modifications thereto shall be communicated to the Court and the parties."

Conclusion

Impartiality duty is committed to insulating arbitrators from bias, while efficiency duty is committed to ending the arbitration within a reasonable time limit. They are, on the one hand, complementary, thus maintaining the quality and limiting the costs of the arbitration, and on the other hand, conflicting, thus requiring a balance of competing interests between private justice and high efficiency.

第七章

临时仲裁在中国有它的生命力

金　鑫

随着现代国际关系、经济贸易的发展，商事争议逐渐复杂化、多元化、全球化，具有高度自治性和准司法性的商事仲裁在世界范围内受到商事纠纷当事人的普遍欢迎。商事仲裁依照组织形式可以分为机构仲裁和临时仲裁，临时仲裁作为仲裁的初始形式，具有悠久的历史和较大的实践灵活性。《中华人民共和国仲裁法》只承认机构仲裁，不承认临时仲裁。但随着自由贸易区、"一带一路"等政策的推进，中国的立法者和司法者也逐渐认识到了临时仲裁的生命力，通过相关规范性文件及个案裁判为中国的临时仲裁的发展创造了新的可能。

本章首先对临时仲裁的概念和优势进行了阐述，指出临时仲裁生命力的源泉。其次，分析了临时仲裁在中国的独特意义。最后，基于临时仲裁的法律渊源和司法现状，进一步强调了临时仲裁在中国有它的生命力。

一、什么是临时仲裁？

临时仲裁是商事仲裁的最初形式，有着悠久的历史。相较于在仲裁组织的框架内进行的机构仲裁，临时仲裁则并非通过机构主导和管理，而是依照当事人之间合意的程序规则，组成临时仲裁庭进行裁决。大部分国家和地区的仲裁规则允许当事人依据个案需要在机构仲裁与临时仲裁中自由选择。

在实践中，对于争议不太复杂的案件，当事人往往会寻求一种快速、经济、灵活的解决方式，临时仲裁可以满足这种需求。协调良好的临时仲裁在解决争议时通常更有效率，不受仲裁机构时间表、开庭时的举证、质询等程序限制，以便仲裁庭能够以更高的效率对个案作出裁决。同时，临时仲裁程序的费用也可以较为灵活，能够满足当事人的经济需求。由于临时仲裁依赖于仲裁庭与当事人的密切合作，泄露商业秘密的风险也可能更小。

20世纪初，国际商事贸易频繁，发达国家的企业迫切地呼吁通过立法的方式促进国内和国际仲裁争端解决机制的发展。1958年，在国际商事联盟和联合国经社理事会的帮助下，各国签订了《承认及执行外国仲裁裁决公约》（《纽约公约》）。到目前为止，已有170余个国家签署这一条约。[①]《纽约公约》明确将仲裁分为机构仲裁和临时仲裁两种形式，承认其他成员国仲裁裁决的义务并不区分机构裁决和临时裁决。

临时仲裁在商事纠纷解决中具有重要价值，并在多数司法管辖区与国际公约中受到普遍支持。其生命力植根于其在自主性、效率性、经济性和保密性方面独特的优势。从实现仲裁制度的目的上讲，应当允许临时仲裁与机构仲裁并行，赋予当事人根据个案需求充分的选择权。

二、临时仲裁为何在中国具有生命力？

近年来，中国的对外贸易急剧增长，成为世界第一大贸易国。现代中国不再是一个传统的农业强国，而是一个商业和工业强国，自然需要一个基于当事人选择的强有力的争议解决机制，承认和发展临时仲裁制度有其

---

① 请见 https://www.newyorkconvention.org/countries（2022.12）。

重要意义。

　　然而，我国目前的《仲裁法》只允许机构仲裁，而不允许临时仲裁，这会造成与国际商事纠纷解决机制的脱节。例如，如某商事仲裁的一方当事人为中国国籍或中国注册企业，而另一方当事人为外国国籍或境外注册企业，而双方当事人希望以临时仲裁的方式作为争议解决机制，则只能选择在中国境外临时仲裁。这是因为虽然《仲裁法》不承认临时仲裁协议的效力，但是基于最高人民法院确定的冲突规则，递交至我国法院予以审查的临时仲裁协议并不会当然地会被认定为无效。由此可见，这样的法律障碍并不能彻底阻止当事人进行临时仲裁，反而使我国的当事人处在不便的地位。

　　如今国际范围内的商事纠纷日益复杂化，传统的诉讼争议解决机制往往不能够很好地满足需求，世界各国都在逐渐探索争议解决的多元化机制。随着"一带一路"沿线发展，以仲裁为主的非诉讼争议解决机制逐渐展现出制度性优势，临时仲裁这种相对自主、高效、隐秘的仲裁模式更是受到了国际商事纠纷当事人的欢迎。从立法和司法层面确认临时仲裁的合法性和有效性，有助于推动多元纠纷解决机制建设，对中国仲裁业的进一步发展具有重要意义。

三、临时仲裁在中国的生命力如何体现？

　　中国仲裁制度的法律渊源一方面是国内立法，另一方面是签署的国际条约中规定的权利与义务。

　　国际条约方面，《纽约公约》于 1987 年对中国生效。根据国际条约的优先效力原则，中国需要履行对其他缔约国仲裁裁决的承认及执行义务，其中既包括机构仲裁也包括临时仲裁。中国加入《纽约公约》后第一例承认与执行外国临时仲裁的案件是"广州远洋运输公司诉 Marships of Connecticut

公司执行案"①。申请人于 1989 年在英国提起了临时仲裁并于 1990 年向广州海事法院申请承认和执行仲裁裁决。广州海事法院则根据《纽约公约》的条约义务，承认了该仲裁裁决的约束力。由此可见，对于约定在域外临时仲裁的案例，中国法院需要承认与执行该外国仲裁裁决。

国内立法方面，是否也存在临时仲裁的可能性？中国仲裁立法相对较晚，第一部《仲裁法》于 1994 年颁布。根据《仲裁法》和《法律适用法》②的规定，无论是否为涉外争议，约定为我国境内仲裁的协议应当受我国《仲裁法》管辖。《仲裁法》第十六条、第十八条及第二十条明确规定，仲裁协议必须约定仲裁委员会，因此临时仲裁的协议无效。然而，2021 年 7 月，司法部就《仲裁法》的修订发布了《征求意见稿》，其中第九十一——九十三条明确对临时仲裁作出了规定。第九十一条中允许有涉外因素的当事人约定临时仲裁，且其并未区分域内或域外仲裁，即有涉外因素的争议双方当事人有约定在境内临时仲裁的可能性。

对于不存在涉外因素的国内争议，原则上不允许临时仲裁。但与国内传统企业相比，自贸区企业在商业活动上有很大区别，为了促进自贸区商业活动，提高自贸区对国际投资者的吸引力，最高院在 2016 年印发了《关于为自由贸易试验区建设提供司法保障的意见》（《自贸区意见》），初步承认了"特定人员、特定规则、境内特定地点"的条件下临时仲裁协议的效力。2017 年，中国首部临时仲裁规则《横琴自由贸易试验区临时仲裁规则》发布，进一步为临时仲裁机制的实践运用提供了指导。此外，中国的行业协会也逐渐发布临时仲裁的行业规则，如 2022 年 3 月的《海协仲裁规则》和《海仲服务规则》。

事实上，中国仲裁立法与国际条约规定的临时仲裁义务存在一定的脱

---

① 广州远洋运输公司诉美国 Marships of Connecticut 公司执行案，请见《人民法院案例选》（1992 年第 1 辑），人民法院出版社 1992 年版，第 163 — 167 页。
② 请见《中华人民共和国涉外民事关系法律适用法》第十八条。

节，长期以来未对临时仲裁放开"涉外"的限制，导致了商事争议解决中的一些问题。但中国的立法和司法部门并未全盘否定临时仲裁，而是倾向于从立法层面认可临时仲裁的效力，并在后续仲裁法律和仲裁规则的发展中逐步解决这一问题。

结语

临时仲裁作为无须仲裁机构参与的争议解决机制，是商事仲裁的初始形式，历史悠久。其生命力源自其独特的优势，对我国商事纠纷解决机制的国际化、多元化有重要意义，有助于推动我国仲裁产业发展。尽管我国《仲裁法》并未承认临时仲裁的效力，但国际条约与相关规范性文件都为当事人选择临时仲裁机制提供了可能性。

随着社会经济发展和商业、法治理念的进步，中国目前已经具备建立和发展临时仲裁制度的土壤，中国立法机关及司法机关对临时仲裁也有了更多的认识，认为其是一种具有机构仲裁所不具备的优势的纠纷解决机制。此外，中国的仲裁员队伍也在逐渐壮大，能够以仲裁方式高效、公正地处理跨境纠纷，并在以仲裁庭的名义出具的仲裁裁决书上署名。仲裁的社会认可度不断提高，商事纠纷的当事人愿意选择仲裁，尤其是选择临时仲裁。

因此，临时仲裁在中国有其生命力，构建和发展中国的临时仲裁机制具有必然性和可行性。我们应借鉴国际先进经验，及时完善中国的临时仲裁制度，逐步增强临时仲裁在中国的生命力。

参考文献

[1] Blanke, G. , "Institutional versus ad hoc arbitration: A European perspective," *ERA Forum,* 9. Available at: https://doi.org/10.1007/s12027-008-0055-6, 2008.

[2] Born, G. , *International Commercial Arbitration,* Wolters Kluwer, 2021.

[3] Moses, M.L. , *The principles and practice of International Commercial Arbitration.*

Cambridge University Press, 2017.

[4] Black, E.A. and Bell, G.F. , *Law and legal institutions of asia: Traditions, adaptations and Innovations,* Cambridge University Press, 2011.

[5] 陆炯：《对临时仲裁制度的法律思考》，《仲裁研究》2005 年第 1 期，第 70—77 页。

[6] 杨良益：《国际商务仲裁》，中国政法大学出版社 1997 年版。

[7] 高菲、徐国建：《中国临时仲裁实务指南》，法律出版社 2017 年版。

[8] 张铁铁：《无法禁止的临时仲裁及当事人的应对策略——兼谈仲裁协议准据法及〈纽约公约〉》，《师大法学》2019 年第 1 期，第 96—122 页。

[9] 黄佳贝：《我国国际商事争端多元解决机制：创新、影响与展望》，《商事仲裁与调解》2021 年第 4 期，第 122—141 页。

[10] 程敏：《中国临时仲裁制度发展的三种路径探析》，载刘晓春、潘剑锋《中国国籍仲裁评论第 3 卷》法律出版社 2021 年版。

Chapter 7

Ad Hoc Arbitration Has its Life in China

Xin Jin

With the development of modern international relations, economic activities and trade, commercial disputes have become more complicated, diversified, and globalized. As a result, commercial arbitration, with a high degree of autonomy and quasi-judicial feature, has been widely welcomed by parties to commercial disputes around the world. Commercial arbitration can be divided into institutional arbitration and *ad hoc* arbitration based on the organization forms. As the initial form of arbitration, *ad hoc* arbitration has a long history and greater flexibility in practice. In *the Arbitration Law of the People's Republic of China (the PRC Arbitration Law)*, only institutional arbitration is recognized while *ad hoc* arbitration is denied. But with the promotion of the free trade zone, the "Belt and Road Initiative" and other policies, Chinese legislators and judicial officials gradually realize the vitality of *ad hoc* arbitration, and create new possibilities for the development of *ad hoc* arbitration in China through relevant regulatory documents and judgments of cases.

This chapter first describes the concept and advantages of *ad hoc* arbitration, pointing out the source of life of *ad hoc* arbitration. Secondly, this chapter analyzes the unique significance of *ad hoc* arbitration in China. Finally, based on the legal sources and current judicial status, this chapter further emphasizes that *ad hoc* arbitration has its life in China.

1. What is Ad Hoc Arbitration?

Ad hoc arbitration is the original form of commercial arbitration with a long history. Compared with institutional arbitration which is conducted within the framework of an arbitration organization, *ad hoc* arbitration is not directed or managed by an institution. It is rendered by an *ad hoc* arbitral tribunal formed in accordance with procedures and rules mutually agreed upon by the parties. Arbitration rules in most countries and regions allow the parties to choose between institutional arbitration and *ad hoc* arbitration, depending on the needs of individual cases.

In practice, for cases involving less complicated disputes, the parties tend to seek a quick, economical, and flexible resolution, and *ad hoc* arbitration can meet the demand. Well-coordinated *ad hoc* arbitration is usually more efficient in resolving disputes, not subject to procedural restrictions such as timetable of the arbitration institution, presenting evidence and making inquiries at oral hearings, etc., so that the arbitral tribunal can render awards for individual cases with higher efficiency. Meanwhile, the costs of *ad hoc* arbitration procedures may be more flexible, which can satisfy the economic needs of the parties. There may also be fewer risks of disclosure of commercial secrets as *ad hoc* arbitration relies on close cooperation between the arbitral tribunal and the parties.

At the beginning of the 20th century, the international commercial trade was frequent. The enterprises of developed countries urgently called for legislation to promote the development of domestic and international arbitration mechanisms. In 1958, with the help of the United Nations Economic and Social Council (ECOSOC), countries signed *the New York Convention on the Recognition and Enforcement of Foreign Arbitral Awards* (*the New York Convention*). So far, more than 170 countries have signed this significant treaty[1] *The New York Convention* explicitly divides arbitration into two forms, institutional arbitration and *ad hoc* arbitration, and the obligation to recognize arbitral awards of other member states does not distinguish between institutional and *ad hoc* awards.

---

① Please see http://www.newyorkconvention.org/countries/ (2022.12).

Ad hoc arbitration is of great value in the resolution of commercial disputes, and is generally recognized in most jurisdictions and international conventions. Its vitality is rooted in its unique advantages in respects of autonomy, efficiency, economy, confidentiality. To truly realize the purpose of arbitration, *ad hoc* and institutional arbitration ought to be allowed to run side by side, and the parties given the right to choose according to the needs of individual cases.

2. Why Ad Hoc Arbitration Has its Life in China?

China's foreign trade increased dramatically in recent years, making it the number 1 trading nation in the world. Modern China is no longer a traditionally rural strength country but now a commercially and industrially strong country. It is natural to need a strong dispute resolution system based on the choice of the parties, so it is of great significance to recognize and develop *ad hoc* arbitration system.

However, the current *PRC Arbitration Law* only allows institutional arbitration, not *ad hoc* arbitration, which will disconnect from the international commercial dispute resolution mechanism. For example, if one of the parties in commercial arbitration is a Chinese national or is a Chinese-registered enterprise, while the other is a foreign national or is a foreign-registered enterprise, and both parties wish to use *ad hoc* arbitration as the dispute resolution mechanism, then the only option to conduct *ad hoc* arbitration is to be used outside of China. This is because although *the PRC Arbitration Law* does not recognize the validity of *ad hoc* arbitration agreements, based on the conflict rules determined by the Supreme People's Court, the *ad hoc* arbitration agreement submitted to the Chinese courts for review will not be certainly determined as invalid. Therefore, such legal obstacle cannot completely hinder the parties to conduct *ad hoc* arbitration, but instead puts the parties in an inconvenient position.

As international commercial disputes become more and more complicated, countries are exploring the diversified dispute resolution mechanism. With the developments along the "Belt and Road Initiative", the trend of arbitration-oriented and non-litigation dispute resolution has gradually displayed its institutional advantages. *Ad hoc* arbitration, as a relatively autonomous, efficient and confidential mode, has gained greater popularity among parties involved in international commercial disputes. Recognizing the legitimacy and validity of *ad hoc* arbitration from the legislative and judicial levels is conducive to promoting the development of a pluralistic dispute resolution mechanism, and is of great significance for the further development of arbitration industry in China.

3. How Ad Hoc Arbitration Has its Life in China?

The sources of law of China's arbitration system are domestic legislation as well as the rights and obligations provided in the international treaties signed by China.

In terms of international treaties, *the New York Convention* entered into force on China in 1987. According to the priority of international treaties, the signatories to *the New York Convention* are required to perform the obligation of recognition and enforcement of the arbitral awards of other member states, including both institutional arbitration and *ad hoc* arbitration. The first case on recognition and enforcement of foreign *ad hoc* arbitration after China's accession to the *New York Convention* was *Guangzhou Ocean Shipping Co., Ltd. v. Marships of Connecticut, Inc. (Enforcement Case)*. The claimant applied for an *ad hoc* arbitration in the U.K. in 1989 and the respondent applied to Guangzhou Maritime Court for recognition and enforcement of the arbitral award in 1990.[1] The Guangzhou Maritime Court then recognized the binding force of the arbitral award based on its treaty obligations under *the New York Convention*. It can be seen that a PRC court should recognize and enforce such foreign arbitral award after the arbitration is conducted abroad.

In terms of domestic legislation, is there a possibility of *ad hoc* arbitration? China's arbitration legislation is relatively late. The first *PRC Arbitration Law* was promulgated in 1994. According to *the PRC Arbitration Law* and *the Law of the Application of*

---

[1] Guangzhou Ocean Shipping Co., Ltd. v. Marships of Connecticut, Inc. (Enforcement Case). Please see Selected Cases of the People's Courts (Series 1 of 1992), People's Court Press, October 1992, pp. 163-167.

Law[1], whether a foreign-related dispute involves a PRC party, an agreement for domestic arbitration shall be governed by *the PRC Arbitration Law*. Articles 16, 18 and 20 stipulate that an arbitration commission must be agreed upon in an arbitration agreement, thus the agreement on *ad hoc* arbitration shall be deemed invalid. However, in July 2021, the Ministry of Justice issued a draft revision to *the PRC Arbitration Law* for public comment, of which Articles 91-93 provide for *ad hoc* arbitration. Article 91 allows parties involving foreign elements to agree on *ad hoc* arbitration, and it doesn't distinguish between intra-territorial and extra-territorial arbitration, which means that parties to a dispute involving foreign elements may agree on *ad hoc* arbitration domestically.

For domestic disputes without foreign related elements, *ad hoc* arbitration is not allowed in principle. However, compared with traditional enterprises in China, there are great differences in the commercial activities of enterprises in free trade zones. In order to promote commercial activities and enhance the attractiveness of free trade zones to international investors, the Supreme People's Court issued *the Opinions on Providing Judicial Guarantees to the Construction of Free Trade Pilot Zones* (the *FTZ Opinions*) in 2016, which preliminarily recognized the validity of *ad hoc* arbitration agreements under the "specific person, specific rules, and specific place within mainland China". In 2017, the first *ad hoc* arbitration rule in China, *the Ad Hoc Arbitration Rules of the Hengqin Pilot Free Trade Zone*, was released, further providing guidance for the practical application of *ad hoc* arbitration. In addition, Chinese trade associations have gradually issued industry rules for *ad hoc* arbitration. For example, the *CMLA Ad Hoc Arbitration Rules* and the *CMAC Ad Hoc Arbitration Service Rules* were released in March, 2022.

In fact, arbitration legislation in China is disjointed from the obligations of *ad hoc* arbitration provided in the international treaties, and has not abandoned the limitation of "foreign-related" for a long time, causing some problems in commercial dispute resolution. However, Chinese legislative and judicial authorities do not completely deny

---

[1] Please see Article 18 of Law of the Application of Law for Foreign-related Civil Relations of the People's Republic of China.

ad hoc arbitration, but tend to recognize the effectiveness of *ad hoc* arbitration from the legislative level, and gradually resolve this issue during the subsequent development of the arbitration law and rules.

Conclusion

Ad hoc arbitration, as a dispute resolution mechanism without the participation of arbitration institutions, is the initial form of commercial arbitration with a long history. Its vitality stems from its unique advantages, which is of great significance to the internationalization and diversification of the commercial dispute settlement mechanism and helps promote the development of the arbitration industry in China. Although *the PRC Arbitration Law* does not recognize the validity of *ad hoc* arbitration, international treaties and relevant normative documents provide the possibility for the parties to choose *ad hoc* arbitration.

With the development of the socialist economy and the progress of the rule of law, China has had the soil to establish and develop the *ad hoc* arbitration system. The legislature and legal system in China have also gained a better understanding of *ad hoc* arbitration, regarded as a dispute resolution system having its own advantages over institutional arbitration. In addition, the team of arbitrators are also growing progressively, well capable of handling cross-border disputes efficiently and impartially by way of arbitration, and signing the arbitration awards issued in the names of the arbitral tribunal. The social recognition of arbitration has been improved, and the parties to commercial disputes are willing to choose arbitration and especially *ad hoc* arbitration.

Therefore, *ad hoc* arbitration has its life in China, and it is inevitable and feasible to build and develop an *ad hoc* arbitration mechanism in China. We should learn from international advanced experience and timely improve our *ad hoc* arbitration system in order to progressively enhance the vitality of *ad hoc* arbitration in China.

第八章
败诉方针对裁决书的救济

高雅菲

　　在仲裁裁决作出之后，败诉方有权寻求救济。本章首先将介绍仲裁裁决撤销制度的一般理论，其次说明在中国大陆撤销裁决的途径，最后分析一个案例。

一、一般理论

　　仲裁制度通过使裁决难以被撤销来贯彻其终局性优势。因此，若仲裁中的败诉方想要撤销裁决，等待它的将是一场艰苦的战斗。尽管如此，只要足够坚定，对裁决结果有异议的一方并非无路可走。①

（一）不同救济途径的辨析
　　败诉方有两种救济途径：第一种是申请撤销仲裁裁决，第二种是申请裁定不予执行。人们有时候会混淆这两种途径。在程序上，这两种途径的

---

① Margaret L. Moses, *The Principles and Practice of International Commercial Arbitration*, 1ˢᵗ edn. New York: Cambridge University Press, 2008, p. 213.

申请人、法院的审查和证明责任等均有所不同。除了程序的不同之外，这两种救济的结果也不同。被撤销的裁决是无效的，而如果法院裁定不予执行一项裁决，该裁决仍然有效，并可以在其他法院申请执行。[①]

（二）撤销裁决的事由

撤销裁决的申请所在区域的适用法律决定了具体的撤销事由。在大部分地区，撤销事由被分为两大类：管辖权异议和程序性事由。大多数情况下撤销事由为程序性事由，但是也有例外，如中国、英国等国家，法院会审查实体性事由。[②]这被认为是司法权的扩张，从而引发争议。

（三）除斥期间

当事人应当及时提起撤销仲裁裁决之诉。如果没有在规定时间内行使该权利，即使该仲裁裁决存在瑕疵，也仍然有效。《示范法》或许赋予了法院一定的自由裁量权，因为它规定的是"当事人不得自收到裁决书之日起三个月后申请撤销裁决"。[③]

（四）撤销仲裁裁决的效力

在法院撤销裁决之后，裁决无效，当事人可以根据不同的撤销事由起诉或者重新申请仲裁。

---

① Randall Peerenboom, 'The Evolving Regulatory Framework for Enforcement of Arbitral Awards in the PRC', *Asian-Pacific Law & Policy Journal*, Vol. 1, No. 2, 2000, p. 42.

② Margaret L. Moses, The Principles and Practice of International Commercial Arbitration. 1st edn. New York: Cambridge University Press, 2008, p. 195.

③ 《联合国国际商事仲裁示范法》第 34 条。

二、在中国大陆撤销仲裁裁决的途径

（一）仲裁裁决的不同类型

在中国大陆，仲裁裁决被分为三类，它们分别为外国仲裁裁决、涉外仲裁裁决和国内仲裁裁决。通常来说，外国仲裁裁决指的是所有在中国境外作出的裁决。国内仲裁裁决指的是在国内仲裁机构作出的，不涉及任何外国因素的裁决。对于涉外仲裁裁决，法律没有准确的定义。但是 2012 年最高院的司法解释中提及了"涉外"一词，或许可以使其有所明晰。该司法解释规定，民事关系具有下列情形之一的，人民法院可以认定为涉外民事关系：（1）当事人一方或双方是外国公民、外国法人或者其他组织、无国籍人；（2）当事人一方或双方的经常居所地在中华人民共和国领域外；（3）标的物在中华人民共和国领域外；（4）产生、变更或者消灭民事关系的法律事实发生在中华人民共和国领域外；（5）可以认定为涉外民事关系的其他情形。[①]

（二）撤销裁决的事由

中国仲裁法区分对待了国内仲裁裁决和涉外仲裁裁决，赋予涉外仲裁裁决优惠待遇。下面将解释这两类仲裁裁决的撤销事由。

1. 国内裁决

《中华人民共和国仲裁法》第 58 条规定，当事人提出证据证明裁决有下列情形之一的，可以向仲裁委员会所在地的中级人民法院申请撤销裁决：（1）没有仲裁协议的；（2）裁决的事项不属于仲裁协议的范围或者仲裁委员会无权仲裁的；（3）仲裁庭的组成或者仲裁的程序违反法定程序的；（4）裁决所根据的证据是伪造的；（5）对方当事人隐瞒了足以影响

[①] 最高人民法院关于适用《中华人民共和国涉外民事关系法律适用法》若干问题的解释（一）(2020 修正)，第 1 条。地址：https://www.pkulaw.com/（登录时间：2022 年 11 月 4 日）。

公正裁决的证据的；（6）仲裁员在仲裁该案时有索贿受贿，徇私舞弊，枉法裁决行为的。此外，本条第 2 款还规定了应当撤销违背公共利益的裁决。

在中国大陆，"公共利益"的含义复杂而富有争议。不了解的人往往会批评中国法院以公共利益为借口试图干预实体问题。[①] 但是近十年来，中国法院审慎地适用公共利益这一事由，体现了对仲裁员自由裁量权的尊重。

中国法院在处理撤销仲裁裁决案件时，有意识地减少对实体问题的干涉，除非存在明显不公正的情形。即使进行干预，也大多以证据的合法性为切入口。[②]

2. 涉外仲裁裁决

《仲裁法》第 70 条规定，当事人提出证据证明涉外仲裁裁决有民事诉讼法第 258 条第 1 款规定的情形之一的，经人民法院组成合议庭审查核实，裁定撤销。根据民事诉讼法第 258 条（现为第 291 条）第 1 款，撤销事由列举如下：（1）当事人在合同中没有订有仲裁条款或者事后没有达成书面仲裁协议的；（2）被申请人没有得到指定仲裁员或者进行仲裁程序的通知，或者由于其他不属于被申请人负责的原因未能陈述意见的；（3）仲裁庭的组成或者仲裁的程序与仲裁规则不符的；（4）裁决的事项不属于仲裁协议的范围或者仲裁机构无权仲裁的。

《民事诉讼法》第 291 条规定的理由比《仲裁法》第 58 条规定的撤销国内裁决的事由范围要窄得多，这反映了尽量减少干预实体问题的政策，以期尽量与国际保持一致。此外，应当注意的是，《民事诉讼法》第 291 条第 2 款中的"公共利益"事由，《仲裁法》第 70 条未明确规定。第 70 条只参引了第 291 条的第 1 款。本条第 2 款规定，如果人民法院认为执行

[①] Gu, Weixia, 'Recourse Against Arbitral Awards: How Far Can a Court Go? Supportive and Supervisory Role of Hong Kong Courts as Lessons to Mainland China', Chinese Journal of International Law, 4(2) [online]. Available at SSRN: https://ssrn.com/abstract=2641321 (Accessed: September 2022).

[②] 肖建国：《仲裁法学》，高等教育出版社 2021 年版，第 218 页。

仲裁裁决有悖于公共利益，人民法院应当作出不予执行的裁定。如前所述，"公共利益"事由的解释非常模糊，在实践中可能适用于对实体问题的审查。对第 291 条第 2 款的排除体现了立法上只审查程序性问题的承诺。

3. 撤销裁决的程序

（1）提出申请

根据《仲裁法》第 58 条规定，有管辖权的人民法院是仲裁委员会所在地的中级人民法院。第 59 条规定，当事人申请撤销仲裁裁决的，应当自收到裁决书之日起 6 个月内提出。申请既可以采用书面形式，也可以口头进行。

（2）对申请的审查

根据仲裁法的规定，法院应组成合议庭审查，以示司法监督仲裁的慎重。第 60 条规定，人民法院应当在受理申请之日起 2 个月内审查，并且作出撤销裁决或驳回申请的裁定。

（3）重新仲裁制度

《仲裁法》规定，受理撤销国内裁决或者涉外裁决申请的法院，可以指示仲裁庭重新审理。法院必须给法庭一定期限审理，并必须在此期间暂停撤销程序。仲裁庭拒绝重新仲裁的，应当恢复撤销程序。[1]

4. 撤销仲裁裁决的救济

（1）不可上诉

司法解释规定，法院对仲裁司法审查案件作出的裁决，在送达时产生法律效力。当事人申请复议、上诉、再审的，除法律和司法解释另有规定的外，法院不予受理。从 1997 年到 2004 年，最高人民法院通过一系列通知逐步建立了该制度。

---

[1] Han Ping, *A Comparative Study of the Chinese Abitration Law and the Arbitration Laws of the UK*, Xiamen: Xiamen University Press, 2019.

（二）内部报告制度

为了解决 20 世纪 90 年代的地方保护主义问题，最高人民法院于 1998 年专门为涉外仲裁裁决的撤销设立了内部报告制度。该机制的目的是确保涉外仲裁裁决的撤销和重新仲裁，未经最高人民法院的事先审查和确认不得进行。[1] 需要特别注意的是，近年来这一制度也开始适用于国内仲裁裁决[2]。

三、案例分析

北京康卫医药咨询服务中心有限公司申请撤销仲裁裁决案。[3]

（一）基本案情

申请人北京康卫医药咨询服务中心有限公司与被申请人亚洲医疗资源开发有限公司就北京国际医疗中心有限公司的经营产生争议，向中国国际经济贸易仲裁委员提出了两份仲裁申请。2006 年 9 月 7 日，中国贸仲委作出第 268 号仲裁裁决，裁定申请人与被申请人签订的补充协议有效，因此双方应履行协议，被申请人应支付拖欠的六个月承包利润共计人民币 675500.00 元。随后，由于被申请人拖欠其他合同款项，申请人根据第 268 号裁决书的内容再次提出仲裁申请，要求被申请人支付 2003 年 8 月 8 日至 2009 年

---

[1] See Jingzhou Tao, *Arbitration Law and Practice in China*, 2nd edn. , Kluwer Law International, 2004, p. 445.

[2] 最高人民法院关于仲裁司法审查案件报核问题的有关规定（2021 年修正）。根据该司法解释第 2 条、第 3 条的规定，各中级人民法院或者专门人民法院办理非涉外涉港澳台仲裁司法审查案件，经审查拟认定仲裁协议无效，不予执行或者撤销我国内地仲裁机构的仲裁裁决，应当向本辖区所属高级人民法院报核；待高级人民法院审核后，方可依高级人民法院的审核意见作出裁定。高级人民法院经审查，拟同意中级人民法院或者专门人民法院以违背社会公共利益为由不予执行或者撤销我国内地仲裁机构的仲裁裁决的，应当向最高人民法院报核，待最高人民法院审核后，方可依最高人民法院的审核意见作出裁定。

[3] （2012）民四他字第 57 号。

11 月 7 日期间发生的承包费，贸仲委作出第 181 号裁决，裁定《补充协议》无效，驳回了被告应支付其他合同利润的请求。贸仲委基于同一协议和事实做出的相互矛盾的裁决给申请人造成了巨大的经济损失，因此申请人请求人民法院撤销第 181 号裁决。

（二）分析

这一涉外仲裁裁决能否被撤销取决于仲裁程序是否违反了仲裁规则。根据《仲裁法》第 70 条和《民事诉讼法》（2007 年）第 258 条第 1 款的规定，当事人提出证据证明仲裁的程序与仲裁规则不符的，人民法院必须撤销裁决。《仲裁法》第 9 条规定，仲裁实行一裁终局制度。"一裁终局"原则是中国仲裁制度的基石。因此，不遵守该原则是对基本仲裁程序的严重违反。

最高人民法院和北京市高级人民法院对于贸仲委对 181 号案件的受理是否违反了《一裁终局》原则持不同意见。北京市高级人民法院在向给最高人民法院的报告中认为，贸仲委在此前的 268 号裁决中确认了《补充协议》的有效性，因此 181 号裁决构成对《补充协议》效力的再次审理，违反了《一裁终局》原则。最高人民法院在答复中认为不应撤销当前的仲裁裁决。部分答复如下："一裁终局原则应理解为仲裁裁决作出后，当事人就同一纠纷再申请仲裁或者向人民法院起诉的，仲裁机构或者人民法院不予受理。然而，本案仲裁所涉纠纷与先前 268 号仲裁所涉纠纷不是同一纠纷，因此，仲裁机构受理本案仲裁纠纷并不违反一裁终局原则。你院关于本案仲裁裁决对相关合同效力的认定与先前生效的人民法院判决以及 268 号仲裁裁决的认定不同违反了一裁终局原则而应予撤销的意见，实质上是对本案仲裁裁决的实体结果是否正确进行审查，违背了程序性审查原则，缺乏法律依据。"[1]

---

[1] 最高人民法院关于北京康卫医药咨询服务中心有限公司申请撤销中国国际经济贸易仲裁委员会仲裁裁决案件的请示的复函，见北大法宝官网。地址：https://www.pkulaw.com/（登陆时间：2022 年 11 月 24 日）。

后续裁决如果基于与先前裁决相同或部分相同的事实，则可能构成对一裁终局原则的违反，但尚未有明确的法律规则。在东莞浩庆纸业有限公司申请撤销仲裁裁决一案中，最高人民法院认为，深圳仲裁委员会根据不同当事人的申请，根据不同的仲裁协议，就不同的仲裁请求做出的仲裁裁决，并非重复仲裁。[①]一般认为，该批复提供了一个标准：如果当事人、仲裁协议、仲裁请求相同，则裁决违反了一裁终局原则。但是可能会被批评的是，过于明确的标准会造成恶意的规避，因此，应适当灵活处理。[②]

本案有两个值得关注的点：第一，这是一个涉外仲裁内部报告制度的例子，体现了中国对涉外仲裁司法审查的审慎态度；第二，这一案件反映了减少对实体性问题进行干预的趋势，以与国际接轨。

结语

撤销仲裁裁决是法院对仲裁监督职权的一部分。作为一种救济制度，它必须符合其存在的目的，尽量与仲裁的理念相统一：首先，公正性是仲裁的基本原则，救济制度存在的意义之一，就是要减少不公正裁决。其次，为了与仲裁裁决的终局性和高效率相统一，撤销制度也应尽量快捷。最后，考虑到法院的职能及其公共属性，在审查裁决时需要将公共利益纳入考量范围之内。在决定是否撤销仲裁裁决时，存在着自由与公平、个人利益与集体利益的权衡取舍，我们期待其中能够涌现更多的中国智慧。

[①] 参见最高人民法院（2015）民四他字第 35 号复函。
[②] 董少谋：《"一裁终局"下仲裁裁决的司法救济途径》，《仲裁研究》2015 年第 3 期，第 21—29 页。

Chapter 8

The Losing Party's Recourse against the Arbitral Award

Yafei Gao

After an arbitral award is made, the losing party is entitled to seek recourse against it. This chapter first introduces a general system of setting aside arbitral awards from the theoretical perspective. Then, the approach of setting aside awards in Chinese mainland is reviewed. Finally, some important cases are noted.

1. A General Legal Theory

One of the advantages of arbitration is the finality of the award. Arbitration laws and rules support finality by making it difficult to set aside an award. So a party that has lost before an arbitral tribunal faces an uphill battle if it wishes to set aside the award. Nonetheless, there are steps that can be taken by a determined party that believes the award was improperly made.[1]

---

[1] Margaret L. Moses, *The Principles and Practice of International Commercial Arbitration*, 1st edn. New York: Cambridge University Press, 2008, p. 213.

(1) Disambiguation of Methods of Challenge

The losing party has two opportunities to challenge an award: first, apply to set aside the award in the court of the situs and, second, oppose the prevailing party's efforts to enforce the award. People have sometimes confused the two actions. The procedure of setting aside differs from a challenge to the recognition and enforcement of an award in several respects, such as the burden of proof, the supervision of the court, and the applicants. Apart from the procedural differences, the consequences of the two actions are different. An award that is set aside becomes invalid. By contrast, if a court refuses to recognize or enforce an award, the award remains valid, provided the court has jurisdiction, and the applicant may still apply for enforcement in another court in that country.[①]

(2) Grounds of Revocation

The applicable law in the jurisdiction where the challenge is brought defines the grounds that can be used. In most jurisdictions, the grounds for a challenge tend to fall into two broad categories: jurisdictional and procedural. Awards are most often challenged on procedural grounds. There are exceptions, though. In some countries, such as the UK and China, the merits of the award might be reviewed.[②] It causes some problems and debates as an expansion of judicial review.

(3) Time Limitations

Challenges to an award must be brought promptly. Failure to act within the time limitations may preclude the challenge. Article 34 (3) of *the UNCITRAL Model Law* stipulates that an application for setting aside may not be made after three months have elapsed from the date on which the party making that application had received the award.[③] This article means that the parties may apply to set aside within the three

---

① Randall Peerenboom, 'The Evolving Regulatory Framework for Enforcement of Arbitral Awards in the PRC', *Asian-Pacific Law & Policy Journal*, Vol.1, No. 2, 2000, p. 42
② Margaret L. Moses, *The Principles and Practice of International Commercial Arbitration, 1ˢᵗ edn.* New York: Cambridge University Press, 2008, p. 195
③ Article 34, the UNCITRAL Model Law.

months from receipt of the award, and after three months, they cannot do so.

(4) Effects of a Successful Application

After the court renders the award null and void, there will be a court action or another arbitration depending on the grounds of revocation.

2. Setting Aside Arbitral Awards in Chinese Mainland

(1) Types of Awards

There are three main types of arbitral awards: foreign, foreign-related, and domestic. It is generally believed that foreign arbitral awards refer to any awards made outside of China. Domestic awards are awards by local arbitration commissions that do not involve foreign elements. There is no statutory definition of 'foreign-related awards'. However, the latest judicial guidance on the general use of the term 'foreign-related' can be found in the the SPC interpretation issued in 2012, which may help to define a foreign-related award. The SPC interpretation stipulates that the following may be regarded as foreign-related civil matters:

a. where either party or both parties are foreign citizens, foreign legal persons or other organizations or stateless persons;

b. where the habitual residence of either party or both parties is located outside the territory of the People's Republic of China;

c. where the subject matter is outside the territory of the People's Republic of China;

d. where the legal fact that leads to establishment, change or termination of civil relationship happens outside the territory of the People's Republic of China; or

e. other circumstances under which the civil relationship may be determined as foreign-related civil relationship.[1]

---

[1] Interpretations of the Supreme People's Court on Several Issues Concerning Application of the Law of the People's Republic of China on Choice of Law for Foreign-Related Civil Relationships (I) (2020 Amendment), Article1. Available at: https://www.pkulaw.com/ (Accessed: 4 November 2022).

(2) Grounds for Setting Aside Awards

Domestic awards and foreign-related awards are treated differently by *the Arbitration Law of the People's Republic of China,* and obvious priority is enjoyed by the latter. The grounds for each sort of award will be listed and interpreted as below:

i.Domestic Awards

Article 58 of *the Arbitration Law of the PRC provides* that where a party can provide evidence proving that the arbitration award involves one of the following circumstances, he/she may apply to the intermediate people's court in the place where the arbitration commission is located to set aside a domestic award where:

a. there is no arbitration agreement;

b. the matters decided in the award exceed the scope of the arbitration agreement or are beyond the arbitral authority of the arbitration commission;

c. The formation of the arbitration tribunal or the arbitration procedure was not in conformity with the statutory procedure;

d. the evidence on which the award is based was forged;

e. the other party has withheld evidence sufficient to affect the impartiality of the arbitration;

f. the arbitrators committed embezzlement, accepted bribes, practiced graft or made an award that perverted the law.

In addition, the second paragraph of Article 58 provides that the court could rule ex officio to set aside a domestic award if the award is contrary to the social and public interest.

In Chinese mainland, "social and public interest" carries a complicated and controversial meaning. It has remained a common criticism that outsiders lay against the Chinese courts that they sometimes try to review the merits of the award under the pretext of public interest.[1] In recent ten years, however, courts in China have applied the public interest ground sparingly, showing respect to the jurisdiction of arbitrators.

There is a tendency that courts in China are becoming reluctant to apply substantial

---

[1] Gu, Weixia, 'Recourse Against Arbitral Awards: How Far Can a Court Go? Supportive and Supervisory Role of Hong Kong Courts as Lessons to Mainland China', Chinese Journal of International Law, 4(2) [online]. Available at SSRN: https://ssrn.com/abstract=2641321 (Accessed: September 2022).

grounds to set aside an award unless the award is unfair. Even if they try to intervene, in most cases they resort to the legality of evidence as an approach.

ii.Foreign-related Awards

Under Article 70 of *the Arbitration Law of the PRC*, if the party that initiates the action for setting aside can present to the competent People's Court proof that a foreign-related award involved one of the circumstances set forth in the first paragraph of Article 281 of the Chinese Civil Procedure Law now , the court shall, after examination and verification, set aside the award. The grounds are stated as follows:

a. no arbitration clause in the contract nor written arbitration agreement concluded after the occurrence of the dispute by the parties;

b. the failure of the respondent to receive the notice of appointment of arbitrators or of commencement of arbitral proceedings or the inability of the respondent to present his/her case for reasons not due to his own fault;

c. the formation of the tribunal or the arbitration procedure was not consistent with the arbitration rules;

d. the matters decided in the award being out of scope of the arbitration agreement or beyond the authority of the arbitration institution.

The grounds set out in Article 291 of *the Civil Procedure Law* are significantly narrower than those governing domestic awards in Article 58 of *the Arbitration Law*; this is a reflection of the policy of minimizing interference with the merits of the award and consistent with the growing international trend. Furthermore, it shall be noted that the "social and public interest" ground in the second paragraph of Article 291 of *the Civil Procedure Law*, is not expressly provided by Article 70 of *the Arbitration Law*.[①] Article 70 concerns only the first paragraph of Article 291, and the second paragraph stipulates that if a People's Court holds that the enforcement of an arbitration award is contrary to the public interest, the People's Court shall issue a ruling not to enforce the award. As mentioned above, the "social and public interest" ground can be interpreted

---

[①] Gu, Weixia, 'Recourse Against Arbitral Awards: How Far Can a Court Go? Supportive and Supervisory Role of Hong Kong Courts as Lessons to Mainland China', Chinese Journal of International Law, 4(2) [online]. Available at SSRN: https://ssrn.com/abstract=2641321 (Accessed: September 2022).

flexibly, which might be applied to the review of the merits of the award in practice. The exclusion of the second paragraph of Article 291 demonstrates the legislature's commitment to review only procedural issues.

(3) Procedure for Setting Aside Awards

i.Application

Under Article 58 of *the Arbitration Law of the PRC*, the competent court in an application to set aside a domestic award is the intermediate court of the place where the arbitration commission is situated. Article 59 provides that an application must be submitted within 6 months of receipt of the award. The application form can be either oral or written.

ii.Judicial Review

According to the Arbitration Law, a collegial panel will be formed by the People's Court, which shows prudence in judicial supervision. Article 60 then indicates that the court shall cancel the award or reject the application, within 2 months of receipt of the application.

iii.Remitting Awards for Reconsideration

The Arbitration Law allows the court which receives an application for setting aside a domestic or a foreign-related award to direct that the case be reconsidered by the arbitral tribunal. The court must give the tribunal a certain period of time to take this step, and must suspend the cancellation procedure in the meantime. If the tribunal refuses to re-arbitrate, the court shall resume the cancellation procedure. [1]

(4) The Remedy against Setting Aside Awards

i.The Ruling is Unappealable

The SPC Interpretation provides that a ruling made by a court in an arbitration-related judicial review case shall produce a legal effect upon service. Where a party applies for reconsideration, files an appeal, or applies for re-trial, the court shall grant no acceptance unless otherwise provided by the law or any other judicial interpretation. The system was set up gradually by a series of notices by the SPC from 1997 to 2004.

---

[1] Han Ping, *A Comparative Study of the Chinese Abitration Law and the Arbitration Laws of the UK*, Xiamen: Xiamen University Press, 2019.

ii.The Prior Reporting System

To deal with local protectionism in the 1990s, a special prior reporting system was established only for foreign-related awards in 1998. The mechanism serves to ensure that the revocation of a foreign-related arbitral award, or the issuing of an order to an arbitration commission to re-arbitrate the dispute, may not occur without the prior examination and confirmation of the SPC.[1] What calls for special attention is that the Reporting System also applies to domestic awards in recent years.[2]

3. Case Study

Beijing Kang Wei Pharmaceutical Consultation Centre Co. Ltd. v. Asia Medical Resources Development (Holdings) Limited[3].

Facts

Due to disputes arising from the operation of Beijing International Medical Centre Co. Ltd. between Beijing Kang Wei Pharmaceutical Consultation Centre Co Ltd□ the applicant, and Asia Medical Resources Development (Holdings) Limited, the respondent, two arbitration applications had been made to CIETAC. On 7 September 2006, CIETAC rendered Arbitral Award No.268, ruling that the Supplementary

---

① See Jingzhou Tao, *Arbitration Law and Practice in China*, 2nd edn. Kluwer Law International, 2004, p. 445.

② Relevant Provisions of the Supreme People's Court on Issues concerning Applications for Verification of Arbitration Cases under Judicial Review (2021 Amendment).

Articles 2 and 3 of the 2021 Amendment stipulate that in the handling of domestic arbitration cases under judicial review, where, upon review, any Intermediate People's Court or Special People's Court is to determine to revoke an arbitral award rendered by an arbitration institution in the Chinese mainland, the Intermediate People's Court or Special People's Court shall file an application for verification with the Higher People's Court within the jurisdiction; upon review of the Higher People's Court, the Intermediate People's Court or Special People's Court may render a ruling based on the review opinions of the Higher People's Court. If the Higher People's Court intends to grant the application for revocation of an arbitral award in the Chinese mainland shall apply to the Supreme People's Court for review.

③ No.32 of the Fourth Civil Tribunal of the Supreme People's Court [2010].

Agreement signed between the applicant and the respondent was valid and enforceable, and so the parties should perform the agreement accordingly. The respondent should pay the applicant contract profits in arrears amounting to 675500.00 RMB. Subsequently, due to the respondent's default on other contracting payments, the applicant made another arbitration application based on the contents of Award No. 268, demanding the respondent's payment for the contracting fees incurred between 8 August 2003 and 7 November 2009. CIETAC rendered Award No.181, ruling that the Supplementary Agreement was invalid. The commission dismissed the submission that the respondent should pay other contract profits. CIETAC's contradictory ruling based on the same agreement and facts generated huge economic losses to the applicant, so the applicant requested that the People's Court set aside Award No. 181.

Discussion

Whether this foreign-related award can be set aside depends on whether the arbitration procedures violated the Arbitration Rules. Pursuant to Article 70 of *the Arbitration Law of the PRC* and paragraph 1, Article 258 of *the Civil Procedure Law of the PRC* (2007), if a party presents evidence that proves that the arbitration procedure is not in conformity with arbitration rules, the People's Court must set aside the award. Article 9 of *the Arbitration Law* stipulates that a system of a single and final award shall be practiced for arbitration. The "single and final award" principle is the cornerstone of the arbitration system in China. Non-compliance with the principle is therefore a serious violation of the fundamental arbitration procedure.

The Supreme People's Court and the High People's Court of Beijing held different views on whether the arbitration institution's acceptance of case No. 181 was in violation of the 'single and final award principle. In its Report to the Supreme People's Court, the High People's Court of Beijing held that CIETAC confirmed the Agreement's validity in its prior Award No. 268, so Award No.181 constituted a re-trial of the issue regarding the validity of the Supplementary Agreement and was in violation of the principles. In its Reply, the Supreme People's Court disagreed and held that the current arbitral award should not be annulled. Part of its reply was as follows:

...the system of a single and final award shall be interpreted as "if a party applies

for arbitration to an arbitration commission or institutes an action in a people's court regarding the same dispute after an arbitration award has been made, the arbitration commission or the People's Court shall not accept the case. Nevertheless, since the disputes to be arbitrated by the arbitration institution here were different from the previous Arbitration Case No.268, the arbitration institution's acceptance of this case was therefore not in violation of the 'single and final award principle. Your court's holding that the arbitral award in question's confirmation of the validity of the relevant contract, the people's court's decision previously in force, and the determination of Arbitral Award No.268 was in violation of the 'single and final award' principle and so shall be set aside is a de facto review of the correctness of the substantive outcome of the arbitral award in question. Therefore, the holding violated the principle that only procedural review is allowed and lacked legal basis.[1]

The latter award might violate the single and final award principle if it is made on the same or partly the same facts which have been decided by other arbitral awards, but it has not formed a legal rule. This case is one of them. In the case that Dongguan Haoqing Paper Co. Ltd applying for setting aside arbitral award, the SPC held that the arbitral award made by Shenzhen Arbitration Commission on different arbitration requests according to the applications of different parties and based on different arbitration agreements is not the repeated arbitration for the same dispute. It is generally believed that the precedent provides a standard: if the parties, the arbitration agreement, and arbitration application are the same, the award is in violation of the single and final award principle.[2] What might be criticized is that the definite standard will cause malicious evasion, therefore, the recognition should be more flexible.[3]

There are two key points for readers in this case: It is an example of the Prior Reporting System for foreign-related awards, which shows China's prudent attitude toward the judicial review of foreign-related arbitrations. Besides, it is also a reflection

---

[1] See Yang Fan, *Foreign-related arbitration in China : commentary and cases*, 1st edn. UK: Cambridge University Press, 2016, pp. 447-458.

[2] See Letter No.35 of the Fourth Civil Court of the Supreme People's Court.

[3] 董少谋:《"一裁终局"下仲裁裁决的司法救济途径》,《仲裁研究》2015 年第 3 期,第 21—29 页。

of the policy of minimizing interference with the merits of an award and is consistent with the growing international trend.

Conclusion

The authority to set aside an award is part of the court's supervisory authority. As a relief system, it needs to be consistent with the purpose for which it exists. First, impartiality is one of the fundamental principles of arbitration. One of the reasons that the relief system exists is to uphold the principle by reducing unjust awards. Besides, arbitral awards are considered final and binding, and the system of revocation should preserve the speediness and convenience of arbitration. Also, given the function of the court, public interests will be considered when awards are reviewed. There is a trade-off between freedom and equity, individual interests and collective interests when setting aside an arbitral award. We are looking forward to more Chinese wisdom both in theory and in practice.

第九章
胜诉方的执行路线

袁一凡

《纽约公约》（"NYC"）为承认和执行缔约国之间的裁决提供了普遍适用的标准。一旦在争议中作出裁决，获胜方就必须寻求执行的途径，而《纽约公约》是承认和执行裁决的法律基础。在本章中，我们将讨论仲裁裁决不被承认和执行的情况。

一般来说，根据《纽约公约》第 1 条，一项仲裁裁决是否属于外国仲裁裁决主要取决于仲裁地或裁决地。出于当事人意思自治原则，仲裁地通常是经双方当事人同意在仲裁协议中共同选择。如今，涉外商事活动占据了很大的市场份额。在中国，《民事诉讼法》第 290 条和《仲裁法》第 72 条都对仲裁地在中国的仲裁裁决的执行路径作了相关规定。

一、《纽约公约》和强制执行

实际执行或强制执行是整个仲裁过程中最重要的程序，因为双方当事人所追求的正是适当的解决方案和实质性的赔偿。最理想的情况是，裁决作出后，败诉方履行裁决的义务。然而，在现实中，败诉方拒绝履行或拒绝遵守裁决的情况屡屡发生。那么，胜诉方可以寻求法院的强制执行。

一般来说，有两种方式可以将裁决转化为更具强制力的判决：（1）直接将仲裁裁决视为判决；（2）根据仲裁裁决启动法律程序。在英国《1996年仲裁法》中，第101（3）条规定："如获许可，可根据裁决书作出判决。"选定的法院可以根据实际情况采取各种措施，让败诉方遵守裁决。这些措施包括：（1）扣押令；（2）执行货物；（3）第三方债务令；（4）提供信息的命令；（5）公司的清算和清盘；（6）接管等。

二、拒绝承认和执行裁决的理由

《纽约公约》在其内容中没有直接列明裁决可以执行的情况，而是规定了裁决可能无法获得承认和执行的情况。通过了解哪些情况不能执行，选定的法院将拥有更大的自由裁量权。在《纽约公约》第5条中，总共有七个理由，唯有在该七个理由任何一个被证明存在时，才可以拒绝承认和执行外国仲裁裁决。

（一）第5条第(1)款第(a)项：根据适用的法律或无效的协议，无行为能力

第5条第(1)款第(a)项的这一理由有两个抗辩。一个是根据当事人的适用法律，当事人没有能力；另一个是协议无效。在纠纷或分歧中，当事人可以是个人、公司或政府。当败诉方以无行为能力作为辩护理由时，这通常与适用法律有关。一般来说，"该条款明确指出，订约能力不是由当事人选择的法律决定的，而是由适用于他们的法律，或他们的属人法决定的，对于自然人来说，属人法指的是他们的国籍或住所的法律"[1]。而对于公司

---

[1] George A. Bermann, *Recognition and Enforcement of Foreign Arbitral Awards The Interpretation and Application of the New York Convention by National Courts,* Springer International Publishing AG, 2017, p. 285.

来说，适用的法律应该是其注册地的管辖法律。仲裁协议的准据法可以是当事人选择的合同的准据法。有关这一主题的更多细节，请参见第十六章（Myo Su Thant 的章节）。

（二）第 5 条第 (1) 款第 (b) 项：没有适当的通知或没有能力陈述案情

第 5 条第 (1) 款第 (b) 项与整个仲裁程序的公正性密切相关。该理由包括两个重要的抗辩理由，即（1）被援引裁决的一方没有得到关于指定仲裁员或仲裁程序的适当通知，或；（2）因其他原因无法陈述案情。第一个理由规定保证了正当程序的原则。虽然该条款只要求适当通知仲裁员的任命和仲裁程序，但在实践中，它"适用于程序的所有基本步骤的通知，包括开庭日期和地点的通知，以及最终裁决的通知"[1]。第二个理由规定事实上保证了陈述案情和提交证据的权利。当事人在仲裁程序中必须被给予机会陈述案情。有多种未给予机会的情况可能发生，比如，在仲裁过程中：（1）败诉方提交补充证据的请求被仲裁委员会或仲裁员以某些理由拒绝；（2）当事人没有得到适当的通知或因某些特殊原因没有出席仲裁庭的程序性事项（缺席庭审者例外）。

（三）第五条第 (1) 款第 (c) 项：裁决涉及的分歧不符合提交仲裁的规定

根据第 5 条第 (1) 款第 (c) 项的规定，裁决书中做出的决定可能面临以超出仲裁庭权限为理由的抗辩。"仲裁协议赋予了仲裁庭全面的权力。然而，仲裁协议不仅是仲裁庭权力的来源，也是对仲裁庭权力的限制。"[2] 裁决应

---

[1] George A. Bermann, *Recognition and Enforcement of Foreign Arbitral Awards The Interpretation and Application of the New York Convention by National Courts,* Springer International Publishing AG, 2017, p. 291.

[2] George A. Bermann, *Recognition and Enforcement of Foreign Arbitral Awards The Interpretation and Application of the New York Convention by National Courts,* Springer International Publishing AG, 2017, p. 322.

在当事人的上述协议范围内作出，这就指向了仲裁庭的管辖权。有关这个话题的更精彩的内容，请见本书第五章。

根据 1996 年《仲裁法》第 30 条详细描述的仲裁庭管辖权自治原则，即"仲裁庭可裁定其实体管辖权，亦即关于：按照仲裁协议何等事项已提交仲裁"，仲裁庭有责任遵循仲裁协议。但是，如果裁决是最终的，但裁决中的一些条款超出了仲裁庭的权限，那么可以援引部分执行，而不是否定整个裁决。

（四）第 5 条第 (1) 款第 (d) 项：仲裁机构的组成或仲裁程序有违当事人的意愿

仲裁协议是任何其他进一步仲裁行为的前提条件。国际商事仲裁的第一条规则是当事人自治原则，而仲裁协议是根据这一原则制定的。鉴于第 2 条和第 5 条第 (1) 款第 (a) 项的部分已经强调了仲裁协议的意义，即上述协议是仲裁的基石，因此解释这一理由就容易多了。一般来说，该理由包括不遵守的两个方面：仲裁庭和仲裁程序。在大多数情况下，当事人应明确写明仲裁地点的选择、仲裁庭、仲裁员的指定等。但如果在协议中没有作出确定的指定，那么当事人应寻求仲裁地的法律作为管辖法律来确定这些事项。

（五）第 5 条第 (1) 款第 (e) 项：裁决尚未对各方当事人产生约束力，或在某些情况下被国家主管当局撤销或中止

第 5 条第 (1) 款第 (e) 项可分为两部分作为拒绝裁决的理由。该条款中的第一个理由是"尚未对当事人产生约束力"，而第二部分提出了裁决"已被主管机关撤销或中止"的情况。对于前者，应该注意的是，该条款使用了裁决"具有约束力"而不是"最终"一词。这实际上导致了对"具有约束力"的含义的理解。如果裁决对当事人具有约束力，那就意味着"寻求

执行裁决的当事人不需要在裁决的原籍国获得豁免权"①。这符合避免双重许可、维护效率和正义的意图。这里有一个例子，*Egypt No. 3. Misr Foreign Trade (nationality not indicated) v. R.D Harboties (Mercantile) (nationality not indicated), 2010 / JY 64*②。在本案中，在根据双方的仲裁协议作出裁决后，败诉方 Misr 外贸公司拒绝执行该裁决，并提出索赔，但已被南开罗法院驳回。然而，Misr 外贸公司对该判决提出质疑，并声称"对其作出的仲裁裁决是初步裁决，而不是最终裁决，这违反了《纽约公约》第 5 条第 (1) 款第 (e) 项"。针对这一主张，法院认为，鉴于一事不再审，裁决一旦作出就应具有约束力。

对于后者来说，什么身份或条件的主管部门是理解这一理由的关键。根据《纽约公约》第 5 条第 (1) 款第 (e) 项，对主管当局有两个要求：（1）在作出裁决的国家；或（2）在依据其法律规定作出裁决的国家。因此，撤销或中止的情形基本上是指由主管当局"在其原籍国"③撤销或中止裁决，或者"可以在寻求执行裁决的国家对裁决提出质疑"④。

（六）第 5 条第 (2) 款第 (a) 项：根据该国法律，分歧的主题不能通过仲裁解决

第 5 条第 (2) 款意在裁决的实体的可执行性。第 5 条第 (2) 款第 (a) 项这一理由要求提交的争议的可仲裁性，因为它影响到仲裁协议的有效性。第 5 条第 (1) 款第 (a) 项和第 (2) 款第 (a) 项这两条规定的不同之处在于，在

---

① Dr. Reinmar Wolff, *New York Convention Convention on the Recognition and Enforcement of Foreign Arbitral Awards of 10 June 1958 Article-by-Article Commentary,* Verlag C.H.Beck oHG Wilhelmstr. 9, 80801 München, 2019, p. 372.

② General Assembly, Distr.: General, 2013, CASE LAW ON UNCITRAL TEXTS (CLOUT), available from: 〈https://www.uncitral.org/clout/clout/data/egy/clout_case_1325_leg-3105.html〉.

③ Dr. Reinmar Wolff, *New York Convention Convention on the Recognition and Enforcement of Foreign Arbitral Awards of 10 June 1958 Article-by-Article Commentary,* Verlag C.H.Beck oHG Wilhelmstr. 9, 80801 München, 2019, p. 381.

④ Ibid.

第 5 条第（1）款第 (a) 项中，不可仲裁性取决于仲裁地或 / 和仲裁协议的法律，而在第 5 条第（2）款第 (a) 项中，不可仲裁性是由裁决执行地的法律决定的。在国际商事仲裁中，援引这一理由来拒绝执行的情况不太常见。然而，这个相关案例的存在可以作为例证。在 *Shipping Services A/S v. RAB Sevnaučflot, Fishery Group LLC 13 May 2011*[①] 一案中，双方发生了纠纷，Shipping Services A/S 提起了诉讼，但在诉讼过程中，双方都被强调正在经历破产。法院认为，根据 1996 年《立陶宛共和国商业仲裁法》第 5 条第（2）款第 (a) 项，破产公司之间的争议缺乏可仲裁性，该争议不可仲裁。

（七）第五条第 (2) 款第 (b) 项：承认或执行裁决将违反该国的公共政策

这是第 5 条中最有争议的条款，它规定，当裁决违背国家的公共政策时，将不被承认和执行。公共政策不仅仅是一个简单的法律概念，更是指向了对外国商事仲裁的政治影响。鉴于公共政策通常是由某些国家部门设计的，其形式也各不相同，它们可能会根据国家情况频繁地改变或修正。对于裁决的承认和执行而言，这种公共政策的不稳定性在一定程度上是危险的。正如 *Richardson v. Mellish* (1824) 2 Bing 228[②] 一案所指出的，"公共政策是一匹非常不稳定的马，当你一旦骑上它，你永远不知道它会把你带到哪里。它可能会把你带离健全的法律"，公共政策在具体案件中确实很难处理。

《纽约公约》缔约国在使用这一理由作为拒绝承认和执行外国裁决的理由时会非常谨慎。在中国有一个著名的案例，其中援引了第 5 条第（2）款第（b）项并被法院接受，那就是 *Hemofarm DD, MAG International Trade*

---

① Lithuania, 13 May 2011, 'Lithuania, Lietuvos Apeliacinis Teismas (Court of Appeal of Lithuania) / Shipping Services A/S v. RAB Sevnaučflot, Fishery Group LLC / 2-1545/2011', available from: 〈https://newyorkconvention1958.org/index.php?lvl=categ_see&id=46〉.

② Burrough, J, Richardson v Mellish , 2 Bing 229 at 252, 130 ER 294 (CP1824).

Holding DD, Suramu Media Ltd. v. Jinan Yongning Pharmaceutical Co., Ltd[①] 。
在该案中，Jinan–Hemofarm 对法院的管辖权提出质疑，并将租金合同问题
提交巴黎国际商会国际仲裁院进行仲裁。但是，租金合同纠纷不属于本案
当事人之间达成的仲裁协议的范围，因此不能进行仲裁。最高人民法院在
给山东省高级人民法院的答复中认为，"承认和执行该裁决有悖于中国的
公共政策"，拒绝承认和执行国际商会的裁决。在这个例子中，援引公共
政策是为了获得中国的司法主权和中国法院的管辖权。在国际商事仲裁中，
"公共政策的目的是为缔约国提供一个安全阀，使其能够防止裁决侵入其
认为与之不相容的法律体系"[②]。

结论和展望

在承认和执行仲裁裁决方面，最重要的原则是当事人意思自治。当事
人自治原则是仲裁协议和整个仲裁程序的基石。然而，仲裁程序不过是达
成解决方案的工具，所以认识执行裁决的途径有其实际意义。

在中国，《纽约公约》还没有成为一个社会上广为人知的公约。希望
将来它能帮助当事人在外国商事仲裁中争取自己的权利，同时也能成为巩
固法治社会的基础。

参考文献

[1] 杨良宜、莫世杰、杨大明：《仲裁法 从开庭审理到裁决书的作出与执行》法律出版社
2010 年版。

---

① hemofarm dd v jinan yongning pharmaceutical co ltd [2008] min si ta zi no.11.Available from: 〈https://
arbitrationlaw.com/library/hemofarm-dd-v-jinan-yongning-pharmaceutical-co-ltd-2008-min-si-ta-zi-
no-11〉；〈http://www.lawinfochina.com/display.aspx?lib=law&id=14615&CGid=〉.

② Dr. Reinmar Wolff, *New York Convention Convention on the Recognition and Enforcement of Foreign
Arbitral Awards of 10 June 1958 Article-by-Article Commentary,* Verlag C.H.Beck oHG Wilhelmstr. 9,
80801 München, 2019, p. 419.

[2] 齐湘泉：《外国仲裁裁决承认及执行论》法律出版社 2010 年版。

[3] 宋航：《国际商事仲裁裁决的承认与执行》法律出版社 2000 年版。

[4] Zheng Sophia Tang, *Jurisdiction and Arbitration Agreements in International Commercial Law,* First published by Routledge, 2014.

[5] Dr. Reinmar Wolff, *New York Convention Convention on the Recognition and Enforcement of Foreign Arbitral Awards of 10 June 1958 Article-by-Article Commentary,* Verlag C.H.Beck oHG Wilhelmstr. 9, 80801 München, 2019.

[6] George A. Bermann, *Recognition and Enforcement of Foreign Arbitral Awards The Interpretation and Application of the New York Convention by National Courts,* Springer International Publishing AG, 2017.

Chapter 9

The Winning Party's Route towards Enforcement

Yifan Yuan

The New York Convention ("NYC") provides universally applicable standards for the recognition and enforcement of the foreign arbitral awards made among the State Parties. Once the award is made in a dispute, the winning party will have to seek a route towards enforcement and NYC is the legal basis for recognition and enforcement. In this chapter, we discuss the circumstances when the arbitral award is not recognized and enforced.

Generally, based on NYC Article 1, deciding whether an arbitration award is foreign or not mainly depends on the place of arbitration or where the award is made. Due to the principle of party autonomy, the place of arbitration usually is chosen in the arbitration agreement upon both parties' agreement. Nowadays foreign-related commercial activities occupy a significant market share. In China, Article 290 of *the Civil Procedure Law* and Article 72 of *the Arbitration Law* both state relevant provisions to deal with the route of enforcement of arbitral awards when the place of arbitration is in China.

1.*The New York Convention* and Enforcement

The actual execution or enforcement is the most significant proceeding during the whole arbitration process, because the proper solution and substantive compensation are what the two parties are seeking. The ideal situation is that after the award is made, the losing party fulfills the obligation of the award. However, in reality, the circumstance that the losing party refuses to perform or comply with the award happens time and again. Then the winning party may seek the court for enforcement.

Generally, there are two ways to transform the award into a judgment which is more coercive: (i) consider the arbitral award as a judgment directly; (ii) initiate legal proceedings in terms of the arbitral award. *In the UK Arbitration Act 1996*, Section 101 (3) provides "Where leave is so given, judgment may be entered in terms of the award." The selected court is able to take a variety of measures to get the losing party to comply with the award depending on the circumstances of the case. Such measures may include: (i) charging order; (ii) execution goods; (iii) third party debt orders; (iv) order to provide information; (v) liquidation and winding-up of company; (vi) receivership, etc.

2. Grounds for Refusal to Recognize and Enforce the Award

The New York Convention does not directly suggest in its content the circumstances in which the award is enforceable, but rather sets forth the circumstances in which and only in which the award may be not recognized or be unenforceable. By knowing what cannot be enforced, the selected court will have greater discretion. There are seven grounds in total in Article V from NYC, only seven grounds, the proof of each of which will result in refusal of recognition and enforcement of foreign arbitral awards.

2.1 Article V (1)(a) Incapacity under applicable law or invalid arbitration agreement

There are two defenses in this ground of Article V (1)(a). One is the parties' incapacity pursuant to the applicable law of the parties and the other is null or invalid agreement. In a dispute or difference, the parties can be persons, companies or government or non-governmental bodies. When the losing party uses incapacity as a defence, this is usually related to the applicable laws. Generally, "this provision makes clear that capacity is to be determined not by the law chosen by the parties, but rather by the law applicable to them, or their personal law, which for natural persons refers to the law of their nationality or domicile."[1] And for corporations, the applicable law should be the governing law of its incorporation. The governing law of the arbitration agreement may be the governing law of the contract chosen by the parties. Please see Chapter 16 [Myo Su Thant's chapter] for more details of this topic.

2.2 Article V (1)(b) No proper notice or no ability to present the case

Article V (1)(b) is closely linked to the justice of the whole arbitration proceedings. The ground consists of two significant defenses, which are: (i) the party against whom the award is invoked was not given proper notice of the appointment of the arbitrator or of the arbitration proceedings or; (ii) it was otherwise unable to present its case. The first provision guarantees the principle of due process. Although the provision only requires the proper notice of the appointment of the arbitrator and of the arbitration proceedings, in practice, it "applies to notifications of all essential steps of the proceedings, including the notice of the date and the place of hearing, and notice of the final award."[2] The second provision in fact guarantees the right of the presentation of the case and the submission of evidence. Parties must be given the opportunity to present their case in arbitration proceedings. There are various circumstances that could have happened, denying such opportunities. For example, during the process of arbitration (i) the losing party's request to submit supplementary evidence was rejected by the arbitration commission or the arbitrator for certain reasons; (ii) the party was not given proper notice or for some specific reasons failed to attend to the procedural matters from the arbitration tribunal (default proceedings excepted).

---

[1] George A. Bermann, *Recognition and Enforcement of Foreign Arbitral Awards The Interpretation and Application of the New York Convention by National Courts,* Springer International Publishing AG, 2017, p. 285.

[2] George A. Bermann, *Recognition and Enforcement of Foreign Arbitral Awards The Interpretation and Application of the New York Convention by National Courts,* Springer International Publishing AG, 2017, p. 291.

2.3 Article V(1)(c) Award deals with a difference that is not in accordance with the submission to arbitration

Pursuant to Article V (1)(c), the decisions made in the award may face a plea for they art beyond the arbitral tribunal's authority. "The arbitration agreement gives comprehensive powers to the arbitral tribunal. The arbitration agreement, however, is not only the source, but also the limit to the arbitral tribunal's authority."[1] The award should be made within the scope of the parties' said agreement and this leads to the jurisdiction of the arbitral tribunal. [For more discussion of this topic, please refer to Chapter 5 in this book.]

According to the principle of competence-competence, which is described in detail in the Arbitration Act 1996 Section 30, "the arbitral tribunal may rule on its substantive jurisdiction......as to what matters have been submitted to arbitration in accordance with the arbitration agreement", so it is the duty of the arbitral tribunal to follow the arbitration agreement. However, if the award is made final but some of the terms in the award exceed the arbitral tribunal's authority, then partial enforcement can be invoked instead of denying the whole award.

2.4 Article V (1)(d) Composition of the arbitral authority or the arbitral procedure is against the will of the parties

Arbitration agreement is the prerequisite for any other further arbitral act. The first rule of international commercial arbitration is the principle of party autonomy which the arbitration agreement is made in line with. Given that the significance of the arbitration agreement has been stressed in the part of Article II and Article V (1)(a), i.e., the said agreement is the cornerstone of arbitration, it is much easier to interpret this ground. Generally, the ground includes two aspects in non-compliance: the arbitral tribunal and the arbitral procedure. In most circumstances, the parties should write clearly on the choice of the place of arbitration, the arbitration tribunal, the appointment

---

[1] George A. Bermann, *Recognition and Enforcement of Foreign Arbitral Awards The Interpretation and Application of the New York Convention by National Courts,* Springer International Publishing AG, 2017, p. 322.

of arbitrators and so on. But if no certain appointment is made in the agreement, then the parties should seek for the law of the place of arbitration as the governing law to determine these matters.

2.5 Article V (1)(e) Award has not yet become binding on the parties, or has been set aside or suspended by a competent authority of the country in some conditions

Article V (1)(e) can be divided into two parts as grounds for the refusal of the award. The first ground in this provision is that the award "has not yet become binding on the parties" while the second part presents the circumstance when the award "has been set aside or suspended by a competent authority". For the former one, it should be noted that the provision uses the word "binding" rather than "final". This actually leads to the understanding of the meaning of "binding". If the award has become binding on the parties, that means "the party seeking the enforcement of the award is not required to obtain exequatur in the award's country of origin."[①] This is in line with the intention of avoiding double exequatur and maintaining the efficiency and justice. Here's an example, *Egypt No. 3. Misr Foreign Trade (nationality not indicated) v. R.D Harboties (Mercantile) (nationality not indicated), 2010 / JY 64*[②]. In this case, after the award was made in accordance with the arbitration agreement between the two parties, the losing party, Misr Foreign Trade Co. refused to enforce the award and filed a claim which has been rejected by the South Cairo Court. However, Misr Foreign Trade challenged the judgement and alleged that "the arbitral award issued in its regard was a preliminary award and not a definitive one, which is contrary to Article V (1)(e) NYC". In response to this claim, the court considered that in light of the *res judicata*, the award should have binding force once it is made.

For the latter, the competent authority of what capacities or conditions is the key to comprehend this ground. In light of the Article V (1)(e) in NYC, there are two

---

① Dr. Reinmar Wolff, *New York Convention Convention on the Recognition and Enforcement of Foreign Arbitral Awards of 10 June 1958 Article-by-Article Commentary,* Verlag C.H.Beck oHG Wilhelmstr. 9, 80801 München, 2019, p. 372.

② General Assembly, Distr.: General, 2013, CASE LAW ON UNCITRAL TEXTS (CLOUT), available from: ⟨https://www.uncitral.org/clout/clout/data/egy/clout_case_1325_leg-3105.html⟩.

requirements for the competent authority that it should be: (i) in the country in which the award was made; or (ii) in the country under the law of which the award was made. Thus basically the award can be set aside or suspended by the competent authority "in its country of origin"[1]or "can be challenged in the country where its enforcement is sought."[2]

2.6 Article V (2)(a) Subject matter of difference is not capable of settlement by arbitration under the law of the country

Article V (2) intends to have more relationship with the awards' substantial enforceability. This ground, Article V (2)(a), requires the arbitrability of the submitted dispute as it affects the validity of the arbitration agreement. Pursuant to the two provisions of Article V(1)(a) and Article V(2)(a), the difference is that in Article V (1) (a), the non-arbitrability depends on the law of the arbitration seat or/and the arbitration agreement, whereas in Article V (2)(a), the non-arbitrability is determined by the law of the place where the award is to be enforced. In foreign commercial arbitration, it is less common to invoke this ground for a refusal of enforcement. However, the existence of relevant cases can be supportive. In the case, *Shipping Services A/S v. RAB Sevnaučflot, Fishery Group LLC 13 May 2011*[3], a dispute arose between the two parties and the Shipping Services A/S lifted a lawsuit, but in the course of the proceedings, both of the parties are stressed to be going through a bankruptcy. The court considered the dispute was non-arbitrable pursuant to Article V (2)(a) on the ground that in respect *of the Republic of Lithuania Law on Commercial Arbitration, 1996*, the difference between companies of bankruptcy is lack of arbitrability.

---

[1] Dr. Reinmar Wolff, *New York Convention Convention on the Recognition and Enforcement of Foreign Arbitral Awards of 10 June 1958 Article-by-Article Commentary,* Verlag C.H.Beck oHG Wilhelmstr. 9, 80801 München, 2019, p. 381.

[2] Id.

[3] Lithuania, 13 May 2011, 'Lithuania, Lietuvos Apeliacinis Teismas (Court of Appeal of Lithuania) / Shipping Services A/S v. RAB Sevnaučflot, Fishery Group LLC / 2-1545/2011', available from: 〈https:// newyorkconvention1958.org/index.php?lvl=categ_see&id=46〉.

2.7 Article V (2)(b) Recognition or enforcement of the award would be contrary to public policy of the country

This is the most controversial provision in Article V and it states that the award will not be recognized and enforced under the situation when it is contrary to the country's public policy. Public policy is more than a simple legal concept but indicates to the political influence on foreign commercial arbitration. Given that the public policies are commonly designed by certain country department and vary in their forms, they might be changed or fixed in high frequency pursuant to the national circumstances. This kind of unstable character of public policy is dangerous for recognizing and enforcing the award to some extent. As noted in *Richardson v. Mellish* (1824) 2 Bing 228[1], "public policy is a very unruly horse, and when once you get astride it you never know where it will carry you. It may lead you from sound law"; public policy is indeed hard to handle in specific cases.

The Contracting States to NYC are very discreet on using this ground as a refusal to recognize and enforce the foreign award. There's one famous case in China in which the Article V (2)(b) was invoked and accepted by the court, that is *Hemofarm DD, MAG International Trade Holding DD, Suramu Media Ltd. v. Jinan Yongning Pharmaceutical Co., Ltd*[2]. In this case, Jinan-Hemofarm challenged the court's jurisdiction and submitted the rent contract issue to the ICC international Court of Arbitration in Paris for arbitration. However, dispute in the rent contract is out of the scope of the arbitration agreement made between the parties in this case thus it cannot be arbitrated. The Supreme People's Court, in its reply to the Higher People's Court of Shandong, held that "it would be contrary to the public policy of China to recognize and enforce the award," and refused to recognize and enforce the award made by ICC. In this example case, public policy is invoked to obtain PRC's judicial sovereignty and the jurisdiction of PRC courts on matters beyond the scope to the . In foreign commercial

---

① Burrough, J, Richardson v Mellish, 2 Bing 229 at 252, 130 ER 294 (CP1824).

② HEMOFARM DD V JINAN YONGNING PHARMACEUTICAL CO LTD [2008] MIN SI TA ZI NO. 11. Available from: 〈 https://arbitrationlaw.com/library/hemofarm-dd-v-jinan-yongning-pharmaceutical-co-ltd-2008-min-si-ta-zi-no-11 〉; 〈 http://www.lawinfochina.com/display.aspx?lib=law&id=14615&CGid= 〉.

arbitration, "public policy serves the purpose of providing the Contracting States with a safety- valve which allows them to prevent the intrusion of awards into their legal system which they consider irreconcilable with it."[①]

Conclusion and Outlook for the future

In the recognition and enforcement of an arbitration award, the most significant principle is party autonomy. The principle of party autonomy is the cornerstone of the arbitration agreement and the whole arbitration proceedings. However, the arbitration proceedings are no more than a tool for reaching a solution, so the route to enforcement of foreign arbitral awards has its practical significance.

In China, the NYC has not become a widely known convention in the general public. Many hope in the future it can help parties to fight for their rights in international commercial arbitration and meanwhile help strengthen the foundation of society with rule of law.

---

① Dr. Reinmar Wolff, *New York Convention Convention on the Recognition and Enforcement of Foreign Arbitral Awards of 10 June 1958 Article-by-Article Commentary,* Verlag C.H.Beck oHG Wilhelmstr. 9, 80801 München, 2019, p. 419.

附件一

Convention on the Recognition and Enforcement of Foreign Arbitral Awards

Article I

1. This Convention shall apply to the recognition and enforcement of arbitral awards made in the territory of a State other than the State where the recognition and enforcement of such awards are sought, and arising out of differences between persons, whether physical or legal. It shall also apply to arbitral awards not considered as domestic awards in the State where their recognition and enforcement are sought.

2. The term "arbitral awards" shall include not only awards made by arbitrators appointed for each case but also those made by permanent arbitral bodies to which the parties have submitted.

3. When signing, ratifying or acceding to this Convention, or notifying extension under article X hereof, any State may on the basis of reciprocity declare that it will apply the Convention to the recognition and enforcement of awards made only in the territory of another Contracting State. It may also declare that it will apply the Convention only to differences arising out of legal relationships, whether contractual or not, which are considered as commercial under the national law of the State making such declaration.

Article II

1. Each Contracting State shall recognize an agreement in writing under which the parties undertake to submit to arbitration all or any differences which have arisen or which may arise between them in respect of a defined legal relationship, whether contractual or not, concerning a subject matter capable of settlement by arbitration.

2.The term "agreement in writing" shall include an arbitral clause in a contract or an arbitration agreement, signed by the parties or contained in an exchange of letters or telegrams.

3. The court of a Contracting State, when seized of an action in a matter in respect of which the parties have made an agreement within the meaning of this article, shall, at the request of one of the parties, refer the parties to arbitration, unless it finds that the said agreement is null and void, inoperative or incapable of being performed.

Article III

Each Contracting State shall recognize arbitral awards as binding and enforce them in accordance with the rules of procedure of the territory where the award is relied upon, under the conditions laid down in the following articles. There shall not be imposed substantially more onerous conditions or higher fees or charges on the recognition or enforcement of arbitral awards to which this Convention applies than are imposed on the recognition or enforcement of domestic arbitral awards.

Article IV

1. To obtain the recognition and enforcement mentioned in the preceding article, the party applying for recognition and enforcement shall, at the time of the application, supply:

(a) The duly authenticated original award or a duly certified copy thereof;

(b) The original agreement referred to in article II or a duly certified copy thereof.

2.If the said award or agreement is not made in an official language of the country in which the award is relied upon, the party applying for recognition and enforcement of the award shall produce a translation of these documents into such language. The translation shall be certified by an official or sworn translator or by a diplomatic or consular agent.

Article V

1. Recognition and enforcement of the award may be refused, at the request of the party against whom it is invoked, only if that party furnishes to the competent authority where the recognition and enforcement is sought, proof that:

(a) The parties to the agreement referred to in article II were, under the law applicable to them, under some incapacity, or the said agreement is not valid under the law to which the parties have subjected it or, failing any indication thereon, under the law of the country where the award was made; or

(b) The party against whom the award is invoked was not given proper notice of the appointment of the arbitrator or of the arbitration proceedings or was otherwise unable to present his case; or

(c) The award deals with a difference not contemplated by or not falling within the terms of the submission to arbitration, or it contains decisions on matters beyond the scope of the submission to arbitration, provided that, if the decisions on matters submitted to arbitration can be separated from those not so submitted, that part of the award which contains decisions on matters submitted to arbitration may be recognized and enforced; or

(d) The composition of the arbitral authority or the arbitral procedure was not in accordance with the agreement of the parties, or, failing such agreement, was not in accordance with the law of the country where the arbitration took place; or

(e) The award has not yet become binding on the parties, or has been set aside or suspended by a competent authority of the country in which, or under the law of which, that award was made.

2. Recognition and enforcement of an arbitral award may also be refused if the competent authority in the country where recognition and enforcement is sought finds that:

(a) The subject matter of the difference is not capable of settlement by arbitration under the law of that country; or

(b) The recognition or enforcement of the award would be contrary to the public policy of that country.

Article VI

If an application for the setting aside or suspension of the award has been made to a competent authority referred to in article V (1) *(e)*, the authority before which the award is sought to be relied upon may, if it considers it proper, adjourn the decision on the enforcement of the award and may also, on the application of the party claiming enforcement of the award, order the other party to give suitable security.

Article VII

1. The provisions of the present Convention shall not affect the validity of multilateral or bilateral agreements concerning the recognition and enforcement of arbitral awards entered into by the Contracting States nor deprive any interested party of any right he may have to avail himself of an arbitral award in the manner and to the extent allowed by the law or the treaties of the country where such award is sought to be relied upon.

2. The Geneva Protocol on Arbitration Clauses of 1923 and the Geneva Convention on the Execution of Foreign Arbitral Awards of 1927 shall cease to have effect between Contracting States on their becoming bound and to the extent that they become bound, by this Convention.

Article VIII

1.This Convention shall be open until 31 December 1958 for signature on behalf of any Member of the United Nations and also on behalf of any other State which is or hereafter becomes a member of any specialized agency of the United Nations, or which is or hereafter becomes a party to the Statute of the International Court of Justice, or any other State to which an invitation has been addressed by the General Assembly of the United Nations.

2. This Convention shall be ratified and the instrument of ratification shall be deposited with the Secretary-General of the United Nations.

Article IX

1. This Convention shall be open for accession to all States referred to in article VIII.

2. Accession shall be effected by the deposit of an instrument of accession with the Secretary-General of the United Nations.

Article X

1. Any State may, at the time of signature, ratification or accession, declare that this Convention shall extend to all or any of the territories for   the international relations of which it is responsible. Such a declaration shall take effect when the Convention enters into force for the State concerned.

2. At any time thereafter any such extension shall be made by notification addressed to the Secretary-General of the United Nations and shall take effect as from the ninetieth day after the day of receipt by the Secretary-General of the United Nations of this notification, or as from the date of entry into force of the Convention for the State concerned, whichever is the later.

3. With respect to those territories to which this Convention is not extended at the time of signature, ratification or accession, each State concerned shall consider the possibility of taking the necessary steps in order to extend the application of this Convention to such territories, subject, where necessary for constitutional reasons, to the consent of the Governments of such territories.

Article XI

In the case of a federal or non-unitary State, the following provisions shall apply:

(a) With respect to those articles of this Convention that come within the legislative jurisdiction of the federal authority, the obligations of the federal Government shall to this extent be the same as those of Contracting States which are not federal States;

(b) With respect to those articles of this Convention that come within the legislative jurisdiction of constituent states or provinces which are not, under the constitutional system of the federation, bound to take legislative action, the federal Government shall bring such articles with a favourable recommendation to the notice of the appropriate authorities of constituent states or provinces at the earliest possible moment;

(c) A federal State Party to this Convention shall, at the request of any other Contracting State transmitted through the Secretary-General of the United Nations, supply a statement of the law and practice of the federation and its constituent units in regard to any particular provision of this Convention, showing the extent to which effect has been given to that provision by legislative or other action.

Article XII

1. This Convention shall come into force on the ninetieth day following the date of deposit of the third instrument of ratification or accession.

2. For each State ratifying or acceding to this Convention after the deposit of the third instrument of ratification or accession, this Convention shall enter into force on the ninetieth day after deposit by such State of its instrument of ratification or accession.

Article XIII

1. Any Contracting State may denounce this Convention by a written notification to the Secretary-General of the United Nations. Denunciation shall take effect one year after the date of receipt of the notification by the Secretary-General.

2. Any State which has made a declaration or notification under article X may, at any time thereafter, by notification to the Secretary-General of the United Nations, declare that

this Convention shall cease to extend to the territory concerned one year after the date of the receipt of the notification by the Secretary-General.

3.This Convention shall continue to be applicable to arbitral awards in respect of which recognition or enforcement proceedings have been instituted before the denunciation takes effect.

Article XIV

A Contracting State shall not be entitled to avail itself of the present Convention against other Contracting States except to the extent that it is itself bound to apply the Convention.

Article XV

The Secretary-General of the United Nations shall notify the States contemplated in article VIII of the following:

(a) Signatures and ratifications in accordance with article VIII;

(b) Accessions in accordance with article IX;

(c) Declarations and notifications under articles I, X and XI;

(d) The date upon which this Convention enters into force in accordance with article XII;

(e) Denunciations and notifications in accordance with article XIII.

Article XVI

1. This Convention, of which the Chinese, English, French, Russian and Spanish texts shall be equally authentic, shall be deposited in the archives of the United Nations.

2. The Secretary-General of the United Nations shall transmit a certified copy of this Convention to the States contemplated in article VIII.

附件二

承认及执行外国公断裁决公约

第一条

一、公断裁决，因自然人或法人间之争议而产生且在声请承认及执行地所在国以外之国家领土内作成者，其承认及执行适用本公约。本公约对于公断裁决经声请承认及执行地所在国认为非内国裁决者，亦适用之。

二、"公断裁决"一词不仅指专案选派之公断员所作裁决，亦指当事人提请裁断之常设公断机关所作裁决。

三、任何国家得于签署、批准或加入本公约时，或于依本公约第十条通知推广适用时，本交互原则声明该国适用本公约，以承认及执行在另一缔约国领土内作成之裁决为限。任何国家亦得声明，该国唯于争议起于法律关系，不论其为契约性质与否，而依提出声明国家之国内法认为系属商事关系者，始适用本公约。

第二条

一、当事人以书面协定承允彼此间所发生或可能发生之一切或任何争议，如关涉可以公断解决事项之确定法律关系，不论为契约性质与否，应提交公断时，各缔约国应承认此项协定。

二、称"书面协定"者,谓当事人所签订或在互换函电中所载明之契约公断条款或公断协定。

三、当事人就诉讼事项订有本条所称之协定者,缔约国法院受理诉讼时应依当事人一造之请求,命当事人提交公断,但前述协定经法院认定无效、失效或不能实行者不在此限。

第三条

各缔约国应承认公断裁决具有拘束力,并依援引裁决地之程序规则及下列各条所载条件执行之。承认或执行适用本公约之公断裁决时,不得较承认或执行内国公断裁决附加过苛之条件或征收过多之费用。

第四条

一、声请承认及执行之一造,为取得前条所称之承认及执行,应于声请时提具:

(1)原裁决之正本或其正式副本;

(2)第二条所称协定之原本或其正式副本。

二、倘前述裁决或协定所用文字非为援引裁决地所在国之正式文字,声请承认及执行裁决之一造应备具各该文件之此项文字译本。译本应由公设或宣誓之翻译员或外交或领事人员认证之。

第五条

一、裁决唯有于受裁决援用之一造向声请承认及执行地之主管机关提具证据证明有下列情形之一时,始得依该造之请求,拒予承认及执行:

(1)第二条所称协定之当事人依对其适用之法律有某种无行为能力情形者,或该项协定依当事人作为协定准据之法律系属无效,或未指明以何法律为准时,依裁决地所在国法律系属无效者;

（2）受裁决援用之一造未接获关于指派公断员或公断程序之适当通知，或因他故，致未能申辩者；

（3）裁决所处理之争议非为交付公断之标的或不在其条款之列，或裁决载有关于交付公断范围以外事项之决定者，但交付公断事项之决定可与未交付公断之事项划分时，裁决中关于交付公断事项之决定部分得予承认及执行；

（4）公断机关之组成或公断程序与各造间之协议不符，或无协议而与公断地所在国法律不符者；

（5）裁决对各造尚无拘束力，或业经裁决地所在国或裁决所依据法律之国家之主管机关撤销或停止执行者。

二、倘声请承认及执行地所在国之主管机关认定有下列情形之一，亦得拒不承认及执行公断裁决：

（1）依该国法律，争议事项系不能以公断解决者；

（2）承认或执行裁决有违该国公共政策者。

第六条

倘裁决业经向第五条第一项（5）款所称之主管机关声请撤销或停止执行，受理援引裁决案件之机关得于其认为适当时延缓关于执行裁决之决定，并得依请求执行一造之声请，命他造提供妥适之担保。

第七条

一、本公约之规定不影响缔约国间所订关于承认及执行公断裁决之多边或双边协定之效力，亦不剥夺任何利害关系人可依援引裁决地所在国之法律或条约所认许之方式，在其许可范围内，援用公断裁决之任何权利。

二、1923年日内瓦公断条款议定书及1927年日内瓦执行外国公断裁决公约在缔约国间，于其受本公约拘束后，在其受拘束之范围内不再生效。

第八条

一、本公约在 1958 年 12 月 31 日以前听由任何联合国会员国及现为或嗣后成为任何联合国专门机关会员国或国际法院规约当事国之任何其他国家，或经联合国大会邀请之任何其他国家签署。

二、本公约应予批准。批准文件应送交联合国秘书长存放。

第九条

一、本公约听由第八条所称各国加入。

二、加入应以加入文件送交联合国秘书长存放为之。

第十条

一、任何国家得于签署、批准或加入时声明将本公约推广适用于由其负责国际关系之一切或任何领土。此项声明于本公约对关系国家生效时发生效力。

二、嗣后关于推广适用之声明应向联合国秘书长提出通知为之，自联合国秘书长收到此项通知之日后第九十日起，或自本公约对关系国家生效之日起发生效力，此两日期以较迟者为准。

三、关于在签署、批准或加入时未经将本公约推广适用之领土，各关系国家应考虑可否采取必要步骤将本公约推广适用于此等领土，但因宪政关系确有必要时，自须征得此等领土政府之同意。

第十一条

下列规定对联邦制或非单一制国家适用之：

（1）关于本公约内属于联邦机关立法权限之条款，联邦政府之义务在此范围内与非联邦制缔约国之义务同；

（2）关于本公约内属于组成联邦各州或各省之立法权限之条款，如各州或各省依联邦宪法制度并无采取立法行动之义务，联邦政府应尽速将此等条款提请各州或各省主管机关注意，并附有利之建议；

（3）参加本公约之联邦国家遇任何其他缔约国经由联合国秘书长转达请求时，应提供叙述联邦及其组成单位关于本公约特定规定之法律及惯例之情报，说明以立法或其他行动实施此项规定之程度。

第十二条

一、本公约应自第三件批准或加入文件存放之日后第九十日起发生效力。

二、对于第三件批准或加入文件存放后批准或加入本公约之国家，本公约应自各该国存放批准或加入文件后第九十日起发生效力。

第十三条

一、任何缔约国得以书面通知联合国秘书长宣告退出本公约。退约应于秘书长收到通知之日一年后发生效力。

二、依第十条规定提出声明或通知之国家，嗣后得随时通知联合国秘书长声明本公约自秘书长收到通知之日一年后停止适用于关系领土。

三、在退约生效前已进行承认或执行程序之公断裁决，应继续适用本公约。

第十四条

缔约国除在本国负有适用本公约义务之范围外，无权对其他缔约国援用本公约。

第十五条

联合国秘书长应将下列事项通知第八条所称各国：

（1）依第八条所为之签署及批准；

（2）依第九条所为之加入；

（3）依第一条、第十条及第十一条所为之声明及通知；

（4）依第十二条本公约发生效力之日期；

（5）依第十三条所为之退约及通知。

第十六条

一、本公约应存放联合国档库，其中文、英文、法文、俄文及西班牙文各本同一作准。

二、联合国秘书长应将本公约正式副本分送第八条所称各国。

主编◎张玉林　周立新

New York Convention
To Know Itself in China

纽约公约
在中国见证成长

下册
Book II

新华出版社

图书在版编目（CIP）数据

纽约公约：在中国见证成长 . 下册 / 张玉林，周立新主编 .
-- 北京：新华出版社，2024. 6.
ISBN 978-7-5166-7439-0

Ⅰ . D997.4

中国国家版本馆 CIP 数据核字第 20242XK169 号

纽约公约：在中国见证成长 . 下册

主编：张玉林　周立新
出版发行：新华出版社有限责任公司
　　　　　（北京市石景山区京原路 8 号　邮编：100040）
印刷：三河市君旺印务有限公司

成品尺寸：170mm×240mm　1/16　　　　印张：12.75　字数：180 千字
版次：2024 年 7 月第 1 版　　　　　　印次：2024 年 7 月第 1 次印刷
书号：ISBN 978-7-5166-7439-0　　　　定价：58.00 元（上下册）

微店

视频号小店

抖店

京东旗舰店

微信公众号

喜马拉雅

小红书

淘宝旗舰店

扫码添加专属客服

双循环经济包括内循环经济和外循环经济。外循环经济是国际仲裁的背景和摇篮。越多的国际合同中包含有关中国的仲裁条款，就会成就更多的国际仲裁裁决对国际外循环经济的贡献。读者在本书下册将看到近几年双循环经济中的诸多有趣的仲裁案例，说明中国外部环境中产生的涉及中国的故事，包括在香港的案例和新加坡的涉及上海仲裁地的案例。

　　Dual economic circulation includes the inner economic circulation and the external economic circulation. The latter serves as the backgrounder and the birthplace of international arbitration. More and more international contracts include arbitration clauses involving the place of arbitration in China. This contributes to the increasing dynamics of integration of world economy into China by way of enforcement of international arbitral awards. Readers will see many interesting cases in the dual economic circulation in recent years, and understand stories how China has been involved in the external economic circulative environment. Such stories demonstrate the landscape where Hong Kong SAR is selected as the place of arbitration in China, and where Shanghai is selected as the place of arbitration in China in cases conducted in Singapore.

序 言

  联合国《承认及执行外国仲裁裁决公约》(《纽约公约》)是国际贸易法领域最重要和最成功的国际条约之一，也是国际仲裁制度的基石。到目前为止，已有多达 172 个国家加入《纽约公约》。这些国家有义务使仲裁协议生效，并且承认和执行在其他缔约国作出的裁决。这一跨国承认和执行仲裁裁决的统一国际方案为国际仲裁在全球的繁荣发展奠定了基础，并极大地促进了对外贸易和经济活动的发展。

  中国国际经济贸易仲裁委员会（CIETAC）（以下简称"贸仲委"）是中国第一个仲裁机构，设立于 1956 年，比《纽约公约》早两年。贸仲委设立的初衷即为发展中国的涉外仲裁。得益于这一特殊使命，贸仲委熟知国际仲裁规则、拥有更多的国际仲裁实践经验，并在促进中国于 1986 年加入《纽约公约》方面扮演了积极的角色。《纽约公约》于 1987 年 4 月在中国正式生效。中国的境外仲裁开始融入国际仲裁界，这极大地促进了中国仲裁的发展。

  根据《纽约公约》的相关规定，贸仲委的涉外裁决已在全世界得到承认和执行。截至目前，贸仲委已经办理了 5 万多件国际和国内仲裁案件，涉及 150 多个国家和地区的当事人。在世界这么多不同的司法管辖区执行贸仲委的裁决对于《纽约公约》的实践和私法一体化努力也有非常大的贡献。贸仲委因裁决的被承认及执行度高、仲裁服务的专业性强得到了国际上的

广泛认可，并被评为世界上最受欢迎的 5 家仲裁机构之一。贸仲委的发展
也反映了《纽约公约》的成功及其在国际仲裁中的关键作用。

深入了解这样一个重要的公约是非常值得花时间和精力的。本书以《纽
约公约》的一般知识为中心。它由资深仲裁员与外国专家和从业人员跨界合
作编辑，并设有由北京大学学生和本地从业人员组建的特别兴趣小组。我们
珍视《纽约公约》的精神。作为国际法治系统的重要组成部分，它熠熠生辉。
我们鼓励读者阅读本书，在阅读中了解国际仲裁、对外贸易和经济的世界，
并从中受益。

作为贸仲委的副主任兼秘书长，以及一个有着 30 多年仲裁经验和激情
的从业者，我借此机会向本书的编者和作者表示衷心的感谢，并祝愿本书
取得巨大成功，希望它能成为引领大家进入国际仲裁世界的工具书。

王承杰

中国国际经济贸易仲裁委员会的副主任兼秘书长

2023 年 2 月 15 日

Preface

The United Nations Convention on the Recognition and Enforcement of Foreign Arbitral Awards (better known as *the New York Convention*), is one of the most important and successful international treaties in the area of international trade law and the cornerstone of the international arbitration system. Up till now, as many as 172 States have acceded to *the New York Convention*, and are obligated to give effect to an agreement to arbitrate, and to recognize and enforce awards made in other Contracting States. This unified international scheme for the recognition and enforcement of arbitral awards across borders has set the foundation for the prosperous development of international arbitration globally, and greatly contributed to the promotion of foreign trade and economic activities.

China International Economic and Trade Arbitration Commission (CIETAC) is the first arbitration institution in China, which was born in 1956, two years earlier than *the New York Convention*, with the mission to develop China's foreign-related arbitration. Because of this special mission, CIETAC is very familiar with international rules and practice, and has played an active role in facilitating China's accession of the New York Convention in 1986. The New York Convention took effect in China since April 1987. China's foreign arbitration began to integrate into the international arbitration community, which significantly promoted the development of arbitration in China.

Under the scheme of *the New York Convention*, CIETAC's foreign-related awards have been recognized and enforced worldwide. Up till now, CIETAC has concluded over 50,000 international and domestic arbitration cases involving parties from more than 150 countries and regions. The enforcement of its awards in so many different jurisdictions in the world also contribute to the unification efforts under *the New York Convention*. CIETAC has now become a well-known brand in international arbitration community for the professionality and credibility of its awards and arbitration service, and has been recognized as one of the 5 most preferred arbitration institutions in the world. CIETAC's development is also a reflection of the success of *the New York Convention* and its key role in international arbitration.

It is well worth devoting time and attention to learn more about such an important convention, This book centers on the general knowledge of *the New York Convention*. It is edited by a senior arbitrator in collaboration with foreign experts and practitioners across borders, with a special interest group of PKU students and local practitioners. We appreciate that the spirit of *the New York Convention* shines as part of the international rule of law. Readers are encouraged to read the texts of the Book on *the New York Convention* and will be benefited from the reading in understanding the world of international arbitration, foreign trade and economics.

As the Vice Chairman & Secretary General of CIETAC and a practitioner with over 30 years of experience and passion in arbitration, I take this opportunity to extend my sincere thanks and gratitude to the editors and writers of this book, and wish this book great success, to become a useful book to lead you to the world of international arbitration.

Wang Chengjie

Vice Chairman & Secretary General of CIETAC

February 15, 2023

前　言

　　《纽约公约》是联合国在国际贸易法领域最重要的条约之一，也是国际商事仲裁制度的基石。迄今为止，它已在 172 个国家和地区生效，覆盖了世界主要的贸易国，极大地推动了国际商事仲裁事业的发展。本书围绕《纽约公约》的英文写作展开，汇集了北京大学法律英语暑期课程中优秀学生的法律英语写作成果，邀请多名来自律所、仲裁机构和学界的专家学者参与撰写。通过深入解析公约条文，结合大量案例分析公约在中国和世界各国的适用，本书向读者展示了扎实的法律英语写作水平、批判性思维能力和中英文法律语言运用能力。本书内容丰富全面，案例分析翔实深入，中英文表达通顺流畅，法律语言精练地道，法律术语翻译准确严谨，是一本兼具专业性和可读性的佳作。

　　当前，中国日益走近世界舞台中央，亟须推进国际传播能力建设，向世界展示真实、立体、全面的中国形象。法治是国际交往的最大公约数，法治传播则是实现精准传播的关键抓手。国际传播离不开翻译，法律翻译是实现法治国际传播的必然途径。通过阅读本书，读者不仅能够深入了解《纽约公约》的精神、条款和相关案例，还能够接触到鲜活生动的法律英语，并通过对照地道的中英文内容，研习法律翻译。希望本书能够激发更多学习者的兴趣，帮助他们深入理解法治内涵，更精准地传播法治理念，为国际传播做出积极贡献。学好法律英语，做好法律翻译，是成为合格涉外法治专业人才的前提保障，也是为国家涉外法治建设做出贡献的必由之路。

张法连

中国政法大学教授，博士生导师

Forward

The New York Convention, as the cornerstone of the international commercial arbitration system, is one of the most important treaties in the field of international trade law. It has been ratified by 172 countries and regions, encompassing major trading nations worldwide, and has greatly facilitated the development of international commercial arbitration. This book compiles outstanding legal writings by students from Peking University's summer Legal English course and focuses on the English writing of *the New York Convention*. Under the guidance of experts and scholars from law firms, arbitration institutions and academia, the students conduct in-depth analysis of the Convention's provisions and present abundant case studies on its application in China and other countries. Through this, the book showcases the students' solid legal English writing skills, critical thinking abilities, and proficiency in applying both Chinese and English legal languages. With comprehensive contents and insightful case analysis, this book features smooth and fluent writing in both Chinese and English, concise and idiomatic legal language, and accurate translation of legal terminology. It is a remarkable work combining professionalism and readability.

As China continues to gain prominence on the global stage, it is crucial that we enhance our ability to communicate internationally and present an authentic, multifaceted and holistic China to the world. The rule of law serves as a common foundation for global exchange, making it essential to effectively communicate legal principles for accurate cross-cultural understanding. Translation plays a vital role in international communication, with legal translation being essential for conveying rule of law across borders. This book provides readers with a comprehensive understanding of the spirit, provisions, and relevant cases of *the New York Convention*, while also exposing them to dynamic and vivid legal English. What is more, by comparing the Chinese and English content, readers can thoroughly study legal translation. My aspiration is that this book will inspire more learners of legal English and translation, enabling them to deeply comprehend the significance of the rule of law and convey these ideas more precisely, thereby making positive contributions to international communication. Mastering legal English and translation is a prerequisite for becoming qualified professionals in foreign-related legal affairs and a necessary pathway to fostering the development of rule of law engagement between China and other nations.

Zhang Falian

Professor and Ph.D. Supervisor at China University of Political Science and Law

第十章
某些案件中仲裁与调解相结合的实践

马瑞璟

本章着重于仲裁与调解相结合的独特争议解决方式在中国的实践。仲裁程序产生仲裁裁决，调解程序产生当事人和解协议。这两种程序如何结合使用，是中国国际经济贸易仲裁委员会在几十年前实践探索的问题。唐厚志先生在中国积极推动了这一相结合的仲调进程，他被誉为该种相结合方式的大师，协助各方通过仲裁与调解协同达成和解。

一、什么是调解?

调解作为一种纠纷解决机制，在我国有着悠久的历史。然而，我国现行的调解制度和实践与现代意义上的"国际商事调解"相去甚远。顾名思义，"国际商事调解"是指在跨境商事活动发生纠纷后，由当事各方共同选择中立的第三方作为调解人，调解人在自愿的基础上，通过说服、劝导或其他方式达成和解的争议解决方式。与法官或仲裁员不同，调解员的作用不是作出裁决或决定，而是协助当事人达成自愿和解，最终达成具有法律约束力的和解。国际商事调解通常与国际商事诉讼、国际商事仲裁一起讨论，构成了国际商事争议解决的三种主要方式。

在过去几十年中，最流行的跨境商事纠纷解决方式实际上是国际商事仲裁，几乎 90% 的国际商事合同都包含仲裁条款。国际商事仲裁发展迅速的一个重要原因在于其跨境执行的便利性。自 1958 年《承认及执行外国仲裁裁决公约》（《纽约公约》）正式开放签署以来，缔约国已达 170 多个国家和地区。因此，当事人通常会选择国际商事仲裁作为解决跨境商事纠纷的手段，以确保在未来的纠纷中救济措施能够得到跨境执行。

调解制度在国际上的运用相对较晚，主要是由联合国国际贸易法委员会（"贸易法委员会"）推动。该委员会制定了两项旨在统一国际商事调解的文书：《联合国国际贸易法委员会调解规则》（1980 年）（《调解规则》）和《联合国国际商法委员会调解示范法》（2002 年)(《2002 年调解示范法》）。这两个文书共同构成了国际商事调解制度的框架，为各国国内法商事调解制度的完善作出了巨大贡献，为解决国际商事纠纷提供了一整套实施方案，包括调解人、调解程序、保密原则等方面的规定。2018 年 12 月 20 日，联合国大会通过了《联合国调解达成国际和解协议公约》《新加坡调解公约》），为承认和执行不同国家之间的国际商事调解协议提供了法律依据。

二、调解能否适用于仲裁?

近年来，国际商事仲裁因其费用高、周期长、程序复杂等问题受到质疑。当事人和律师开始探讨国际商事调解作为替代性争议解决办法的可能性。根据康奈尔《财富》1000 强公司法律调查（1997 年）和《财富》1000 强公司法律调查（2011 年），1994 年至 1997 年，87% 的《财富》1000 强公司使用过调解来解决纠纷，40% 的公司尝试过这样做；2008 年至 2011 年，《财富》1000 强企业中使用调解解决纠纷的公司数量上升了 11 个百分点，达到 98%；而使用调解解决纠纷的公司数量上升了 11 个百分点，达到 51%，相比之下，使用仲裁解决纠纷的公司数量仅为 3 个百分点。[①]

　　另一个例子是国际律师事务所赫伯特·史密斯对 21 家大型跨国公司（包括摩根士丹利、BP、壳牌、沃特福德、通用汽车等）的纠纷解决方式进行的调查。调查显示，19 家公司表示，当出现纠纷时，它们将使用调解。其中 7 家企业在发生纠纷时选择先调解，6 家企业在纠纷标的较大、影响企业形象时选择调解，6 家企业在纠纷需要诉讼或仲裁时选择庭审前调解解决争议。[②] 一些跨国公司（如通用电气和西门子）也在公司治理层面逐步探索和公开推行替代性争端解决办法，如国际商事调解。[③]

　　在处理跨境商事争议方面，相比仲裁，国际商事调解具有独特的吸引力和优势。

（一）成本低、周期短

　　国际商事调解的最大优势在于成本低、周期短。与诉讼、仲裁等对抗性很强的纠纷解决机制不同，调解的首要目标既不是查明事实真相，也不是分配法律责任，更不是打败对方当事人，而是帮助当事人达成和解合意。因此，调解程序通常不需要耗时持久的取证、调查过程，比如文件互相送达、专家证人出庭等。通常情况下，国际商事调解要求只指定一名调解员。与通常需要三名仲裁员的复杂国际商事仲裁案件相比，调解所需的调解员费用和案件协调管理费用要低得多。

　　根据 2010 年的一项估计，国际商会仲裁院（ICC）在伦敦组成了一个由三名仲裁员组成的仲裁庭，审理一个标的 2500 万美元的争端，费用约为

---

① Harvard Negotiation Law Review, "Living with ADR: Evolving Perceptions and Use of Mediation, Arbitration and Conflict Management in Fortune 1000 Corporations", Stipanowich & Lamare, 2013.

② Herbert Smith, The Inside Track-How Blue-chips are using ADR, November 2007.

③ Walter G. Gans & David Stryker, ADR, The Siemens' Experience, 51 DISP. RESOL. J.40, 41(1996) Michael A. Wheeler & Gillian Morris, GE's Early Dispute Resolution Initiative (A), Harvard Business School 2, 2001.

2836000 美元。整个仲裁过程需要 18–24 个月，听证通常需要一周左右。如果同样的纠纷由伦敦的调解员调解，费用仅为 1.2 万美元（包括调解员、代理和律师费），整个调解过程仅需 2–3 个月，听证时间通常为 1–2 天。在这种情况下，国际商事调解的费用仅为国际商事仲裁程序费用的 5% 左右，而所需时间仅为 10%–15%。[1]

（二）促进维持合作关系

国际商事调解可以帮助当事人维护现有的和未来的合作关系。调查显示，这也是继成本和时间之后，当事人选择调解的第三个关键考虑因素。[2]

在某些类型的纠纷中（如国际工程项目、合资企业等纠纷），由于双方需要继续合作，双方希望解决争端，但不希望完全断绝关系。

国际商事调解不拘泥于法律层面的"是非"，更容易达到"双赢"的效果。调解过程通过第三方调解员的介入和沟通，可以帮助双方找到争议问题背后的真实意图和需求，达成互利合作共识。在专业调解员的组织下，当事人通过协商谈判解决纠纷，也是为了澄清误会，重新建立信任。由于最终和解协议是在当事人意愿的基础上达成的，结果更容易被各方接受，从而达到合作、持续经营的效果。相比之下，对抗性较强的国际商事诉讼和国际商事仲裁程序，可能会在旷日持久的程序对抗中加剧双方矛盾，彻底破坏互信和继续合作的可能性，从而无法满足当事人对继续合作的商业期待。

---

[1] Thomas Gaultier, Cross-Border Mediation, "A New Solution for International Commercial Dispute Settlement?", N*YSBA International Law Practicum*, Vol. 45, No. 46, 2013.

[2] 当事人可以约定适用国际争议解决中心或者 UNCITRAL 的现行规则，如 ICDR 国际调解规则、ICC 替代争议解决规则、UNCITRAL 调解规则等。

三、贸仲委与香港调解实践之比较

在国际商事活动中，多层次争议解决条款符合商业合同拟定的需求。多层次争议解决条款"（Multi-tiered Dispute Resolution Clauses 或 Escalation Clauses）是在"替代性纠纷解决机制"（Alternative Dispute Resolution, ADR）基础上发展而来的复合型条款。双方合意将和解（conciliation）、调解（mediation）、专家决定（expert decision）等作为仲裁或者诉讼的前置性层次，只有完成该前置性层次后才能进入第二层次，仲裁或诉讼将成为最终的救济途径。

根据中国《仲裁法》的规定，仲裁和调解也可以进行结合。当事人申请仲裁后，可以自行和解。达成和解协议的，可以请求仲裁庭根据和解协议作出裁决，也可以撤回仲裁申请。仲裁庭作出裁决前，当事人可以先行调解。调解达成协议的，仲裁庭应当根据协议制作调解书或者裁决书。

《中国国际经济贸易仲裁委员会仲裁规则》第47条之规定，允许在仲裁机构受理案件并完成组庭工作后，仲裁庭可以根据当事人的请求或者在征得当事人同意的情况下进行调解。当事人达成调解协议的，可以请求仲裁庭根据调解协议的内容制作调解书或者裁决书。《北京仲裁委员会仲裁规则》，也同样允许这样做。值得注意的是，一些国际仲裁机构对于仲裁庭调解存在不同意见。例如，《香港国际仲裁中心调解规则》在调解之后的程序中对调解员的回避作出了规定，当事人承诺不得委任调解员作为任何后继的审裁、仲裁或司法程序中任何一方当事人的审裁员、仲裁员或代表、大律师或专家证人，不论该等程序是否因是次调解或因同一合同中其他争议而引起。

四、我国法院诉讼中的调解结合

调解制度的地位和作用在我国发生了许多变化。从 1949 年到 1980 年，我国一直强调"调解为主，诉讼为辅"的司法政策。在这一历史时期，调解在解决民间纠纷过程中发挥了比司法裁判更显著的作用，出现了"重调解，轻裁判"的现象。

1991 年 4 月颁布的《民事诉讼法》首次确立了"调解自愿、合法"原则。《民事诉讼法》第 6 条明确规定："人民法院审理民事案件，应当以调解为主；调解不成的，人民法院应当及时判决。"此后，"重调解，轻判决"的局面有所改变，调解在审判活动中的作用逐渐减弱，更多的民事案件通过诉讼方式审结。

2003 年以来，由于法院受理案件数量剧增，最高人民法院（以下简称"最高法"）开始重新强调调解的重要性。在一系列司法解释和规定中，最高法提出了"重调解""先调解""以调解为主、调判结合"等原则，并通过"调解案件费用减半"的规定鼓励当事人调解。2012 年修订的《民事诉讼法》除保留原有的"着重审判"原则和调解专章的规定外，首次将"调解在先"确立为民事审判的一项原则，规定除非当事人拒绝调解，对向法院提起的适合调解的纠纷应当先行调解。至此，"调解"再次成为我国司法活动中民事诉讼程序的一个关键环节。

五、《新加坡调解公约》与调解的未来运用

近年来，调解作为一种重要的纠纷解决方式越来越受到人们的关注。2018 年 12 月 20 日，第 73 届联合国大会审议通过了《联合国关于调解所产生的国际和解协议公约》（以下简称《公约》或《新加坡调解公约》）。《公约》旨在针对通过调解达成的和解协议建立一个统一有效的跨境执行机制，

从而促进国际商事调解活动的发展和应用。随着《新加坡调解公约》的签署和各国相继批准，和解协议的跨境执行这一障碍也将逐步得到解决。新加坡被视为亚太地区乃至全球领先的争议解决中心，其商事调解制度自20世纪90年代以来一直在发展。而新加坡作为一个有着丰富民事调解历史的东方国家，在其发展过程中也面临着诸多问题和挑战。

近十年来，国内各种商事调解组织如雨后春笋般涌现，尤其是在北京、上海、天津、深圳、广州等大城市。目前，我国商事调解机构主要包括以下几种类型。

（一）依靠行业协会的调解机构

如上所述，国际商事调解不拘泥于法律层面的"是非"，其目的在于达到"双赢"的效果。调解过程通过第三方调解员的介入和沟通，可以帮助双方找到争议问题背后的真实意图和需求，达成互利合作共识。在专业调解员的组织下，当事人通过协商谈判解决纠纷，也是为了澄清误会，重新建立信任。由于最终和解协议是在当事人意愿的基础上达成的，结果更容易被各方接受，从而达到合作、持续经营的效果。例如，2012年成立的中国证券业协会调解中心是中国证券业协会的内设机构，履行《证券法》赋予中国证券业协会的相关职责，调解会员之间、会员与客户之间的证券业务纠纷。[①]

（二）仲裁委员会设立的调解中心

《中国国际经济贸易仲裁委员会调解规则》（CIETAC）第24条包含"调解与仲裁结合"的规定，规定当事人可以根据调解协议的条款向CIETAC申请仲裁裁决，而在CIETAC仲裁程序中，各方当事人还可请求由仲裁庭以外

---

① 吴俊：《中国商事调解年度观察（2013）》，《北京仲裁》2013年第1辑，第29页。

的人进行独立调解。

（三）专业商事调解机构

近年来，中国出现了专门从事商事调解活动的调解机构。其中，探索最早的是中国国际贸易促进委员会/中国国际商会调解中心（原名"中国国际贸易促进委员会/中国国际商会北京调解中心"），由中国国际贸易促进委员会于 1987 年在北京成立。从 1992 年开始，中国国际贸易促进委员会/中国国际商会先后在中国国际贸易促进委员会在全国各省、直辖市、自治区和一些主要城市设立分支机构调解中心。到目前为止，已经建立了 30 多个调解中心，帮助中外当事人解决商业、海事和其他争端。

这些调解组织致力于组织商事调解活动，并提供相关的法律咨询、培训和交流活动。它们的产生和发展反映了中国市场对商事调解活动的需求和热情。

随着《新加坡调解公约》的生效，我们坚信，调解量将迎来一个新的增长时期，这有助于解决本区域国际商务中的争端。中国独特的仲裁与调解相结合的经验可能具有帮助当事人通过协议解决争议的优势。在该区域这种复合式的争议解决方法也可能面临着挑战。当事人在仲裁过程中对使用调解的共识以及他们达成和解协议和自愿履行和解协议的自主权将成为这一独特方法能否在争议解决领域取得成功的关键。

Chapter 10

In Some Cases, Arb-Med May Well Work in Practice

Ruijing Ma, Reyna

This chapter considers the unique oriental method of Arb-Med in practical use in China. Arbitration process results in an arbitral award, while mediation process results in a settlement agreement between the parties. How can these two processes be used in combination with each other is something explored by the predecessors of the CIETAC arbitration practice decades ago. Mr. Tang Houzhi who actively promoted this combined process in China was accredited as the master of this process in assisting the parties to get to settlement through Arb-Med synergy.

1. What is Mediation?

As a dispute resolution mechanism, mediation has a long history in China. However, China's current mediation system and practice are far from the modern sense of "international commercial mediation". As its name implies, "international commercial mediation" refers to a dispute resolution method whereby, after a dispute over cross-border commercial activities arises, all parties concerned jointly choose a neutral third party as the mediator, and the mediator assists the parties in reaching a settlement on a voluntary basis through persuasion, persuasion or otherwise. Unlike a judge or arbitrator, the mediator's role is not to make a decision , but to assist the parties in reaching a voluntary settlement and ultimately reaching a legally binding settlement. International commercial mediation is usually discussed together with international commercial litigation and international commercial arbitration, which constitute the three main ways of international commercial dispute resolution.

In the past few decades, the most popular form of cross-border commercial dispute resolution has been international commercial arbitration, with almost 90 percent of international commercial contracts containing arbitration clauses. An important reason for the rapid development of international commercial arbitration lies in its convenience of cross-border enforcement. Since the 1958 *Convention on the Recognition and Enforcement of Foreign Arbitral Awards* (*"New York Convention"*) was officially opened for signature, more than 170 countries and regions have adopted the convention. Therefore, the parties usually choose international commercial arbitration as a means of settling disputes over cross-border commercial disputes to ensure that remedies can be enforced across borders in future disputes.

The relatively late model practice of the mediation system at the international level was promoted mainly by the United Nations Commission on International Trade Law ("UNCITRAL"), which developed two instruments aimed at unifying international commercial mediation: *the United Nations Commission on International Trade Law Mediation Rules* (1980) (the "Mediation Rules") and *the United Nations Commission on International Commercial Law Mediation Model Law* (2002) (the "Mediation Model Law 2002"). Together, these two instruments constitute the framework of the international commercial conciliation system for mediation and contribute greatly to the improvement of the commercial conciliation system in the domestic law of each country, providing a complete set of implementation plans for the settlement of international commercial disputes, including the provisions on conciliators, conciliation procedures, confidentiality principles, etc. On December 20, 2018, *the United Nations General Assembly adopted the United Nations Convention on International Settlement Agreements Resulting from Mediation* (*"the Singapore Mediation Convention"*), which provides a legal basis for the recognition and implementation of international commercial mediation agreements between different countries.

2. Can Mediation Be Used in Arbitration?

In recent years, international commercial arbitration has been questioned because of its high cost, long cycle and complicated procedure. The parties and lawyers began to explore the possibility of international commercial mediation as an alternative dispute resolution. For example, according to the Cornell Fortune 1000 Corporate Legal Survey (1997) and the Fortune 1000 Corporate Legal Survey (2011), 87% of Fortune 1000 companies had used mediation to resolve disputes between 1994 and 1997, and 40% had tried to do so; between 2008 and 2011, the number of companies using mediation to resolve disputes jumped 11 percentage points to 98% of Fortune 1000 companies, while the number using mediation to resolve disputes rose 11 percentage points to 51%, compared with just 3 percentage points for arbitration.[1]

Another example is an interview conducted by Herbert Smith, an international law firm, with 21 big multinationals (including Morgan Stanley, BP, Shell, Watford, General Motors, etc.) that rank high in the world. The survey showed that 19 companies said they would seek mediation when a dispute arises. Seven of them chose to use mediation first when any dispute arises, six chose mediation in cases in which the subject matter of the dispute was large and affected their corporate image, and six chose mediation before a court hearing when the dispute required litigation or arbitration.[2] Some multinationals (such as General Electric and Siemens) are also gradually exploring and openly pursuing alternative dispute resolution methods, such as international commercial mediation, at the corporate governance level.[3]

International commercial mediation has unique attractions and advantages over arbitration in dealing with cross-border commercial disputes:

---

[1] Harvard Negotiation Law Review, "Living with ADR: Evolving Perceptions and Use of Mediation, Arbitration and Conflict Management in Fortune 1000 Corporations", Stipanowich & Lamare, 2013.

[2] Herbert Smith, The Inside Track-How Blue-chips are using ADR, November 2007.

[3] Walter G. Gans & David Stryker, ADR, The Siemens' Experience, 51 DISP. RESOL. J.40, 41(1996) Michael A. Wheeler & Gillian Morris, GE's Early Dispute Resolution Initiative (A), Harvard Business School 2, 2001.

(1) Low Cost and Short Cycle

The biggest advantage of international commercial mediation lies in its low cost and short time period. Unlike litigation, arbitration and other adversarial dispute resolution mechanisms, the primary objective of mediation is neither to ascertain the truth, nor to allocate legal liability, nor to defeat the opposing party, but rather to help the parties reach a settlement agreement. Therefore, the mediation procedure usually does not need the time-consuming evidence-taking and discovery process, for example, the document disclosure, the expert witness appearing in court and so on. International commercial mediation also usually requires the appointment of only one mediator. Compared to complex international commercial arbitration cases where three arbitrators are normally required, mediation requires much lower mediator fees and case coordination management costs.

According to one 2010 estimate, a three-member tribunal in London formed by the International Chamber of Commerce (ICC) to hear disputes worth $25 million costs about $2836000. The process takes 18-24 months and usually takes about a week for the heaving alone. If the same dispute is mediated by a mediator in London, the cost would be only US $120, 000 (covering mediator, agency and lawyer fees), the entire mediation process takes only 2-3 months, and the hearing time is usually 1-2 days. In this case, the cost of international commercial conciliation is only about 5 per cent of the cost of international commercial arbitration proceedings, while the time required is only 10-15 percent.[1]

(2) Facilitating the Maintenance of Cooperative Relations

International commercial mediation can help the parties to maintain the existing and future cooperative relationship. According to the survey, this is also the third key consideration for the parties in choosing mediation after cost and time.[2]

---

[1] Thomas Gaultier, Cross-Border Mediation, "A New Solution for International Commercial Dispute Settlement?", *NYSBA International Law Practicum*, Vol. 45, No. 46, 2013.

[2] 当事人可以约定适用国际争议解决中心或者 UNCITRAL 的现行规则, 如 ICDR 国际调解规则、ICC 替代争议解决规则、UNCITRAL 调解规则等。

In certain types of disputes (such as disputes over international engineering projects, joint ventures, etc.), due to the need for continued cooperation between the parties, the parties wish to resolve the dispute but do not wish to destroy the relationship completely.

International commercial mediation does not adhere to the legal level of "right and wrong", more likely to achieve a "win-win" effect. Through the intervention and communication of third-party mediators, the mediation process can help both parties find the true intention and need behind the disputing issues and reach a mutually beneficial cooperation consensus. Under the organization of professional mediators, the parties resolve disputes through consultation and negotiation, but also to clarify misunderstandings and re-establish trust. Because the final settlement agreement is reached on the basis of the parties' willingness, the result is more easily accepted by all parties, thus achieving the effect of cooperation and continuous operation. By contrast, international commercial litigation and international commercial arbitration proceedings with strong antagonism may aggravate the contradictions between the two parties in the protracted procedural confrontation, completely undermine the possibility of mutual trust and continued cooperation, and thus fail to meet the commercial expectations of the parties for continued cooperation.

3. CIETAC Practice and Comparison with HK Practice

In international commerce, Multi-tiered Dispute Resolution Clauses are in line with the development of commercial contracts. "Multi-tiered Dispute Resolution Clauses or Escalation Clauses are composite clauses based on Alternative Dispute Resolution (ADR). The ADR clause is a composite clause that has been developed from the traditional ADR clause. In the multi-level dispute resolution clause, the parties agree to use conciliation, mediation, and expert decision as the first level of arbitration or litigation, and only after the completion of the first level can they enter the second level, making arbitration or litigation the final route to relief.

According to *the Chinese Arbitration Law*, arbitration and mediation can also be combined. After the parties apply for arbitration, they can settle the case on their own.

If a settlement agreement is reached, they may request the arbitral tribunal to issue an award based on the settlement agreement, or they may withdraw their application for arbitration. Before the arbitral tribunal makes an award, the parties may first seek mediation. If an agreement is reached in the mediation, the arbitral tribunal shall prepare a mediation statement or an award based on the result of the agreement.

Article 47 of *the CIETAC Arbitration Rules* allows the arbitral tribunal to conduct conciliation[①] at the request of the parties or with the consent of the parties after the arbitral institution has accepted the case and completed the constitution of the tribunal. If the parties reach a conciliation agreement, they may request the arbitral tribunal to produce a conciliation statement or an award based on the content of the conciliation agreement. *The Beijing Arbitration Commission Arbitration Rules*, likewise, allow for this, but it is noteworthy that some international arbitration institutions have different views on arbitral tribunal's involvement in mediation. *The HKIAC Mediation Rules*, for example, provide with respect to the role of the mediator in subsequent proceedings that the parties undertake not to appoint the mediator as an adjudicator, arbitrator or representative, barrister or expert witness for any party in any subsequent adjudication, arbitration or judicial proceedings, whether or not such proceedings arise out of this sub-mediation or out of other disputes in the same contract.

4. Mediation Combined in Court Proceedings in China

The status and function of mediation system in China has undergone many changes. From 1949 to 1980, China has been emphasizing the judicial policy of "mediation first, litigation second". In this historical period, mediation played a more significant role than judicial decision in the process of settling civil disputes and there appeared the phenomenon of "attaching importance to mediation but neglecting judgment".

The principle of "voluntary and lawful mediation" was first established in *the Civil Procedure Law* promulgated in April 1991. Article 6 of *the Civil Procedure Law* clearly stipulates: "When trying a civil case, the people's court shall lay emphasis on

---

① The term "conciliation" is used interchangeably with "mediation".

mediation; if mediation fails, the people's court shall make a judgment without delay." Since then, the situation of "attaching more importance to mediation than judgment" has changed, the role of mediation in trial activities has gradually weakened, and more civil cases have been concluded through litigation.

Since 2003, the Supreme People's Court (the "Supreme Court") has begun to re-emphasize the importance of mediation due to the sharp increase in the number of cases accepted by the courts and the need to conclude cases. In a series of judicial interpretations and provisions, the Supreme People's Court has put forward such principles as "emphasizing mediation", "first mediation" and "giving priority to mediation and combining mediation with sentencing", and encouraged the parties concerned to mediate through the provision of "halving the expenses for mediation cases". In addition to retaining the original principle of "voluntary and lawful mediation" and the provisions of the special chapter on mediation, *the Civil Procedure Law* revised in 2012 for the first time establishes "prior mediation" as a principle for civil trials, stipulating that unless the parties concerned refuse to mediate, disputes brought to the court that are suitable for mediation shall be firstly mediated. At this point, "mediation" once again becomes China's judicial activity as a key part of the civil litigation process.

5. Singapore Mediation Convention and the Use of Mediation in the Future

In recent years, mediation as an important way of dispute resolution has attracted more and more attention. With the signing of *the Singapore Mediation Convention and the successive ratifications of various countries*, this obstacle to the cross-border implementation of the settlement agreement will be gradually resolved. Singapore is regarded as a leading dispute resolution center in the Asia-Pacific region and even in the world. Its commercial mediation system has been developed since the 1990s. As an oriental country with a rich history of civil mediation, Singapore has also faced many problems and challenges in the process of its development.

In the past decade, various commercial mediation organizations have sprung up in China, especially in large cities such as Beijing, Shanghai, Tianjin, Shenzhen, and Guangzhou. At present, commercial mediation institutions in China mainly include the following types:

(1) Mediation Institutions Relying on Industry Associations

As noted above, international commercial mediation does not adhere to the legal level of "right and wrong", more likely to achieve "win-win" effect. Through the intervention and communication of third-party mediators, the mediation process can help both parties find the true intention and need behind the disputing issues and reach a mutually beneficial cooperation consensus. Under the organization of professional mediators, the parties resolve disputes through consultation and negotiation, but also to clarify misunderstandings and re-establish trust. Because the final settlement agreement is reached on the basis of the parties' willingness, the result is more easily accepted by all parties, thus achieving the effect of cooperation and continuous operation. By contrast, international commercial litigation and international commercial arbitration proceedings with strong antagonism may aggravate the contradictions between the two parties in the protracted procedural confrontation, completely lose the possibility of mutual trust and continued cooperation, and thus fail to meet the commercial expectations of the parties for continued cooperation. For example, the Mediation Center of the Securities Association of China established in 2012 is an internal body of the Securities Association of China, which performs the relevant duties vested in the Securities Association of China by *the Securities Law* to mediate securities business disputes between members and between members and clients.[1]

(2) Mediation Centres Established by the Arbitration Commission

Article 24 of *the Mediation Rules of the China International Economic and Trade Arbitration Commission* (CIETAC) contains the provision of "docking between mediation and arbitration", which provides that the parties may apply to CIETAC for

---

[1] Wu Jun, "Annual Observation on Commercial Mediation in China", *Beijing Arbitration*, No. 1, 2013, p. 29.

an arbitral award in accordance with the terms of the conciliation agreement, while in CIETAC arbitration proceedings, the parties may also request that an independent conciliation be conducted by a person outside the arbitral tribunal.

(3) Professional Commercial Mediation Institutions

In recent years, China has produced mediation institutions dedicated to commercial mediation activities. Among them, the earliest exploration is the China Council for the Promotion of International Trade/China Chamber of International Commerce Mediation Center (formerly known as the "China Council for the Promotion of International Trade/China Chamber of International Commerce Beijing Mediation Center"), which was established by the China Council for the Promotion of International Trade in Beijing in 1987. Since 1992, the China Council for the Promotion of International Trade/China Chamber of International Commerce have successively set up mediation centers in branches of the China Council for the Promotion of International Trade in all provinces, municipalities directly under the Central Government, autonomous regions and some major cities throughout the country. So far, more than 30 mediation centers have been set up to help Chinese and foreign parties to resolve commercial, maritime and other disputes.

These mediation organizations are committed to organizing commercial mediation activitie, and provide relevant legal advice, training and exchange activities. Their emergence and development reflect the needs and enthusiasm of the Chinese market for commercial mediation activities.

With the *Singapore Mediation Convention* in place, we hold a strong belief that mediation will have a new time of growth in helping resolution of disputes in the international commerce in the region. China's unique experience of arbitration combined with mediation (Arb-Med) may have its advantage of helping parties settle their disputes through new agreements. It may also have challenges in relation to the acceptance of such combined method in the region. The parties' consensus on the use of mediation in the arbitration process and their autonomy to reach a settlement agreement and to perform their settlement agreement voluntarily is the key to the success of this unique method in the dispute resolution field.

第十一章
仲裁员是否在法律上免责？

刘心仪

　　正如 Jean Flavien Lalive 所写，仲裁的好坏取决于其仲裁员。仲裁员遵守他们的法律义务，对于高效和高质量的争端解决至关重要。在大多数法域，法律都明示或默示地赋予仲裁员一定程度的豁免权。这就产生了一个问题：仲裁员在法律上是否可以免除责任？

一、仲裁员责任制度总体性介绍

　　首先，读者应牢记仲裁的双重性质，即契约性和司法性。与之相应，仲裁员的角色也具有双重属性。一方面，他们从私人性质的仲裁协议中得到任命和授权，并基于合同关系提供仲裁服务以获得报酬。另一方面，他们以准司法官员的身份裁决争端。对仲裁员角色的不同认识会产生关于仲裁员责任或仲裁员豁免权的不同理论。

　　与明确给予仲裁员豁免权的华盛顿公约不同[1]，国际商事公约中没有关于仲裁员责任或豁免权的统一规定。贸易法委员会示范法也在此问题上保

---

[1] 《关于解决国家和他国国民之间投资争端公约》第21条、第22条。

持沉默。因此，我们有必要查看各国仲裁立法和机构规则如何规定仲裁员的责任范围或豁免范围。

（一）各国立法

1. 大陆法系做法[①]

一般来说，大多数大陆法系国家采取仲裁员有限责任制度。在这一契约范式下，仲裁员被视为基于商业合同关系提供仲裁服务的私人。因此，他们应承担不履行或严重过失的民事责任。瑞士、德国、法国和荷兰等国家都采用这种方式。[②]

同时，大陆法系的国家在仲裁员刑事责任的规制上转向了司法范式。仲裁员受到了和公务员相似的规制，他们要对渎职行为（通常涉及贿赂和腐败）承担刑事责任。日本、法国、西班牙和韩国等国家的立法中都有这些罪名。[③]

2. 英美法系做法

相比之下，普通法系国家的做法基本支持仲裁员豁免权或仲裁豁免权。这一理论源于司法豁免权，即法官受法律保护，可以独立公正地行事，而不必担心个人所要承担的后果。这一理论以类推论证为基础，延伸应用到仲裁员身上。一个判决为这种司法范式提供了简洁的描述："……在履行裁决职能时，他们所扮演的角色与法官相似，因而需要同样的保护以确保决策的独立性。"[④]

[①] 此处，"大陆法系做法"是指大多数大陆法域国家的做法，而非全部国家的做法。后面的"英美法系做法"同理。

[②] Martinez-Fraga Pedro J. , *The American Influence on International Commercial Arbitration, Doctrinal Developments and Discovery Methods* , 2nd Ed. Cambridge University Press, 2020, p. 110.

[③] 彭丽明：《仲裁员责任制度比较研究》，法律出版社 2017 年版，第 144—147 页。

[④] CanLII. Hazel v. Ainsworth Engineered, 2009 HRTO 2180, https://www.canlii.org/en/on/onhrt/doc/2009/2009hrto2180/2009hrto2180.html.

美国是唯一采用基于这种司法范式的绝对豁免权的国家。在 1996 年英国仲裁法(《1996 年法案》)之前，英国法院也采用了广泛的豁免权，豁免的唯一可能的例外是欺诈。[①] 然而，从《1996 年法案》第 29 条可以推断这一立场得以缓和，仲裁员在两种情况下应当承担法律责任：第一，该行为或不行为被证明是恶意的；第二，法院认为仲裁员辞职是不合理的。加拿大、澳大利亚、新西兰和新加坡等其他普通法地区的法院也采取了类似的立场。[②]

(二)机构规定

许多一流的仲裁机构在它们的规则中纳入了限制或排除民事责任的条款。特别是它们中的大多数都将有限豁免权赋予了广泛的主体，包括仲裁员、仲裁机构及其下属机构和雇员。此外，对豁免权的限制一般有两种类型。一种与仲裁员的主观意图有关。例如，"有意识的和故意的错误行为"[③] "故意的不法行为"[④] "不诚实地做"[⑤]，以及 "故意违反职责或严重疏忽"[⑥]。另一种限制则更为灵活，取决于所适用法律的禁止性规定。[⑦]

(三)初步观察

对仲裁员适用责任豁免有利也有弊。一方面，它有利于确保仲裁员的独立性和公正性，保证仲裁的终局性，吸引有技能的人担任仲裁员，以及

---

① Gary B. Born, *International Commercial Arbitration*, 3rd Ed. Kluwer Law International, 2021, p. 2182.
② 同上。
③ 《伦敦国际仲裁院仲裁规则 2020》第 31 条。
④ 《贸易法委员会仲裁规则 2021》第 16 条。
⑤ 《香港国际仲裁中心机构仲裁规则 2018》第 46 条。
⑥ 《德国仲裁院仲裁规则 2018》第 45.2 条。
⑦ 《贸易法委员会仲裁规则 2021》第 16 条；《香港国际仲裁中心机构仲裁规则 2018》第 46 条；《国际商会仲裁规则 2021》第 41 条。

通过减少诉累来使公众受益。① 另一方面，赋予仲裁员豁免权可能会有以下风险：不鼓励仲裁员谨慎和小心行事；为了终局性而牺牲个体正义；违反了默示的诚信义务；以及未给当事人提供充分的替代救济措施。更好的立场是采取有限豁免，因为它在两端之间取得了平衡。这为中国仲裁员责任制度的发展提供了启迪。

二、中国仲裁员责任制度

中国大陆的《仲裁法》和《刑法》都有明文规定，要求仲裁员在特定情况下承担责任。但是，该仲裁员责任制度还有待完善。

（一）中国大陆
1. 仲裁法下的责任

《仲裁法》第 38 条规定，在两种情况下，仲裁员应承担法律责任。第一种情况是第 38 条第 4 项，仲裁员私自会见当事人、代理人，或者接受当事人、代理人的请客送礼，这也是仲裁员应回避的情形。这一规则的适用要求达到"情节严重"。第二种情况是依据第 58 条第 6 项，仲裁员在仲裁该案时有索贿受贿、徇私舞弊、枉法裁决行为，这也是撤销仲裁裁决的理由。在这些情况下，仲裁委员会也将仲裁员从仲裁员小组中除名。

在实践中，鲜有商业仲裁的公开案件会援引仲裁法第 38 条。此外，根据第 58 条第 6 项撤销裁决也很难成功。这部分是因为最高人民法院的司法解释要求当事人必须提供生效的刑事法律文书或纪律处分决定作为证据。②

---

① Susan D. Franck. "The Liability of International Arbitrators: A Comparative Analysis and Proposal for Qualified Immunity", *New York Law School Journal of International and Comparative Law*, Vol.20, No. 1, 2000, pp. 28-30.

② 《最高人民法院关于审理仲裁司法审查案件若干问题的规定》第 18 条。

然而，当事人很难在申请撤销的有限期限内获得这些证据。如果没有这样的证据，法院一般会驳回申请。①

2. 刑法下的责任

中国是极少数对仲裁员施加刑事责任的国家之一。依据刑法第 399 条之一（枉法仲裁罪），依法承担仲裁职责的人员，在仲裁活动中故意违背事实和法律作枉法裁决，情节严重的，处三年以下有期徒刑或者拘役；情节特别严重的，处三年以上七年以下有期徒刑。

尽管刑法修正时对于这一罪名的存废有着激烈的争议，但在过去的几十年里，仲裁员的刑事责任引起的关注相对较少。这在一部分体现为实践中很少有公开的案例，而且大部分案例大多是劳动仲裁而非商事仲裁。

3. 纪律责任

中国关于仲裁员纪律责任尚没有统一的规则。以中国国际经济贸易仲裁委员会为例，人们可以在其发布的《仲裁员守则》和《仲裁员行为考察规定》中找到关于仲裁员职责和对仲裁员不当行为的惩戒措施的详细规定。

根据《中国仲裁法》第 5 条的规定，中国仲裁协会（"协会"）是一个监督仲裁委员会及其组成人员、仲裁员违纪行为的自律性组织。该协会已于 2022 年 10 月 14 日在民政部登记为社会团体，预计将制定仲裁行业规则，加强监管，加强信用建设。②

（二）中国港澳台地区

香港特区也在香港仲裁条例中明确规定了对仲裁员责任的限制。第 104 条的特点是责任主体范围广泛，包括仲裁庭的雇员或代理人，或调解员的雇员或代理人。此外，该条例强调不诚实，因为他们"只有在证明该作为

---

① (2022) 粤 01 民特 13 号、(2022) 粤 01 民特 73 号、(2022) 苏 08 民特 9 号、(2021) 黑 03 民特 16 号
② 中国仲裁协会, https://xxgs.chinanpo.mca.gov.cn/gsxt/newDetails?b=eyJpZCI6IjUxMTAwMDAwMTUUow
　MDAwOTgySyJ9.

是不诚实地作出或该不作为是不诚实的情况下"才承担法律责任。在 2018 年香港国际仲裁中心的仲裁规则第 26 条中也有类似的表述。

新的澳门仲裁法对仲裁员适用有限豁免权。第 35 条规定，仲裁员不对其以仲裁员身份所作的决定承担责任。但是，这种豁免权不包括其执行职务时违反合同或法律上须遵守的义务的情况。此外，责任可以是民事、刑事或纪律性的。

在台湾地区，仲裁员根据其刑法可能会承担刑事责任。其刑法将仲裁员视为公职人员，在第 121—124 条规定了渎职罪，主要针对收受贿赂和枉法仲裁行为。中华民国仲裁协会规则中也规定了免责条款，但"该行为或不行为构成故意不当行为的"除外。

结语

本章简要介绍了仲裁员的有限豁免规则，这一规则基于仲裁员契约—司法双重地位的认识。这些规则背后有着平衡仲裁员的保护和惩罚的基本的政策考虑。许多国家立法和机构规则都采用这种方法。大多数普通法国家对仲裁员适用有限豁免来作为司法豁免权的延伸，但美国支持绝对豁免权。大多数大陆法系国家倾向于在其国家法律中对仲裁员实施有限的民事和刑事责任，这对中国大陆产生了影响。

中国大陆的仲裁员责任制度仍有一定的改进空间。第一，中国大陆仲裁员的刑事责任具有独特性和争议性。第二，没有将仲裁员的行为建立在诚信的底线上。不过，中国也有一些进步的迹象，比如正在进行的《仲裁法》的修订和中国仲裁协会的建立。随着 CMAC 规则中责任限制条款的引入，更多的中国仲裁机构可能会采用这种方式来和国际惯例保持一致。通过这些共同努力，我们可以设想中国将会建立更好的仲裁员责任制度，规定仲裁员们的权利和义务，促使他们公正和独立地行事。

Chapter 11

Are Arbitrators Legally Exempt From Liability?

Xinyi Liu, Angela

As Jean Flavien Lalive wrote, arbitration is only as good as its arbitrators. It's essential to have arbitrators comply with their legal obligations for efficient and quality dispute resolution. In most jurisdictions, arbitrators are expressly or impliedly entitled to a certain degree of immunity. That begs the question: are arbitrators legally exempt from liability?

1. Arbitrators' Liability System in General

To start with, readers shall bear in mind the dual nature of arbitration, both contractual and quasi-judicial. Correspondingly, the arbitrators' role is twofold. On one hand, their appointment and power derive from private arbitration agreements and they get remuneration in return for their arbitral services as a result of contractual relationships. On the other hand, they adjudicate disputes in a quasi-judicial capacity. Different perceptions of the arbitrator's role can lead to different theories on arbitrators' liability or immunity.

Unlike the ICSID Convention which expressly grants immunity to arbitrators,[1] there are no uniform provisions concerning arbitrators' liability or immunity in

---

[1] ICSID Convention, Arts. 21-22.

international commercial conventions. The UNICITRAL Model Law is also silent on this issue. Thus, it is necessary to review national arbitration legislation and institutional rules as to how they regulate the scope of arbitrators' liability or immunity.

(1) National Laws

a. A Civil Law Approach[①]

Generally speaking, most civil law jurisdictions impose limited liability on arbitrators. Under a contractual paradigm, arbitrators are treated as private persons providing arbitral services based on commercial contractual relationships. As a result, they shall assume civil liability for non-performance or gross negligence. This approach is adopted by countries like Switzerland, Germany, France, and the Netherlands.[②]

Meanwhile, the civil law approach turns to the judicial paradigm for criminal liability. Arbitrators are regarded as counterparts of public actors and are held criminally liable for malfeasances, typically involving bribery and corruption. Countries like Japan, France, Spain, and South Korea have these offenses in their legislation.[③]

b. A Common Law Approach

In contrast, the premise of a common law approach is primarily in favor of arbitrator immunity or arbitral immunity. This theory originates from judicial immunity that judges are protected under the law to act independently and impartially without fear of personal consequences to themselves, and extends to arbitrators grounded in argument by analogy. A decision provides a succinct description of this judicial paradigm: *"...in discharging their adjudicative functions, they are performing a similar role to that of judges, and require the same protection to ensure independence in decision making."*[④]

---

① Here, the "civil law approach" refers to the approach adopted by the majority of countries in civil law jurisdictions, but not all civil law countries. And the same applies to the "common law approach".

② *See* Martinez-Fraga Pedro J. , *The American Influence on International Commercial Arbitration, Doctrinal Developments and Discovery Methods,* 2nd edn., Cambridge University Press, 2020, p. 110.

③ *See* Peng Liming , *A Comparative Study on Arbitrator's Liability Institution*, Law Press, 2017, pp. 144-147.

④ *Hazel v. Ainsworth Engineered*, 2009 HRTO 2180 (CanLII), Available from 〈 https://www.canlii.org/en/on/onhrt/doc/2009/2009hrto2180/2009hrto2180.html 〉. [8 October 2022].

America stands alone in adopting absolute immunity based on this judicial paradigm. Before the 1996 English Arbitration Act ("1996 Act"), English courts also adopted a broad immunity with the only (possible) exception for fraud.[①] However, Section 29 of the 1996 Act infers that position is tempered by holding arbitrators liable under two circumstances: (i) the act or omission is shown to have been in bad faith, and (ii) the court finds it unreasonable for the arbitrator to resign. Other common law courts in Canada, Australia, New Zealand, and Singapore have adopted similar positions.[②]

(2) Institutional Rules

Many leading arbitral institutions have incorporated a limitation or exclusion of civil liability clause into their rules. In particular, most of them accord qualified immunity to a broad scope of entities, including arbitrators, arbitral institutions, and their organs and employees. Moreover, there are generally two types of limitations on immunity. One concerns the intention of arbitrators. For example, *"conscious and deliberate wrongdoing"*[③], *"intentional wrongdoing"*[④], *"done dishonestly"*[⑤], and *"intentional breach of duty or gross negligence"*[⑥]. The other exception is more flexible, relying on the prohibition by the applicable law.[⑦]

(3) A Preliminary Observation

Applying immunity to arbitrators has its pros and cons. On one hand, it is conducive to (i) ensuring the independence and impartiality of arbitrators, (ii) guaranteeing the finality of arbitration, (iii) attracting skilled people to act as arbitrators, and (iv) benefiting the public by reducing the burden of litigation. On the

---

① *See* Gary B. Born, *International Commercial Arbitration (3rd Edition)*, Kluwer Law International, 2021, p. 2182.

② Ibid.

③ LCIA Arbitration Rules 2020, Art. 31.

④ UNCITRAL Arbitration Rules 2021, Art. 16.

⑤ HKIAC Administered Arbitration Rules 2018, Art. 46.

⑥ DIS Arbitration Rules 2018, Art. 45.2.

⑦ UNCITRAL Arbitration Rules 2021, Art. 16; HKIAC Administered Arbitration Rules 2018, Art. 46; ICC Arbitration Rules 2021, Art. 41.

other hand, entitling arbitrators to immunity may risk (i) discouraging caution and carefulness, (ii) sacrificing individual justice for finality, (iii) breaching implied duty of good faith, and (iv) providing inadequate alternative remedies.① Qualified immunity is a better position because it strikes a balance between the two ends. This is an enlightening view of the development of the arbitrators' liability system in China.

2. Arbitrators' Liability System in China

(1)Mainland China

In Mainland China, there are express provisions in *the Arbitration Law* and *the Criminal Law* holding arbitrators liable under enumerative circumstances. However, the general liability system of arbitrators in Mainland China leaves much to be desired.

a. Liability under the Arbitration Law

Article 38 of *the Arbitration Law* provides that an arbitrator shall assume legal responsibility under two circumstances. First, the arbitrator has privately met with a party or its agent or accepted an invitation under Article 38(4), which is also a ground for the withdrawal of an arbitrator. A degree of seriousness is required for this rule to apply. Second, the arbitrators have committed embezzlement, accepted bribes or done malpractices for personal benefits, or perverted the law in the arbitration of the case under Article 58(6), a ground for setting aside an arbitration award. In these circumstances, the arbitrators will also be removed from the panel of arbitrators by the arbitration commission.

In practice, there is rarely any public case involving commercial arbitrators which invokes Article 38. Moreover, setting aside an award based on Article 58(6) is hardly successful. That is partly because the judicial interpretation by SPC requires that the parties must produce evidence such as an effective criminal legal instrument or a

---

① See Susan D. Franck , "The Liability of International Arbitrators: A Comparative Analysis and Proposal for Qualified Immunity" , *New York Law School Journal of International and Comparative Law, vol. 20, no. 1,* 2000, pp. 28-30.

disciplinary action decision.[1] However, it is hard for parties to obtain such evidence within the limited period for applying for the annulment. Absent such evidence, courts generally reject the application.[2]

b. Liability under the Criminal Law

China is among the very few countries that impose criminal liability on arbitrators. Under Article 399 of the Criminal Law, if the person who undertakes the duties of arbitration intentionally goes against the facts or law and makes any wrongful ruling in the process of arbitration, he shall be sentenced to fixed-term imprisonment of not more than three years or incarceration. If the circumstances are extremely serious, he shall be sentenced to fixed-term imprisonment of not less than three years but not more than seven years.

Despite fierce controversy over the existence of this crime around the amendment, the criminal liability of arbitrators has drawn relatively little attention over the past decades. This is in part evidenced by very few public cases in practice and the majority of these cases are labor arbitration rather than commercial arbitration.

c. Disciplinary Liability

There is no unified rule concerning disciplinary liability. Take CIETAC as an example, one can find detailed provisions about arbitrators' duties and disciplinary measures on arbitrators' misconduct in the Code of Conduct for Arbitrators and the Rules for Evaluating the Behaviors of Arbitrators issued by CIETAC.

According to Article 5 of *the Arbitration Law of PRC*, the China Arbitration Association ("CAA") shall serve as a self-discipline organization that supervises arbitration commissions and their members and arbitrators as to whether or not they breach discipline. CAA has been registered with the Ministry of Civil Affairs as a social organization on October 14, 2022, which is expected to formulate rules for the

---

[1] Provisions of the Supreme People's Court on Several Issues concerning Trying Cases of Arbitration-Related Judicial Review, Art. 18.

[2] Guangzhou Intermediate People's Court, Guangdong Civil Ruling No.13, No.73, 2022; Huai'an Intermediate People's Court, Jiangsu Civil Ruling No.9, 2022; Jixi Intermediate People's Court, Heilongjiang Civil ruling No.16, 2021.

arbitration industry, strengthen supervision and enhance credit construction.[①]

(2) Hong Kong, Macao and Taiwan

Hong Kong SAR also explicitly imposes a limitation on arbitrators' liability in the Cap. 609 Arbitration Ordinance. Section 104 features a broad scope of the subject of liability, from employees or agents of an arbitral tribunal to that of the mediators. In addition, the Ordinance stresses dishonesty as such liability exists *"only if it is proved that the act was done or omitted to be done dishonestly."* Similar expressions can be found in Article 26 of the 2018 HKIAC Administered Arbitration Rules.

The new Macau Arbitration Law applies qualified immunity to arbitrators. Article 35 stipulates that *an arbitrator shall not be liable for decisions made in his capacity as arbitrator.* However, such immunity will not extend to breach of contractual or legal obligations in the exercise of his functions. Moreover, the liability can be of a civil, criminal, or disciplinary nature.

In Taiwan, arbitrators may be subject to criminal liability under its Criminal Code. The Code provides offenses of malfeasance in office in Articles 121 to 124, regarding arbitrators as counterparts of public officials and mainly targeting the offense of bribery and the offense of perverting the law in rendering an arbitral award. Chinese Arbitration Association (Taipei) International Arbitration Rules provide *exclusion of liability with the exception "where such act or omission constitutes willful misconduct".*

Concluding Remarks

This chapter briefly introduces qualified immunity rules about arbitrators' liability for their contractual-judicial status. There are underlying policy considerations to balance protection and punishment for arbitrators. This approach is adopted by many national laws and institutional rules. Most common law countries apply qualified immunity to arbitrators as an extension of judicial immunity, except that America

---

① Available from 〈 https://xxgs.chinanpo.mca.gov.cn/gsxt/newDetails?b=eyJpZCI6IjUxMTAwMDAwTUo wMDAwOTgySyJ9.%5B15〉. [15 January 2023].

espouses absolute immunity. Most civil law countries tend to impose limited civil and criminal liabilities on arbitrators in their national laws, which has influenced Mainland China.

For the arbitrators' liability system in Mainland China, there is still some room for improvement. Firstly, the criminal liability of arbitrators in Mainland China is unique and contentious. Secondly, there is no bottom line of basing the conduct of arbitrators on honesty. Nevertheless, there are signs of progress, such as the ongoing revision of *the Arbitration Law* and the establishment of the Chinese Arbitration Association. With the introduction of the limitation of liability clause in CMAC Rules, more Chinese institutions may follow this approach to comply with international practice. With these joint efforts, we may envisage a better system of arbitrators' liability in China that stipulates their rights and duties and impels them to act impartially and independently.

第十二章

元宇宙业务中的仲裁 [①]

彭 竹

本章旨在探讨元宇宙仲裁中的裁决执行机制与《纽约公约》下传统裁决执行路径之间的关系。为此，我们将从仲裁的起点，即元宇宙中仲裁协议的有效性入手（第一节）。其后，聚焦于元宇宙为仲裁程序带来的便利（第二节）。最后，讨论在元宇宙中仲裁裁决执行的影响（第三节）。

一、 元宇宙中的仲裁协议

本节主要论点为元宇宙的出现使得电子商务业务中仲裁协议的有效性呈现出显著的不确定性。如下文所述，对于大多数元宇宙公司在其用户协议等线上合同中所采用的仲裁条款，境内外法院始终对其有效性保持怀疑和审慎态度。

1. 元宇宙的定义

"元宇宙"的概念缘起于 1992 年的科幻小说《雪崩》，在该书中，元

[①] 彭竹、Michael Edwards 和陈子木，方达律师事务所。

宇宙被形象地描述为一个虚拟现实世界，用户可以像在现实世界中那样进行互动、游戏和体验。

2. 元宇宙中仲裁协议的有效性

元宇宙中开展商业交易产生的争议通常是合同性的，典型如线上消费者合同。该等合同中的仲裁条款经常受到质疑，原因在于有观点认为该类仲裁条款系显失公平的、不可协商的格式条款，用户对该等条款的"同意"本质上并非其真实的意思表示。因此，各地法院对于此类协议中仲裁条款的有效性认定持不同态度，导致各地司法判决之间存在矛盾之处，缺乏统一的司法指引。此外，各国消费者相关法律的差异，特别是在线上消费者合同中仲裁条款有效性缺乏统一国际规则的情况下，更是加剧了仲裁条款效力的不确定性。联合国国际贸易法委员会曾发布《在线纠纷解决机制技术指引》[1]，尝试解决该问题。然而，该指引最终仍将在线仲裁条款有效性的决定权交给了当地法院，致使统一司法标准缺位这一关键问题至今仍未得到妥善解决。

（1）中国案例

中国法院在审查"点击同意"类型线上合同中的仲裁条款有效性时呈现出不同的裁判思路。具体而言，在一些案件中[2]，法院认为案涉平台仅将已"同意"的条款列于单独页面中，而未给消费者提供可以自由选择的明显提示，并据此认定用户并未真正同意通过仲裁方式解决双方之间的争议，进而否认了该等仲裁条款的效力。与之相反，在另一些案件中[3]，法院立足于对字体大小、颜色和页面布局等具体情况的全面分析，综合认定平台已经采取"合理方式通知"用户相关仲裁条款的存在，并认为用户事实上已经通过"点击同意"的方式与平台就协议中的仲裁条款达成了合意。

（2）境外案例

其他法域的司法裁判也存在类似的分歧。一方面，由于电子商务业务（包括元宇宙业务）属于蓬勃发展、快速增长的经济领域，裁判者逐渐倾向于承认和支持"点击同意"类型协议中仲裁条款的有效性 [4]。另一方面，部分法院仍驳回了当事方要求强制仲裁的申请，理由在于电商平台没有"询问并通知" [5] 消费者该等强制仲裁条款 [6]。

3. 小结

从上述内容可以看出，各地法院对"点击同意"类型协议中仲裁条款效力的认定，很大程度上取决于具体案件事实。因此，与传统合同中的仲裁条款相比，元宇宙平台通常采用的用户协议中仲裁条款的有效性存在更大程度的不确定性。

二、仲裁程序中的元宇宙技术

本节聚焦于作为元宇宙核心的区块链技术如何在仲裁程序中发挥作用。事实上，商事仲裁越来越受益于区块链具有的可靠性以及高效率等优势。更进一步来讲，区块链甚至有机会创造一种新的仲裁形式，即由随机选择且受利益驱动的仲裁员主导的，仲裁裁决可实现自动执行的去中心化争议解决机制。

1. 提高仲裁程序效率

元宇宙可以作为一个证据保全和认证体系。由于区块链上的记录不可篡改，涉案数据可以实现自动存储，在申请和执行财产保全和 / 或证据保全时，可以节省大量的时间和费用 [7]。在实践中，一些机构已经将区块链纳入其案件管理系统之中。例如，广州仲裁委员会在证据保全和认证过程中使用了区块链技术。据报道，该等技术明显提升了案件处理效率 [8]。

2. 创建争议解决的乌托邦：元宇宙仲裁

区块链技术的大规模应用促使"元宇宙仲裁"的诞生，这一发展对商事仲裁具有潜在的革命性影响。

（1）去中心化的争议解决机制

所谓元宇宙仲裁的核心属性即去中心化。传统的争议解决模式有赖于权威的第三方裁判者作为案件审理的中心，如法官或仲裁员等。当事方向其诉诸司法正义、寻求法律保护。而去中心化的司法模式则移除了第三方裁判者的角色，取而代之的是严格的算法程序。

（2）随机选择的裁判者

随机选择裁判者是元宇宙仲裁实现去中心化的重要步骤，该等做法可以在最大限度上消除人为的不当影响。一旦争议产生且当事方将争议提交仲裁，该案的裁判者将会从预先设立的裁判者池中自动抽取。裁判过程依靠一种内置的激励机制使得裁判者达成一致的决定，即形成多数意见的裁判者会获得针对构成少数意见裁判者征收的罚款以及当事方支付的仲裁费用[9]。在该等激励机制下，裁判者更有动力作出会被其他裁判者同样采纳的裁决，从而使得裁决结果一致。

（3）自动执行机制

有别于传统仲裁，自动执行是元宇宙仲裁的另一个关键特征。这个过程依赖于智能合约，即存储在区块链上，在满足某些预设条件时会自动触发的程序代码。借由这种方式处理纠纷可以有效减少执行过程中个体的投机行为，并实现传统仲裁模式中所缺乏的法律确定性。更重要的是，自动执行所消耗的时间和费用远远低于传统模式。因此元宇宙仲裁能够以及时、有效和安全的方式简化仲裁裁决的执行过程。鉴此，元宇宙仲裁，相较于耗时又昂贵的传统仲裁，对于解决小额标的的批量纠纷具有明显优势。

3. 小结

元宇宙仲裁是一项具有变革性的发明，它通过消除人为干预，特别是人为错误和道德风险，实现了更快、更高效的裁判和执行过程。元宇宙或区块链的价值不仅仅是作为提高仲裁程序效率的技术工具，更在于它有能力从根本上创造去中心化的司法系统，使其不再依赖于既有的政治和社会机构[10]。然而，正如下文所述，当争议涉及较多主观和价值判断时，元宇宙并非理想的争议解决机制。

三、仲裁裁决的执行

本节主要讨论元宇宙领域仲裁裁决的执行，这也是裁决价值的核心体现之一。为便于阐述这个问题，我们设定了如下三种情形，其中区块链的参与度依次递进。我们将以《纽约公约》作为蓝本，对每种情形下的优势和局限性进行具体分析。

1. 情形一：传统裁决 + 区块链技术

该情形下，仲裁裁决仍由传统仲裁庭作出，裁令当事方以加密货币履行裁决。裁决中的指令被记录在区块链上。

（1）优势

得益于区块链的不可篡改性和可追溯性，裁决有机会实现链上溯源和追踪，并完成公证认证手续。因此，区块链技术可以使得仲裁裁决更高效地获得承认。

（2）挑战 / 局限性

首先，仲裁裁决执行地对加密货币所持态度具有决定性意义。许多法域出于加密货币存在管制缺位，以及潜在的逃税和洗钱风险等原因，对其持否定态度。例如，深圳市中级人民法院最近裁定撤销深圳国际仲裁院作出了一项仲裁裁决，理由即为该裁决裁令以美元或人民币代替加密货币进行赔偿的做法违反了中国的公共政策[11]。该裁定释放出了明确的警示信号，即在中国执行涉及加密货币的仲裁裁决存在较大难度。同时，该裁定也预留了一个问题，即该等违反公共政策的理由是否也同样适用于《纽约公约》项下境外裁决的承认和执行[12]。

此外，情形一仍然受限于传统裁决执行机制，即依托国际公约或互惠原则实现跨法域执行。这意味着裁决执行仍取决于国家的司法体制，仅在《纽约公约》的签署国或存在相互承认安排的国家间适用。总而言之，在情形一中，区块链或元宇宙仲裁并没有实现自动执行，而只是为传统执行过程提供了有限的技术上的便利，在一定程度上加速了原有执行程序，特别是对于跨境裁决而言。

2. 情形二：传统裁决 + 智能合约

该情形下，裁决仍由传统仲裁庭作出，裁令当事方以加密货币履行裁决。当事方事先签订智能合约以便自动执行裁决，支付指令也记载于智能合约之中。

（1）优势

如上所述，元宇宙仲裁的真正价值并不局限于为执行程序提供技术上的便利，而更在于实现仲裁裁决的自动执行。通过智能合约执行传统的裁决的做法更接近于这一内核价值的实现。情形二有机会使裁决的执行完全自动化，并确保裁决的执行不受债务人的拖延、抵抗等外在影响。

（2）挑战

理论上这种模式是很具有吸引力的，但实际操作中仍存在复杂难题。首先，当事方必须明确同意将与争议数额等值的虚拟货币置于代管账户[13]。该行为与临时措施较为相似，即要求当事方缴纳具有保证性质的预付款作为获得临时救济的条件。鉴于该模式下需要锁定当事方资产以保证后续执行，且其目的仅是为了担保假设的、尚未发生的争议，当事方出于现实原因可能不会同意适用该等模式。

另一个局限在于该等模式的适用的争议范围较窄，仅限于二元争议，即在是或否两种答案中作出选择。当涉及"混合"裁决时，比如需要在链上支付前满足某些链下条件。虽然有些"混合"裁决可以通过设计更复杂的、功能性更强的智能合约来解决，但随之而来的不确定性会消减区块链执行具有的优势。

3. 情形三：全链上仲裁

"全链上仲裁"是指仲裁的整个过程都发生在区块链上，即原始交易记录在区块链上，争议系由随机选择的仲裁员进行审理并作出裁决，并最终依靠智能合约自动执行仲裁裁决。

（1）优势

如情形二中所述，自动执行是元宇宙仲裁的核心优势。"全链上仲裁"充满雄心勃勃的愿景，致力于为数字领域的争议创造一个更高效、实惠、经济的纠纷解决机制。一些国家的法院已经率先建立了类似支持系统。例如，杭州互联网法院开创性地设立了区块链平台[14]，符合审查条件的当事方可以自行缔结智能合约，以确保裁决的自动执行。这一举措大幅提高了裁判执行效率，据报道，截至 2022 年 7 月，电子商务平台的纠纷率已从 5% 降至 0.01% 以下[15]。

（2）挑战

首先，如前所述，区块链有效解决的纠纷类型大多限于二元争议，而现实世界中的多数案件更加复杂且多元，需要主观和价值判断的综合考量，即需要引入裁判者的自由裁量过程。

其次，"全链上仲裁"赖以实现的底层技术尚不成熟，仍不足以解决复杂案件。况且，距离当事方和裁判者完全接受、利用并采纳这种新的仲裁形式还需一定准备时间和工作。

再次，"全链上仲裁"作出的裁决质量和公正性仍值得怀疑。具体而言，链上仲裁的裁决是由受利益驱动的裁判者根据公平公正的共识来认定的，并非经过严格法律而得出的结论。

最后,"全链上仲裁"裁决的可执行性面临《纽约公约》项下的诸多挑战。其中包括,区块链上记录的仲裁协议是否符合《纽约公约》中协议必须是"书面"的,或在"交互电函中所载明"[16]的要求。另一挑战则是仲裁地与管辖法院的确定。鉴于仲裁程序全过程均在链上进行,并未进行实际庭审,最终裁决也不存在有形副本。在缺乏上述要素的前提下,链上仲裁裁决能否在《纽约公约》框架内予以裁决仍存在相当争议。

4. 小结

仲裁过程中的自动化程度越高,取得的结果未必越好。虽然运用区块链技术可以使当事方从更高效经济的裁决执行中获益,但执行过程中也存在实际困难。

结语

区块链和元宇宙技术在一定程度上促使仲裁成为更高效经济的争议解决方式,并提高其竞争力。与此同时,认识到元宇宙中仲裁的局限性也同样重要。从境内外法院对元宇宙仲裁协议有效性的不同裁判;到执行仲裁裁决面临《纽约公约》项下的障碍;更何况区块链技术本身也有待成熟。据此,本章得出的结论为,元宇宙中仲裁的发展应立足于发挥并增强区块链技术的优势和价值,例如,可以将链上仲裁应用于小额批量纠纷等可使其发挥积极作用的特定类型纠纷,与此同时,努力寻求与《纽约公约》等既有机制的协调而非取代,以便在简化仲裁程序的同时提高效率。

参考文献

[1] United Nations Commission on International Trade Law, *Technical Notes on Online Dispute Resolution*, https://uncitral.un.org/sites/uncitral.un.org/files/media-documents/uncitral/en/v1700382_english_technical_notes_on_odr.pdf.

[2] 浙江省杭州市中级人民法院，(2016) 浙 01 民辖终 1070 号民事裁定书；江苏省常州市中级人民法院，(2020) 苏 04 民终 999 号民事裁定书。

[3] 北京市第四中级人民法院，(2020) 京 04 民特 672 号民事裁定书；江苏省淮安市中级人民法院，(2021) 苏 08 民终 2436 号民事裁定书。

[4] *Dialogue Consulting Pty Ltd v Instagram, Inc.* (2020) FCA 1846; *Instagram Inc v Dialogue Consulting Pty Ltd.* (2022) FCAFC 7; *Bridgecrest Acceptance Corporation v. Kelly Donaldson and Robert Haulcy*, No. SC99269.

[5] *Schnabel v. Trilegiant Corp.*, 697 F.3d 110, 120 (2d Cir. 2012)，"询问并通知"系指将合同条款合理地通知给用户，使一个合理谨慎的人能够注意到该等合同条款。

[6] *Scotti v Tough Mudder Inc.*, 63 Misc. 3d 84.

[7] Nimrod Tauber. Block Chain and Evidence Law, https://www.legalbusinessworld.com/post/2018/12/17/blockchain-and-evidence-law.

[8] 广州仲裁委员会：《广仲战"疫""放大招"——区块链＋互联网仲裁》，https://www.gzac.org/gzxw/741.

[9] Bruce Greig, What can mediators learn from Kleros, a platform which uses cryptocurrency and game theory to resolve disputes? http://mediationblog.kluwerarbitration.com/2022/03/06/what-can-mediators-learn-from-kleros-a-platform-which-uses-cryptocurrency-and-game-theory-to-resolve-disputes/.

[10] Herian, R. *Taking blockchain seriously*, https://doi.org/10.1007/s10978-018-9226-y.

[11] 广东省深圳市中级人民法院，(2018) 粤 03 民特 719 号民事裁定书。

[12] Brad Wang, Xianyue Bai, *Award Concerning Bitcoin Exchange – Bit Too Risky to Enforce?* http://arbitrationblog.kluwerarbitration.com/2021/04/02/award-concerning-bitcoin-exchange-bit-too-risky-to-enforce/.

[13] Zhen Er Low, *Commentary,* Execution of Judgements on the Blockchain- A Practical Legal Commentary, [J/OL]. Harv. J.L. & Tech. Dig, https://jolt.law.harvard.edu/digest/execution-of-judgements-on-the-blockchain-a-practical-legal-commentary.

[14] 杭州互联网法院司法区块链网站：https://blockchain.netcourt.gov.cn/first；另参见 Miranda Wood. Chinese internet court adopts blockchain smart contracts, processes 1.9bn transactions, https://www.ledgerinsights.com/chinese-internet-court-blockchain-smart-contracts/.

[15] 景汉朝：《互联网法院的时代创新与中国贡献》，《中国法学》2022 年第 4 期，https://www.court.gov.cn/zixun-xiangqing-367851.html.

[16] 《纽约公约》第 2 条："1. 当事方以书面协议承允彼此间所发生或可能发生之一切或任何争议……2. 称"书面协定"者，谓当事方所签订或在互换函电中所载明之契约公断条款或公断协定。"（注：公断指仲裁）

Chapter 12

Arbitration in Metaverse Business[①]

Zhu Peng, Diane

The ultimate goal of this chapter is to discuss the relationship between enforcement mechanisms in Metaverse arbitration and the conventional path under the New York Convention (the "**NYC**"). To this end, we will start with the cornerstone of arbitration, that is, the validity of arbitration agreements in the Metaverse (Section I), followed by the benefits the Metaverse has for arbitration proceedings (Section II). The final section (Section III) discusses enforcement implications of arbitral awards in the Metaverse.

1. Arbitration Agreements in the Metaverse

The main contention of this section is that the Metaverse has injected significant uncertainty as to the validity of arbitration agreements in e-commerce business. As illustrated below, courts both in China and overseas continue to express skepticism over, and go to great lengths to deny, the validity of arbitration clauses in online contracts, which are adopted by a majority of Metaverse companies.

1) Definition of Metaverse

The term "Metaverse" originated in the 1992 science fiction novel *Snow Crash*,

---

① Diane Peng, Michael Edwards and Zimu Chen, Fangda Partners.

where it was described, in a colloquial sense, as a virtual reality world where users can interact, game and experience things as they would in the real world.

2) Validity of Arbitration Agreements for Metaverse Business

Disputes arising out of commerce transacted in the Metaverse are normally contractual, typically online consumer contracts. A recurrent criticism of arbitration clauses in these contracts is that they are unfairly one-sided and non-negotiable standardized terms, with users' "agreement" to those terms essentially a form of non-genuine consent. Therefore, the validity of arbitration clauses in such agreements has been discussed extensively in court decisions, resulting in an unstable legal framework driven by diverging judgments in different jurisdictions. Moreover, differences in national consumer law reinforce this uncertainty, particularly in the absence of any unified international rules as to the validity of arbitration clauses contained in online consumer contracts. One of the few attempts at addressing this lacuna is the **UNCITRAL Technical Notes on Online Dispute Resolution** (UNCITRAL 2017). However, this document also leaves the determination of the validity of online arbitration clauses in the hands of local courts, thus resulting in the critical issue of the lack of a unified standard unresolved.

(1)PRC Cases

In China, courts have reached varying results when considering the validity of arbitration clauses in "click-wrap" online contracts. Specifically, in some cases[1], the courts have denied the effect of the arbitration clauses by determining that the delivery of such clauses, which in those cases was simply to display the "agreed" terms on a separate webpage without requiring users to explicitly indicate their assent to the arbitration clauses, did not establish that users actually agreed to resolve their disputes through arbitration. Conversely, in other cases[2], the courts, based on a comprehensive

---

[1] *Hangzhou Netease Leihuo Technology Co., Ltd. v. Hu, Yunhe* (2016) Zhe 01Min Xia Zhong No.1070; *Pu, Ping v. Hangzhou Youmai Technology Co., Ltd.* (2020) Su 04 Min Zhong No.999.

[2] *Xiao, Chong v. Beijing Baikeluoke Technology Co., Ltd.* (2020) Jing 04 Min Te No.672; *Zhu, Lang v. Hangzhou Netease Yanxuan Trading Co., Ltd.* (2021) Su 08 Min Zhong No.2436.

analysis, such as the font size, the color and the layout of the page, held that users had "reasonable notice" of the arbitration provisions and thus found that a consensus had been reached in respect of arbitration clauses contained in "click-wrap" agreements.

(2)Foreign Cases

Court opinion in other jurisdictions is similarly divided. On the one hand, as e-commerce business (including the Metaverse) represents an exponential growth economic area, decision-makers are progressively tending to recognize and uphold the validity of "click-wrap" agreements[①]. On the other hand, there are still courts dismissing applications to compel arbitration on the grounds that the ecommerce platform had failed to put the consumer on "inquiry notice" (*Schnabel v. Trilegiant Corp.* 697 F.3d 110, 120) of mandatory arbitration provisions (*Scotti v. Tough Mudder Inc.* 63 Misc. 3d 84).

3) Summary

It is inferred that courts' recognition of arbitration clauses in "click-wrap" agreements is highly dependent on the factual matrix. It follows that, compared to arbitration clauses in traditional contracts, there is far greater uncertainty surrounding the validity of arbitration clauses in the terms of use normally adopted by Metaverse platforms.

2. Metaverse Technology in Arbitration Proceedings

This section focuses on how the blockchain technology utilized in the Metaverse can be deployed in arbitration proceedings. As a matter of fact, commercial arbitration is increasingly benefiting from blockchain in terms of reliability and efficiency. It is even possible that blockchain will facilitate the creation of a new form of arbitration where a decentralized dispute resolution is conducted by randomly-chosen and

---

① *Dialogue Consulting Pty Ltd v. Instagram, Inc, (2020) FCA; Instagram Inc v Dialogue Consulting Pty Ltd (2022) FCAFC 7; Bridgecrest Acceptance Corporation v. Kelly Donaldson and Robert Haulcy* No. SC99269.

commercially-minded arbitrators and supported by a self-executing mechanism.

1) Improving the Efficiency of the Arbitral Proceedings

The Metaverse can serve as an evidence preservation and authentication system. Owing to the immutability of blockchain records, relevant data at issue can be automatically preserved and stored, saving significant time and expense when it comes to applying for and enforcing asset attachment and/or evidence preservation (Tauber 2018). In practice, some institutions have adopted blockchain technology in their case management system. For instance, the Guangzhou Arbitration Commission has adopted blockchain into the evidence preservation and authentication process. It is reported that blockchain technology has remarkably boosted the efficiency of case handling (Guangzhou Arbitration Commission 2020).

2) Creating a Utopian System of Dispute Resolution: Metaverse Arbitration

The massive and advanced application of blockchain technology has led to the birth of "Metaverse arbitration", a development that is of potentially revolutionary consequence for the conduct of commercial arbitration.

(1)Decentralized Dispute Resolution

The core attribute of so-called Metaverse arbitration is decentralization. In particular, whilst traditional dispute resolution systems are premised on the existence of authoritative third-party decision-makers such as judges or arbitrators acting as a central authority from whom parties seek justice, decentralized justice systems remove the position of the third-party adjudicator and instead rely on strict algorithms.

(2)Randomly-Selected Adjudicators

One of the crucial components of decentralized Metaverse arbitration is the random constitution of the decision-maker(s), which eradicates undue influence to the greatest extent possible. Once a dispute arises and a party refers the dispute to arbitration, the decision-makers are automatically drawn from a pre-constituted pool of adjudicators. There is commonly an in-built incentive for the adjudicators to reach a consensus decision: if they form part of the majority, the adjudicators are commonly rewarded with a share of the penalty levied against the minority adjudicator, plus the fee that the parties have paid (Greig 2022). The adjudicators are thus incentivized to arrive at the decision that is most likely to be adopted by arbitrators operating under the same incentives.

(3)Self-Executing Enforcement Apparatus

Self-executing enforcement is another key feature of Metaverse arbitration that distinguishes it from traditional arbitration. This process involves smart contracts, which are programmes stored on blockchain and triggered when certain pre-conditions are met. In this way, blockchain can handle disputes in a way that reduces the opportunistic behavior of human beings and provides the legal certainty that is absent in traditional systems. More importantly, automated enforcement consumes significantly less time and expense than the traditional enforcement process. Accordingly, Metaverse arbitration offers the prospect of streamlining the enforcement of arbitration outcomes in a timely, effective and secure manner. This is particularly appealing for high-volume, low-value disputes, where the length and cost of traditional arbitration are often prohibitive.

3) Summary

Metaverse arbitration is a transformative invention, which allows for a quicker and more cost-effective decision-making process by removing human intervention, in particular human errors and moral hazard. The value of Metaverse or blockchain is not merely as an advanced instrument for facilitating arbitration proceedings, but, at a more fundamental level, resides in its capacity to achieve a system of decentralized justice without the need for existing political and social institutions (Herian 2018). However, as further elaborated below, automated arbitration is unlikely to be an exemplary solution for disputes involving the application of more subjective and qualitative standards.

3. Enforcement of Arbitral Awards

This section focuses on the enforcement of arbitral awards in relation to the Metaverse, which is one of the most crucial steps in crystalizing the value of the award. To elaborate on this issue, we formulate three scenarios, each involving a greater level of involvement than the last for blockchain in the process of enforcement. Further, in each scenario, advantages and challenges are analyzed specifically in parallel with the NYC.

1) Scenario 1—Traditional Award + blockchain Technology

The award is issued by a traditional tribunal and specifies payment in cryptocurrency. The orders made in the award are recorded on the blockchain.

(1)Advantages

Given that the certification and authentication of award can be tracked and verified due to the immutability and traceability of blockchain, it is feasible that the award can be more efficiently recognized in the execution jurisdiction using blockchain evidence.

(2)Challenges/Limitations

As a starting point, the attitude of the jurisdiction where recognition and enforcement are sought towards cryptocurrency will be of decisive importance in the execution of the arbitral award. There are many jurisdictions expressing concerns regarding cryptocurrencies owing to the lack of regulatory oversight and potential tax evasion and money laundering concerns. For example, the Shenzhen Intermediate People's Court recently ordered that an arbitral award made by the Shenzhen Court of International Arbitration be set aside on the ground that awarding damages in USD/ RMB in lieu of cryptocurrency would be contrary to Chinese public policy (*Gao Zheyu v. Shenzhen Yunsilu Innovation Development Fund (Limited Partnership) & Lin Bin.* (2018) Yue 03 Min Te No. 719) . This ruling sends a clear warning that enforcing a crypto-related arbitral award may be difficult in China and raises questions as to whether same public policy reasoning could also apply to the recognition and enforcement of foreign awards under the NYC (Wang& Bai 2021).

Furthermore, scenario 1 is still trapped in the traditional legal mechanism for enforcing an award, i.e., pursuant to an international convention or mutual recognition. This means that enforcement is dependent upon the judicial machinery of the state and is only feasible in countries which are signatories to the NYC or where mutual recognition arrangements exist. To conclude, in this scenario, blockchain or Metaverse arbitration does not achieve fully automated enforcement, but only provides limited convenience in the conduct of traditional enforcement, ameliorating to some extent the unwieldy procedures involved in enforcing arbitral awards, especially cross-border awards.

2) Scenario 2— Traditional Award + Smart contract

The award is issued by a traditional tribunal and specifies payment in cryptocurrency. Parties have entered into a smart contract automating execution of the award. The orders made in the award are communicated by smart contract.

(1)Advantages

As discussed above, the true value of Metaverse arbitration lies not in providing technical convenience for execution, but in the self-enforcement of arbitral awards. The execution of a traditional award by smart contract comes closer to realizing this inherent value. It can make the enforcement of the award fully automated and ensure that the satisfaction of the award is not vulnerable to any delay or resistance from the debtor.

(2)Challenges

This model is theoretically appealing, but there are practical complexities. The parties must explicitly agree to place monetary amounts in escrow up to the quantum in dispute (Zhen, 2021). An analogy can be drawn between such commitments and interim measures, where parties are commonly required to advance guarantees as a condition of obtaining interim relief. Parties may be reluctant to agree to a system that locks up their assets in the name of securing automated enforcement of a hypothetical future dispute.

Another limitation is the narrow scope of application to the extent of binary disputes, where a decision is to be made between two alternatives. When it comes to "mixed" awards, calling for fulfillment of certain off-chain condition(s) before on-chain payment. Although some of the conditions can be tackled through a more sophisticated and sometimes multi-functional smart contract, it instills uncertainty and undermines the advantages of blockchain enforcement.

3) Scenario 3—Full on-chain Arbitration

The "full on-chain" arbitration means that the entire process of the arbitration occurs on the blockchain: the original transaction is recorded in blockchain, the adjudication is performed by randomly-chosen jurors and the award is to be enforced on an automated basis by virtue of a smart contract.

(1)Advantages

As with scenario 2, automated enforcement is core advantage of this approach. A "full on-chain" arbitration is an ambitious project and truly capable of providing a more efficient, affordable, and cost-effective dispute resolution *forum* for digital disputes. Some national courts have pioneered structural support systems. For example, Hangzhou Internet Court initially set up a blockchain platform (Hangzhou Blockchain net court 2017; Wood 2019), where eligible contracting parties could execute a smart contract to ensure automated enforcement. This initiative has improved the efficiency of enforcement proceedings, having reduced the rate of e-commerce platform disputes from 5% to less than 0.01% by July 2022 (Jing 2017).

(2)Challenges

Firstly, the type of dispute appropriate for resolution by blockchain is limited to binary disputes, while most real-world cases are more complex and multi-dimensional, necessitating subjective and qualitative consideration and thus adjudicatory discretion.

Secondly, the underlying technology to facilitate full on-chain arbitration is not yet mature and may not be sophisticated enough to solve complicated cases. The preparedness of parties as well as adjudicators to accept, utilize and adopt this novel form of arbitration is a work-in-progress.

Thirdly, there are concerns regarding the quality of awards rendered through on-chain arbitration and the level of justice achieved. Specifically, on-chain awards are determined by profit-driven adjudicators following a communal sense of what is fair and equitable rather than rigorous application of the law.

Finally, the enforceability of on-chain arbitral awards faces challenges under the NYC. One question is whether the arbitration agreements recorded in code fulfil the requirement under the NYC that the agreement must be *in writing* or concluded through *an exchange of letters or telegrams* (New York Convention 1958)[①]. Another challenge

---

① Article II of New York Convention: *"1. Each Contracting State shall recognize an agreement in writing ... 2. The term "agreement in writing" shall include an arbitral clause in a contract or an arbitration agreement, signed by the parties or contained in an exchange of letters or telegrams."*

is the determination of the seat of arbitration and the supervisory court, since the entire arbitration is conducted on-chain, with no physical hearings, or any tangible copies of the final award. In the absence of those elements, enforcing on-chain awards within the NYC framework is likely to be beset by controversy.

4) Summary

It is not necessarily the case that the greater the degree of automation introduced in the arbitration process, the better the result that will be achieved. Whilst parties using blockchain can benefit from easier access to more efficient and cost-effective forms of execution, this comes at the cost of certain practical difficulties, particularly when it comes to the enforcement of the award.

Concluding remarks

Blockchain provides a potential competitive advantage for arbitration, by making it more efficient and cost-effective in some circumstances. Yet it is equally important to realize the limitations of arbitration in the Metaverse, from the diverse judicial opinions as to the validity of Metaverse arbitration agreements, to the obstacles faced in enforcing Metaverse awards under the NYC, not to mention the immaturity of blockchain technology. This chapter concludes that it is pivotal to improve the value proposition of blockchain technology, for instance, by identifying particular kinds of disputes where on-chain arbitration could exert positive effects like high-volume and low-value disputes, while seeking co-ordination with rather than wholesale replacement of current mechanisms such as the NYC, so as to boost efficiency whilst streamlining the arbitration process.

Reference list:

[1] United Nations Commission on International Trade Law. (2017). UNCITRAL Technical Notes on Online Dispute Resolution. Available from: 〈https://uncitral.un.org/sites/uncitral.un.org/files/media-documents/uncitral/en/v1700382_english_technical_notes_on_odr.pdf〉. [19 December 2022].

[2] *Hangzhou Netease Leihuo Technology Co., Ltd. v. Hu, Yunhe* (2016) Zhe 01Min Xia Zhong No.1070 ; *Pu, Ping v. Hangzhou Youmai Technology Co., Ltd.* (2020) Su 04 Min Zhong No.999.

[3] *Xiao, Chong v. Beijing Baikeluoke Technology Co., Ltd* (2020) Jing 04 Min Te No.672; *Zhu, Lang v. Hangzhou Netease Yanxuan Trading Co., Ltd.* (2021) Su 08 Min Zhong No.2436.

[4] *Dialogue Consulting Pty Ltd v. Instagram, Inc.* (2020) FCA 1846;*Instagram Inc v. Dialogue Consulting Pty Ltd.* (2022) FCAFC 7; *Bridgecrest Acceptance Corporation v. Kelly Donaldson and Robert Haulcy* (2021) No. SC99269.

[5] *Schnabel v. Trilegiant Corp.* 697 F.3d 110, 120 (2d Cir. 2012), "inquiry notice" means the terms of the contract are reasonably communicated to the user such that a reasonably prudent person would be put on notice of the terms of the contract.

[6] *Scotti v. Tough Mudder Inc.* 63 Misc. 3d 84.

[7] Tauber, N., 'Blockchain and Evidence Law', *Legal Business World*, 2018, Available from: 〈 https://www.legalbusinessworld.com/post/2018/12/17/blockchain-and-evidence-law 〉 . [19 December 2022].

[8] Guangzhou Arbitration Commission 2020, *GAC's reaction towards the pandemic-Blockchain + online arbitration.* Available from: 〈 https://www.gzac.org/gzxw/741 〉 (only in Chinese). [19 December 2022].

[9] Greig, B., "What can mediators learn from Kleros, a platform which uses cryptocurrency and game theory to resolve disputes?", *Kluwer Mediation Blog,* 2022, Available from:〈 http:// mediationblog.kluwerarbitration.com/2022/03/06/what-can-mediators-learn-from-kleros-a-platform-which-uses-cryptocurrency-and-game-theory-to-resolve-disputes/ 〉 . [19 December 2022].

[10] Herian, R., "Taking blockchain seriously", *Law and Critique*, Vol. 29, No. 2, 2018, pp.163-171. Available from: 〈 https://doi.org/10.1007/s10978-018-9226-y 〉 . [19 December 2022].

[11] *Gao Zheyu v. Shenzhen Yunsilu Innovation Development Fund (Limited Partnership) & Lin Bin.* (2018) Yue 03 Min Te No. 719

[12] Wang, B.& Bai, X., "Award Concerning Bitcoin Exchange – Bit Too Risky to Enforce?" , *Kluwer Arbitratio* ■ *Blog*, 2021 Available from: 〈 http://arbitrationblog.kluwerarbitration. com/2021/04/02/award-concerning-bitcoin-exchange-bit-too-risky-to-enforce/ 〉 . [19 December 2022].

[13] Zhen, E., "Execution of Judgements on the Blockchain- A Practical Legal Commentary" , *Harv. J.L. & Tech. Dig, 2021* Available from: 〈 https://jolt.law.harvard.edu/digest/execution-of-judgements-on-the-blockchain-a-practical-legal-commentary 〉 . [19 December 2022].

[14] Hangzhou Blockchain Netcourt, Available from: 〈 https://blockchain.netcourt.gov.cn/ first 〉 , [19 December 2022]; Wood, M., "Chinese internet court adopts blockchain smart contracts, processes 1.9 bn transactions" , *Ledger Insights, Blockchain for business*, 2019,

Available from: 〈https://www.ledgerinsights.com/chinese-internet-court-blockchain-smart-contracts/〉. [19 December 2022].

[15] Jing, H., 'The Innovation and China's Contribution to the Internet Court', *China Legal Science*. Available from: 〈https://www.court.gov.cn/zixun-xiangqing-367851.html〉. [19 December 2022].

[16] New York Convention 1958 Article 2 states that "*1. Each Contracting State shall recognize an agreement in writing ... 2. The term "agreement in writing" shall include an arbitral clause in a contract or an arbitration agreement, signed by the parties or contained in an exchange of letters or telegrams.*"

第十三章

条约必须履行——近年来根据《纽约公约》在中国及其他地区（涉及中国）的执行案例

刘乐阳

仲裁裁决得到司法承认和执行是仲裁制度存在和发展的基础和依托。《纽约公约》是有关承认和执行外国仲裁裁决的国际条约中最重要的法律文件。中国政府于 1987 年 4 月 22 日加入了《纽约公约》。随着中国经济更加积极地融入世界经济，中国不仅面临着对越来越多的外国仲裁裁决的承认和执行问题，而且越来越多在中国境内作出的裁决需要得到外国法院的承认和执行。本章主要通过系统的案例分析的方法，介绍和分析《纽约公约》在中国的执行以及根据《纽约公约》在其他地区执行中国仲裁裁决的状况。

一、《纽约公约》关于承认和执行的相关条款

《纽约公约》第 5 条明确了缔约国法院得拒绝承认和执行外国仲裁裁决的理由，且第 1 款规定的 5 种情形是由当事人提出、法院才予以审查的理由，只有第 2 款规定的两种情形是法院可以依职权主动审查的理由。

根据中国加入《纽约公约》时所作的互惠保留声明，中国只在互惠的基础上对在另一缔约国领土内作出的仲裁裁决的承认和执行适用公约，这

意味着，中国实际上排除了对"非内国裁决"的执行。最高人民法院在（2016）最高法民他 11 号《关于保罗·赖因哈特公司向湖北省宜昌市中级人民法院申请承认和执行国际棉花协会在英国作出的仲裁裁决案给湖北省高级人民法院的复函》中，明确指出："人民法院对仲裁裁决是否存在《纽约公约》第 5 条第 1 款拒绝承认和执行的情形，必须依当事人的请求进行审查，当事人未请求的，人民法院不予审查；对仲裁裁决是否存在《纽约公约》第 5 条第 2 款规定的违反可仲裁性和公共政策情形，人民法院则可以依职权主动审查。"最高人民法院强调，只有存在《纽约公约》第 5 条规定的情形之一的，人民法院才能裁定拒绝承认和执行外国仲裁裁决，且对每项理由均予严格解释，以提高拒绝承认和执行外国仲裁裁决的门槛。以下分别介绍最高人民法院对《纽约公约》第 5 条规定的 7 种得拒绝承认和执行外国仲裁裁决理由的具体掌握情况。

中国是成文法传统国家，法院、法官必须根据法律的规定行事。《中华人民共和国民事诉讼法》（2021）第 290 条为外国仲裁裁决如何在中国得到承认和执行提供了基本法律依据。该条规定："国外仲裁机构的裁决，需要中华人民共和国人民法院承认和执行的，应当由当事人直接向被执行人住所地或者其财产所在地的中级人民法院申请，人民法院应当依照中华人民共和国缔结或者参加的国际条约，或者按照互惠原则办理。"

《中华人民共和国民事诉讼法》第 281 条规定，对中华人民共和国涉外仲裁机构作出的裁决，被申请人提出证据证明仲裁裁决有下列情形之一的，经人民法院组成合议庭审查核实，裁定不予执行：

（一）当事人在合同中没有订有仲裁条款或者事后没有达成书面仲裁协议的。

（二）被申请人没有得到指定仲裁员或者进行仲裁程序的通知，或者由于其他不属于被申请人负责的原因未能陈述意见的。

（三）仲裁庭的组成或者仲裁的程序与仲裁规则不符的。

（四）裁决的事项不属于仲裁协议的范围或者仲裁机构无权仲裁的。

（五）人民法院认定执行该裁决违背社会公共利益的，裁定不予执行。

可见，在涉外仲裁机构裁决的承认与执行的法律规定方面，《纽约公约》与中国法律对于有证据证明无有效仲裁协议的、未进行适当通知的、仲裁机关及仲裁程序不符合约定或者规定的、超裁的，以及违背公共利益的裁决，才可以不予执行。

二、近期《纽约公约》在中国的执行案例分析

1. 案例数据定量分析

通过检索威科先行法律数据库[①]，通过筛选共收集到 26 起于近三年结案的承认与执行外国仲裁裁决案件。从检索到的 26 起承认与执行外国仲裁裁决案件的审理结果来看，有三起案件的当事人在达成和解后，申请人撤诉；一起案件因被申请人主体错误、不符合受理条件而被驳回申请；一起因管辖权问题再审被撤销原裁定；一起案件申请人自愿撤回申请；一起案件部分支持了申请人承认与执行外国仲裁裁决的申请；剩下的 19 起案件的外国仲裁裁决得到了我国法院的承认与执行（其中三起案件只涉及承认不涉及执行）。

从这些案件的裁判结果来看，外国仲裁裁决在我国实现了较高的承认和执行率。从管辖法院来看，根据《民事诉讼法》第 304 条，申请承认、执行外国仲裁裁决的当事人应向被执行人住所地或者其财产所在地的中级人民法院申请。此外，根据《海事诉讼特别程序法》和相关司法解释，申请承认、执行外国海事仲裁裁决的，申请人应向被执行人的财产所在地或被执行人住所地海事法院提出。前文提到的 26 起案件中，5 起案件的受理法院是专门法院，即 1 起为金融法院、4 起为海事法院，21 起案件的受理法院是普

---

① https://www.wkinfo.com.cn/login/index.

通中级人民法院。从被申请人提出异议的依据来看，由于有10起案件被申请人因双方当事人达成和解或申请人撤案而未发表意见，在剩余16起案件中，针对被申请人提出的《纽约公约》第5条的异议统计如下：1起案件的被申请人提出了《纽约公约》第5条第1款（a）项的异议，14起案件的被申请人均提出了《纽约公约》第5条第1款（b）项的异议，7起案件的被申请人提出了《纽约公约》第5条第1款（c）项的异议，3起案件的被申请人提出了《纽约公约》第5条第1款（d）项的异议，3起案件的被申请人提出了《纽约公约》第5条第2款（e）项的异议。

从上述案件来看，近三年来我国法院对《纽约公约》第5条的理解和适用，总体上来看延续了以往的观点，如部分法院将仲裁协议存在与否视为事实问题审理、对程序性事项（未受适当通知或未能申辩、仲裁庭组成或仲裁程序与约定不符）的审理倚重证据和当事人约定、对公共政策进行严格解释等。同时我国法院在对《纽约公约》第5条第1款（c）项超裁的理解与适用上，与以往相比有所进步：一是从结果来看，7起被申请人提出超裁异议的案件，有6起法院认定仲裁庭未超裁；二是从审理思路来看，法院较为倚重仲裁规则对仲裁庭管辖权的规定，也较为尊重仲裁庭的管辖权认定。

2. 外国仲裁裁决在中国大陆不执行的原因

就近三年检索到的案例而言，仅有一例法院驳回了申请人的申请[（2017）鲁06民初382号]，主要是依据《纽约公约》第4条第1款第（a）项、第（b）项的规定，申请承认和执行裁决的申请人应当在申请时提供经正式认证的裁决正本或经正式证明的副本、仲裁协议正本或经正式证明的副本。前述规定中的裁决及仲裁协议应当是对申请人与被申请人具有约束力的仲裁裁决及仲裁协议，而申请人未提交充分证据证明仲裁裁决及合同的当事人为被申请人，不符合受理条件。

还有一例，被申请人的部分申请因符合《纽约公约》第5条第1款（c）

项的规定而裁定不予承认和执行[（2015）琼海法他字第1号]。因其中一个被申请人仅为案涉协议之一的缔约方，而非其他五份协议的缔约方，故其他五份协议中的仲裁条款对该被申请人不具有约束力。海口海事法院进而认定涉案裁决该被申请人就其他五份协议向申请人承担责任超出了仲裁协议约定的范围。因为超裁部分与有权裁决部分不可分，因此根据《纽约公约》第5条第1款第（c）项的规定，海口海事法院裁定，对于案涉仲裁裁决涉及该被申请人部分的裁决，应当不予承认和执行。

三、根据《纽约公约》在其他地区执行中国仲裁裁决

1. 案例数据分析

通过检索 Westlaw Classic 法律在线数据库，共检索到11起于近10年结案的外国承认与执行我国仲裁裁决的案件。从检索到的11起承认与执行我国仲裁裁决案件的审理结果来看，有一起在上诉阶段被发回重审，两起因未向被申请人充分通知仲裁程序而不予承认和执行，两起案件因违反其他规定被驳回申请，剩余六起案件获得确认（其中一起案件部分承认部分拒绝），从裁判结果来看，我国仲裁裁决在国外的承认与执行率达到了50%以上，足以印证我国涉外仲裁案件的质量逐步受到其他国家的认可。从被申请承认与执行的仲裁裁决作出机构来看，主要是中国国际经济贸易仲裁委员会作出的仲裁裁决。从不予承认和执行中国仲裁裁决的原因来看，主要是仲裁程序通知不当。

2. 外国法院认为中国仲裁裁决的主要异议和执行情况

在收集到的11个中国作出的仲裁裁决在其他国家执行的案例中，有10个案例都受到被申请人的异议，这说明，中国作出的仲裁裁决在国外的执行确实充满挑战。从被承认和执行的情况来看，那些不被支持的异议主要集中

于对于中国的仲裁程序和规则、仲裁范围、基本的仲裁程序以及违背中国或者执行国的公共政策。由此可见，申请执行国很少基于中国的仲裁机构的程序和规则以及公共政策相关的异议拒绝承认和执行中国的仲裁裁决。例如，在 21-CV-84 案件中，被申请人认为 CIETAC 作出的裁决违背了《纽约公约》第 5 条第 1 款第（d）项：仲裁没有按照中国国际经济贸易仲裁委员会自己的程序和规则进行；第（c）项：裁决包括律师费，超出了双方仲裁协议的范围以及第 2 款第（b）项：违反美国的公共政策。但是，美国纽约地方法院并没有支持被申请人 New Monarch Machine Tool，Inc. 的拒绝承认和执行的请求。

在收集到的 11 个案例中，有 5 起案件没有得到充分的承认和执行。外国法院认为，中国仲裁裁决不能得到承认和执行的主要原因包括三个方面。第一，对仲裁协议有效性的不恰当确定。例如，在 21-3143 号案件中，被申请人根据《纽约公约》第 5 条第 1 款第（d）项提出异议，认为 CIETAC 上海分会作出的裁决无可执行的仲裁协议。针对 CIETAC 作出的仲裁裁决，美国上诉法院，第三巡回法院不同意双方的论点，其认为"首先，《联邦仲裁法》（FAA）第 2 章要求地区法院独立确定是否存在仲裁协议，即使外国的仲裁庭已经作出了裁决。法院不必也不应该服从外国专家组对可仲裁性的裁定，因为这将使执行《纽约公约》第 4 条规定的裁决的先决条件变得多余，并使他们成为毫无意义的手续；其次，中国法院裁定，根据中国国内法，7 月谅解备忘录是可以执行的，但没有分析以下单独问题: (a) 根据《纽约公约》第 4 条，仲裁裁决是否需要在外国得到确认，或 (b) 当事人的电子邮件往来是否符合第 2 条的'书面'要求。虽然美国法院在许多情况下会承认外国的司法行为，根据国际礼让原则，外国法院无权就法院未裁决的问题享有礼让；最后，被申请人并没有因为同时反对在中国仲裁而放弃其由美国法院就可仲裁性作出独立裁决的权利"。如果一方当事人反对可仲裁性，但仍参与仲裁程序，则不推定放弃对仲裁管辖权的质疑。因此，地区法院正确的裁定不受中国仲裁庭裁决的约束，被申请人并未放弃其对执行提出异议的权利，决定发回重审，发回重审后区域法院应根据指示就可仲裁性作出独立决定。

第二，初步仲裁通知不充分。仲裁程序通知不当是国外法院不支持中国仲裁裁决的最主要原因。在 5 项没有被充分执行的案例中，有 3 个案例都是因为被申请人对仲裁通知程序提出了异议（SACV 21–441 PSG；2：20–cv–08412–RGK–JC；15–1256）。其中，15–1256 号案例最为典型。在这一案例中，被申请人 LUMOS 提出异议认为，根据纽约公约第 5 条第 1 款第（b）项，被申请人未收到仲裁程序的通知，且仲裁当局的组成或仲裁程序不符合当事各方的约定。美国上诉法院第十巡回法院认为"中文通知的计算不合理，无法向被申请人通报诉讼程序。申请人和被申请人之间之前所有的通信都是英文，合同要求以英语作为双方沟通的语言，协议要求双方所有互动和争议解决程序都将以英文进行。通知发出近一个月后，申请人回复被申请人的一封电子邮件，用简短的英文解释说中文文件构成通知。因此，申请人表示其本可以用被申请人能够理解的语言发出通知，简单地说，申请人不可能合理地计算出用被申请人高管无法理解的语言向被申请人通报仲裁程序的时间。根据这些事实，我们的结论是，中文通知没有合理地计算向被申请人通报贸仲程序"。因此，美国上诉法院第十巡回法院根据《纽约公约》第 5 条第 1 款第（b）项"受裁决约束的执行对象未接获关于指派仲裁员或仲裁程序之适当通知，或因他故，致未能申辩者"的规定作出了不予支持仲裁裁决的的决定。

第三，仲裁庭组成或仲裁程序不当。在搜集到的 11 个案例中，有一个中国作出的裁决没有得到全部支持的理由是仲裁庭组成不当。在民事诉讼第 13–276 号案件中，被申请人 ACC RESOURCES CO. 认为，根据《纽约公约》第 5 条第 1 款第（b）项：被申请人没有机会向北京专家组辩称上海裁决无效；《纽约公约》第 5 条第 1 款第（c）项：北京专家组就上海裁决达成的结论超出了提交北京仲裁小组仲裁的范围；《纽约公约》第 5 条第 1 款第（d）项：北京专家组作出的仲裁裁决与当事人的合同不符。美国宾夕法尼亚州地区法院认为"针对被申请人的第一项抗辩，被申请人没有证据证明其因没有收到北京专家组正在考虑上海裁决作为证据的通知而受到损害，被申请人也不会因为北京专家组没有向被申请人发出通知以及没有充分和公平的陈述机会而受到损害；针对被申请人的第二项抗辩，北京专家组在确定被申请人必须向申请人支付剩余 30% 价款并未超出提交仲裁的范围；针对被申请人的第三项抗辩，没有证据证明被申请人知道上海宣布独立于中国国际经济贸易仲裁委员会以及该行动的后果，被申请人在可以质疑上海裁决的时间内，被申请人未能举出足够的证据证明它因北京专家组不遵守合同约定而受到损害"。因此，申请人申请执行的裁决不符合《纽约公约》第 5 条第 1 款第（b）项"受裁决约束的执行对象未接获关于指派仲裁员或仲裁程序之适当通知，或因他故，致未能申辩者"、第（c）项"裁决所处理的争议非为交付仲裁之标的或不在其条款之列，或裁决载有关于交付仲裁范围以外事项之决定者，但交付仲裁事项之决定可与未交付仲裁之事项划分时，裁决中关于交付仲裁事项之决定部分得予以承认及执行"及第（d）项"仲裁机关之组成或仲裁程序与各当事人之间的协议不符，或无协议、与仲裁地所在国法律不符"的规定。但对于申请人要求律师费的请求，法院认为被申请人的起诉并未达到"非常高的标准"，不属于"恶意、无理取闹或出于压迫性原因提起诉讼"，且扣留所欠申请人款项并非没有正当理由，因此法院最终决定，驳回申请人关于律师费的请求，承认与执行 CIETAC 作出的裁决。

四、外国仲裁裁决的执行展望

1. 合同订立阶段

首先，仲裁条款的正确订立有利于提高权利主张的效率。有效的仲裁条款是仲裁机构能够行使管辖权的基本前提，《纽约公约》及我国民事诉讼法关于涉外仲裁裁决执行的规定方面均不承认、执行没有仲裁协议的裁决。

在仲裁条款的订立方面也需要注意仲裁条款无效情形，不同国家在仲裁条款效力认定方面存在一定差异，虽然越来越多的国家加入了《纽约公约》，但依然有国家不受《纽约公约》的约束，这就需要在订立仲裁条款之前了解意向仲裁地仲裁法的具体规定。

其次，约定有效的送达地址有利于建立畅通的纠纷解决通道。仲裁文件的有效送达是当事人权利保障的前提。《纽约公约》和我国民诉法都规定受裁决约束的执行对象未获得关于指派仲裁员或仲裁程序之适当通知，导致未能陈述意见的裁决不予执行。上述案例的定量分析也可以发现大部分承认与执行外国仲裁裁决案件中被申请人都主张仲裁庭未进行有效送达，导致无法有效申辩。因此，在合同订立阶段就需要约定有效的送达地址。

2. 仲裁阶段

在仲裁阶段，为了保障仲裁裁决的执行，需要做好材料文书的准备工作。《纽约公约》对于材料文书的准备有明确规定。根据其第4条第1款规定，申请人应当提交原裁判正本或其正式副本、仲裁协议之原本或其正式副本。如果前述文件所用文字不是申请与执行地所在国正式文字的，还应提交由公设或宣誓之翻译员或外交或领事人员认证的译本。所以需要做好材料文书的收集、准备工作。

同时，在实践中，可能会出现申请人地址无效、无法送达、恶意拒签等情况。此时，申请人可聘用仲裁执行地律师委托公证机构向被申请人进行公证送达，可有效防止被申请人以未送达为理由提出执行异议。同时，申请人向仲裁机构提交仲裁申请或者向被申请人送达仲裁通知时应附上英文翻译，以防止被申请人以语言不通为由提出抗辩。

3. 中国仲裁法修订后临时仲裁的前景

临时仲裁（Ad-hoc Arbitration）是相对于熟知的机构仲裁（Institutional

Arbitration）的一个概念。临时仲裁中，当事人无须受制于某个特定的仲裁机构管理。他们可以以更加灵活、自由的方式，根据他们的需要量身定做仲裁协议，并将争议提交给他们临时组成的仲裁庭进行审理。仲裁最早就是以临时仲裁的方式出现的，随后逐渐产生出机构仲裁。而机构仲裁的蓬勃发展并未能削弱临时仲裁的生命力。现如今，在以西方欧洲国家为代表的众多国家和地区，如德国、美国、意大利等，以"双轨并行"的模式在其仲裁制度下明确了临时仲裁；而以葡萄牙、希腊为代表的少数国家，则将临时仲裁作为主要的仲裁形式在全国范围内推行。《纽约公约》第1条第2款对临时仲裁也明确约定，即"本公约所述'仲裁裁决'不仅包括由每一案件指定的仲裁员所作出的裁决；同样也包括当事人将争议提交的仲裁机构所作出的裁决"。

与国际通常做法不同，我国现行《仲裁法》是以机构仲裁为主体，并不认可"临时仲裁"。但这并不表明我国完全禁止临时仲裁。对于域外临时仲裁而言，我国作为《纽约公约》缔约国，有义务对外国临时仲裁裁决予以承认与执行。随着我国仲裁制度的发展，"一带一路"倡议的推行，我国《仲裁法》与国际接轨的必要性日渐凸显。中国也开始就"临时仲裁"的制度构建进行了一系列探索。2016年12月，在自贸区运行三周年之际，最高院发布《最高人民法院关于为自贸试验区建设提供司法保障的意见》（以下简称《司法保障的意见》）。《司法保障的意见》第9.3条规定："在自贸试验区内注册的企业相互之间约定在内地特定地点、按照特定仲裁规则、由特定人员对有关争议进行仲裁，可以认定该仲裁协议有效。"该项规定突破了现行《仲裁法》对于有效的仲裁协议应当包括"明确约定的仲裁委员会"的要求，允许各级法院认可自贸试验区企业之间约定在"特定地点"、按照"特定仲裁规则"并由"特定人员"仲裁（以下简称"特定仲裁"）的仲裁协议。换句话说，《司法保障的意见》通过该种方式实质上承认了在自贸区进行临时仲裁协议的有效性。为更好地与最高院《司法保障意见》接轨，有效推进临时仲裁落地，满足当事人实际需求，最高院发布了一系列意见以规范和深化规制"特定仲裁"。虽然临时仲裁制度尚未完善，但中国政府的支持和市场的支持已经呈现。

在对"临时仲裁"经年的积极探索和制度铺垫的大背景下，2021 年 7 月 30 日《仲裁法征求意见稿》正式公布，其中便引入了"临时仲裁"制度。

临时仲裁作为仲裁的基本方式之一，在长期的历史发展过程中，对于民商事争议纠纷的解决发挥着重要的作用；对于未来，它也能够积极面对现代经济生活而担当应有的角色。由于历史以及社会政治经济体制等原因，我国没有承认和建立临时仲裁制度，导致机构仲裁一枝独秀。随着社会政治经济体制的巨变和经济全球一体化，缺少临时仲裁制度的弊端日益显现和严重。尽快在我国确立和完善临时仲裁制度不仅是社会主义市场经济体制发展和完善的需要，也是仲裁制度乃至整个法律制度健全的需要。临时仲裁制度的建立，不仅将增加经济生活的参与者对于争议纠纷解决方式的选择机会，也有利于促进机构仲裁制度自身的进一步完善，最终使仲裁制度以一个完善的整体服务于社会，促进国内和国际经济贸易的健康发展。

Chapter 13

Treaty Must Be Performed — Recent Enforcement Cases under the New York Convention in China and Beyond (Involving China)

Leyang Liu

Judicial recognition and enforcement of arbitral awards are fundamental requirements for development of an arbitration system. *The New York Convention* is the most important legal document among international treaties on the recognition and enforcement of foreign arbitral awards. The People's Republic of China acceded to *the New York Convention* on April 22nd,1987, declaring it would reserve the rights of "reciprocity reservation" and "commercial reservation". As China more vigorously integrates into the world economy, China needs recognition and enforcement of an increasing number of foreign arbitral awards, and simultaneously, a growing number of awards made in China need to be recognized and enforced by foreign courts.

This chapter introduces and analyzes the enforcement of *the New York Convention* in China and the status of enforcement of Chinese arbitral awards in other regions under *the New York Convention* through a systematic case study approach.

1. Relevant Provisions of the New York Convention on Recognition and Enforcement of Foreign Arbitral Awards

Article V of *the New York Convention* specifies the conditions under which the court of a Contracting State may refuse to recognize and enforce a foreign arbitral award. The five conditions outlined in paragraph 1 are raised by the parties and only reviewed by the court. The two conditions outlined in paragraph 2 Article V are the only conditions that the court *ex officio* can review on its own initiative.

According to the declaration of reciprocity made by China upon signing *the New York Convention*, China applies the Convention only to the recognition and enforcement of arbitral awards made in the territory of another Contracting State on the basis of reciprocity. This means that China *de facto* excludes the enforcement of "non-domestic awards" as defined in Article I (2) of *the New York Convention*.

In terms of the applicable domestic laws, China is a country with a statutory tradition, and courts and judges must act following the provisions of the law. Article 290 of *the Civil Procedure Law of the People's Republic of China* (2021) provides the essential legal basis for how foreign arbitral awards can be recognized and enforced in China. This article provides that: "If an award of a foreign arbitral institution requires recognition and enforcement by the people's courts of the People's Republic of China, the parties shall apply directly to the intermediate people's court of the place of the person subjected to execution or the place where his property is located, and the people's court shall handle the application in accordance with the international treaties concluded or participated by the People's Republic of China, or in accordance with the principle of reciprocity."

Article 281 of the *Civil Procedure Law of the People's Republic of China* specifies that where an award made by a foreign arbitration institution in the People's Republic of China is proven by the respondent to have one of the following circumstances, the People's Court shall, after examination and verification by a collegial panel, adjudge that the award shall not be enforced:

(1) The parties did not have an arbitration clause in the contract or did not reach a written arbitration agreement afterwards.

(2) The respondent has not been notified of the appointment of the arbitrator or of

the conduct of the arbitration proceedings, or was unable to present its case for reasons that are not attributed to the respondent's responsibility.

(3) The composition of the arbitral tribunal or the arbitration procedure is not in accordance with the arbitration rules.

(4) The matter to be arbitrated does not fall within the scope of the arbitration agreement, or the arbitration institution does not have the competence to arbitrate.

(5) If the People's Court concludes that the enforcement of the award is contrary to the public interest, it shall rule that it shall not be enforced.

In general, there is consistency between *the New York Convention* and Chinese law with respect to the legal provisions on the recognition and enforcement of foreign arbitral awards. The courts do not support the enforcement of foreign related awards without evidence of a valid arbitration agreement, without proper notice to the parties, or where the arbitration tribunal and the arbitration procedure do not comply with the agreement or the provisions, or if the award is beyond the scope of arbitration agreement, or if it is contrary to the public interest.

2. Analysis of Recent Enforcement Cases of the New York Convention in China

1) Analysis of Cases

By searching the Wolters Kluwer Legal Database (威科先行)[①], we have collected 26 cases of recognition and enforcement of foreign arbitral awards closed in the last three years. In three of these cases, the parties withdrew their claims after reaching a conciliation. One case was rejected because the respondent's subject matter was wrong and did not meet the admissibility requirements; one case in which the original decision was reversed following a retrial on jurisdictional issues; one case where the applicant voluntarily withdrew the application. In the remaining 19 cases, the foreign arbitral awards were recognized and enforced by Chinese courts (three of which involved only recognition and not enforcement).

---

① https://www.wkinfo.com.cn/login/index.

From the analytical results of these cases, it is clear that foreign arbitral awards have achieved a high rate of recognition and enforcement in China. In terms of the jurisdictional court, according to Article 304 of *the Civil Procedure Law*, the party applying for recognition or enforcement of a foreign arbitral award shall apply to the intermediate people's court of the place of the person subjected to execution or the place where its property is located. In addition, according to *the Maritime Litigation Special Procedures Law* and relevant judicial interpretations, if an application for recognition or enforcement of a foreign maritime arbitral award is made, the applicant shall submit it to the marine court at the place where the property of the person subjected to execution is located or where he is domiciled. Of the 26 cases mentioned earlier, five cases were handled by specialized courts, i.e., one was a financial court, four were maritime courts, and 21 cases were handled by general intermediate people's courts. In terms of the reasons for the respondents' objections, there were 10 cases in which the respondents did not submit comments because the parties reached a settlement or the applicant withdrew the case. In the remaining 16 cases, the objections raised by the respondents under Article V of the New York Convention are as follows: one case in which the respondent raised the objection following Article V(1)(a) of the New York Convention; 14 cases in which the respondents filed objections following Article V(1)(b) of the New York Convention; 7 cases in which the respondents filed objections following Article V(1)(c) of the New York Convention; three cases in which the respondents filed objections following Article V(1)(d) of the New York Convention; three cases in which the respondents raised objections following Article V(2)(b) of the New York Convention.

From the case analysis results, the application of Article V of *the New York Convention* by Chinese courts in the past three years is generally consistent with the previous views. For example, some courts consider the existence of an arbitration agreement as a question of legal fact, rely on evidence and party agreement for procedural matters (lack of proper notice or failure to defend, the composition of the arbitral tribunal or inconsistency with the arbitration procedure), and strictly interpret public policy. Meanwhile, compared to the past, Chinese courts have improved their understanding and application of Article V(1)(c) of the New York Convention for matters beyond the scope. On the one hand, in terms of the results, in six of the seven cases where the respondent challenged beyond the scope of the award, the court found that the tribunal did not exceed the scope. On the other hand, from the viewpoint of hearings, the court relied more on the arbitration rules on the jurisdiction of the arbitral tribunal, and also respect for the tribunal's jurisdictional determination.

2) Reasons for Non-enforcement of Foreign Arbitral Awards in China

With respect to the cases retrieved in the past three years, there is only one case where the court rejected the applicant's enforcement application [(2017) 鲁 06 民 初 382 号]. The rejection was based primarily on the provisions of Article IV(1)(a) and (b) of the New York Convention, i.e., the party applying for recognition and enforcement shall supply the duly authenticated original award or a duly certified copy thereof and the original agreement or a duly certified copy thereof. In this case, the arbitration agreement was binding. However, the applicant did not submit sufficient evidence to prove that the parties to the arbitration award and contract were the respondent and did not meet the conditions of admissibility.

There is also a case [(2015) 琼海法他字第 1 号] where part of the respondent's application was not recognized or enforced on the basis of Article V(1)(c) of the New York Convention. Because one of the respondents was a party to only one of the agreements at issue, and not to the other five sub-agreements. Therefore, the arbitration clauses in the other five agreements are not binding on the respondent. The Haikou Maritime Court concluded that the respondent's liability to the claimant for the other five agreements was beyond the scope of the arbitration agreement. Because the parts beyond the scope were indistinguishable from the entitled parts, following the provisions of Article V(1)(c) of the New York Convention, the Haikou Maritime Court decided that the arbitral award should not be recognized and enforced in respect of the respondent's portion of the award.

3. Enforcement of Chinese Arbitration Awards in Other Regions under the New York Convention

1) Analysis of Cases

A search of the Westlaw Classic legal online database yielded 11 cases of foreign recognition and enforcement of Chinese arbitral awards in the last ten years. Of the 11 cases, one case was remanded at the appeal stage, two cases were not recognized and enforced because the respondent was not given sufficient notice of the arbitration proceedings, two cases were dismissed for violation of other provisions, and the remaining six cases were recognized (one of which was partially recognized and partially rejected). In terms of adjudication results, the recognition and enforcement rate of China's arbitral awards abroad has reached over 50%, indicating that other countries gradually recognize China's foreign-related arbitration awards. In terms of the institutions that have been applied for recognition and enforcement of arbitral awards, the main one is CIETAC. In terms of the reasons for not recognizing and enforcing Chinese arbitral awards, the main reason given in these cases is an improper notice of the arbitration proceedings.

2) **Main Deficiencies of Chinese Arbitral Awards as Perceived by Foreign Courts**

Of the 11 cases collected on the enforcement of arbitral awards made in China in other countries, 10 of them were objected to by the respondents, suggesting that the enforcement of arbitral awards made in China abroad is indeed fraught with challenges. In terms of the awards that were recognized and enforced, objections that were not supported centered on challenges to the Chinese arbitration proceedings and rules, the scope of the arbitration, the arbitration procedures, and the violation of the public policy of China or the country of enforcement. It suggests that applicant-enforcing countries rarely refuse to recognize and enforce Chinese arbitral awards based on the procedures and rules of Chinese arbitral institutions and on public policy-related objections. For example, in Case 21-CV-84, the respondent argued that the award made by CIETAC was contrary to Article V(1)(c)(d) and Article V(1)(b) of *the New York Convention*. However, the U.S. District Court in New York did not support the respondent's request for refusal of recognition and enforcement.

Of the 11 cases reviewed, 5 cases were not fully recognized and enforced. There were several reasons why Chinese arbitral awards were not recognized and enforced.

First, inappropriate determination of the validity of the arbitration agreement. For example, in Case No. 21-3143, the respondent objected under Article V(1)(d) of *the*

New York Convention, arguing that the award made by the Shanghai Sub-Commission of CIETAC had no enforceable arbitration agreement. The U.S. Court of Appeals, Third Circuit disagree with each contention. It upheld that "First, Chapter 2 of the FAA requires a district court 'to determine independently the existence of an agreement to arbitrate even though an arbitration panel in a foreign state already had rendered an award.' A court need not, and should not, defer to a foreign panel's finding of arbitrability because this would 'render the prerequisites to enforcement of an award set forth in Article IV of the New York Convention superfluous' and make them 'a meaningless formality.'; Second, the Chinese Court determined that the July MOU was enforceable under Chinese domestic law but did not analyze the separate issues of (a) whether an arbitration award would be subject to confirmation in a foreign nation under Article IV of the New York Convention or (b) whether the parties' email exchange satisfies the 'writing' requirement of Article II. While United States courts will in many cases 'give effect to ... judicial acts of a foreign nation' under principles of international comity, a foreign court is 'not entitled to comity on issues the court did not decide.'; Third, Angle World did not waive its right to an independent ruling on arbitrability by a United States court because it contemporaneously objected to arbitration in China. 'Where a party objects to arbitrability but nevertheless participates in the arbitration proceedings, waiver of the challenge to arbitral jurisdiction will not be inferred.' Accordingly, the District Court correctly determined that it was not bound by the decisions of Chinese tribunals and that Angle World did not waive its right to contest enforcement." and decided to remand for a new hearing. On remand, the District Court should make an independent determination as to arbitrability in accordance with our instructions above.

Second, inadequate initial notice of arbitration. Improper notice of arbitration proceedings is the most important reason why foreign courts do not support Chinese arbitration awards. Of the five cases that were not fully enforced, three were due to the respondent's objection to the notice of arbitration proceedings (SACV 21-441 PSG; 2: 20-cv-08412-RGK-JC; 15-1256). The case (#15-1256) is the most typical among them. In this case, the respondent LUMOS objected that it had not received notice of the arbitration proceedings under Article V(1)(b) of *the New York Convention* and that the composition of the arbitration tribunal or the arbitration proceedings were not following the agreement of the parties. The U.S. Court of Appeals for the Tenth Circuit held that "the Chinese-language notice was not reasonably calculated to apprise LUMOS of the proceedings. All previous communications between CEEG and LUMOS had been in English, the Contract reinforced that English would govern the relationship by requiring that the English language version of the Contract would control, and the Agreement memorialized the parties' understanding that all interactions and dispute resolution proceedings would be in English. Nearly a month after the notice had been sent, CEEG responded to an email from LUMOS with a short English-language explanation that the Chinese documents constituted notice. Thus, CEEG demonstrated the ease with which it could have sent notice in a language it knew LUMOS would understand. Simply, CEEG could not have reasonably calculated that notice in a language it knew LUMOS' executives would be unable to comprehend would apprise LUMOS of the arbitration proceedings. On these facts, we conclude that notice in Chinese was not reasonably calculated to apprise LUMOS of the CIETAC proceedings." Accordingly, the U.S. Court of Appeals for the Tenth Circuit relied on article V(1)(b) of *the New York Convention* provides that enforcement of an award may be refused when "The party against whom the award is invoked was not given proper notice of the appointment of the arbitrator or of the arbitration proceedings or was otherwise unable to present his case" issued a decision not to enforce the arbitration award.

Third, improper composition of the arbitral tribunal or arbitration procedures. Of the 11 cases collected, one award made by China was not fully upheld because the tribunal was improperly constituted. In the case Civil Action No. 13-276, the Respondent ACC Resources. objected that under Article V(1)(b) of the New York Convention, the Respondent had no opportunity to defend the invalidity of the Shanghai Award to the Beijing Panel; Article V(1)(c) of the New York Convention, the conclusions reached by the Beijing Panel on the Shanghai Award were beyond the scope of the arbitration referred to the Beijing Arbitration Panel; Article V(1)(d) of the New York Convention, the arbitral award made by the Beijing panel was not in line with the parties' contract. The U.S. District Court for the District of Pennsylvania held that "For the respondent's first defense, ACC submitted three statements from CIETAC about the Shanghai sub-commission declaring its independence from CIETAC and the ramifications of that action, but there is no evidence of record that ACC knew about the statements or their contents at a time during which ACC could have objected to the Beijing panel's reliance upon the Shanghai award. Without that kind of evidence, ACC cannot show it was prejudiced by not receiving notice that the Beijing panel was considering the Shanghai award as evidence. Under those circumstances, there could not have been a factual dispute in need of resolution by the Beijing panel and ACC could not be prejudiced by the Beijing panel failing to provide ACC notice and a full and fair opportunity to be heard. ACC's reliance on the Article V(1)(b) defense will not, therefore, preclude the entry of summary judgment in favor of Calbex;For the respondent's secend defense,act beyond the scope of the submission of arbitration when it determined that ACC was required to pay Calbex the remaining 30% of the purchase price of the 2010 contract; For the respondent's third defense,because there is no evidence of record that—even if the Beijing panel provided ACC notice and a full and fair opportunity to be heard—ACC knew about Shanghai declaring its independence from CIETAC and the ramifications of that action within a time it could have challenged the Shanghai award, ACC failed to adduce evidence sufficient to show it was prejudiced by the Beijing panel's failure to abide by Article 41(3). Based upon the foregoing, ACC's reliance on the Article V(1)(d) defense will not preclude the entry of summary judgment in favor of Calbex. "Therefore, the award applied for enforcement by the applicant was not in conformity with article V(1)(b) of the New York Convention provides that enforcement of an award may be refused when "The party against whom the award is invoked was not given proper notice of the appointment of the arbitrator or of the arbitration proceedings or was otherwise unable to present his case"; (c) "The award deals with a difference not contemplated by or not falling within the terms of the submission to arbitration, or it contains decisions on matters beyond the scope of the submission to arbitration, provided that, if the decisions on matters submitted to arbitration can be separated from those not so submitted, that part of the award which contains decisions on matters submitted to arbitration may be recognized and enforced"; (d) "The award deals with a difference not contemplated by or not falling within the term "The composition of the arbitral authority or the arbitral procedure was not in accordance with the agreement of the parties, or, failing such agreement, was not in accordance with the law of the country where the arbitration took place". However, with regard to the applicant's request for attorneys' fees, the court held that the respondent's lawsuit did not meet a "very high standard", did not constitute a "malicious, vexatious or oppressive lawsuit", and that the withholding of the money owed to the applicant was not without justification. Ultimately decided that "Calbex's motion for summary judgment (ECF No. 31) will be granted in part and denied in part. The motion for summary judgment will be denied with respect to Calbex's request for attorneys' fees. The motion for summary judgment will be granted in all other respects. The Beijing award will be confirmed."

4. Prospects for the Enforcement of Foreign Arbitral Awards

1) Contract Formation Stage

First of all, the correct formulation of the arbitration clause is essential to improve the efficiency of the claim. A valid arbitration clause is a critical prerequisite in an arbitral institution to be able to exercise jurisdiction. Neither *the New York Convention* nor the provisions of *China's Civil Procedure Law* on the enforcement of foreign arbitral awards recognize and enforce awards without an arbitration agreement. The New York Convention and the Civil Procedure Law of China do not recognize and enforce awards without an arbitration agreement with respect to the enforcement of foreign arbitral awards. It is also necessary to pay attention to the invalidity of the arbitration clause at the time of its formation. There are some differences in the validity of arbitration clauses in different countries. Although an increasing number of countries have signed up to the New York Convention, there are still countries that are not bound by the New York Convention, requiring knowledge of the specific provisions of the arbitration law of the intended place of arbitration prior to signing the arbitration clause.

Second, the agreement of a valid delivery address is conducive to establishing a smooth dispute resolution channel. The effective delivery of arbitration documents is a prerequisite for the protection of the rights of the parties. Both the New York Convention and our Civil Procedure Law provide that an award is not to be enforced if the person against whom the enforcement is sought has not been given proper notice of the appointment of an arbitrator or of the arbitration proceedings, resulting in a failure of presentation. The analysis of the above cases also reveals that in most cases of recognition and enforcement of foreign arbitral awards, the respondents claim that the arbitral tribunal failed to make effective delivery, resulting in the inability to plead the case effectively. Therefore, it is necessary to agree on a valid address for service at the contract formation stage.

2) Arbitration Stage

During the arbitration stage, the preparation of material documents is required in order to guarantee the enforcement of the arbitral award. *The New York Convention* has explicit provisions for the preparation of material instruments. According to Article IV (1), "the party applying for recognition and enforcement shall supply the duly authenticated original award or a duly certified copy thereof and the original agreement referred to in article II or a duly certified copy thereof. If the said award or agreement is not made in an official language of the country in which the award is relied upon, the party applying for recognition and enforcement of the award shall produce a translation of these documents into such language. The translation shall be certified by an official or sworn translator or by a diplomatic or consular agent." Therefore, the parties need to do a good job of collecting and preparing the material documents.

Meanwhile, in practice, there may be cases where the applicant's address is invalid, undeliverable, and malicious refusal to sign. In this case, the claimant can hire a lawyer in the place of arbitration enforcement to appoint a notary to make notarized delivery to the respondent, which can effectively prevent the respondent from objecting to the enforcement for the reason of non-delivery. In addition, the applicant should submit the arbitration application to the arbitration institution or deliver the notice of arbitration to the respondent with an English translation in order to prevent the respondent from defending on the ground of a language barrier.

3) Prospects for Ad Hoc Arbitration after the Revision of the Chinese Arbitration Law

Ad hoc arbitration is a concept used in comparison to the familiar institutional arbitration. In *ad hoc* arbitration, the parties are not subject to the administration of a particular arbitration institution. They can customize their arbitration agreements to their needs in a more flexible and free-form manner and submit disputes to their *ad hoc* constituted tribunal for arbitration. Arbitration first emerged as *ad hoc* arbitration, and then gradually institutional arbitration arose. The boom in institutional arbitration has not diminished the vitality of *ad hoc* arbitration. Today, many countries and regions, represented by Western countries, such as Germany, the United States, Italy, etc., have adopted a "dual-track" model in which *ad hoc* arbitration is specified under their arbitration systems. In contrast, a few countries, represented by Portugal and Greece, have introduced *ad hoc* arbitration as the main form of arbitration on a national level. Article I (2) of the New York Convention also explicitly stipulates for *ad hoc* arbitration, i.e., "The term 'arbitral awards' shall include not only awards made by arbitrators appointed for each case but also those made by permanent arbitral bodies to which the parties have submitted."

Unlike the usual international practice, China's current Arbitration Law is mainly based on institutional arbitration and does not recognize *ad hoc* arbitration. However, this does not indicate that *ad hoc* arbitration is completely prohibited in China. In the case of foreign *ad hoc* arbitration, China, as a party to *the New York Convention*, is obliged to recognize and enforce foreign *ad hoc* arbitral awards. With the development of China's arbitration institution and the "One Belt, One Road" initiative, the need for China's Arbitration Law to be in line with international standards has become increasingly evident. China has also begun a series of explorations on the institutional framework for *ad hoc* arbitration. In December 2016, the Supreme Court issued the Opinions of the Supreme People's Court on Providing Judicial Guarantees for the Construction of the Pilot Free Trade Zone (referred to as "Opinions on Judicial Guarantees"). Article 9.3 of the Opinions on Judicial Guarantees provides that "if enterprises registered in the Pilot Free Trade Zone agree among themselves to arbitrate the relevant disputes at a specific location in the Mainland, in accordance with specific arbitration rules and by specific personnel, the arbitration agreement may be deemed valid." This provision breaks the current Arbitration Law's requirement that a valid arbitration agreement should include a "clearly agreed arbitration committee" and allows courts at all levels to recognize arbitration agreements between enterprises in the Free Trade Pilot Zone that agree to arbitrate in a "specific place", under "specific arbitration rules" and by "specific personnel" (referred to as "specific arbitration"). In other words, the Opinions on Judicial Guarantees substantially recognizes the validity of *ad hoc* arbitration agreements in the Free Trade Zone. In order to better align with the Opinions on Judicial Guarantees and effectively promote *ad hoc* arbitration, a series of rules and opinions were issued by the Supreme Court of the PRC to explore and deepen the "specific arbitration." So far, even though a complete system of laws and regulations has not yet been developed, the exploration reflects the relaxation of the official position on *ad hoc* arbitration in China and the positive response of the private sector to the promotion of an *ad hoc* arbitration system. In the context of years of active exploration and institutional development of *ad hoc* arbitration, the draft Arbitration Law was published on July 30, 2021, introducing the institution of *ad hoc* arbitration.

As one of the basic forms of arbitration, *ad hoc* arbitration has played an important role in settling disputes in civil and commercial matters over a long time. In the future, it can also play an important and active role in the face of modern economic life. For historical as well as socio-political and economic reasons, China has not recognized and established an *ad hoc* arbitration system, resulting in institutional arbitration being the only one. With the huge changes in the socio-political and economic system and the global integration of the economy, the drawbacks of the lack of an *ad hoc* arbitration system have become increasingly apparent and severe. The establishment and improvement of the *ad hoc* arbitration system in China as soon as possible is not only a need for the development and advancement of the socialist market economy regime, but also a need for the soundness of the arbitration system and the legal system as a whole. Establishing an *ad hoc* arbitration system will not only increase the opportunities for economic participants to choose the tools of dispute resolution, but also contribute to the further improvement of the institutional arbitration system. Ultimately, the arbitration system will serve society as a sound whole, promoting the healthy development of domestic and international economic trade.

第十四章

香港地区适用《纽约公约》仲裁裁决的执行现况

廖咏诗

众所周知，香港是一个对仲裁友好的司法管辖区，大多数寻求在香港执行的适用纽约公约的裁决（以下简称"公约裁决"）均被批准。

最近的仲裁统计数据证实了其作为全球最受欢迎的仲裁中心的地位。根据香港国际仲裁中心（以下简称"HKIAC"）的统计，在 2021 年提交 HKIAC 的 277 起仲裁案件中，超过 80% 为国际案件，即至少有一方当事人不是来自香港[①]。HKIAC 提供的仲裁裁决执行记录亦展现了法院支持执行的态度。在 2021 年执行仲裁裁决的 70 份申请中，有 54 份获批强制执行令[②]。

虽然上述数据并未单独计算公约裁决的执行情况，但香港法院在被认为是执行公约裁决的里程碑式案例 *Hebei Import & Export Corp v Polytek Engineering Co Ltd* [1999] HKCFA 40（"Hebei"）一案中阐明法院倾向于根据纽约公约所载的终局性和礼让原则执行公约裁决[③]。

---

① 香港国际仲裁中心，"2021 统计数据"，https://www.hkiac.org/about-us/statistics。

② 香港国际仲裁中心，"2021 仲裁裁决执行数据"，https://www.hkiac.org/about-us/statistics/enforcement-awards。

③ [82] 段 (Sir Anthony Mason NPJ)。

一、《纽约公约》适用于香港特别行政区的理据

《纽约公约》长期以来一直适用于香港特别行政区，尽管在中国恢复行使主权前后的法律依据有所不同。当香港还是英国殖民地时，英国于1975年加入《纽约公约》并于1977年将该公约扩展至其附属领土，《纽约公约》因此适用于香港。1997年7月1日后，中国将《纽约公约》的领土适用范围延伸至香港，使其继续受益于《纽约公约》。由于中国在加入《纽约公约》时作出了两项保留，即互惠保留和商业保留，香港也受两项保留约束。

《纽约公约》已被充分纳入香港的法律制度中。2011年生效的《仲裁条例》①是规范香港仲裁的主要立法，取代了1963年颁布的旧条例，主要建基于《联合国国际贸易法委员会国际商事仲裁示范法》（《示范法》）。现行版本的第10部分涉及仲裁裁决的承认和执行，第2部分专门针对公约裁决的执行（第87-91条）。这些条款将《纽约公约》的规则纳入《仲裁条例》。例如，《仲裁条例》第89条中列出的拒绝强制执行公约裁决的理由与《纽约公约》第5条是一致的。

《纽约公约》对不同类型的裁决适用范围不一。需要注意的是，香港并非独立于中国内地的"缔约国"，因此只有在《纽约公约》的其他缔约国作出的裁决才能根据《纽约公约》在香港执行，反之亦然。其他裁决，如内地作出的裁决，不能依据《纽约公约》在香港承认及执行。《仲裁条例》第10部分根据裁决的性质，将有关执行裁决的条款分类，即一般裁决、公约裁决、内地裁决和台湾裁决。

① 第609章。

二、香港法院支持执行仲裁的立场

在 *KB v. S and others* [2015] HKCFI 1787 案中，香港法院简要概括了其对执行仲裁协议和仲裁裁决的态度，总结了十项处理仲裁裁决的基本原则。引文如下 [①]：

(1) 法院的主要目标是促进仲裁程序和协助执行仲裁裁决。

(2) 根据《仲裁条例》，只有在条例明文规定的情况下，法院才应干预仲裁。

(3) 在遵守公共利益所需的保障措施的前提下，争端各方应可自由商定如何解决争端。

(4) 仲裁裁决的执行应该"几乎是行政程序的问题"，法院应该"尽可能地机械化"处理。

(5) 除非反对执行的理由充分，否则法院应执行仲裁裁决。反对执行的一方必须证明存在损害的真实风险，而且其权利已被证明受到实质性的侵犯。

(6) 在处理撤销仲裁裁决或拒绝执行裁决的申请时，无论是基于未收到仲裁程序通知、无法陈述案情或仲裁庭的组成或仲裁程序不符合当事人的协议，法院关注的重点是仲裁程序的结构完整性。在这方面，被投诉的行为"必须是严重的，甚至是过分的"，否则法院不会认定存在严重到足以破坏正当程序的错误。

(7) 在考虑是否拒绝执行裁决时，法院不审查案件的实体问题或基础交易。

(8) 未能及时向仲裁庭或管辖法院提出异议可能构成禁止反言或违反诚信原则。

---

① [5] 段（Mimmie Chan J）。

(9) 即使任何拒绝执行或撤销仲裁裁决的理由成立，法院仍具有自由裁量权执行裁决。

(10) 终审法院在 *Hebei Import & Export Corp v. Polytek Engineering Co Ltd* 一案中明确认定仲裁当事人负有诚实信用的义务，或善意行事的义务。

在以下各节中，笔者将借助最近的案例分析一些关键的指导原则。

值得强调的是，即使拒绝执行的理由已经成立，法院仍有自由裁量权予以执行。在 *Hebei Import & Export Corp v. Polytek Engineering Co Ltd* 一案中，终审法院遵循 *China Nanhai Oil Joint Service Corp., Shenzhen Branch v. Gee Tai Holdings Co. Ltd* [1994] HKCFI 215[①] 的判决，重申香港法院可以不顾已经证实的拒绝执行理由，行使执行仲裁裁决的自由裁量权。这是因为《纽约公约》第 V 条和《香港行政法》第 89 条的法律用语显示，当任何指定的理由成立时，法院"可以"拒绝执行仲裁裁决——这表明法院也可以批准执行。法院在作出强制执行决定前，会综合考虑程序违规的程度、提出程序异议的时间等多种因素。

首先，法院只会在程序违规足够严重的情况下拒绝执行仲裁裁决。*Pacific China Holdings Ltd (in liq) v. Grand Pacific Holdings Ltd* [2012] HKCA 200 一案展示了法院如何在证实程序违规的情况下仍然执行裁决。本案中，Pacific China 和 Grand Pacific 之间的一项贷款协议规定在香港进行仲裁，其后双方将争议提交国际商会并根据其规则进行仲裁，Grand Pacific 胜诉。Pacific China 向香港高等法院原讼法庭申请撤销裁决，基于《示范法》第 34(2) 条（现行《仲裁条例》第 81 条；《纽约公约》第 5 条），辩称其在仲裁程序中无法陈述其案情或仲裁程序不符合当事人的协议。原讼法庭基于这两个程序上的理由撤销裁决，Grand Pacific 其后上诉。

在决定法院以何标准行使自由裁量权不撤销裁决时，上诉法庭参考了

---

① [93] 段 (Sir Anthony Mason NPJ)。

多个权威案例和对《示范法》和《纽约公约》的解释。其中，上诉法庭引用了 van den Berg 教授的评注，该评注表明《纽约公约》第 5 条中拒绝执行的理由应作狭义的解释，即只有在严重的情况下才接受 [1]。上诉法庭随后引用了一个加拿大最高法院的案例，该案例与 van den Berg 教授的观点一致。最终上诉法庭裁定，Pacific China 辩称的无法陈述其案情的行为必须"足够严重或过分"，法院才可以裁定违反了正当法律程序。

本案中，Pacific China 基于三个理由提出申诉：(i) 仲裁庭允许 Grand Pacific 在 Pacific China 就实体问题提交材料 10 天后才提交，不仅违反公平，也背离了约定的程序时间表；(ii) 仲裁庭拒绝 Pacific China 援引三个外国判例，因为其认为让 Grand Pacific 在证据听证会前三周内检阅这些判例是"不公平的"，这使 Pacific China 无法提出最有说服力的诉讼理由；(iii) 仲裁庭拒绝 Pacific China 回应 Grand Pacific 就香港法律问题提交的意见书。上诉法庭最终推翻了原讼法庭的决定，并裁定 Pacific China 提出的程序违规理由皆不成立。尽管如此，上诉法庭重申即使程序违规被证实，法院也可以行使自由裁量权允许执行仲裁裁决。法院应考虑的问题是，如果没有程序违规，仲裁结果是否会有所不同 [2]。如果没有，那么法院可以批准执行。

其次，当一方违反诚信原则时，法院可能会在程序违规的情况下批准执行，比如在当事人得以陈述其案情的情况下仍然有策略地延迟提出程序性异议。

在 Hebei 一案中，终审法院确认仲裁当事人负有诚实信用义务，如果未能及时在仲裁庭前提出异议，可能违反此义务。常见的是，抵制执行的一方本可以在仲裁程序的早期纠正程序违规问题，而不是等到执行阶段才提出。Hebei 案中的争议源于 Polytek 向 Hebei 出售有缺陷的设备，导致根本

---

[1] [91] 段 (Tang VP)。

[2] 该判定标准被 *Paklito Investment Ltd v. Klockner East Asia Ltd* [1993] HKCFI 147 和 *Apex Tech Investment Ltd v Chuang's Development (China) Ltd* [1996] HKCA 593 采用。

性违约。双方将此事提交给中国国际经济贸易仲裁委员会进行仲裁，Hebei 胜诉并随后获准在香港执行裁决。Polytek 申请撤销强制执行令起初未获批准，其后上诉成功，主要基于首席仲裁员和专家证人在 Polytek 缺席的情况下去工厂检查设备并接受了工厂技术人员的来信。Polytek 根据前《仲裁条例》第 44(2)(c) 条及第 44(3) 条指出其未能陈述案情并且在该程序违规的情况下强制执行会违反公共政策。终审法院推翻了该决定，裁定 Polytek 不能以这些程序性理由为依据申请撤销裁决，因为它本可以及时向仲裁庭提出这些理由来修正程序上的缺陷。

三、援引《纽约公约》的实际案例

为了更清楚地了解香港法院的做法，笔者将举出几个拒绝执行的案例。值得再次强调的是，程序上的缺陷必须足够严重，法院才会拒绝执行仲裁裁决。

（一）未能陈述案情

Paklito Investment Ltd v. Klockner East Asia Ltd [1993] HKCFI 147 一案中，法院以抵制执行一方未能陈述其案情为由拒绝执行仲裁裁决。案中争议源于 Paklito 和 Klockner 之间的协议，双方将此事提交给中国国际经济贸易仲裁委员会进行仲裁。Klockner 对仲裁庭指定的一名专家提出异议，并告知仲裁庭其打算就专家报告提出意见。然而，在 Klockner 提交意见之前，仲裁庭就作出了有利于 Paklito 的裁决。法院认为这是一个严重的程序违规行为，因为专家报告提出了新的证据，并提出了与 Klockner 所面对的案件非常不同的情况。因此，法院认为，Klockner 显然被剥夺了公平和平等的听证机会，故拒绝执行仲裁裁决。

X v. Y [2020] HKCFI 2782 是另一个较新的例子，它为程序违规行为应

有的严重程度提供了一个参考。本案中，一项有利于保险公司 X 的裁决在台湾作出。X 公司获许在香港执行该裁决，但另一方以未能陈述其案情为由成功地撤销了该裁决。该争议涉及 X 公司资产的质押，法庭认为根据台湾"保险法"第 146 条，该质押是无效的。然而，这是 X 公司在审讯后提交的材料中才提出的新观点。在此之前，双方的专家都认为台湾"保险法"第 146 条并不具有使质押无效的效力，质押的有效性受新加坡法律管辖。 由于听证会后提交的材料是同时交换的，另一方未能就新观点进一步提交材料。因此，法院认为法庭的裁决"严重偏离"了双方在听证会后提交的案件，拒绝执行仲裁裁决①。

（二）当事人无行为能力

这一理由很少出现。在 *A Consortium Comprising TPL and ICB v. AE Limited* [2021] HKCFI 2341 一案中，抵制执行方以该理由寻求撤销执行命令，但法院灵活地修正了程序上的不规范。本案的裁决是在迪拜作出的，申请人获准在香港执行该裁决。争议源于双方之间的分项咨询协议，其中申请人被称为"TPL 和 ICB 的合资公司"。后来在仲裁和执行程序中，申请人却被称为"由 TPL 和 ICB 组成的财团"。 被申请人试图辩称，香港法院在执行程序中应尽量"机械式"地遵循程序，即裁决只能由所述的"合资公司"执行，可是这种僵硬的解释会使裁决无法执行。

法院阐明，机械化地执行仲裁裁决法并不意味着它不能通过对裁决的文义解释使其生效。本案中，法院有合理理由认定"合资公司"由 TPL 和 ICB 组成，他们共同有权对被申请人执行裁决。最终，法院通过将 TPL 和 ICB 作为额外的申请人加入，修正了当事人行为能力上的程序性缺陷，再次展现了香港法院支持执行的态度。

---

① 在 [87](Mimmie Chan J)。

（三）无效的仲裁协议

伴随这一理由的常见问题是：协议当事人的关联公司是否也受仲裁协议的约束。*AB v. CD* [2021] HKCFI 327 一案中，法院认为一方当事人的关联公司不是仲裁协议方，撤销了裁决。案中纠纷源于 AB 与 CD 公司之间的协议，该协议将 "AB" 定义为 "AB 机构或任何其他关联实体"。CD 公司最初在仲裁通知中指定 "AB 机构" 为被申请人，但后来将名称改为 "AB 工程"，误以为前者在重组后被改名为后者。然而，在签订协议时，AB 工程公司只是 AB 机构的一个子公司，此后它又成为另一家公司的子公司。

X v. Jemmy Chien [2020] HKCFI 286 案涉及一种不同的情况。本案中，原告声称与被告签订的服务协议是一个虚假协议，被告不是协议的实际当事人。法院指出尽管其审查仲裁庭管辖权的标准是 "正确性"，但这并不意味着 "对仲裁庭所作裁决的案情进行无端和无限的审查"[1]。因此，在审查本案中仲裁员作出的关于案情的裁决时，法院认定有关当事人证据和事实调查的可信度应由仲裁员而非法庭判断[2]，故法院只审查了仲裁员在解释协议时采用的方法。最终，法院同意了仲裁庭的结论，认定仲裁条款有效。

（四）公共政策

与大多数司法管辖区一致，香港法院对公共政策理由采取了狭义的解释[3]。在 *Hebei* 一案中，终审法院指出，案件必须 "违反法院的道德和正义的基本概念" 才能被裁定违反公共政策[4]。这一高门槛使大多数以这一理由提出的拒绝执行仲裁裁决申请失败。

---

① [4]—[6] 段（Mimmie Chan J）。

② [13] 和 [21] 段 (Mimmie Chan J)。

③ Tiffany Chan, Adam Lee, "A Tale of Two Cases: 在香港执行裁决的公共政策辩护"，http://arbitrationblog.kluwerarbitration.com/2020/06/03/a-tale-of-two-cases-public-policy-defence-to-award-enforcement-in-hong-kong/，2022 年 10 月 15 日访问。

④ [99] 段（安东尼 - 梅森爵士 NPJ）。

前文已经概括了 *Hebei* 的案情概要。简而言之，Polytek 以其未能陈述案情为由申请撤销强制执行令，被法院拒绝。Polytek 还提出了公共政策的理由认为在未能陈述案情执行裁决是违反公共政策的。有言这是以公共政策理由为幌子的同一抗辩理由 ①。由于法院并未认定 Polytek 未能陈述其案情，公共政策的辩护理由不成立。在笔者看来，即使前者的程序违规理由成立，也没有达到违反公共政策的地步。正如 Kaplan J. 所正确指出，抵制执行方往往 " 试图在所有情况提出 [公共政策理由]" ②。

那么，什么时候能以违反公共政策拒绝执行仲裁裁决？可能的情况包括欺诈、贪污和其他不合理的行为。在 *Z v. Y* [2018] HKCFI 2342 案中，法院拒绝执行裁决，因为相关协议是虚假的，根据中国法律构成了"欺诈性合同"的罪行。法院认为，该裁决可能有"非法性的污点"，而仲裁庭又没有以充分的理由处理非法主张时，执行裁决将违反公平和正义的原则 ③。

四、承认和执行内地裁决

在中国恢复对香港的主权后，香港与内地之间相互承认和执行仲裁裁决方面出现短暂的法律空白。"一国两制"政策下，两地法律制度不同，缺乏法律依据相互执行仲裁裁决。*Ng Fung Hong Ltd v. ABC* [1998] 1 HKC 213 一案中，法院拒绝在香港执行一项内地裁决，指出香港和内地在回归后不再是《纽约公约》的独立缔约方。这在当时的商界引起轩然大波，因为有

---

① Nadia Darwazeh 和 Friven Yeoh, "Recognition and Enforcement of Awards under the New York Convention:China and Hong Kong Perspectives", *Journal of International Arbitration*, Vol. 25, No.6, 2008, pp. 837-856.

② [77] 段（Palikto）。

③ [14] 段（Mimmie Chan J）。

人质疑在香港审理与中国有关的纠纷是否合适①。

1999 年，中国最高人民法院和香港特区政府签署了《关于内地和香港特别行政区相互执行仲裁裁决的安排》（以下简称《安排》），填补了这一空白，为两地之间执行裁决提供了法律依据。在 2020 年，两地又签署了一系列补充安排（以下简称《补充安排》），对《安排》进行了修改和补充。

《补充安排》带来了在两地同时进行申请执行程序的可能性。在以前的安排中，如果当事人希望在两个地区执行裁决，只能在第一个司法管辖区执行裁决不足以偿还其债务②时才能诉诸第二个司法管辖区。虽然理论上也可以同时进行执行程序，但花费时间较长。《补充安排》的规定显示，一方当事人可以同时启动程序③。

结语

香港特区是中华人民共和国境内的一个普通法司法管辖区，使中国获得了类似于加拿大（魁北克省行大陆法而其他省份行普通法）和美国（路易斯安那州行大陆法而其他州行普通法）的普通法体系与大陆法体系的联合力量。这种法律体系倾向于逐渐产生有利于法治的先例，日趋一致和稳定。类似的案件都以类似的方法处理，这一规则将在未来的应用中继续沿用。

我们希望《纽约公约》以及最新的中港两地相互执行仲裁裁决的安排会在"一国两制"的框架下，自然而然地、充满活力地推动两地的国际商事仲裁法律和实践的共同发展。

---

① Jack W. Nelson, "International Commercial Arbitration in Asia: Hong Kong, Australia and India Compared", *Asian International Arbitration Journal*, Vol. 10, 2024, pp. 105-136.

② 第2(3)条，《关于内地和香港特别行政区相互执行仲裁裁决的安排》。

③ 第3条，《关于内地和香港特别行政区相互执行仲裁裁决的安排》（补充安排）。

Chapter 14

Enforcement of Convention Awards in the HKSAR

Liu Wing Sze, Daisy

The Hong Kong courts are well-known for their pro-arbitration and, correspondingly, pro-enforcement approach. Most awards under the UN Convention on the Recognition and Enforcement of Foreign Arbitral Awards (the "NYC" or the "Convention") seeking enforcement in Hong Kong succeeded.

Hong Kong's recent arbitration statistics confirm its status as the world's favoured arbitration hub. According to the Hong Kong International Arbitration Centre ("HKIAC"), over 80% of the 277 arbitrations submitted to the HKIAC in 2021 were international in nature, which means having at least one party not from Hong Kong[1]. The records of enforcement of arbitral awards rendered by the HKIAC clearly demonstrate the court's pro-enforcement attitude. Out of 70 applications to enforce arbitral awards in 2021, 54 were granted enforcement orders[2].

Although the above data does not count the enforcement of Convention awards alone, the Hong Kong court inclines to enforce Convention awards with regard to the principles of finality and comity enshrined in the NYC. This was enunciated in *Hebei*

---

[1] HKIAC, "2021 Statistics", 〈https://www.hkiac.org/about-us/statistics〉 accessed 15 October 2022.

[2] HKIAC, "2021 Enforcement of Awards", 〈https://www.hkiac.org/about-us/statistics/enforcement-awards〉 accessed 15 October 2022.

Import & Export Corp v Polytek Engineering Co Ltd [1999] HKCFA 40 ("Hebei")[1], the landmark case on enforcement of arbitral awards under the NYC.

1. Applicability of the NYC to the HKSAR

The NYC has long been applicable to the HKSAR, although on a different basis before and after China resumed sovereignty over the city. Before 1 July 1997, when Hong Kong was still a British colony, it became a party to the NYC by virtue of the UK's ratification of the Convention in 1975 and the extension of the Convention to its dependent territories in 1977. After the handover, Hong Kong continued to benefit from the NYC owing to China's extension of the territorial application of the Convention. As China made two reservations upon accession to the NYC, namely the reciprocity reservation and the commercial reservation, Hong Kong is also subject to both reservations.

The NYC is well-incorporated into Hong Kong's statutory regimes. The *Arbitration Ordinance*[2] ("HKAO") entered into force in 2011 is the primary legislation that governs arbitration in Hong Kong, replacing the previous ordinance enacted back in 1963. It is primarily based on the UNICITRAL Model Law with certain modifications. Part 10 of the current version deals with the recognition and enforcement of arbitral awards, with Division 2 specifically addressing the enforcement of Convention awards (ss. 87-91). These sections incorporate the NYC into the HKAO. For instance, the grounds of refusal for enforcement listed in s.89 replicate those under art. V of the NYC.

As to the scope of the NYC's application to different types of awards, it should be noted that Hong Kong is not a "contracting state" independent of the mainland, such that only awards rendered in other state parties to the NYC may be enforced by virtue of the Convention, and vice versa. Other awards, such as Mainland awards, do not fall within the ambit of the NYC. Part 10 of the HKAO helpfully categorises the provisions regarding the enforcement of awards according to the nature of awards, namely awards in general, Convention awards, Mainland awards and Taiwan awards.

---

[1] At [82] (Sir Anthony Mason NPJ).
[2] Cap. 609.

2. The Hong Kong Court's Pro-Enforcement Approach

In *KB v. S and others* [2015] HKCFI 1787, the court succinctly summarized the Hong Kong court's attitude towards enforcing arbitration agreements and awards. Ten guiding principles were laid down and have since been regarded as "ten commandments" by the legal world. The principles are produced below in verbatim (citations omitted)[1]:

(1) The primary aim of the court is to facilitate the arbitral process and to assist with enforcement of arbitral awards.

(2) Under the Arbitration Ordinance, the court should interfere in the arbitration of the dispute only as expressly provided for in the Ordinance.

(3) Subject to the observance of the safeguards that are necessary in the public interest, the parties to a dispute should be free to agree on how their dispute should be resolved.

(4) Enforcement of arbitral awards should be "almost a matter of administrative procedure" and the courts should be "as mechanistic as possible".

(5) The courts are prepared to enforce awards except where complaints of substance can be made good. The party opposing enforcement has to show a real risk of prejudice and that its rights are shown to have been violated in a material way.

(6) In dealing with applications to set aside an arbitral award, or to refuse enforcement of an award, whether on the ground of not having been given notice of the arbitral proceedings, inability to present one's case, or that the composition of the tribunal or the arbitral procedure was not in accordance with the parties' agreement, the court is concerned with the structural integrity of the arbitration proceedings. In this regard, the conduct complained of "must be serious, even egregious", before the

---

[1] At [1] (Mimmie Chan J).

court would find that there was an error sufficiently serious so as to have undermined due process.

(7) In considering whether or not to refuse the enforcement of the award, the court does not look into the merits or at the underlying transaction.

(8) Failure to make prompt objection to the Tribunal or the supervisory court may constitute estoppel or want of bona fide.

(9) Even if sufficient grounds are made out either to refuse enforcement or to set aside an arbitral award, the court has a residual discretion and may nevertheless enforce the award despite the proven existence of a valid ground.

(10) The Court of Final Appeal clearly recognized in *Hebei Import & Export Corp v. Polytek Engineering Co Ltd* that parties to the arbitration have a duty of good faith, or to act bona fide.

In the following sections, some of the key guiding principles will be analysed with the aid of recent cases.

At the outset, it should be emphasized that the court has a residual discretion to permit enforcement even if a ground for refusal of enforcement has been established. In *Hebei Import & Export Corp v. Polytek Engineering Co Ltd*, the CFA reiterated that the Hong Kong court retains residual discretion to enforce an arbitral award even when a ground for refusal has been made out, following the reasoning in *China Nanhai Oil Joint Service Corp., Shenzhen Branch v. Gee Tai Holdings Co. Ltd* [1994] HKCFI 215[1]. This is because Art. V of the NYC and s.89 of the HKAO provide that the court "may" refuse enforcement when any of the specified grounds has been established — which suggests that the proof of a ground for refusal does not lead to automatic refusal for enforcement. Various factors, such as the degree of procedural irregularities and the time of making such procedural objections, would be considered before the court makes the enforcement decision.

First, the procedural irregularities must be sufficiently serious for the court to refuse enforcement. *Pacific China Holdings Ltd (in liq) v. Grand Pacific Holdings*

---

[1] At [93] (Sir Anthony Mason NPJ).

Ltd [2012] HKCA 200 illustrates how the court nonetheless enforced a case despite establishing a procedural ground. Pacific China and Grand Pacific had an alleged loan agreement, which provided for arbitration in Hong Kong. Disputes later arose, and an ICC award was made in favour of Grand Pacific. Pacific China applied to the CFI to set aside the award on grounds that it was unable to present its case and/or that the arbitral procedure was not in accordance with the agreement of the parties under Art. 34(2) of the Model Law (incorporated as s.81 of the current AO; has its equivalent in Art. V of the NYC), emphasizing the first ground. The CFI set aside the award on two procedural grounds. Grand Pacific appealed to the CA.

In deciding the relevant standard for the court to exercise its discretion not to set aside an award despite establishing a procedural ground, the CA made references to several authorities and commentaries on the interpretation of the Model Law and the NYC. In particular, the CA cited Professor van den Berg's commentary, which suggests that the grounds for refusal of enforcement in Art.V shall be construed narrowly such that they are only accepted in serious cases[①]. The CA then cited a Canadian Supreme Court case which concurs with Professor van den Berg's view. Eventually, it was concluded that Pacific China's alleged inability to present its case must be "sufficiently serious or egregious" before the court could say that it has been denied due process.

In the present case, Pacific China based its complaint on three grounds: (i) the arbitral tribunal allowed Grand Pacific to file submissions on a material issue 10 days after Pacific China did so, giving Grand Pacific an unfair advantage and departing from the agreed procedural timetable; (ii) Pacific China was refused to adduce three foreign law authorities because the tribunal thought it was "unfair" for Grand Pacific to review them within three weeks before an evidential hearing, rendering it unable to present its best case; and (iii) the tribunal refused Pacific China to respond to Grand Pacific's submissions on an issue on Hong Kong law. The CA eventually overturned the CFI's decision and found no violation of either the impugned ground. Nonetheless, the CA affirmed that the court may exercise its discretion to permit enforcement even when there is a violation of any procedural grounds. The relevant test is whether the arbitral

---

① At [91] (Tang VP).

result would not have been different without the violation[①]. If not, then the court may permit enforcement.

Second, the court would likely permit enforcement when a party breaches the good faith principle, for instance, keeping a procedural objection "up its sleeves", with the ability to present its case.

In *Hebei,* it was recognized by the CFA that the parties to the arbitration have a duty of good faith, and it may be breached by failing to make prompt objections before the tribunal. There have been many instances that the party resisting enforcement could have cured the procedural defect it wishes to rely upon earlier in the arbitral proceedings, instead of raising it at the enforcement stage. The *Hebei* case is one such illustration. The dispute arose from Polytek selling defective equipment to Hebei, resulting in a fundamental breach of contract.

As the parties referred the matter to CIETAC, an award was made in favor of Hebei. Later, Hebei was granted leave to enforce the award in Hong Kong. Polytek applied to set aside the enforcement order but failed. It then appealed to the CA and succeeded, primarily because the chief arbitrator and the experts inspected the equipment and received communications from the technicians at the end user's factory in the absence of Polytek. It resisted enforcement on the s.44(2)(c) ground that it had been unable to present its case and the s.44(3) ground that enforcement in such circumstances would be contrary to public policy (the section references are made in relation to the old HKAO). The CFA overturned the decision, ruling that Polytek was estopped from relying on such procedural grounds when it could have raised them promptly before the tribunal.

3. Practical Cases Invoking the Provision of the NYC

A few cases invoking the grounds for refusal of enforcement would be illustrated to give a clearer picture of the Hong Kong court's approach. It should be remembered that the procedural defects must be sufficiently serious to render a refusal for enforcement.

---

① The test was adopted in *Paklito Investment Ltd v. Klockner East Asia Ltd* [1993] HKCFI 147 and *Apex Tech Investment Ltd v Chuang's Development (China) Ltd* [1996] HKCA 593.

(1) Lack of opportunity to present one's case

Paklito Investment Ltd v. Klockner East Asia Ltd [1993] HKCFI 147 is an example of the court refusing enforcement on the ground of the resisting party's inability to present its case. A dispute arose from the contract between Paklito and Klockner, the parties referred the matter to CIETAC for arbitration.

Klockner objected to an expert appointed by the tribunal and informed the tribunal that it intended to make submissions on the expert report. However, the award was rendered in favour of Paklito before Klockner was able to present its submissions to the tribunal. The court considered this a serious procedural irregularity because the expert report adduced new evidence and presented a very different case from what Klockner was dealing with. As such, the court held that Klockner was clearly denied a fair and equal opportunity to be heard and refused enforcement.

X v. Y [2020] HKCFI 2782 is another more recent example, giving a reference as to how serious the alleged procedural irregularity should be to render it refused enforcement. In this case, an award was made in Taiwan in favour of an insurance company, X against a bank. X obtained leave to enforce the award in Hong Kong, but the bank later successfully set aside the award based on, among others, its inability to present its case.

The dispute concerns a pledge over X's assets, which the tribunal held to be void under article 146 of the Taiwanese Insurance Act. However, this is a new point advanced by X only in its post-hearing submissions. Before that, the parties' experts shared the view that article 146 of the Taiwanese Insurance Act did not have the effect of rendering the pledge void and that the validity of the pledge was governed by Singapore law.

Since the post-hearing submissions were exchanged simultaneously, the bank was confronted with this new argument and was deprived of the fair opportunity to make further submissions. Thus, the court considered the tribunal's ruling a "significant departure" from the parties' cases presented before the post-hearing submissions and refused enforcement[①].

(2) Incapacity of the party

This ground is rarely invoked. In *A Consortium Comprising TPL and ICB v. AE Limited* [2021] HKCFI 2341, the resisting party sought to set aside the enforcement order on this ground but failed as the court "cured" the procedural irregularity. The award, in this case, was made in Dubai against the respondent, and the applicant was granted leave to enforce it in Hong Kong. The dispute arose from a sub-consultancy agreement between the parties, in which the applicant was named "the Joint Venture of TPL and ICB". Later in the arbitration and enforcement proceedings, the applicant was referred to as the "Consortium comprising TPL and ICB". The respondent sought to argue that the Hong Kong court should adopt a "mechanistic" approach in enforcement proceedings such that the award may only be enforced against the "Consortium" as stated, even though such rigid interpretation would render the award unenforceable.

The court enunciated that a mechanistic approach in enforcing arbitral awards does not mean it cannot give effect to an award on its plain reading. In the present case, it was reasonably apparent to the court that the "Consortium" comprised TPL and ICB, and they are jointly entitled to enforce the award against the respondent. Eventually, the court demonstrated its pro-enforcement approach by joining TPL and ICB as additional applicants, curing the procedural defect on the party's capacity.

(3) Invalid arbitration agreement

Under this ground, one often encountered issue is whether a contracting party's affiliate is also subject to the arbitration agreement. *AB v. CD* [2021] HKCFI 327 is a recent case where the court held that a party's affiliate was not a party to the arbitration agreement and set aside the award. The dispute, in this case, arose under an agreement between AB Bureau and CD, which defined "AB" as "AB Bureau or any other Affiliated entity". CD initially named "AB Bureau" as the respondent in the

---

① At [87] (Mimmie Chan J).

notice of arbitration but later corrected the name to "AB Engineering" on the belief that the former had been renamed as the latter after restructuring. However, AB Engineering was only a subsidiary of AB Bureau at the time of the agreement, and it has since become a subsidiary of another company.

X v. Jemmy Chien [2020] HKCFI 286 concerns a different situation, where the plaintiff X claimed that the underlying service agreement was a sham such that the defendant, Mr Chien, was not the true party to the agreement. The court first reminded itself that the standard of the court's reviewing the arbitral tribunal's jurisdiction is "correctness", but this does not suggest "an unwarranted and unlimited review of the merits of the findings made by the tribunal"[①]. Thus, when reviewing the award on merits made by the arbitrator, the court carefully observed that the credibility of the parties' evidence and fact-finding is a question for the arbitrator[②] and only reviewed the approach adopted by the arbitrator in constructing the agreement. Eventually, the court agreed with the tribunal's conclusion and held the arbitration clause valid.

(4) Public policy

In line with most jurisdictions, the Hong Kong court adopts a narrow construction of the public policy ground[③]. In *Hebei*, the CFA pointed out that the case must be "contrary to the fundamental conceptions of morality and justice of the forum" before the court can say it is contrary to public policy[④]. The high threshold rendered most applications on this ground unsuccessful.

The facts of *Hebei* have been discussed above. Essentially, Polytek's application to set aside the enforcement order based on its inability to present its case failed because it did not make a timely complaint. Polytek also raised the public policy ground,

---

① At [4]—[6] (Mimmie Chan J).

② At [13] and [21] (Mimmie Chan J).

③ Tiffany Chan, Adam Lee, "A Tale of Two Cases: Public Policy Defence to Award Enforcement in Hong Kong", ⟨http://arbitrationblog.kluwerarbitration.com/2020/06/03/a-tale-of-two-cases-public-policy-defence-to-award-enforcement-in-hong-kong/⟩ accessed 15 October 2022.

④ At [99] (Sir Anthony Mason NPJ).

arguing to enforce the award despite its alleged inability to present its case would be contrary to public policy. Commentators consider this to be the same argument in the guise of the public policy ground[①]. As the court considered that Polytek was not unable to present its case, the public policy defence failed. In my view, even if the former ground succeeded, it would be unlikely for the parties to elevate it to the standard of contravening public policy. As rightly observed by Kaplan J, the resisting parties often have "the attempt to wheel [the public policy ground] on all occasions"[②].

When, then can the public policy ground successfully be established? Possible cases include fraud, corruption and other unconscionable conduct. In *Z v. Y* [2018] HKCFI 2342, the court refused to enforce the award as the underlying agreements were a sham and constituted the offence of "fraudulent contracts" under PRC law. The court held that enforcing the award when it might be "tainted by illegality" and when the tribunal did not address the illegality claims with adequate reasons would contravene the notions of fairness and justice[③].

4. Recognition and Enforcement of Mainland Awards

A legal lacuna followed the resumption of Chinese sovereignty over Hong Kong in the mutual recognition and enforcement of arbitral awards between Hong Kong and the Mainland. The "One Country, Two Systems" policy entails different legal systems and calls for a legal framework for enforcing Mainland awards in Hong Kong and vice versa. In *Ng Fung Hong Ltd v. ABC* [1998] 1 HKC 213, a 1998 case, the court refused to enforce a Mainland award in Hong Kong as it recognised that Hong Kong and the Mainland were no longer separate parties to the NYC after the handover. This sparked anxiety in the commercial world back then as some questioned whether it was suitable

---

① Nadia Darwazeh and Friven Yeoh, "Recognition and Enforcement of Awards under the New York Convention: China and Hong Kong Perspectives", *Journal of International Arbitration*, Vol. 25, No.6, 2008, pp. 837-856.

② Paklito at [77].

③ At [14] (Mimmie Chan J).

to seat China-related disputes in Hong Kong[①].

In 1999, the Supreme People's Court of the PRC and the HKSAR government filled the lacuna by signing the Arrangement Concerning Mutual Enforcement of Arbitral Awards between Mainland China and the HKSAR (the Arrangement), which provides a legal framework for ready enforcement of awards between the regions. Recently in 2020, a supplemental arrangement (the Supplemental Arrangement) was entered into force to amend and supplement the Arrangement.

One significant amendment concerns the possibility of simultaneous enforcement proceedings in the Mainland and Hong Kong. In the previous Arrangement, if a party wishes to enforce an award in both regions, it can only do so if the enforcement of the award in the first jurisdiction cannot satisfy the liability[②]. Although theoretically, simultaneous enforcement proceedings were possible, they came with unnecessary delays. In the Supplemental Arrangement, a party can initiate the proceedings concurrently[③].

Conclusion

HKSAR is a common law jurisdiction within the territory of the PRC. This rendered China having obtained the combined force of a common law system with a civil law system, similar to Canada (Quebec civil law and rest of the provinces common law), and USA (Louisiana civil law and rest of the states common law). This combined force of the legal system tends to generate precedents in favor of the rule of law rather gradually, increasingly consistently and steadily. Similar cases are handled similarly. This rule will forward look at itself in its application in the future.

We hope that the NYC and the practice surrounding the recognition and enforcement of the foreign arbitral awards in HKSAR and the Mainland under the latest

---

① Jack W. Nelson, "International Commercial Arbitration in Asia: Hong Kong, Australia and India Compared", *Asian International Arbitration Journal*, Vol. 10, 2014, pp. 105-136.

② Art. 2(3), the Arrangement.

③ Art. 3, the Supplemental Arrangement.

mutual arrangements will naturally and dynamically, under the policy of One Country Two Systems, guide the mutual development of the law and practice of international commercial arbitration in the region.

第十五章
新加坡涉上海合同关系的最新案例

Myo Su Thant

本章旨在探究由《纽约公约》下订立的仲裁协议产生的合同关系。本章深入讨论了新加坡和上海的最新案例，以求从亚洲视角进行一些思考。

仲裁具有私密性、独立性、公正性和灵活性。当事人可以选择仲裁地、管辖法律、仲裁员的任命和其他程序事项。当事人亦可根据自己的需要设计程序，例如，指定具有特定专长的仲裁员。[①] 这对投资者极具吸引力。

新加坡和中国都是1958年联合国《承认及执行外国仲裁裁决公约》(《纽约公约》)的缔约国。在两国作出的仲裁裁决可在170个缔约国执行。[②] 新加坡和中国（如香港特区和澳门特区）都采用了《联合国国际贸易法委员会国际商事仲裁示范法》（1985年）及2006年通过的修正案。

借助仲裁的优势，当事人可以利用当事人意思自治，以灵活的条款制定仲裁协议。但重要的是，当事人不应作出有缺陷或无法执行的仲裁协议。为此，本章将从以下几个方面探讨：

(1) 仲裁地；

[①] Yves, D & Eric, S. *A Guide to the New ICC Rules on Arbitration*, Kluwer Law International, 1998, p. 258.

[②] https://uncitral.un.org/en/texts/arbitration/conventions/f0reign arbitral awards/status2.

(2) 仲裁协议的适用法律；

(3) 仲裁协议的有效性；

(4) 仲裁裁决的执行。

一、仲裁地

当事人应在协议中明确规定仲裁地，同时谨记"案件审理地点"和"仲裁地"之间的区别。在"BNA"① 一案中，仲裁协议载有某个地址，但当事人的意图并不明确，无法说明该地是"案件审理地点"还是"仲裁地"。当事人在其仲裁协议第 14.2 条中如是说：

"……争议应最终提交至新加坡国际仲裁中心（SIAC）在上海进行仲裁，仲裁将按照其仲裁规则进行。"

新加坡最高法院裁定，"在上海仲裁"这一短语足以表明"上海是仲裁地"。② 法院援引了英国的权威判例，如"Naviera"③ 和"ABB Lummus"④ 案，其中使用了完全相同的措辞："在［地点］仲裁。"因此，如果当事人的仲裁协议只载有某个地址，则应自然地解释为当事人选择了该地点作为仲裁地。如果协议中并无确定地点，则要根据仲裁机构的规则来确定。就 SIAC 而言，"仲裁地"为新加坡。⑤ 仲裁地在国际仲裁中非常重要，因为：

(1) 仲裁程序将以仲裁地当地的法律为准；

---

① BNA v. BNB [2019] SGCA 84.

② BNA v. BNB [2019] SGCA 84, [65].

③ Naviera Amazonica Peruana SA v. Compania Internacional de Seguros del Peru [1988] 1 Lloyd's Rep 116.

④ ABB Lummus Global Ltd v. Keppel Fels Ltd [1999] 2 Lloyd's Rep 24.

⑤ Rule 18.1 of the Investment Arbitration Rules of the Singapore International Arbitration Centre, 2017 (SIAC Rules).

(2) 当地法院对仲裁享有监督管辖权；

(3) 当地法院有权撤销裁决或司法判决；[①]

(4) 如果没有明示或默示的法律选择，因具有最密切联系，仲裁地的法律可以作为仲裁协议及其有效性的适用法律。[②]

在当事人没有明示或默示协议的情况下，当事人须遵守的法律很可能是仲裁地法。

二、仲裁协议的适用法律

新加坡高等法院在"BCY v. BCZ"[③]一案中采用了三层次的法律选择分析方法，为确定仲裁协议管辖法律提供了明确的法律框架。这三个层次分别是：

(1) 当事人明确选择的法律；

(2) 从缔约时的意图中得出的当事人的默示选择；或

(3) 与仲裁协议有最密切和最真实联系的法律体系。

如果当事人明确约定其仲裁协议的管辖法律，适用法律的问题便不复存在。如无约定，法院或仲裁庭必须分析当事人是否以默示方式选择了适用法律。仲裁协议的适用法律可以是：

(1) 主合同法律；或

(2) 仲裁地法律。

（一）适用法律为主合同法律

如果仲裁协议作为主合同的一部分，且如果主合同选择了明确的管辖

---

① BNA v. BNB [2019] SGCA 84, [65].

② FirstLink Investments Corp Ltd v. GT Payment Pte Ltd and others [2014] SGHCR 12.

③ BCY v. BCZ [2017] 3 SLR 357, [40].

法律，则法院将其解释为"强烈表明"当事人意图用同一法律来管辖仲裁协议和主合同。① 否则，当事人应具体约定另一法律管辖仲裁协议。②

在协议中使用"产生于或与之相关的义务"等措辞，也表明仲裁协议和主合同不是独立的协议，且应适用相同的管辖法律。例如，在"BCY"③一案中，双方在协议第 9.13.1 条中使用了该表述。新加坡法院决定适用主合同的管辖法律（纽约法）来管辖仲裁协议。

即使某一法律管辖主合同的某一特定部分，这种推定仍然适用。例如，在"BMO v. BMP"④案中，越南法律管辖主合同的第 27 条和第 28 条，但法院认定越南法律管辖整个合同。

可分性原则在此并不适用。可分性原则只表明仲裁协议的有效性独立于主合同的有效性或无效性，这并不意味着仲裁协议在各方面都与主合同不同。可分性原则不适用于考虑仲裁协议的适用法律。⑤ 因此，如果当事人没有明确约定或规定不同的法律将适用于合同的不同部分，同一法律可以适用于整个合同。

（二）适用法律为仲裁地法律

在 2014 年的"FirstLink"⑥案中，新加坡高等法院认为根据仲裁协议推定，当事人默示选择仲裁地法律。该协议第 16 条的法律选择条款规定：

"本协议由斯德哥尔摩商会仲裁院（SCC）的法律管辖和解释，因该等法律适用于完全在斯德哥尔摩签订和履行的协议。"⑦

---

① BCY v. BCZ [2017] 3 SLR 357, [40].

② Gary, B., 'The Law Governing International Arbitration Agreements: An International Perspective', SAcLJ, vol. 26, 2014, para.34.

③ BCY v. BCZ [2017] 3 SLR 357, [14].

④ BMO v. BMP [2017] SGHC 127, [39].

⑤ BCY v. BCZ [2017] 3 SLR 357, [60].

⑥ FirstLink Investments Corp Ltd v. GT Payment Pte Ltd and others [2014] SGHCR 12, [14], [15].

⑦ FirstLink Investments Corp Ltd v. GT Payment Pte Ltd and others [2014] SGHCR 12, [9].

即使瑞典法律不是默示的法律选择，"根据三层次的法律选择分析方法很可能得出瑞典法律是与仲裁协议关系最密切的法律"①，因为斯德哥尔摩商会即位于瑞典，这也是仲裁的地点。

因此，当主合同中没有明示或默示的法律选择，仲裁地的法律将被认定为与协议有最密切和最真实联系的法律。

三、仲裁协议的有效性

仲裁协议的有效性决定了仲裁庭审理案件的管辖权。仲裁庭不能从无效的仲裁协议中获得管辖权。在"BCY"②案中，纽约法是管辖仲裁协议的适用法律，根据纽约法，有约束力的仲裁协议并未形成。因此，仲裁员没有审理该等请求的管辖权。

最近一个涉及上海当事人的新加坡案例是"信安"案③。该案中的仲裁条款存在缺陷，当事人未能根据 1994 年《中华人民共和国仲裁法》（《仲裁法》）第 16 条第 3 款正确表达所选的"仲裁委员会"，不符合《仲裁法》第 18 条的规定。双方约定将合同及争议提交至"中国国际仲裁中心"④，而该中心在大陆并不存在。新加坡高等法院认为，该仲裁协议有效，而且双方有益将争议提交至中国国际经济贸易仲裁委员会（CIETAC），因为名称中存在相同的词汇，如"中国""国际"和"仲裁"。⑤因此，中国国际经济贸易仲裁委员会拥有审理该案的管辖权。这一决定使有缺陷的仲裁协议仍然有效和可行，从而保护了当事人意思自治。

---

① BCY v. BCZ [2017] 3 SLR 357, [54].

② BCY v. BCZ [2017] 3 SLR 357, [93]-[97].

③ Re Shanghai Xinan Screenwall Building & Decoration Co, Ltd [2022] SGHC 58.

④ Re Shanghai Xinan Screenwall Building & Decoration Co, Ltd [2022] SGHC 58, [4].

⑤ Re Shanghai Xinan Screenwall Building & Decoration Co, Ltd [2022] 58, []45]-[49].

另一个案例是"BNA v. BNB and Another"案。该案所涉仲裁条款如下：

"ARTICLE 14 DISPUTES

14.1 This Agreement shall be governed by the laws of the People's Republic of China.

14.2 With respect to any and all disputes arising out of or relating to this Agreement, the Parties shall initially attempt in good faith to resolve all disputes amicably between themselves. If such negotiations fail, it is agreed by both parties that such disputes shall be finally submitted to the Singapore International Arbitration Centre (SIAC) for arbitration in Shanghai, which will be conducted in accordance with its Arbitration Rules. The arbitration shall be final and binding on both Parties." (BNA v. BNB [2019] SGHC 142)

新加坡高等法院首先裁定，仲裁地是新加坡，适用法律是新加坡法律，仲裁协议具有约束力[①]。但上诉法院推翻了这一裁决，认为仲裁地是上海，适用法律是中国法律，仲裁协议的有效性由中国法院决定[②]。

该案件在上海提起诉讼[③]，《中华人民共和国仲裁法》第 10 条和第 66 条要求中国国际商会组织设立"涉外仲裁委员会"，新加坡国际仲裁中心的管辖权再次受到质疑。上海市第一中级人民法院确认不禁止设在上海的外国仲裁机构组织仲裁活动，否则将有损国际商事仲裁的发展。[④]

上海法院注意到了中国最高人民法院（SPC）在 2013 年"龙利得"案中首次正式确认了将仲裁条款提交至在中国设立的外国仲裁机构的有效性。[⑤] 最高人民法院认为，约定国际商会仲裁的仲裁协议符合《中华人民共和国仲裁法》第 16 条的规定，仲裁庭对审理所涉 ICC 仲裁条款的案件有管

---

① BNA v. BNB and Another [2019] SGHC 142.

② BNA v. BNB [2019] SGCA 84.

③ Daesung Industrial Gases Co. Ltd. v. Praxair (China) Investment Co. Ltd. [2020] Hu 01 Min Te No. 83.

④ Daesung Industrial Gases Co. Ltd. v. Praxair (China) Investment Co. Ltd [2020] Hu 01 Min Te No. 83, [16].

⑤ Anhui Longlide Packaging Co. Ltd. v. BP Agnati S.R.L. (Longlide) [2013] Min Si Ta Zi No. 13.

辖权。据此，上海法院支持了上文所引述的该案仲裁条款的效力。

四、仲裁裁决的执行

《纽约公约》对外国仲裁裁决的执行至关重要。根据《纽约公约》第5条，中国可以根据《中华人民共和国民事诉讼法》第 283 条拒绝执行，新加坡可根据《国际仲裁法》第 19 条拒绝执行。

在"信安"[①]案中，新加坡高等法院认为，尽管中国国际经济贸易仲裁委员会的管辖权来自于有缺陷的仲裁协议，但其作出的仲裁裁决对各方都有约束力。被告没有参与仲裁程序，并声称包括仲裁通知和裁决在内的文件没有送达其新地址。法院认为，所有文件都以符合《示范法》第 3(1) 条的方式适当地予以送达，即送至了合同中提供的地址。《新加坡国际仲裁法》第 19B 条规定，裁决一旦作出即具有约束力。撤销裁决的时限在中国是 6个月，在新加坡是 3 个月。[②]因此，两国规定的时限都已超过，新加坡法院执行了该裁决。

如果仲裁地采用《示范法》，《示范法》第 34(1) 条规定，"不服仲裁裁决的唯一追诉是申请撤销"。根据《示范法》第 34(2)(a)(i) 条，如果仲裁协议的一方当事人有某种无行为能力情形；或者根据各方当事人所同意遵守的法律，该协议是无效的，则法院可以撤销裁决。

在存在上述理由的情况下，可以根据《纽约公约》第 V(1)(a) 条拒绝承认或执行仲裁裁决。《示范法》第 36(1)(a)(i) 条的规定与《纽约公约》第 5(1)(a)条相同。根据《示范法》，如果仲裁协议的一方当事人处在某种无行为能力状态，或根据当事人所适用的法律判定仲裁协议无效，或裁决本身违反执行

---

① Re Shanghai Xinan Screenwall Building & Decoration Co, Ltd [2022] SGHC 58.

② Re Shanghai Xinan Screenwall Building & Decoration Co, Ltd [2022] SGHC 58, [38].

国的公共政策，则法院可撤销裁决。在具备上述任何理由的情况下，根据《纽约公约》第 5 条和《示范法》第 36（1）条，可以拒绝承认或执行仲裁裁决。

还有一点需要注意，公共政策是一个广泛的概念。但要以公共政策为理由拒绝执行外国仲裁裁决并非易事。例如，在"国奥控股"①案的执行国澳大利亚，仅仅是当事人之间权利和义务的失衡并不被认为是违反了社会正义的基本准则。

结语

中国是大陆法系国家，法院遵从立法而非判例。因此，案例判例在中国的司法程序中发挥的作用较为有限。然而，2020 年 7 月 27 日，最高人民法院发布了一份名为《关于统一法律适用加强类案检索的指导意见（试行）》的指导意见。允许法院在审理类似案件时，以省内同级法院或上级法院审理的或最高人民法院公布的"指导性案例"或"典型案例"为依据。

此举促进了中国司法机构的确定性和一致性，有助于赢得更多外国企业的信心。然而，只有对《中华人民共和国仲裁法》作进一步厘清（如《中华人民共和国仲裁法》第 10 条和第 66 条规定的"委员会"的含义），才能保证仲裁的确定性。

上海法院②和新加坡法院③的共同之处是，二者均试图通过揭示当事人在仲裁协议中的真实意图来维护当事人意思自治原则，而不是保留或改变有缺陷的仲裁协议。另外，当事人有义务为主合同和仲裁协议约定明确的法律框架，以避免漫长的诉讼带来不必要的成本和时间。

---

① Guoao Holding Group Co Ltd v. Xue (No 2) [2022] FCA 1584, [32] - [38].

② Daesung Industrial Gases Co.Ltd. v. Praxair (China) Investment Co.Ltd [2020] Hu 01 Min Te No. 83.

③ BNA v. BNB [2019] SGCA 84.

Chapter 15

Recent Cases from Singapore in Contractual Relationships Involving Shanghai

Myo Su Thant

This chapter aims to understand the contractual relationship between the parties arising out of the arbitration agreements governed by *the New York Convention*. The chapter contains an in-depth discussion of recent cases from Singapore and also from Shanghai, to have some reflections from local Asian perspective.

Arbitration is private, independent, impartial and flexible. The parties may choose the seat of arbitration, governing law, appointment of arbitrators, and other procedural matters. The procedure can be designed by the parties depending on their own needs, for example, appointing arbitrators with specific expertise.[1] This is especially attractive for investors.

Both Singapore and China are parties to the UN Convention on the Recognition and Enforcement of Foreign Arbitral Awards 1958 (the "New York Convention"). Arbitral awards rendered in these countries are enforceable in 170 contracting states.[2] Both Singapore and China (as in Hong Kong SAR and Macao SAR) have subscribed to the UNCITRAL Model Law on International Commercial Arbitration (1985) with

---

[1] Yves, D & Eric, S., *A Guide to the New ICC Rules on Arbitration*, Kluwer Law International,1998, p. 258.

[2] https://uncitral.un.org/en/texts/arbitration/conventions/foreign_arbitral_awards/status2.

amendments as adopted in 2006 (UNCITRAL Model Law).

Taking advantage of the arbitration, the parties can use their party autonomy to make an arbitration agreement in flexible terms. But it is important that the parties do not make a defective or unenforceable arbitration agreement. Therefore, the following discussions will be addressed:

(1)Seat of arbitration,

(2)Proper law of the arbitration agreement,

(3)Validity of the arbitration agreement, and

(4)Enforcement of the arbitral award.

1. Seat of Arbitration

The parties should provide the seat of arbitration in their agreement clearly, bearing in mind the differences between the 'venue to hear the case' and the 'seat of arbitration'. In BNA case,[1] there was a geographical location provided in the arbitration agreement, but the intention of the parties was unclear in that whether they intended it to be the 'venue to hear the case' or the 'seat of arbitration'. The parties concluded in Article 14.2 of their arbitration agreement as:

"....disputes shall be finally submitted to the Singapore International Arbitration Centre (SIAC) for arbitration in Shanghai, which will be conducted in accordance with its Arbitration Rules."

The Supreme Court of Singapore ruled that the phrase "arbitration in Shanghai" is enough to indicate that 'Shanghai is the seat of arbitration'.[2] The Court referred the authority from the English rulings such as, *Naviera*[3] and *ABB Lummus*[4] where the exact same phrases were used, "arbitration in [location]". Therefore, if the parties provide only one geographical location in an arbitration agreement, it is to be naturally

---

[1] BNA v. BNB [2019] SGCA 84.

[2] BNA v. BNB [2019] SGCA 84, [65].

[3] Naviera Amazonica Peruana SA v. Compania Internacional de Seguros del Peru [1988] 1 Lloyd's Rep 116.

[4] ABB Lummus Global Ltd v. Keppel Fels Ltd [1999] 2 Lloyd's Rep 24.

interpreted that the parties have chosen that place as the seat of arbitration. If the geographical location is not identified in the agreement at all, the determination will depend on the rule of the arbitral institution. In case of SIAC, the 'seat' will be Singapore.[①] In international arbitrations, the seat of arbitration is important because:

(1)The local law of the seat of arbitration will govern the arbitration process,

(2)The local courts will have supervisory jurisdiction over the arbitration,

(3)The local courts will have power to set aside the award or judicial rulings,[②] and

(4)Where there is an absence of express or implied choice of law, the law of the seat of arbitration can be taken as the law applicable for the arbitration agreement and its validity because it has the closest connection.[③]

The law that the parties are subjected to is likely to be the law of the seat of arbitration in the absence of an express or implied agreement by the party.

2. Proper Law of the Arbitration Agreement

The three stages of choice-of-law analysis adopted by the High Court in *BCY v. BCZ*,[④] is a clear legal framework to determine the law governing the arbitration agreement. The stages are:

(1)the express choice of law by the parties;

(2)the implied choice of the parties as gleaned from their intentions at the time of contracting; or

(3)the system of law with which the arbitration agreement has the closest and most real connection.

---

① Rule 18.1 of the Investment Arbitration Rules of the Singapore International Arbitration Centre, 2017 (SIAC Rules).

② BNA v. BNB [2019] SGCA 84, [65].

③ FirstLink Investments Corp Ltd v. GT Payment Pte Ltd and others [2014] SGHCR 12.

④ BCY v. BCZ [2017] 3 SLR 357, [40].

It will be very straightforward, if the parties had expressly agreed to their governing law for the arbitration agreement. If not, the court or the arbitral tribunal must analyze whether the parties had impliedly chosen the proper law. The proper law of an arbitration agreement can be;

    (1)the law of the main contract, or

    (2)the law of the seat of arbitration.

(1) Proper Law as the Law of the Main Contract

If the arbitration agreement is formed as a part of the main contract and if there is an express choice-of-law to govern the main contract, the courts interpret this as a 'strong indication' of the intention of the parties for the same law to govern both the arbitration agreement and the main contact.[1] If the intention is otherwise, the parties are to specifically provide so, so that another law governs the arbitration agreement.[2]

The usage of a phrase in the agreement, such as 'obligations arising out of or in connection with' would also indicate that the arbitration agreement and the main contract are not separate agreements and that they would apply the same governing law. For example, in the *BCY* case,[3] such a phrase was used in Article 9.13.1 of the agreement between the parties. The Singapore court decided to apply the governing law of the main contract, New York law, to govern the arbitration agreement.

Such presumption is still adopted even if a particular law was to cover a particular part of the main contract. For example, in *BMO v. BMP*,[4] Vietnamese law was to cover Articles 27 and 28 of the main contract. But the court viewed Vietnamese law to cover the entire contract.

The doctrine of separability does not apply here. It only means that the validity of the arbitration agreement is independent from the validity or invalidity of the main contract. It does not mean that the arbitration agreement is distinct from the main

---

[1] BCY v. BCZ [2017] 3 SLR 357, [59].

[2] Gary, B., 'The Law Governing International Arbitration Agreements: An International Perspective', *SAcLJ*, vol. 26, 2014, para. 34.

[3] BCY v. BCZ [2017] 3 SLR 357, [14].

[4] BMO v. BMP [2017] SGHC 127, [39].

contract in every aspect. Therefore, the doctrine of separability does not apply to considering the proper law of the arbitration agreement.[①] Therefore, the same law can apply to the entire contract, if the parties did not expressly agree nor provided that different laws will apply to different parts of the contract.

(2) Proper Law as the Law of the Seat of Arbitration

In the 2014 *FirstLink* case,[②] the Singapore High Court held the law of the seat of arbitration as the presumed implied choice of the proper law of the arbitration agreement. The choice of law clause in Article 16 of the agreement stated that:

"This Agreement is governed by and interpreted under the laws of Arbitration Institute of the Stockholm Chamber of Commerce (SCC) as such laws are applied to agreements entered into and to be performed entirely within Stockholm".[③]

Even if the Swedish law was not an implied choice-of-law, 'the application of the third stage of the choice-of-law analysis would probably have pointed to Swedish law as the law with which the arbitration agreement had the closest connection,'[④] because the SCC was in Sweden, which is also the place of arbitration.

Therefore, when there is no express choice-of-law nor an implied choice-of-law to be referred from the substantive contract, the law of the seat of arbitration would be assumed as the law having the closest and most real connection with the agreement.

3. Validity of the Arbitration Agreement

The validity of the arbitration agreement determines the jurisdiction of an arbitral tribunal to hear the case. An arbitral tribunal cannot infer its jurisdiction from an invalid arbitral agreement. In the *BCY* case,[⑤] no binding arbitration agreement was formed under New York law which was the proper law to govern the arbitration agreement.

---

① BCY v. BCZ [2017] 3 SLR 357, [60].

② FirstLink Investments Corp Ltd v. GT Payment Pte Ltd and others [2014] SGHCR 12, [14], [15].

③ FirstLink Investments Corp Ltd v. GT Payment Pte Ltd and others [2014] SGHCR 12, [9].

④ BCY v. BCZ [2017] 3 SLR 357, [54].

⑤ BCY v. BCZ [2017] 3 SLR 357, [93]-[97].

Therefore, the Arbitrator did not have jurisdiction to hear the claims.

The most recent Singapore case involving a Shanghai party is the *Xinan* case,[①] where the arbitration clause was defective because the parties failed to express the correct 'arbitration commission chosen' under Article 16(3) of the Arbitration Law of the People's Republic of China, 1994 (PRC Arbitration Law). It did not conform with Article 18 of the PRC Arbitration Law. The contracts between the parties included the dispute to be submitted to 'China International Arbitration Center',[②] which does not exist in mainland China. The Singapore High Court held that the arbitration agreement was valid and that the parties intended to submit the dispute to the China International Economic and Trade Arbitration Commission (CIETAC) because of the common words in the names, such as "China", "International", and "Arbitration".[③] Therefore, the CIETAC had jurisdiction to hear the case. This decision protected party autonomy by making an arbitration agreement effective and workable despite being defective.

Another case is *BNA v. BNB and Another*, which involves the following arbitration clause:

"ARTICLE 14 DISPUTES

14.1 This Agreement shall be governed by the laws of the People's Republic of China.

14.2 With respect to any and all disputes arising out of or relating to this Agreement, the Parties shall initially attempt in good faith to resolve all disputes amicably between themselves. If such negotiations fail, it is agreed by both parties that such disputes shall be finally submitted to the Singapore International Arbitration Centre (SIAC) for arbitration in Shanghai, which will be conducted in accordance with its Arbitration Rules. The arbitration shall be final and binding on both Parties." (BNA v BNB [2019] SGHC 142)

The High Court in Singapore first ruled that the seat of arbitration was Singapore,

---

① Re Shanghai Xinan Screenwall Building & Decoration Co, Ltd [2022] SGHC 58.
② Re Shanghai Xinan Screenwall Building & Decoration Co, Ltd [2022] SGHC 58, [4].
③ Re Shanghai Xinan Screenwall Building & Decoration Co, Ltd [2022] SGHC 58, [45]-[49].

the proper law was Singapore law and the arbitration agreement was binding.① But it was overruled by the Court of Appeal that the seat of arbitration was Shanghai, the proper law was Chinese law and the validity of the arbitration agreement was to be decided by the Chinese court.②

When the case was brought in Shanghai,③ the jurisdiction of the SIAC was challenged again under Articles 10 and 66 of the PRC Law, which require 'foreign arbitration commissions' to be formed by the China International Chamber of Commerce. The Shanghai No.1 Intermediate People's Court, confirmed that foreign arbitral institutions seated in Shanghai are not prohibited from administering arbitrations, otherwise, it would be contrary to the development of international commercial arbitration.④

The Shanghai Court took note from the ruling of the Supreme People's Court of China (SPC) in 2013 that officially confirmed the validity of arbitration clause referring to a foreign arbitral institution seated in China for the first time in the *Longlide* case.⑤ The SPC held that the arbitration agreement referring to the ICC arbitration complies with Article 16 of the PRC Law and that the tribunal had jurisdiction to hear the case. Therefore, the Shanghai Court held that the arbitration clause as quoted above in the case was valid.

4. Enforcement of the Arbitral Award

The New York Convention is crucial for the enforcement of foreign arbitral awards. Enforcement can be refused under Article V of the New York Convention, under Article 283 of the PRC Civil Procedure Law in case of China, and under Section 19 of the International Arbitration Act in case of Singapore.

---

① BNA v. BNB and another [2019] SGHC 142.
② BNA v. BNB [2019] SGCA 84.
③ Daesung Industrial Gases Co. Ltd. v. Praxair (China) Investment Co. Ltd [2020] Hu 01 Min Te No. 83.
④ Daesung Industrial Gases Co. Ltd. v. Praxair (China) Investment Co. Ltd [2020] Hu 01 Min Te No. 83, [16].
⑤ Anhui Longlide Packaging Co. Ltd. v. BP Agnati S.R.L. (Longlide) [2013] Min Si Ta Zi No. 13.

In the *Xinan* case,[①] the Singapore High Court held that the arbitral award made by the CIETAC was binding upon the parties, although the jurisdiction of the CIETAC was derived from a defective arbitration agreement. The respondent did not participate in the arbitration proceedings and claimed that the documents, including the notice of arbitration and the Award, were not served to their new address. The court found that all the documents were properly served in a manner consistent with Article 3(1) of the Model Law by being delivered to the address provided in the contracts. Section 19B of the Singapore International Arbitration Act provides that an award is binding once made. The timeframe to set aside an award is 6 months in China and 3 months in Singapore.[②] Therefore, the timeframe had run out in both countries. The Singapore Court enforced the award.

If the seat of arbitration subscribes to the 'UNCITRAL Model Law', Article 34(1) provides that '[r]ecourse to a court against an arbitral award may be made only by an application for setting aside' of the arbitral award. Under UNCITRAL Model Law, an award may be set aside by the court if a party to the arbitration agreement was under some incapacity, or if the arbitration agreement is invalid under the law to which the parties have subjected it, or if the award itself is contrary to the public policy of the enforcement country.[③] In a case of having any of such grounds mentioned above, an arbitral award can be refused to recognize or enforce under Article V of the New York Convention and Article 36(1) of the UNCITRAL Model Law.

One more thing to note is that the public policy ground is a wide concept. But it is not easy to constitute a public policy exception to enforcement of the foreign arbitral award. For example, a mere imbalance of rights and obligations occurred between the parties is not considered to be contrary to fundamental norms of social justice in Australia, the enforcing country in *Guoao Holding* case.[④]

---

① Re Shanghai Xinan Screenwall Building & Decoration Co, Ltd [2022] SGHC 58.
② Re Shanghai Xinan Screenwall Building & Decoration Co, Ltd [2022] SGHC 58, [38].
③ Article 34(2) of the UNCITRAL Model Law.
④ Guoao Holding Group Co Ltd v. Xue (No 2) [2022] FCA 1584, [32] - [38].

Conclusion

China practices a civil law system. The courts rely on legislation rather than precedents. Therefore, case precedents play a very limited role in the judicial process in China. However, on 27 July 2020, the SPC issued a guidance note named "Opinion on Strengthening the Search for Similar Cases to Unify the Application of Law (for Trial Implementation)". This allowed the courts to rely, in similar cases, on the "guiding cases" or "typical cases" held by the same court or higher court in the province, or published by the SPC.

This promotes certainty and consistency in the Chinese Judiciary. This will gain more reliance by foreign businesses. However, certainty for arbitration can only be afforded by further clarification of the PRC Arbitration Law. For example, the meaning of 'commission' under Articles 10 and 66 of the PRC Arbitration Law.

What is common in both the Shanghai Courts[1] and the Singapore Courts[2] is that they try to maintain the party autonomy by revealing the real intention of the party in the arbitration agreement, rather than to save or change a defective arbitration agreement. Also, it is the duty of the parties to have a clear legal framework governing the main contract and the arbitration agreement in order to avoid unnecessary cost and time from long litigation.

---

[1] Daesung Industrial Gases Co. Ltd. v. Praxair (China) Investment Co. Ltd [2020] Hu 01 Min Te No. 83.

[2] BNA v. BNB [2019] SGCA 84.

第十六章

《示范法》在哪里与《纽约公约》相吻合？

赵逸之

通过于 1958 年的《纽约公约》和 1985 年的《示范法》共同构成了国际商事仲裁法的基石。随着中国继续履行其作为一个负责任的世界大国的义务，这一条约体系也对中国仲裁的发展产生了较大影响，指导着中国仲裁的法律框架、实践应用和行业环境。本章希望通过对这些文件的分析，协助您更好地理解中国仲裁。

一、目的与原则

早在《纽约公约》和《示范法》诞生之前，仲裁就已经是一个历史深厚、备受尊重的普通法传统。由于其灵活性、高效性、保密性和可执行性，它经常被认为是诉讼程序的更好的争议解决替代方案。然而，随着现代国家开始占据决策中心，不同国家的法律制度之间的差异浮出水面，逐渐成为加强非国内仲裁裁决的承认和执行的主要障碍。

《纽约公约》的导言中指出，该公约致力于确保"外国和非内国仲裁裁决不受歧视"，划定了缔约国对仲裁协议和仲裁裁决可施加限制的边界①。它为国际仲裁创造了一个宽松的政策环境，方便了跨国的政策协调与调整。这一愿景贯彻了国际商事仲裁的法律史，特别体现在《示范法》的形成过程中。

20世纪60年代，国际贸易的发展呼唤着一个推动标准化发展的独立机构的建立。于是，联合国国际贸易法委员会成立了。作为一个专门处理国际贸易中的法律框架问题的组织，整合和补充该领域的现有立法是组织议程上的首要任务。在这个过程中，委员会认识到，为了促进形成一个相互认可的国际贸易法体系，各成员国应该首先有一个本质上不相互矛盾的国内仲裁法体系。

应政府和非政府机构的要求，联合国国际贸易法委员会召集了一系列会议，并决定起草一份所有国家都可以参考的示范法作为解决方案。这将有助于各国建立统一的仲裁程序，与国际贸易的发展进程保持一致，从而走向一个更加标准化的未来。

二、《示范法》需要的改进

在《示范法》问世之前，《纽约公约》主要是在已有仲裁和商业传统的国家之间充当协调者，履行着国际交易法律程序的政策润滑剂的职责。然而，当越来越多的新生发展中国家开始登上全球化舞台，一些组织注意到，为了解决《纽约公约》与新生国家国内仲裁法之间的系统性差异，有必要制定一套新的标准化规则②。在这一讨论的过程中《联合国国际贸易法委员会示范法》诞生了。

1976年，亚非法律协商委员会（AALCC）向贸易法委员会提交了意见书，

---

① UNCITRAL, *UNCITRAL Secretariat Guide on the Convention on the Recognition and Enforcement of Foreign Arbitral Awards.* New York: United Nations, 2016, p.2.

② UN Doc. A/CN.9/127. *Note by the Secretariat-General: International Commercial Arbitration*, para. 3.

建议在《纽约公约》之下新增一项议定书，以确保国内法律不成为当事人意思自治下其自由选择仲裁程序的阻碍。经过多轮谈判，委员会一致认为，比起新的公约或议定书而言，制定一套示范法是协调有关跨境仲裁的国内法的最佳解决方案。

一个趋向协调和标准化的国际法体系不仅能很好地适应国际贸易的需要，而且有助于在实现不同社会经济地位的国家之间的公平。此外，《示范法》可以消除一些国家在处理过时的国内法和现代仲裁规则之间的矛盾时所面临的痛苦。由于联合国国际贸易法委员会发布了其版本的仲裁规则，当事人可以在其合同中援引和参考，因此，一部对其有利的示范法将更好地保证跨境仲裁的有效性。最后，《示范法》可有助于适当限制法院撤销仲裁裁决的理由[1]。

总的来说，《示范法》将更好地保证仲裁裁决的可执行性，免受裁决地的限制，也可以防止司法系统任意干预仲裁程序。

三、两文件的关键异同

（一）仲裁协议

根据《纽约公约》的规定，要判断仲裁协议是否有效，需要回答以下四个问题：

（1）是否有书面协议对争端主体进行仲裁？

（2）该协议是否规定在《公约》缔约国的领土上进行仲裁？

（3）该协议是否产生于商事法律关系中（合同关系与否不论）？

（4）该商事关系是否与一个或多个国家有关？

---

① UN Doc. A/CN.9/169. *Secretariat Note Concerning Recommendations on International Commercial Arbitration By The Asian-African Legal Consultative Committee*, para. 6-9.

如果法院对这些问题的回答是肯定的，那么它必须下令进行仲裁，除非它认定协议"无效、无法实施或无法履行"①。

《示范法》第 7 条第 2 款要求仲裁协议为书面形式。这一规定基于《示范法》不应与《纽约公约》相冲突的基本原则②。此外，在开始起草《示范法》之前，秘书处审查了《公约》对仲裁协议的"书面形式"这一要求存在的一些模糊之处，比如使用电子通信手段是否满足书面要求，以及合同中单独提及其他文件是否满足书面要求。考虑到上述因素，《示范法》为仲裁协议设定了以下四种被认为有效的方式。

（1）书面签署的文件

（2）信件、电报、电传或其他提供协议记录的电信往来

（3）索赔和辩护声明往来，其中一方声称协议的存在，而另一方没有否认

（4）在书面合同中提及含有仲裁条款的文件，如果这种提及使该条款成为合同的一部分

《示范法》第 8 条要求法院执行仲裁协议，并在满足某些要素的情况下让仲裁庭优先于司法程序。这一仲裁优先于法院的原则是以《纽约公约》第 2 条第 3 款为蓝本的。

（二）承认与执行仲裁裁决

《纽约公约》第 3 条指出了其所倡导的核心原则，即缔约国应"承认仲裁裁决具有拘束力，并依照裁决地的程序规则和下列各条所在条件予以执行"③。它将执行仲裁裁决的程序性问题留给当地决断，因为起草者意识到各国的裁决执行法可能大相径庭，所以决定在这个问题上保持谨慎，将

---

① Article II (3), New York Convention.

② UN Doc. A/40/17. *Report Of the United Nations Commission on International Trade Law On The Work Of Its 18th Session*, 1985, paras. 85 -86.

③ United Nations Conference on International Commercial Arbitration,1985 *Convention on the Recognition and Enforcement of Foreign Arbitral Awards.* New York: United Nations, Article III , 1958.

自由裁量权交给各国。《纽约公约》也因此在具有不同法律体系的国家得到了尊重和采纳，在这一领域获得了最广泛的共识。然而，后来的实践证明，在某些情况下，这些国内法的差异可能已经到了难以调和的地步。《示范法》的出台正是考虑到了这一问题。

《示范法》第35条是关于仲裁裁决的承认和执行的。它以《纽约公约》为蓝本，意在与这一被广泛接受的国际条约保持一致。根据《纽约公约》的规定，外国仲裁裁决在国内法律体系中不应受到歧视。因此，《示范法》也遵循这一原则，为承认和执行国内外的仲裁裁决制定了统一一致的机制，并不再强调仲裁地的重要性。

（三）示范法的特殊性

在相似点之外，《示范法》还纳入了一些区别于《纽约公约》的独特概念，并以此确立了一套广泛适用的国际仲裁法模式。

1. 司法干预最小化

《示范法》起草时的一个基本原则是，法院应尽可能少地干预仲裁程序。《示范法》的结构与仲裁的每个步骤保持一致，同时考虑到法院只在明确规定的几种有限情况下发挥作用。

2. 自裁管辖权原则

《示范法》第16条第1款规定，"仲裁庭应有权就其自身的管辖权作出裁决，包括对仲裁协议的存在或有效性提出的任何异议"。在大多数示范法国家的实践中，这一原则表明，仲裁庭应被赋予对其自身管辖权进行裁决的权力。在最近的案例中，这一原则被更广泛地解释为，仲裁庭甚至有权决定仲裁协议的有效性和范围，而这正是其权力的来源，从而将对协议的有效性挑战权提交给了仲裁庭而不是法院。

3. 仲裁程序

《示范法》旨在为有关国际商事仲裁的国内立法提供指导；因此，其内容包括从国际商事仲裁的基本定义、承认仲裁协议到仲裁程序的进行、执行和拒绝仲裁裁决等完整的一套仲裁流程。《示范法》直指国际商事仲裁的核心，建立了一套标准化的程序，可以自始至终在仲裁实践中适用。这也使得各国立法机构更容易将其纳入国内法律体系中。

四、《示范法》与中国《仲裁法》

在 1994 年《中华人民共和国仲裁法》颁布之前，中国大陆缺乏一部完整的法律来处理商事仲裁问题。受《纽约公约》和《示范法》的巨大影响，《中华人民共和国仲裁法》首次采用了协议仲裁的概念。

（一）港澳台地区

2010 年 11 月，香港特区颁布了新的《仲裁条例》，统一了《示范法》在国内和国际仲裁中的使用，同时纳入了《示范法》2006 年的修订内容。香港因其发达的仲裁法体系和深厚的法律历史，被认为是目前全球最理想的仲裁地之一。

澳门的第一部《仲裁法》于 1996 年颁布，又于 1998 年通过了以《示范法》为基础的专门规范国际仲裁的条例。这两部法律至今仍是澳门的仲裁管理法。

台湾在 1998 年通过了其最新的仲裁法。该法案主要在《示范法》基础上制成，并参考了其他辖区法律。关于《纽约公约》是否应适用于台湾的争论已持续多年，也深刻影响了台湾在国际商事仲裁中的地位与角色。此处可参考本书第十七章中这一问题的讨论。

（二）《中华人民共和国仲裁法》修正案

自 1987 年中国加入《纽约公约》以来，随着中国逐渐崛起为一个重要的世界大国，中国仲裁也一直是中国法律发展的焦点。尽管立法机关为完善国内的仲裁法律制度做出了持续的努力，但现有的法律框架仍有待改革和完善，尤其是在与《示范法》的接轨上 ①。

2021 年 7 月，司法部公布了《仲裁法》最新修正案的征求意见稿。征求意见稿对跨境仲裁提出了更加开放和包容的态度。这将一个长期被忽视的问题提到了日程上：中国《仲裁法》中是否有可能设置"国际商事仲裁"一章，专门处理所有在中国的外国仲裁，而无论这些仲裁是只包括外国当事人还是完全属于外国性质？

一个完善而健全的"国际商事仲裁"章节将是中国仲裁法体系的一个里程碑式的改革，因为它不仅可以纳入和重组现有法律中的所有与之相关的条款，而且也可以依循《示范法》的结构填补中国现有法律体系中有关外国仲裁的程序空白，包括管辖权的范围、法院对国际仲裁的有限干预、仲裁地点的选择、临时和机构仲裁以及仲裁庭的选择、撤销和拒绝承认及执行仲裁裁决的限制性理由等关键问题。

结语 —— 未来的中国仲裁

自 20 世纪 70 年代改革开放以来，中国的仲裁事业取得了长足的发展，已经一跃成为拥有着 250 多家仲裁机构的繁荣市场。如果没有《纽约公约》和《示范法》形成的完善的国际法律体系的帮助，中国的仲裁事业很难取得如此之大的成就。今后在执行经济发展的双循环政策时，中国将继续学习国外的先进技术和做法，在引进的同时使之适应国内的现实需要。不管是全盘采用《示范法》，还是在其新的仲裁法中接受《示范法》的原则，其最终目的都是为了中国仲裁一个更加和谐的未来。

---

① 张志：《仲裁立法的自由化、国际化和本土化：以贸法会》，中国社会科学出版社 2016 年版，第 152 页。

Chapter 16

Where Does the Model Law Meet the New York Convention?

Yizhi Zhao

The 1958 New York Convention, the UNCITRAL Model Law (1985), and the Amended Model Law (2006) have shaped the standard legal system of international commercial arbitration as we know it. As China continues to fulfill its role as a responsible world power, this treaty-based system has also exerted its influence on the development of Chinese arbitration, guiding its legal framework, general application, and the industrial environment. To understand Chinese arbitration better through these documents is what this chapter intends to do in the following sections.

1. Purpose and Principles

Arbitration has been a long-performed and well-respected common legal tradition long before the birth of *the New York Convention* and *the Model Law*. It has often been considered a better alternative to judicial proceedings for its flexibility, efficiency, confidentiality, and enforceability. However, as modern countries started to take the decision-making center, the discrepancies among the legal systems of different countries surfaced as a major obstacle to enhancing the recognition and enforceability of non-domestic arbitral awards.

It is indicated in the introduction of the document that this Convention is dedicated to ensuring that "foreign and non-domestic arbitral awards will not be discriminated against," defining the maximum level of control that a Contracting State may exert over arbitration agreement and arbitral awards.[①] It has created a lenient policy environment for international arbitration to coordinate despite borders. This aspiration has been well carried out throughout the legal history of international commercial arbitration, especially in the formation of the UNCITRAL Model Law.

In the 1960s, the creation of an independent agency favoring the development of a standardized international trade system was in the public interest, and UNCITRAL was established. As a targeted organization dealing specifically with technical issues about the legal framework of international trade, integrating and complementing the existing legislation in the field was at the top of the agenda. During this process, the Commission realized that to promote a mutually recognizable international trade law system, the member countries should at least have a domestic arbitration law system that does not inherently contradict each other.

At the request of both governmental and non-governmental bodies, UNCITRAL summoned a series of meetings and decided that the optimal resolution would be to draft a model law to which all States could refer. It would facilitate the establishment of uniform arbitral procedures that pace up with the needs of international trade toward a more standardized future.

2. Improvements Needed for the Model Law

Before the advent of *the Model Law, the New York Convention* mainly served as a coordinator between countries with preexisting arbitration and business traditions. It worked smoothly as a policy lubricator for international transactions and legal processes until new-born countries started to pave their way toward the global order. During this process, several organizations noted the urgency to create a set of standardized rules

---

① UNCITRAL, *UNCITRAL Secretariat Guide on the Convention on the Recognition and Enforcement of Foreign Arbitral Awards,* New York: United Nations, 2016, p.2.

to settle the systematic discrepancies spotted between the Convention and domestic arbitration laws.[1] Their discussions were what gradually and necessarily led to the birth of *the UNCITRAL Model Law*.

In 1976, the Asian-African Legal Consultative Committee (AALCC), an intergovernmental organization, submitted their proposal for a new protocol added to the New York Convention to ensure that national laws would not prevent parties from conducting arbitration in accordance with rules they had freely chosen.[2] After rounds and negotiation and preparation, the necessity of a Model Law, instead of a Convention or a protocol, was considered the most proper solution to guide national arbitration law that deals with international commercial arbitration.

A coordinated and standardized international law system would not only fit well with the needs of international trade, but also help to achieve a greater level of fairness among countries of different social-economic statuses. Moreover, a Model Law could eliminate the pains some countries would face when dealing with the contradiction of an outdated national law and modern arbitration rules. Since UNCITRAL published its version of Arbitration Rules that parties can invoke and refer to in their contract, a Model Law adapted in its favor would better facilitate the effectiveness of cross-border arbitrations. Finally, a model law could be helpful in appropriately limiting the grounds for courts setting aside an arbitral award. [3]

A Model Law would better protect the enforceability of an arbitral award – regardless of the place where it was made – and prevent the judicial system from unrestricted intervention in the arbitral procedure.

---

① UN Doc. A/CN.9/127. *Note by the Secretariat-General: International Commercial Arbitration*, para. 3.

② Holtzmann, H.M. & United Nations Commission on International Trade Law, *A guide to the UNCITRAL Model Law on International Commercial Arbitration: Legislative History and Commentary*. Devente: Kluwer Law and Taxation Publishers, 1989, p. 9.

③ UN Doc. A/CN.9/169. *Secretariat Note Concerning Recommendations on International Commercial Arbitration By The Asian-African Legal Consultative Committee*, para. 6-9.

3. Analysis of Key Commonalities

(1) Arbitration Agreement

The following four questions are to be answered under *the New York Convention*:

- Is there an agreement in writing to arbitrate the subject of the dispute?
- Does the agreement provide for arbitration in the territory of a signatory of the Convention?
- Does the agreement arise out of a legal relationship, whether contractual or not, which is considered commercial?
- Does the commercial relationship reasonably relate to one or more foreign States?

If the court resolves those questions in the affirmative, then it must order arbitration unless it finds the agreement "null and void, inoperative or incapable of being performed."[1]

Article 7, Paragraph 2 of *the Model Law*, requires that an arbitration agreement is in writing, based on the fundamental idea that *the Model Law* should not conflict with the *New York Convention*.[2] Moreover, before the drafting of the Model Law kicked off, the Secretariat reviewed some of the existing ambiguities in the interpretation of the Convention's writing requirement of an arbitration agreement, namely whether the writing requirement is satisfied by use of modern means of telecommunications, and whether it is met by references in contracts to general conditions in separate documents.[3] Taking into account the above factors, *the Model Law* set the following four ways for an arbitration agreement to be reckoned valid:

- Signed document
- Exchange of letters, telexes, telegrams, or other means of

---

[1] Article II (3),　New York Convention.

[2] UN Doc., A/40/17. *Report Of the United Nations Commission on International Trade Law On The Work Of Its 18th Session*, 1985, paras. 85 -86.

[3] UN Doc., A/CN.9/216. *Working Group On International Contract Practices On The Work Of Its Third Session*, 1982, para 23.

telecommunications that provide a record of the agreement

    • Exchange of statements of claim and defense in which the existence of an agreement is alleged by one party and not denied by another

    • Reference in a written contract to a document containing an arbitration clause, if the reference makes the clause part of the contract.

Article 8 requires the court to enforce the arbitration agreement and to give the arbitral tribunal priority over judicial proceedings if certain elements are met. The preference of arbitration over the court is modeled on Article II (3) of the Convention.

(2) Recognition and Enforcement of an Arbitral Award

Article III of *the New York Convention* points out the core principle advocated by the Convention, that the Contracting State shall "recognize arbitral awards as binding and enforcing them in accordance with the rules of procedure of the territory where the award is relied upon". [1] It leaves the enforcement of the arbitral award to local procedural rules, for the drafters realized that countries may differ greatly in their award enforcement laws and decided to stay cautious on this matter and give the discretion to the States. This effectively paves the way for the Convention to be adopted and respected by countries with various legal systems, gaining maximum consensus in this field. However, later practices proved that under certain circumstances, the distinctions might be too contradictive to be reconciled. Thus *the Model Law* was brought to the table with this concern in mind.

Article 35 of *the Model Law* deals with the recognition and enforcement of an arbitral award. It is directly modeled upon *the New York Convention* based on common sense to keep *the Model Law* consistent with this widely accepted international treaty. It features a fundamental notion that foreign arbitral awards should not be discriminated against in domestic legal context based on the provisions of *the New York Convention*, as it sets out a single, unified mechanism for recognition and

---

① United Nations Conference on International Commercial Arbitration, *Convention on the Recognition and Enforcement of Foreign Arbitral Awards,* New York: United Nations, Article III , 1958.

enforcement of the arbitral award and de-emphasize the importance of the place of arbitration.

(3) Distinctiveness of the Model Law

The Model Law incorporates several distinct concepts that distinguished it from the Convention and established itself as a widely applicable model for international arbitration laws.

Minimum Court Intervention

The Model Law was drafted on the basic principle that courts should intervene as little as possible in arbitral proceedings. The structure of the Model Law followed each step in arbitration while taking into account the court's role only in limited circumstances expressly provided under the Model Law.

Competence-Competence Principle

Article 16(1) of *the Model Law* provides that "[t]he arbitral tribunal shall have the power to rule on its own jurisdiction, including any objections with respect to the existence or validity of the arbitration agreement."[1] In most practices of Model Law countries, this principle indicates that an arbitral tribunal should be granted such power to rule on its own jurisdiction. In recent cases[2], this principle has been more widely interpreted in the sense that the tribunal has the power to decide even the validity and scope of the arbitration agreement – the very thing that its authority comes from – thus reaffirming the referral of validity challenges to the arbitral tribunal instead of to the courts.

Conduct of Proceedings

The Model Law aims to provide a legislative guide to domestic legislation concerning international commercial arbitrations; therefore, it composes of instructions on how arbitration should be conducted, from basic definition and recognition of arbitration agreements to the conduct of the proceedings, and to the enforcement

---

[1] United Nations Commission on International Trade Law, *UNCITRAL Model Law on International Commercial Arbitration*. New York: United Nations, 1985, Article 16(1).

[2] *Uber Technologies Inc., et al. v. David Heller*, SCC No. 38534, 2020.

and refusal of arbitral awards. *The Model Law* goes to the backbone of international commercial arbitration, establishing a standardized set of procedures that can be applied in practice from start to end, which makes it easier for national legislations to incorporate it in domestic legal systems.

4. Model Law and Chinese Arbitration Law

Before the promulgation of the 1994 Arbitration Law of the People's Republic of China ("PRC Arbitration Law"), mainland China lacked a unified national law to deal with commercial arbitrations. Influenced tremendously by *the New York Convention* and *the Model Law*, the PRC Arbitration Law adopted for the first time the concept of consensual arbitration （协议仲裁）.

(1) Hong Kong, Macao, and Taiwan

In November 2010, Hong Kong SAR enacted a long-awaited Arbitration Ordinance unifying the use of Model Law in domestic and international arbitrations while incorporating amendments from the 2006 Amended Model Law. Hong Kong is now considered one of the ideal places for arbitration for its well-developed arbitration law system and profound legal history.

The first arbitration law of Macao was promulgated in 1996, and in 1998 an ordinance based on the Model Law and specifically regulating international arbitrations was passed. They remain the governing laws of arbitration in Macao until now.

Taiwan passed its latest arbitration law in 1998 based primarily on the Model Law with references to other jurisdictional laws. Whether *the New York Convention* should apply to Taiwan has been debated for years, affecting Taiwan's role in international commercial arbitration. Reference should be made to the discussion of this topic in Chapter 17 of this book.

(2) Amendment of Chinese Arbitration Law

Since China acceded to *the New York Convention* in 1987, Chinese arbitration has been the focal point of Chinese legal development as China has risen as a significant world power. Despite consistent efforts made by legislative organs to refine the national arbitration system, the existing legal framework is still open to reforms and improvements, namely in its engagement with the Model Law.[1]

In July 2021, the Department of Justice published the Consultation Draft of the latest amendments to the Arbitration Law. The Consultation Draft presented a more open and inclusive attitude toward foreign arbitrations, which brings forward a long-overlooked question onto the table: Is it possible for a chapter on "International Commercial Arbitration" in Chinese Arbitration Law that specifically deals with all foreign arbitrations in China, regardless of whether they include only foreign parties or are of complete foreign nature?

A new and wholesome chapter on international commercial arbitration would be a landmark reform to the Chinese arbitration law system, as it would not only incorporate and organize all related clauses in existing laws, but also fill procedural gaps among proceedings in any foreign arbitration in China along the way of the UNCITRAL Model Law, including the scope of jurisdiction, limited court intervention in international arbitration, choice of place of arbitration, ad hoc and institutional arbitrations, and choice of arbitral tribunals, limited grounds for setting aside and for refusing recognition and enforcement of arbitral awards.

Conclusion — Future Chinese Arbitration

Since the reform and opening up in the 1970s, arbitration in China has come a long way into what it is now, a flourishing market with more than 250 arbitration institutions, and it would not achieve so much without the assistance of a well-preserved international legal system formed by *the New York Convention* and *the UNCITRAL Model Law*. In the future in executing the policy of external circulation and internal circulation of economic development, China will continue to learn from

[1] Zhang, Z., *The Liberalization, Internationalization and Nationalization of Arbitration Legislations: in Comparison with UNCITRAL Arbitration Model Law.* 1st ed. Beijing: China Social Sciences Press, 2016, p.152.

advanced techniques and practices abroad while adapting them to the needs of domestic realities. Regardless wholesale adoption of the UNCITRAL Model Law, the Amended Model Law, or acceptance of their principles into its new arbitration law, all together it is a time for a more harmonious future for Chinese arbitration.

第十七章

谁说《纽约公约》不适用于台湾呢?

高 梁

1958 年联合国通过了《纽约公约》,该公约于 1959 年 6 月 7 日正式生效。如今《纽约公约》已成为世界范围内最成功的国际条约之一。因《纽约公约》一般仅对联合国成员国开放会员资格,而中华人民共和国是在联合国代表中国的唯一官方实体,因此,中国国家主权原则阻止了台湾对《纽约公约》的批准。所以台湾不是《纽约公约》的成员国,台湾也不得以《纽约公约》为法律依据以承认并执行外国仲裁之裁决。同样,由于该公约第 1 条第 3 款所规定的互惠要求排除了在非签署国境内执行仲裁裁决,因此,其导致台湾在很大程度上陷入阻碍对外国裁决承认之局面。

一、台湾仲裁立法与纽约公约

尽管如此,从立法的角度来看,台湾的"仲裁法"是参照《纽约公约》而制定的,并吸收了《纽约公约》的一些主要特点。接下来,我将详细阐述它们之间的相似之处。台湾法院原则上承认外国仲裁裁决的法律效力,但前提是该外国仲裁裁决必须符合其《仲裁法》的有关规定。具体而言,台湾"仲裁法"第 47 条规定:"外国仲裁裁决,经申请法院裁定承认后,于当事人间,与法院之确定判决有同一效力，并得为执行名义。"所以，从法律的角度来看，外国仲裁裁决可享有与法院判决同等的效力，因此可在台湾的管辖范围内得以执行。

仲裁庭的管辖权问题在世界范围内都是仲裁立法的核心问题。为了确保仲裁协议能够得到遵守，《纽约公约》第2条第3款规定，在当事双方之间有仲裁协议的情况下，缔约国法院有义务命当事人提交仲裁。"台湾仲裁法"也强调了仲裁庭的管辖权。该"仲裁法"第4条规定，仲裁协议，如一方不遵守，另行提起诉讼时，法院应依他方声请裁定停止诉讼程序，并命原告于一定期间内提付仲裁。仲裁庭的管辖权是为了确保仲裁协议当事人之间的仲裁承诺在实践中得到履行。

关于仲裁协议的无效性问题而言，《纽约公约》授权缔约国法院对仲裁裁决行使权力。台湾的仲裁立法也是如此。根据"台湾仲裁法"第38条第1款规定，有下列各款情形之一者，法院应驳回其执行裁定之申请：（1）仲裁裁决与仲裁协议目标之争议无关，或逾越仲裁协议之范围者。但除去该部分亦可成立者，其余部分，不在此限。这一规定恰恰反映了《纽约公约》第5条第1款第(c)项的法律精神：若裁决所处理之争议非为交付仲裁之标的或不在其条款之列，则可拒绝承认和执行该裁决。仲裁协议在法律上独立于包含它的主合同，因此主合同无效并不等同于仲裁协议被宣布无效。《纽约公约》与"台湾仲裁法"在这一点上有共同之处。

若外国仲裁裁决之承认和执行可能被视为违反某个法域的公共政策和法律时，我们认为以下操作是合理的，即法院应有权就承认该外国仲裁裁决的问题上说"不"。公共政策不是《纽约公约》所特有的概念。早在1927年《日内瓦公约》第1条第2款第（e）项中就已经规定了公共政策的概念，即仲裁的承认或执行对请求承认或者履行该裁决当地所属国家的公共秩序或法律原则并不抵触。考虑到上述观点，公共政策的概念已广泛被引入世界各地的仲裁立法之中。

根据"台湾仲裁法"第 49 条第 1 款之规定，当事人申请法院承认之外国仲裁裁决，有下列各款情形之一者，法院应以裁定驳回其申请：一、仲裁裁决之承认或执行，有悖于台湾地区公共秩序或善良风俗者。该"仲裁法"第 49 条第 1 款的措辞几乎参照《纽约公约》第 5 条第 2 款的有关规定，后者规定：若裁决的承认与执行违反该国公共政策的情况下，可以拒绝承认和执行仲裁裁决。两者都特别关注作为拒绝承认和执行外国仲裁裁决的事实依据的公共政策。

就仲裁立法中的"可仲裁性"问题而言，其超越了仲裁协议中当事人所享有的"自治"原则，并构成一国维护其法律和秩序的核心利益。"可仲裁性"也不是《纽约公约》所特有的概念。根据 1927 年《日内瓦公约》第 1 条第 2 款第 (b) 项的规定，裁决的事项按照请求履行该裁决当地所属国家的法律是可以用仲裁方法解决的。人们也普遍认为，"可仲裁性"这一概念在世界各国的仲裁立法中得到了体现。更具体而言，根据"台湾仲裁法"第 49 条的规定，当事人申请法院承认之外国仲裁裁决，有下列各款情形之一者，法院应以裁定驳回其申请：（2）仲裁裁决依台湾法律，其争议事项不能以仲裁解决者。而根据《纽约公约》第 5 条第 2 款第 (a) 项的规定，依该国法律，争议事项系不能以仲裁解决者，则可以拒绝承认和执行仲裁裁决。在这方面，《纽约公约》与台湾仲裁立法也有共同之处。

为了在撤销程序启动前不使资产被浪费或隐藏，以确保仲裁裁决在驳回撤销诉讼时能够得到切实执行，"担保"这一概念被引入仲裁立法之中。关于申请撤销或中止外国仲裁裁决的问题上，《纽约公约》[①] 和"台湾仲裁法"[②] 都允许法院有权命令申请人提供适当的担保。

此外，无论是《纽约公约》还是"台湾仲裁法"都高度重视"程序正当"

---

① 请参阅《纽约公约》第 6 条。
② 请参阅"台湾仲裁法"第 51 条。

原则。根据《纽约公约》第 5 第 1 款第 (b) 项，受裁决援用之一方未接获关于指派仲裁员或仲裁程序之适当通知，或因他故，致未能申辩者，则可拒绝承认和执行外国裁决。根据"台湾仲裁法"第 51 条第 3 款规定，若当事人之一方，就仲裁人之选定或仲裁程序应通知之事项未受适当通知，或有其他情事足认仲裁欠缺正当程序者，他方当事人可申请法院驳回其申请。早在 1927 年的《日内瓦公约》中，"正当程序"原则就体现在该公约第 2 条第 1 款第 (b) 项中：如果法院认为仲裁程序的进行未及时通知对其请求履行裁决的人以使其有充分的时间提出意见时，法院可以拒绝承认和执行该裁决。

因此，人们普遍认为，《纽约公约》对台湾仲裁立法产生了重大影响。而且，台湾地区在承认和执行外国仲裁裁决方面的司法实践，普遍被认为符合《纽约公约》的有关规定。

《纽约公约》第 10 条讨论了该《公约》适用于国内领土单位的问题。根据该《公约》第 10 条，任何国家在签署、批准或加入时，均可宣布本《公约》适用于其负责管理国际关系的所有或任何领土。中华人民共和国乃《纽约公约》之缔约国，其当然是在国际机构中代表中国的合法实体。在法律上，台湾是中华人民共和国不可分割的一部分。因此，中华人民共和国有权宣布该《公约》将适用于台湾境内。但是，目前台湾实行的是事实上的土地自治、公民自治、资源自治和法律自治，中华人民共和国的法律法规在实际生活中尚未适用于台湾地区。若中华人民共和国宣布将《公约》的适用扩大到台湾地区，那么是否接受该声明将由台湾人民来决定，在相信中国符合国际法程序的情况下，后者自然顺势而为。到目前为止，中华人民共和国尚未通过任何此类宣言，如今《纽约公约》自然还不适用于台湾境内。

二、外国仲裁裁决在台湾的有关案例

尽管台湾不是《纽约公约》的缔约国，但台湾地区的法院对外国仲裁

裁决持开放态度。最近的判决表明，台湾法院越来越有意愿承认和执行外国仲裁裁决。

2010 年，台湾新竹地方法院作出了一项关于外国仲裁裁决在台湾管辖范围内的承认和执行问题的裁定。① 本案中，来自台湾一方的抗告人称，由于台湾不是《纽约公约》的签署国，而芬兰作为《纽约公约》的缔约国，将不承认台湾所作出的仲裁裁决。根据"台湾仲裁法"第 49 条第 2 款的规定，外国仲裁裁决，其裁决地国或裁决所适用之仲裁法规所属国对于台湾之仲裁裁决不予承认者，法院得以裁定驳回其申请。而这正是本案台湾抗告人要求法院拒绝承认芬兰仲裁裁决的法律依据。

在该案中，法院提出："除非外国明确拒绝承认和执行台湾所作出的仲裁裁决，台湾法院将根据国际礼让和互惠原则得首先承认外国仲裁裁决。因此，尽管芬兰与台湾之间没有正式外交关系，且台湾也不是《纽约公约》的签署国，但法院不得基于上述理由驳回承认芬兰仲裁裁决的申请。如果来自台湾的仲裁裁决在芬兰没有被明确否认其法律效力，那么本院宜尽量在互惠的基础上，承认芬兰所作出的仲裁裁决的效力。"

此外，该法院认为，《纽约公约》仅规定各缔约国得申明其仅承认及执行另一缔约国领土内之仲裁裁决，并非要求各缔约国对于不在各缔约国领土内作成之仲裁裁决一概不予承认及执行。因此，各缔约国是否不承认非《纽约公约》缔约国之仲裁裁决，仍须视其于签署《纽约公约》时有无特别声明而定。因芬兰没有根据《纽约公约》作出互惠性保留且台方抗告人未能提交证据证明芬兰拒绝承认台湾作出的仲裁裁决为依据，因此，最终法院没有拒绝承认该来自芬兰的仲裁裁决。

2011 年，台北地方法院亦作出一项关于承认和执行外国仲裁裁决的问

---

① 请参阅台湾新竹地方法院第 2010 号抗字 29 号民事裁定。

题的裁定①。在本案中，抗告人要求法院驳回承认纽约国际商会国际仲裁庭作出的仲裁裁决的申请，理由为相对人未能提供仲裁裁决地国美国承认台湾所作出的仲裁裁决的先例。因此，抗告人认为"台湾仲裁法"第49条第2款适用于本案。

本院认同前一案件中关于承认和执行外国仲裁裁决问题的意见。更具体而言，本院认为，互惠原则并不意味着作出仲裁裁决的国家或裁决所适用之仲裁法规所属国应首先承认台湾的仲裁裁决，台湾法院在此基础上随后才承认该国家的仲裁裁决。此外，法院认为，如果一个国家没有明确拒绝承认在台湾作出的仲裁裁决，那么台湾法院将在互惠精神的基础上承认该国的仲裁裁决。本案中，由于没有证据表明美国拒绝承认台湾作出的仲裁裁决，台北地方法院最终作出驳回抗告的裁定。

以上案例表明，若外国在没有明确拒绝承认台湾仲裁裁决时，台湾法院非常有意愿承认并执行外国仲裁裁决。为了确保外国仲裁裁决能够在台湾执行，申请人首先确认互惠问题是至关重要的。

---

① 请参阅台北地方法院民事判决第2011号抗字107号民事裁定。

Chapter 17

Who Says New York Convention Does Not Apply to Taiwan?

Liang Gao

The *New York Convention* was adopted by the United Nations in 1958 and entered into force on 7 June 1959. Now it has become one of the most successful international agreements ever world-wide. As the Convention is basically open to accession by the member states of the United Nations, the People's Republic of China (PRC) serves as the sole entity representing China in the United Nations. Accordingly, the doctrine of PRC sovereignty has prevented Taiwan from ratifying the New York Convention. Therefore, Taiwan is not a signatory to the New York Convention and it is not possible for Taiwan to seek the recognition and enforcement of foreign arbitral awards on the basis of the New York Convention. Likewise, since the reciprocity requirement as set out in Article I (3) of the treaty precludes enforcement of arbitral awards in non-signatory countries, it therefore would lead Taiwan to a situation where the recognition of foreign awards, to a large extent, is obstructed.

1. Taiwan Arbitration Legislation and the New York Convention

That being said, from the perspective of legislation, the Arbitration Act in Taiwan, however, is modeled on *the New York Convention* and it does incorporate a number of the New York Convention's key features. In what follows, I will elaborate on details of the similarities between them. In principle, the courts in Taiwan recognize the legal effect of foreign arbitral awards, provided that the foreign arbitral awards meet certain requirements as set out in the Arbitration Act. Specifically, according to Article 47 of the Taiwan Arbitration Act, "A foreign arbitral award, after an application for recognition has been granted by the court, shall be binding on the parties and have the same force as a final judgment of a court, and is enforceable." And thus, from a legal point of view, foreign arbitral awards can enjoy the same force as judgments of a court and therefore can be enforced in the jurisdiction of Taiwan.

The jurisdiction of arbitral tribunals is at the heart of arbitration legislation world-wide. In order to ensure that an arbitration agreement can be complied with, Article II (3) of *the New York Convention* provides for the obligation of the courts of the Contracting State to refer the parties to arbitration in the case of an arbitration agreement between them. And the Taiwan Arbitration Act also puts an emphasis on the jurisdiction of arbitral tribunals. According to Article 4 of the Act, in the event that one of the parties to an arbitration agreement commences a legal action contrary to the arbitration agreement the court may, upon application, suspend the legal action and order the plaintiff to submit to arbitration within a specified time. The jurisdiction of arbitral tribunals is to ensure that the commitments to submit to arbitration made between parties to the arbitration agreement can be fulfilled in practice.

With respect to the issue of invalidity of an arbitration agreement, *the New York Convention* authorizes the courts of the Contracting States to exercise power on arbitral awards. That is also the case in Taiwan's arbitration legislation. According to Article 38 (1) of the Arbitration Act, the court shall reject an application for enforcement in any of the following circumstances where:

(1) The arbitral award concerns a dispute not contemplated by the terms of the arbitration agreement, or exceeds the scope of the arbitration agreement, unless the offending portion of the award may be severed and the severance will not affect the remainder of the award. And this provision exactly reflects the legal spirit of Article V(1)(c) of the New York Convention: recognition and enforcement of the award may be refused in the case of the award dealing with a difference not contemplated by or

not falling within the terms of the submission to arbitration. Arbitration agreement is, in law, independent of a contract containing it and thus invalidity of the contract is not tantamount to the arbitration agreement being declared invalid. There is a shared common ground on this point between *the New York Convention* and *the Taiwan Arbitration Act.*

Where recognition and enforcement of a foreign arbitral award is likely to be considered against public policy and law in a particular jurisdiction, it is reasonable to argue that courts should be given the power to say "NO" to recognition of such foreign arbitral award. Public policy is not a concept particular to the New York Convention. As early as the 1927 Geneva Convention, the concept of public policy had been set out in Article 1 (e) thereof: it shall be necessary that the recognition or enforcement of the award is not contrary to the public policy or to the principles of the law of the country in which it is sought to be relied upon. With the above point in mind, the concept of public policy has been widely introduced into arbitration legislation world-wide.

According to Article 49 (1) of the Taiwan Arbitration Act, the court shall issue a dismissal with respect to an application submitted by a party for recognition of a foreign arbitral award, if such award contains one of the following elements:

(1) Where the recognition or enforcement of the arbitral award is contrary to the public order or good morals in Taiwan. The wording of Article 49 (1) of the Arbitration Act is almost modeled on that of Article V (2) of the New York Convention which provides that recognition and enforcement of an arbitral award may be refused in the case that the recognition or enforcement of the award would be contrary to the public policy of that country. Both of them bring particular attention to the public policy serving as a factual basis to refuse the recognition and enforcement of foreign arbitral awards.

As regards the issue of "arbitrable" in arbitration legislation, it goes beyond the principle of "autonomy" parties to arbitration agreement can enjoy and constitutes the core interests of a country in protecting its law and order. "Arbitrable" is not a concept particular to *the New York Convention* as well. According to Article 1 (b) of *the 1927 Geneva Convention*, it shall be necessary that the subject-matter of the award is capable of settlement by arbitration under the law of the country in which the award is sought to be relied upon. It is also widely accepted that the concept of "arbitrable" has been reflected in arbitration legislation in the world. More specifically, According to Article 49 of the Taiwan Arbitration Act, the court shall issue a dismissal with respect to an application submitted by a party for recognition of a foreign arbitral award, if such award contains one of the following elements: (2) where the dispute is not arbitrable under the laws of Taiwan. And Article V (2) (a) of *the New York Convention* provides that recognition and enforcement of an arbitral award may be refused if the subject matter of the difference is not capable of settlement by arbitration under the law of that country. In this regard, *the New York Convention* and *the Taiwan arbitration* legislation share common ground as well.

In order that assets will not be squandered or hidden before the revocation procedure is kick-started so as to ensure that arbitral awards can be enforced practically when dismissing the revocation action, the concept of "security" is introduced in arbitration legislation. With reference to an application for the revocation or suspension of foreign arbitral awards, both *the New York Convention*[①] and *the Taiwan Arbitration Act*[②] allow courts to have the power to order the applicant to give suitable security.

Furthermore, the principle of "due course" has been highly respected by both *the New York Convention* and *the Taiwan Arbitration Act*. According to Article V(1)(b) of *the New York Convention*, recognition and enforcement of foreign awards may be refused, if the party against whom the award is invoked was not given proper notice of the appointment of the arbitrator or of the arbitration proceedings or was otherwise unable to present his case. Pursuant to Article 51(3) of the Taiwan Arbitration Act, the respondent may request the court to dismiss the application, if a party is not given proper notice whether of the appointment of an arbitrator or of any other matter required in the arbitral proceedings, or any other situations which give rise to lack of due process. As early as *the 1927 Geneva Convention*, the principle of "due process" was reflected in Article 2 (1) (b) thereof: recognition and enforcement of the award shall be refused if the Court is satisfied that the party against whom it is sought to

---

① Please see Article VI of the New York Convention.
② Please see Article 51 of the Taiwan Arbitration Act.

use the award was not given notice of the arbitration proceedings in sufficient time to enable him to present his case.

As such, it is widely recognized that *the New York Convention* has exerted a strong influence on the legislation of arbitration in Taiwan. And judicial practices exercised on the recognition and enforcement of foreign arbitral awards in Taiwan have been generally considered as being in line with what is provided for in *the New York Convention*.

Article X of *the New York Convention* discusses the issue of the applicability of the Convention to domestic territorial units. According to Article X, any State may, at the time of signature, ratification, or accession, declare that this Convention shall extend to all or any of the territories for the international relations of which it is responsible. The PRC, as a Party to the Convention, is, of course, the legitimate entity representing China at international institutions. At the legal level, Taiwan constitutes an integral part of the PRC. Therefore, the PRC is vested with the power to declare that the Convention will be applicable to the jurisdiction of Taiwan. However, currently Taiwan is exercising self-governance over its lands, citizens, resources and laws on a de facto basis, to which the PRC laws and regulations are not practically applicable. And if the PRC declares the extension of the Convention to the area of Taiwan, then it will come to Taiwan people to decide whether or not it will accept such declaration, with the belief of China's compliance with procedure of international law, this acceptance naturally being there. So far, the PRC has not adopted any declaration of this kind and naturally, now *the New York Convention* is not applicable within the jurisdiction of Taiwan.

2. Recent Cases concerning Foreign Arbitral Awards in Taiwan

Despite the fact that Taiwan is not a Contracting State *to the New York Convention*, the courts in Taiwan are keeping an open mind towards foreign arbitral awards. Recent judgments have demonstrated that Taiwan is increasingly willing to recognize and enforce foreign arbitral awards.

In 2010, the Hsinchu District Court rendered a ruling[①] concerning the issue of recognition and enforcement of foreign arbitral awards in the jurisdiction of Taiwan. The Taiwanese respondent claimed that since Taiwan was not a signatory to the New York Convention, Finland, a Party thereto, would not recognize arbitral awards made in Taiwan. And according to Article 49 (2) of the Taiwan Arbitration Act, the court may issue a dismissal order with respect to an application for recognition of a foreign arbitral award if the country where the arbitral award is made or whose laws govern the arbitral award does not recognize arbitral awards made in Taiwan. And this exactly constitutes the legal basis by which the Taiwanese respondent asked the Court to refuse the recognition of the Finnish arbitral award.

In the case, the Court submitted that "unless a foreign country expressly refuses recognition and enforcement of arbitral awards rendered in Taiwan, the courts in Taiwan would first recognize the foreign awards on the basis of the principle of international comity and reciprocity. Thus, despite the fact that there are no formal diplomatic relations between Finland and Taiwan and that Taiwan is not a signatory to the New York Convention, the Court would not dismiss the application for the recognition of the Finnish arbitral award on account of the reasons mentioned above. And where arbitral awards from Taiwan are not expressly denied legal effect in Finland, then the Court intends to recognize the effect of arbitral awards rendered in Finland as far as possible on the basis of reciprocity."

In addition, the Court took the view that *the New York Convention* only provides that each Contracting State should declare the recognition and enforcement of awards made in the territory of another Contracting State, without demanding that each Contracting State refuse to recognize and enforce awards made outside of the territory of the Contracting States. As such, whether or not a Contracting State refused to recognize arbitral awards of non-Contracting States depended on whether the Contracting State made a reciprocity reservation under *the New York Convention*. And eventually, the Court did not refuse the recognition of the Finnish arbitral award on the ground that Finland did not make a reciprocity reservation under the Convention

---

① Please see Civil Ruling No. 2010 Kang-Zi 29 in the Hsinchu District Court.

and that the Taiwanese party failed to submit evidence to prove that Finland refused to recognize arbitral awards made in Taiwan.

In 2011, the Taipei District Court also rendered a ruling[①] concerning the issue of recognition and enforcement of foreign arbitral awards. In this case, the appellant asked the Court to dismiss the application for recognition of the arbitral award made by the International Court of the International Chamber of Commerce in New York, on the basis that the respondent failed to present the precedents in which the U.S. where the arbitral award was made recognized arbitral awards made in Taiwan. As such, the appellant argued that Article 49 (2) of the Taiwan Arbitration Act would be applicable in the present case.

The Court echoed the views held in the previous case on the issue of recognition and enforcement of foreign arbitral awards. More specifically, the Court concluded that the principle of reciprocity would not be taken to imply that the country where the arbitral award was made or whose laws govern the arbitral award shall first recognize arbitral awards of Taiwan, and on that basis, the courts in Taiwan would recognize arbitral awards of such country thereafter. Moreover, the Court held that if a country did not expressly refuse the recognition of arbitral awards made in Taiwan, then the Taiwan courts would recognize the arbitral awards of this country on the basis of the spirit of reciprocity. As there was no evidence to indicate that the U.S. refused to recognize arbitral awards made in Taiwan, the Court decided to dismiss the appeal.

The above cases demonstrate that if a foreign country does not expressly refuse the recognition of awards made in Taiwan, then the courts in Taiwan are quite willing to recognize and enforce the foreign arbitral awards. In order to ensure that the foreign arbitral awards may be enforced in Taiwan, it is critically important for applicants to verify the issue of reciprocity in the first place.

---

① Please see Civil Ruling No. 2011 Kang-Zi 107 in the Taipei District Court.

第十八章

跨国法视角下《纽约公约》在中国的理解与适用

杨昆灏　陈思瑞

一、概览：当代中国的仲裁法

在中国，仲裁已成为重要的商事争议解决机制。据《中国国际商事仲裁年度报告（2021—2022）》显示，2021 年中国 270 家仲裁机构共受理415889 个案件。[①]这些案件的总标的金额为 8.593 亿元人民币。[②]与此同时，更多的中国仲裁机构在全球争议解决市场中涌现。伦敦玛丽女王大学（The Queen Mary University of London）和伟凯律师事务所（White & Case LLP）最近进行的一项调查显示，中国国际经济贸易仲裁委员会（CIETAC）在全球最受青睐的仲裁机构名单中排名第五。[③]上述数据展现了中国仲裁在过去

[①] 相关数据可参见中国国际经济贸易仲裁委员会：《中国国际商事仲裁年度报告 (2021—2022)》，法律出版社 2022 年版。

[②] 同上。

[③] The School of International Arbitration, Queen Mary University of London and White & Case LLP, *2021 International Arbitration Survey: Adapting Arbitration to a Changing World*, 2022, p. 10.

几十年中所取得的巨大成功。

仲裁在中国的快速发展根植于民间非司法争议解决的实践经验和民间智慧，同时也得益于现代仲裁法规则的引入。孔子思想深深影响中国社会规范，在传统民间社会主导大众思想。它提倡人们遵守道德和礼制，这也包括在解决争端的过程中。在此基础上，中国民间社会逐渐形成了"无讼"的概念①。换言之，人们倾向于避免将纠纷提交司法程序或诉讼。这为和解、调解或仲裁等非司法纠纷解决机制的广泛使用提供了历史根源。值得注意的是，"仲裁"的概念也是随着时间的推移而演变的。在中国古代，仲裁是一种类似于现代语境下的"调解"，即由双方当事人指定共同信任的第三人协助化解分歧。②通常而言，争议各方往往选择社区中德高望重的成员帮助调解或仲裁争议。

除了历史因素外，中国仲裁还得益于在建立社会主义市场经济体制改革过程中的法律现代化。为了应对从计划经济向市场经济的制度转型所带来的实质性变化，中国出台了一系列新的法律来回应市场所带来的一系列法律问题。③如 1979 年《中外合资经营企业法》、1981 年《经济合同法》、1982 年《商标法》、1984 年《专利法》和 1985 年《涉外经济合同法》等。④其中，1979 年《中外合资经营企业法》规定了调解和仲裁作为争议解决机

---

① *The Analects of Confucius*, translated by Burton Watson, Columbia University Press, 2007, p. 83. 'The Master said, in hearing lawsuits, I am no different from other people. What we need is for there to be no lawsuits!'

② 参见邓瑞平、孙志煜：《论国际商事仲裁的历史演进》，《暨南学报（哲学与社会科学版）》2009 年第 6 期，第 92—93 页。

③ *See* Guiguo Wang and Zhenying Wei (eds.), *Legal Development in China: Market Economy and Law*, Sweet & Maxwell, 1996; Keyuan Zou, *China's Legal Reform: Towards the Rule of Law*, Martinus Nijhoff Publishers, 2006, pp. 73-86.

④ *See* Chenguang Wang and Xianchu Zhang (eds.), *Introduction to Chinese Law*, Sweet & Maxwell, 1997, pp. 171-173.

制；①1981 年《经济合同法》又以专章的形式规定了经济合同纠纷的调解和仲裁。其他一些经济法律法规，如 1988 年的《中外合作经营企业法》，也对调解和仲裁作出了专门规定。这也为后来中国在 1994 年通过第一部《仲裁法》奠定了基础。②

中国加入《纽约公约》通常被认为是中国仲裁事业繁荣发展不可或缺的因素。1986 年 12 月 2 日，根据国务院的建议，全国人民代表大会常务委员会决定批准《纽约公约》。③ 随后，最高人民法院发出通知，要求人民法院根据《纽约公约》统一审查承认和执行外国仲裁裁决申请的程序。④1987 年 4 月 22 日，《纽约公约》在中国正式生效。通过引入外国仲裁裁决的承认和执行机制，中国向外国投资者重申：中国致力于建设一个以规则为基础的开放市场。这代表了中国发展市场经济的坚定雄心。在一定程度上，这也促进了当时跨境交易和中国境内资本流动的显著增长。⑤ 此外，它还将中国法律体系与国际仲裁实践联系起来。根据《纽约公约》，中国有义务审查承认和执行外国仲裁裁决的申请。同样，中国当事人也可以要求承认和执行《纽约公约》其他缔约国在中国境内作出的仲裁裁决。这一互动过程促进了中国仲裁与国际仲裁的既定规则和惯例的接轨。

从跨国法的角度来看，本章聚焦《纽约公约》在中国的实践，并希望回答以下研究问题：《纽约公约》在中国是如何实施的？本章首先简要回顾

---

① 参见 2016 年修订的《中华人民共和国中外合资经营企业法》。其中，该法第 16 条第 1 款规定："合营各方发生纠纷，董事会不能协商解决时，由中国仲裁机构进行调解或仲裁，也可由合营各方协议在其它仲裁机构仲裁。"

② See Jingzhou Tao, *Arbitration Law and Practice in China*, Kluwer Law International, 2004, pp. 2-3.

③ 《全国人民代表大会常务委员会关于我国加入〈承认及执行外国仲裁裁决公约〉的决定》，《中华人民共和国国务院公报》1987 年第 7 号，第 243 页。

④ 最高人民法院：《关于执行我国加入的〈承认及执行外国仲裁裁决公约〉的通知》，法经发〔1987〕5 号，1987 年 4 月 10 日。

⑤ See Harm Zebregs and Wanda S Tseng, *Foreign Direct Investment in China: Some Lessons for Other Countries*, International Monetary Fund Policy Discussion Paper No. 2002/003, February 1, 2002, p. 3.

了中国仲裁发展的背景，并追溯了中国转化适用《纽约公约》的过程。在此基础上，本章进一步梳理《纽约公约》在中国法律实践中的解释问题。对于《纽约公约》实施过程中产生的跨境法律效力，本章还将考虑与中国《仲裁法》相关的案例。最后，本章还将简要回顾了近期中国司法部《中华人民共和国仲裁法（修订）（征求意见稿）》（以下简称司法部《仲裁法修订意见稿》），并探讨《纽约公约》对其产生的影响。

二、中国法院的视角下《纽约公约》在中国的适用

中国致力于通过严格执行《纽约公约》推动国际仲裁。这集中体现在人民法院的判决书、司法解释和审判指导意见中。在中国，人民法院是审查承认和执行外国仲裁裁决的主管机关。如上所述，自中国加入《纽约公约》以来，最高人民法院就《纽约公约》的适用向地方法院发布了统一的指导意见。[①] 在实践中，最高人民法院也采取实质性措施支持《纽约公约》在中国的适用，并要求地方法院在审查承认和执行外国仲裁裁决的申请时严格遵守《纽约公约》的内容。[②]

通常来说，司法审查程序可能会给国际仲裁案件带来挑战。各国法律制度差异可能会对外国仲裁裁决在另一国的承认和执行造成障碍。事实上，这就是《纽约公约》旨在解决的问题。自中国加入《纽约公约》以来，最高人民法院一直在采取措施，规范仲裁案件司法审查的实体和程序要求。对此，最高人民法院专门引入了司法报核制度。对于中国法院拒绝承认和执行的外国仲裁裁决，地方法院作出的不予承认和执行的决定必须经最高人民法院核准后才能生效。换言之，最高人民法院有权对所有拒绝承认和执行外

① 最高人民法院：《关于执行我国加入的〈承认及执行外国仲裁裁决公约〉的通知》。
② 参见高晓力：《中国法院承认和执行外国仲裁裁决的积极实践》，《法律适用》2018年第5期，第4—5页。

国仲裁裁决的案件进行审核并作出最终裁决。① 这体现了司法审查权与国际仲裁独立价值之间的巧妙平衡。

1995年，最高人民法院通过了《关于人民法院处理与涉外仲裁及外国仲裁事项有关问题的通知》。该《通知》规定，地方人民法院对不认可涉外仲裁和外国仲裁案件中的仲裁条款，或者拒绝承认和执行我国涉外仲裁机构裁决或外国仲裁机构的裁决的申请的，应报请本辖区所属高级人民法院进行审查。如果高级人民法院同意不予执行或者拒绝承认和执行，应将其审查意见报最高人民法院。待最高人民法院答复后，地方法院方可裁定不予执行或者拒绝承认和执行。② 这种自下而上的审查机制旨在防止地方法院在适用《纽约公约》过程中滥用监管权。2017年，该机制被明确为仲裁司法审查案件报核制度（以下简称"司法报核制度"）。③ 同年，最高人民法院还通过了《关于审理仲裁司法审查案件若干问题的规定》，进一步明确了仲裁案件的司法审查程序。④

通过司法报核制度，最高人民法院可以对涉外仲裁裁决和外国仲裁裁决在中国不予承认和执行的情况进行监督和复核。这有效防止了司法监督权的滥用，大大降低了地方保护主义的可能性，进一步明确了司法机关对仲裁的支持作用。

此外，多个司法案件在推动中国承认和执行外国仲裁裁决中发挥着重要作用。比如，最高人民法院在对地方法院的复函中澄清了属于第5条第（2）款的中国公共政策的范围。⑤ 该案例表明，与中国法律或法院判决的不一致

---

① 参见肖蓓：《〈纽约公约〉背景下我国对外国仲裁裁决承认及执行的实证研究》，《现代法学》2016年第3期，第188页。

② 最高人民法院：《关于人民法院处理与涉外仲裁及外国仲裁事项有关问题的通知》，1995年。

③ 最高人民法院：《关于仲裁司法审查案件报核问题的有关规定》，2017年制定，2021年修订。

④ 最高人民法院：《关于审理仲裁司法审查案件若干问题的规定》，2017年制定。

⑤ 根据《纽约公约》第五条第2款（b）规定，"承认或执行裁决有违该国公共政策者"，缔约国主管当局可以拒绝承认和执行该外国仲裁裁决。

并不必然违反中国的公共政策，从而导致拒绝承认或执行外国仲裁裁决。通过严格限制公共政策在承认和执行仲裁裁决方面的使用，中国法院旨在尽量最大限度地减少司法机构对仲裁制度的过度干预。在中国法律的语境下，公共政策被称为"社会公共利益"的概念。① 通过法律实践，《纽约公约》所规定的公共政策影响着中国法项下"社会公共利益"的概念。中国法院限制公共政策的适用，人民法院根据具体个案确定"社会公共利益"的范围。现有案例表明，最高人民法院已明确，以下情况并不一定构成对中国社会公共利益的侵犯：（1）仅涉及行业或地区利益；（2）违反中国法律的单一强制性规定。②

　　中国执行《纽约公约》的另一个例子是中国法院对有效仲裁协议的认定。根据《纽约公约》，仲裁协议应是"书面协定"，即"当事人所签订或在互换函电中所载明之契约仲裁条款或仲裁协定"。③ 在此基础上，最高人民法院根据这一定义确立了仲裁协议是否有效的认定标准。现代通信技术为"书面协定"的概念带来了新的内涵，扩大了当事人达成协议的方式。最高人民法院《关于适用〈中华人民共和国仲裁法〉若干问题的解释》中明确规定，"其他书面形式"的仲裁协议包括但不限于合同书、信件和数据电文（包括电报、电传、传真、电子数据交换和电子邮件）等形式达成的请求仲裁的协议。④ 这一说明为中国法院在审查根据《纽约公约》承认和执行外国仲裁裁决的申请时确定"书面协定"提供了务实指导。

---

① 参见林一飞：《商事仲裁实务精要》，北京大学出版社 2016 年版，第 297—298 页。
② 参见万鄂湘：《〈纽约公约〉在中国的司法实践》，《法律适用》2009 年第 3 期，第 5 页。
③ 参见《纽约公约》第 2 条第 1 款、第 2 款。
④ 最高人民法院：《关于适用〈中华人民共和国仲裁法〉若干问题的解释》第 1 条。

三、司法实践中中国法院对《纽约公约》的解释

本章第二部分回顾了《纽约公约》在中国的适用情况。通过研究以下案例，本章注意到中国法院在适用《纽约公约》过程中对仲裁的支持立场。在此基础上，本部分旨在探讨中国法院在具体案件中对《纽约公约》的解释。

解释国际条约通常会参考《维也纳条约法公约》（VCLT）。为了确定《纽约公约》在中国是如何解释的，我们运用关键词在最高人民法院案例数据库"中国裁判文书网"进行检索。我们发现，中国法院通常不明示援引《维也纳条约法公约》或其他国际法律渊源来解释《纽约公约》的条文内容，尽管这并不必然意味着中国法院不考虑《维也纳条约法公约》中规定的条约解释一般原则。现实中，中国法官在解释《纽约公约》时会根据个案的不同情况行使自由裁量权。

司法实践中，中国法官首先需要确定仲裁裁决是否属于《纽约公约》的适用范围。根据该公约，它适用于"在声请承认及执行地所在国以外之国家领土内作成者"或"仲裁裁决经声请承认及执行地所在国认为非内国裁决者"。[①] 在过去很长一段时间内，中国法院习惯于根据仲裁机构所在地来确定"外国仲裁裁决"的定义。在根据《纽约公约》受理承认和执行仲裁裁决的申请时，中国法官需要首先识别作出裁决的仲裁机构所在地。换言之，仲裁裁决籍属仅由管辖仲裁机构所在地决定。然而，这与《纽约公约》第1条对外国仲裁裁决的定义并不兼容。为此，实践中，中国法院逐渐开始采用新的标准来界定外国仲裁裁决，即以仲裁地点而非仲裁机构为依据。

2016年最高人民法院《关于不予执行国际商会仲裁院第18295/CYK号仲裁裁决一案请示的复函》[②] 引入了新规则，明确了确定《纽约公约》项下

---

① 《纽约公约》第1条第1款。
② 最高人民法院：《关于不予执行国际商会仲裁院第18295/CYK号仲裁裁决一案请示的复函》，[2016] 最高法民他8号。

仲裁裁决籍属的标准。在该案中，系争仲裁裁决的仲裁地为香港，但作出裁决的仲裁机构为国际商会国际仲裁院。由于仲裁地与仲裁机构所在地不同，这会导致与《纽约公约》的规定不一致。最高人民法院指出，系争仲裁裁决是在中国香港特别行政区作出的仲裁裁决。由于香港特别行政区是中国的一部分，根据《纽约公约》，该仲裁裁决不能认定为外国仲裁裁决。[①]因此，系争仲裁裁决在中国内地的承认与执行应适用中国内地与香港特别行政区关于承认和执行仲裁裁决方面的特殊安排。[②]通过一系列案例，中国法院关于外国仲裁裁决[③]的认定标准发生了变化。现在中国法院在决定裁决的籍属时，应优先考虑仲裁地，而不是仲裁机构所在地。最高人民法院的一位法官在后来的一篇文章中再次确认了该变化。[④]

　　除了《纽约公约》的适用范围，中国法院还需要考虑《纽约公约》第5条规定的拒绝承认和执行外国仲裁裁决的理由。具体而言，第5条第2款列举了被认为违反该国公共政策的案例。如上所述，中国法院对"公共政策"进行了限缩解释，以限制其在实践中的适用范围。这种做法也体现了中国法院对《纽约公约》相关条款的解释。

　　在现实中，中国法院对利用公共政策作为拒绝承认和执行外国仲裁裁决的依据实施了严格的限制。不过，也有少数案件援引了关于公共政策的第5条第2款。2008年，最高人民法院维持了拒绝承认和执行一项仲裁裁决的决定。这是因为系争仲裁裁决忽视了中国法院之前关于财产保全的裁定，这构成对中国司法主权的挑战，也违背了中国的公共利益。[⑤]总之，中国法

[①] 1997年6月6日，中国政府书面通知联合国秘书长，中国政府自1997年7月1日起将《纽约公约》的领土适用范围延伸至中国香港特别行政区。

[②] 参见最高人民法院：《关于内地与香港特别行政区相互执行仲裁裁决的安排》，2000年制定。

[③] 参见刘敬东、王路路：《"一带一路"倡议下我国对外国仲裁裁决承认与执行的实证研究》，《法律适用》2018年第5期，第33—34页。

[④] 参见高晓力：《司法应依仲裁地而非仲裁机构所在地确定仲裁裁决籍属》，《人民司法》2017年第20期，第68—74页。

[⑤] 参见最高人民法院[2008]民四他字第11号复函。

院对公共政策严格解释，只有在外国仲裁裁决违反中国法律制度或损害核心的社会公共利益或基本法律原则的情况下，才会被拒绝承认或执行。①

结语：中国仲裁法的未来

2021 年 7 月 30 日，中国司法部发布了《仲裁法修订意见稿》，向社会公开征求意见。②《仲裁法修订意见稿》拟对现行《仲裁法》进行实质性修改，旨在使中国仲裁规则与国际仲裁最新实践接轨。总体而言，《仲裁法修订意见稿》体现了中国大多数学者和从业人员的共识。③

《仲裁法修订意见稿》的一些条文值得关注。例如，第 27 条引入了"仲裁地"的概念。这与《纽约公约》保持了一致。在一定程度上，这也重申了中国对仲裁的支持立场。该条还区分了"仲裁地"和"仲裁活动发生地"，后者涵盖的范围更广，包括了案件的合议和开庭地点。④第 28 条规定，仲裁庭有权根据国际商事仲裁的既定惯例确定仲裁协议的有效性。⑤此外，根据《纽约公约》和中国司法实践在确定仲裁裁决籍属的最新发展，⑥《仲裁法修订意见稿》规定，中国法院可以根据国际条约或互惠原则承认和执行在中国境外作出的仲裁裁决。⑦

《仲裁法修订意见稿》第 90 条允许具有涉外因素案件的当事人可以设立"专设仲裁庭"对争议进行仲裁。这是中国首次明确提出在《仲裁法》

---

① 相关判例，可参见最高人民法院 [2013] 民四他字第 46 号复函、[2010] 民四他字第 32 号复函。

② 司法部：《中华人民共和国仲裁法（修订）（征求意见稿）》，2021 年 7 月 30 日。

③ 参见毛晓飞：《法律实证研究视角下的仲裁法修订：共识与差异》，《国际法研究》2021 年第 6 期，第 110—126 页。

④ 参见《仲裁法修订意见稿》第 27 条。

⑤ 参见《仲裁法修订意见稿》第 28 条第 1 款。

⑥ 参见孙巍著：《中国商事仲裁法律与实务》，法律出版社 2020 年版，第 51—52 页。

⑦ 参见《仲裁法修订意见稿》第 87 条。

层面就临时仲裁制定专门规则，这也是中国深化市场开放的重要标志。①《仲裁法修订意见稿》的说明文件指出："临时仲裁作为仲裁的'原初'形式和国际通行惯例，在国际社会中普遍存在并被各国法律和国际公约所认可。考虑到我国加入了《纽约公约》，以及外国的临时仲裁裁决可以在我国得到承认和执行的实际，应平等对待内外仲裁，增加了'临时仲裁'制度的规定，但结合我国国情，将临时仲裁适用范围限定在'涉外商事纠纷'。"《仲裁法修订意见稿》还专门就临时仲裁规定了特殊的程序规则，包括仲裁庭的组成等。② 为加强对临时仲裁行为的监督，《仲裁法修订意见稿》规定："仲裁员因对裁决持不同意见而不在裁决书上签名的，必须向当事人出具书面意见，裁决书及其送达记录要在法院备案。"③

　　总体而言，《仲裁法修订意见稿》参考和回应了《纽约公约》和联合国贸易法委员会《仲裁示范法》等国际立法的经验，突出体现了当事人意思自治的重要性。这重申了中国立法者支持仲裁的积极立场。《仲裁法修订意见稿》旨在实现中国仲裁的现代化，与国际惯例接轨，增强企业经营者和国际仲裁员在中国开展仲裁的信心。同时，这也将提高中国公众对替代性和非司法性争议解决方式的认知，"助力中国经济社会的高质量发展"。

---

① 关于临时仲裁在中国的发展，可参见 Panfeng Fu, "The Complex and Evolving Legal Status of Ad Hoc Arbitration in China", *Journal of International Arbitration,* Vol. 40, Issue 1, 2023, pp. 45-68.

② 参见《仲裁法修订意见稿》第 92 条。

③ 参见《仲裁法修订意见稿》第 93 条。

Chapter 18

The New York Convention in China: From A Transnational Law Aspect

Kunhao Yang and Sirui Chen

1. An Overview: Arbitration Law in Contemporary China

Arbitration has become an increasingly significant mechanism for resolving commercial disputes in China. According to *the Annual Report on International Commercial Arbitration in China* (2021-2022), it was reported that a sum of 415889 cases was accepted in 2021 by 270 arbitration institutions in China.[1] These cases represented the aggregated value of RMB 859300000000.[2] At the same time, more arbitration institutions in China have emerged in the global market of dispute resolution. As per a recent survey conducted by the Queen Mary University of London and White & Case LLP, the China International Economic and Trade Arbitration Commission (CIETAC) has ranked fifth in the list of the most favoured arbitration institutions across the world.[3] The figures mentioned above indicate the great success

---

[1] *See* Annual Report on International Commercial Arbitration in China (2021-2022), Law Press, 2022.

[2] ibid.

[3] The School of International Arbitration, Queen Mary University of London and White & Case LLP, *2021 International Arbitration Survey: Adapting Arbitration to a Changing World*, 2022, p. 10.

that China's arbitration has achieved in the past few decades.

The rapid development of arbitration in China attributes to the combination of practical experience and folk wisdom of non-judicial dispute resolution in civil society, along with the introduction of modern arbitration laws. Deeply embedded in Chinese social norms, Confucianism had a prominent position in the Chinese civil society of ancient times. It called on people to abide by ethics and virtues, including in the process of settling down disputes. On this basis, Chinese civil society developed the general conception of "no lawsuits" (无讼)[1]. In other words, people prefer to avoid referring disputes to judicial proceedings or getting involved in lawsuits. This provides a historical background for the extensive use of non-judicial dispute resolution mechanisms, such as reconciliation, mediation, or arbitration. It is noted that the concept of "arbitration" has evolved over time. In ancient China, arbitration was a process similar to mediation, where neutral arbitrators were appointed by the parties to moderate the disagreement.[2] The parties at issues may select a well-respected member of their community to help with mediating or arbitrating the disputes.

Apart from the historical factor, China's arbitration also benefits from legal modernisation in the course of economic reform to establish a socialist market economy. In response to the substantive changes arising from the systemic transformation from the planned economy to the market economy, China introduced a set of new laws to address the legal issues arising from the market.[3] Such as the 1979 *Sino-Foreign Joint Venture Law*, the 1981 *Economic Contract Law*, the 1982 *Trademark Law*, the

---

[1] *The Analects of Confucius*, translated by Burton Watson, Columbia University Press, 2007, p. 83. "The Master said, in hearing lawsuits, I am no different from other people. What we need is for there to be no lawsuits!"

[2] *See* Ruiping Deng and Zhiyu Sun, "On the Historical Evolvement of International Commercial Arbitration in China", *Journal of Jinan University (Philosophy & Social Science Edition)*, 2009, No. 6, pp. 92-93.

[3] *See* Guiguo Wang and Zhenying Wei (eds.), *Legal Development in China: Market Economy and Law*, Sweet & Maxwell, 1996; Keyuan Zou, *China's Legal Reform: Towards the Rule of Law*, Martinus Nijhoff Publishers, 2006, pp. 73-86.

1984 *Patent Law* and the 1985 *Foreign Economic Contract Law*, etc.[①] Mediation and arbitration are designated as dispute resolution mechanisms in the 1979 *Sino-Foreign Joint Venture Law*.[②] And the 1981 *Economic Contract Law* further includes a chapter specifically in relation to the mediation and arbitration of disputes arising from economic contracts. Some other economic laws and regulations, such as the 1988 *Sino-Foreign Co-operative Joint Venture Law*, also introduce special provisions for mediation and arbitration. This constitutes the main statutory underpinning for later China's adoption of the first *Arbitration Law* in 1994.[③]

China's accession to *the New York Convention* is widely acknowledged as an indispensable factor in the prosperity of arbitration in China. On December 2, 1986, upon the motion by the State Council, the Standing Committee of the National People's Congress decided to ratify the New York Convention.[④] upon the decision, the Supreme People's Court later issued a notification to all Chinese courts regarding the unified procedures for reviewing applications for recognition and enforcement of foreign arbitral awards in accordance with the New York Convention.[⑤] On April 22, 1987, the New York Convention came into force in China. By providing access to the recognition and enforcement of foreign arbitral awards, China reassures foreign investors of its commitment to establishing a rule-based and open market. This represents China's determined ambition to embrace the market-oriewted economy, which has sparked a significant increase in cross-border transactions and inbound capital flow to China

---

① *See* Chenguang Wang and Xianchu Zhang (eds.), *Introduction to Chinese Law*, Sweet & Maxwell, 1997, pp. 171-173.

② *See* Law of the People's Republic of China on Chinese-Foreign Equity Joint Ventures, amended in 2016. *Inter alia*, Paragraph 1 of Article 16 states that, "disputes arising between the parties to an equity joint venture which the board of directors has failed to settle through consultation may be settled through mediation or arbitration by an arbitration institution of China or through arbitration by another arbitration institutions agreed upon by the parties".

③ *See* Jingzhou Tao, *Arbitration Law and Practice in China*, Kluwer Law International, 2004, pp. 2-3.

④ State Council Gazette of the People's Republic of China, No. 530, March 30, 1987, pp. 243-244.

⑤ The Supreme People's Court, Notice on the Implementation of the "Convention on the Recognition and Enforcement of Foreign Arbitral Awards" Acceded to by China, Fafa [1987] No.5 of the Supreme People's Court, April 10, 1987.

in the late 1980s and 1990s.[①] Furthermore, it bridged the Chinese legal system with international arbitration practice. According to the Convention, China is obligated to review the application for recognition and enforcement of foreign arbitral awards. Similarly, Chinese parties can also request recognition and enforcement of arbitral awards rendered within China in other contracting states of the New York Convention. This interactive process has facilitated the alignment of China's arbitration with the established rules and practices of international arbitration.

From a transnational law aspect, this chapter focuses on the practice of the New York Convention in China. It aims to address the following research question: how does China implement *the New York Convention*? The first part briefly reviews the background of the development of arbitration in China, and traces the process that China internalised the content of the New York Convention. On this basis, this chapter will further ascertain how the New York Convention is interpreted in Chinese legal practice. Some selected domestic cases in relation to the application of Chinese Arbitration Law are also considered, when it comes to the cross-border legal effects arising from the implementation of the Convention. Ultimately, the chapter also sheds some light on the recently proposed amendment to *China's Arbitration Law*, exploring to what extent it features in *the New York Convention*.

2. The Application of the New York Convention in China: From the Chinese Court's Perspective

China is dedicated to promoting international arbitration by strictly implementing *the New York Convention*. This features in judgements, judicial interpretations, and trial guidance of the People's Court. In China, the People's Court is the competent authority in reviewing applications for recognition and enforcement of foreign arbitral awards. As noted above, since China's accession to *the New York Convention*, the Supreme People's Court has issued unified guidance to local courts on the application of *the New*

---

① *See* Harm Zebregs and Wanda S Tseng, *Foreign Direct Investment in China: Some Lessons for Other Countries*, International Monetary Fund Policy Discussion Paper No. 2002/003, February 1, 2002, p. 3.

York Convention.[①] In practice, the Supreme People's Court also takes substantive steps to support the application of the Convention in China. It also requires local courts to strictly abide by the content of *the New York Convention* in reviewing the application for recognition and enforcement of foreign arbitral awards.[②]

In general, the process of judicial review may present challenges for international arbitration cases. Differences in national legal systems may give rise to barriers to the recognition and enforcement of foreign arbitral awards in another country. That is what *the New York Convention* aims to tackle. In China, since acceding to the New York Convention, the Supreme People's Court has been taking action to standardise the substantial and procedural requirements for the judicial review of arbitration cases. For this purpose, the Supreme People's Court introduced the judicial verification mechanism of cases in relation to the refusal of recognition and enforcement of arbitral awards by Chinese courts. In regard to foreign arbitral awards, the local court's decision to deny recognition and enforcement must be verified by the Supreme People's Court before this decision ultimately takes effect. In other words, the Supreme People's Court has been granted the authority to make the final decision on all cases in relation to the refusal of recognition and enforcement of foreign arbitral awards in China.[③] This embodies a smart balance between the competence of judicial review and the independent value of international arbitration.

In 1995, the Supreme People's Court adopted a Notice regarding the recognition and enforcement of foreign-related and foreign arbitration.[④] This Notice specifies that, in the event that local people's courts decide not to acknowledge the validity of an arbitration clause in a foreign-related or foreign case, nor recognise and enforce an

---

① The Supreme People's Court, Notice on the Implementation of the "Convention on the Recognition and Enforcement of Foreign Arbitral Awards" Acceded to by China.

② *See* Xiaoli Gao, "Positive Practice of Chinese Courts in Recognizing and Enforcing Foreign Arbitral Awards" *Applicable Law*, 2018, No. 5, pp. 4-5.

③ See Xiao Bei, An Empirical Study on the Recognition and Enforcement of Foreign Arbitral Awards in China under the Background of the New York Convention Modern Law Science, 2016, No. 3, p. 188.

④ The Supreme People's Court, Notice of the Supreme People's Court on the Handling by People's Courts of Issues Concerning Foreign-related Arbitration and Foreign Arbitration, 1995, as amended in 2008.

arbitral award made by a domestic foreign-related arbitration institution or a foreign arbitration institution, the local court is required to report this case to the higher court and the Supreme People's Court for verification. This bottom-up verification system aims to prevent the abuse of judicial review in the implementation of the New York Convention. In 2017, this mechnism was reframed the institution of verification of arbitration cases under judicial review (hereinafter referred to as "The Judicial Verification institution").① In the same year, the Supreme People's Court also adopted an updated Provision further unifying the procedures for the judicial review of arbitration cases.②

The Judicial verification Institution enables the Supreme People's Court to conduct supervision and double-check on the refusal of recognition and enforcement of foreign-related arbitral awards and foreign arbitral awards in China. This effectively prevents the abuse of the judicial supervision power, and greatly reduces the possibility of protectionism. And it also reinforces the role of the judiciary in supporting arbitration.

In addition, multiple judicial cases mark significant milestones in facilitating the recognition and enforcement of foreign arbitral awards in China. For instance, in its reply to a local court, the Supreme People's Court clarifies the scope of public policy in China that falls within Article V (2).③ It demonstrated that the incompatibility with Chinese law or the court's decision does not necessarily constitute a violation of public policy in China, and consequently, does not result in the refusal of recognition or enforcement of a foreign arbitral award. By strictly limiting the use of public policy in the recognition and enforcement of arbitral awards, Chinese courts aim to minimise the interference of the judiciary in the arbitration system. In the context of Chinese

---

① The Supreme People's Court, Relevant Provisions of the Supreme People's Court on Issues concerning Applications for Verification of Arbitration Cases under Judicial Review, 2017, as amended in 2021.

② The Supreme People's Court, Provisions of the Supreme People's Court on Several Issues concerning Deciding Cases of Arbitration-Related Judicial Review, 2017.

③ Point (b), Article V (2), the New York Convention, provides that a contracting state's competent authority may refuse the recognition and enforcement of a foreign arbitral award, in the event that this "would be contrary to the public policy of that country."

law, public policy is always referred to as the concept of "social public interest".[①] Through legal practice, this concept is influenced and shaped by the nature of public policy provided in *the New York Convention*. For China, Chinese Courts adopted a self restrained approach to the application of the public policy clause. People's Courts determine the extent of the "public interest of society" on a case-by-case basis. Existing cases show that the Supreme People's Court has clarified that at least the following circumstances do not necessarily constitute a violation of China's public interest of society: 1) merely sectoral or local interests; or 2) a violation of a single mandatory provision of China's laws. [②]

Another example of how China implements *the New York Convention* can be taken from the Chinese court's identification of an effective arbitration agreement. As per *the New York Convention*, an arbitration agreement is considered to be "an agreement in writing" that "shall include an arbitral clause in a contract or an arbitration agreement, signed by the parties or contained in an exchange of letters or telegrams".[③] Modern communication technology brought new elements to the concept of "an agreement in writing", expanding the ways in which agreements can be made. For the practical reason, the Supreme People's Court established a feasible standard for assessing the existence of an effective arbitration agreement based on this definition. In the judicial interpretation document for the application of the Arbitration Law, the Supreme People's Court clarified that an arbitration agreement "in other written form" includes, but is not limited to, contracts, letters, and data messages, such as telegrams, telexes, facsimiles, electronic data interchange, and emails.[④] This clarification provided Chinese courts with practical guidance on the identification of "an agreement in writing" when examining applications for the recognition and enforcement of a foreign arbitral award under *the New York Convention*.

---

① *See* Yifei Lin, *Essentials of Commercial Arbitration Practice*, Peking University Press, 2016, pp. 297-298.

② See Exiang Wan, "Judicial practice of the New York Convention in China" Journal of Law Application, No. 3, 2009, p. 5.

③ Article II (1)(2), the New York Convention.

④ The Supreme People's Court, Article I, Interpretation of the Supreme People's Court concerning Some Issues on Application of the Arbitration Law of the People's Republic of China.

3. Interpretation of New York Convention in China

In Part II, we review the application of the New York Convention in China. By examining several selected cases, we find out that there is a positive inclination of Chinese courts towards arbitration in upholding the New York Convention. On this basis, Part III aims to gain insight into the Chinese court's interpretation of the New York Convention in specific cases.

When it comes to interpreting international treaties, the Vienna Convention on the Law of Treaties (VCLT) is always referenced. To determine how the New York Convention is interpreted in China, we Look upfor cases in the database of China Judgements Online, which is managed by the Supreme People's Court. From our search, we discover that Chinese courts generally interpret the New York Convention's substantive content without referring to VCLT or other legal resources. Here, it is not correct to jump to the conclusion that Chinese courts completely disregard the general principles of treaty interpretation outlined in VCLT. Rather, Chinese judges exercise their discretion in interpreting the New York Convention based on the various circumstances of individual cases.

In practice, Chinese judges first need to determine whether an arbitral award falls within the scope of the New York Convention. According to the Convention, it applies to the arbitral awards that are "made in the territory of a State other than the State where the recognition and enforcement of such awards are sought" or "not considered as domestic awards in the State where their recognition and enforcement are sought".[1] For a long time, Chinese courts used to determine the definition of "foreign arbitral awards" based on the geographical location of the arbitration institution. When considering an application for recognition and enforcement of an arbitral award in accordance with the New York Convention, Chinese judges need to identify the seat of the arbitration institution that issued the award. In other words, the nationality of an arbitral award was determined solely by the location of the governing arbitration institution. However, this contradicted the definition of foreign arbitral awards outlined

---

[1] Article I (1), the New York Convention.

in Article I of the New York Convention. In response, Chinese courts have begun using a new standard for defining foreign arbitral awards that are based on the location of the arbitration instead of the institution.

More specifically, the Supreme People's Court's Reply to the Instructions on the Non-Enforcement of ICC Court Arbitration Award No. 18295/CYK in 2016[①] establish new rules and provide instructions for courts to rely on the forum or the seat of arbitration to determine the scope of arbitral awards that fall within New York Convention. In that case, the seat of arbitration for the award was Hong Kong, but the arbitral institution that rendered the award was the Court of Arbitration of the International Chamber of Commerce. Here, the seat of arbitration is different from the seat of the arbitral institution, which would lead to uncertainties in the interpretation of the standards of *the New York Convention*. The Supreme People's Court put forward that the arbitral award in question was an arbitral award rendered in the Hong Kong Special Administrative Region of China (HKSAR). As HKSAR is a part of China, this arbitral award cannot be identified as a foreign arbitral award under the New York Convention.[②] Therefore, this case shall fall under the special arrangement between the Chinese mainland and HKSAR in reviewing the recognition and enforcement of the arbitral award at issue in the Chinese mainland.[③] As a result, the criteria for determining foreign arbitral awards have been altered: indirectly by case law, and now Chinese courts should prioritize the seat of arbitration when deciding the nationality of the award over the institution at issue.[④] This change was re-confirmed by a Judge of the Supreme People's Court in an article.[⑤]

---

① *See* the Supreme People's Court, [2016] Minta No.8.
② After China resumed the sovereignty over Hong Kong on July 1997, Chinese government has extended the territorial application of the Convention to Hong Kong, Special Administrative Region of China.
③ Notice of the Supreme People's Court on Issues concerning the Execution of Hong Kong Arbitral Awards in the Mainland.
④ *See* Jingdong Liu, Lulu Wang, "An empirical study on recognition and enforcement of foreign arbitral awards in China under the Belt and Road Initiative", *Applicable Law*, No. 5, 2018, pp. 33-34.
⑤ *See* Xiaoli Gao, "The Judiciary Shall Determine the Nationality of the Arbitral Award According to the Seat of Arbitration but not the Seat of the Arbitral Institution", *People's Judicature (Case)*, No. 7, 2017, pp. 68-74.

Apart from the scope of *the New York Convention*, Chinese courts also need to consider the grounds for refusing to recognize and enforce foreign arbitral awards, as provided in Article V of *the New York Convention*. More specifically, Article V (2) refers to cases that are deemed contrary to the public policy of the country. As noted above, Chinese courts have adopted a narrow interpretation of "public policy" to limit its scope in practice. This approach also represents how Chinese courts interpret the relevant provision of the New York Convention.

In reality, Chinese courts have imposed strict limitations on the utilization of public policy as a basis for denying the recognition and enforcement of foreign arbitration awards. However, there have been a few cases where Article V (2) on public policy was invoked. In 2008, the Supreme People's Court upheld a decision to refuse recognition and enforcement of an arbitral award. This was because the arbitral award at issue ignored a previous Chinese court's decision on property preservation, which was deemed a challenge to China's judicial sovereignty and was contrary to China's public interest.[①] In sum, the Chinese courts follow a strict interpretation of public policy and only refuse recognition or enforcement of a foreign arbitral award, in the event that it goes against China's legal system or is detrimental to China's core social and public interests or fundamental legal principles.[②]

Conclusion: The Future of Chinese Arbitration Law

On July 30, 2021, China's Ministry of Justice released the draft proposal for the amended Arbitration Law (hereinafter referred to as "the Draft") to seek feedback from the public.[③] The Draft proposes to make substantive amendments to the existing Arbitration Law, which aims to align Chinese arbitration rules with the latest practice of international arbitration. In general, the Draft represents the consensus among most

---

① *See* the Supreme People's Court, [2008]Minsi Tazi No.11.
② *Also see* the Supreme People's Court, [2013] Minsi Tazi No. 46, [2010] Minsi Tazi No. 32.
③ Ministry of Justice of the People's of China, the Draft Proposal for the Amended Arbitration Law, 30 July 2021.

of the scholars and practitioners in China.[1]

There are some proposed amendments that are worth paying attention to. One of the examples is Article 27, which introduces the concept of "the seat of arbitration". This aligns with the New York Convention and reiterates China's supportive stance on arbitration. It also differentiates between "the seat of arbitration" and "the seat of arbitration activities". The latter term encompasses a wider range, including places for colligating and hearing cases.[2] Article 28 specifies that it is the competence of the arbitral tribunal' to determine the validity of the arbitration agreement in accordance with established practice of international commercial arbitration.[3] Besides, in line with the New York Convention and the latest development of Chinese judicial practice in determining the nationality of an arbitral award,[4] the Draft clarifies that the arbitral awards rendered outside the territory of China can be recognized and enforced by Chinese courts in accordance with international treaties or the principle of reciprocity.[5]

Article 90 of the Draft allows parties of foreign-related cases to establish an *ad hoc* tribunal to arbitrate on their disputes. It is noted that this is the first time that China proposes a motion to introduce the *ad hoc* arbitration regime in its Arbitration Law.[6] This provision is a significant symbol of market liberalization in China. The explanatory document of the Draft states that *ad hoc* arbitration is widely conducted in international practice and recognized by national laws and international conventions. In line with China's obligations under *the New York Convention*, foreign *ad hoc* arbitration can be recognized and enforced under China. Against this backdrop, the legislator proposes that, as domestic and foreign arbitrations should be treated equally, China shall introduce this *ad hoc* arbitration regime. However, in light of China's

---

[1] See Xiaofei Mao, *Revision of Arbitration Law from the Perspective of Empirical Legal Research: Consensus and Differences*, Chinese Review of International Law, 2021, No. 6, pp. 110-126.

[2] Article 27, the Draft.

[3] Article 28 (1), the Draft.

[4] *See* Wei Sun, *Commercial Arbitration in China: Law and Practice*, Law Press China, 2020, pp. 51-52.

[5] Article 87, the Draft.

[6] For the development of *ad hoc* arbitration in China, see Panfeng Fu, "The Complex and Evolving Legal Status of Ad Hoc Arbitration in China", *Journal of International Arbitration,* Vol. 40, Issue 1, 2023, pp. 45-68.

judicial reality, in the future, China's *ad hoc* arbitration only applies to "foreign-related commercial disputes". The Draft also stipulates special procedural rules for *ad hoc* arbitration, such as the formation of the arbitral tribunal.[①] In order to strengthen the supervision of the practice of *ad hoc* arbitration, the Draft provides that if an arbitrator decides not to sign the award due to his or her disagreement with the award, this arbitrator shall provide a written opinion to the parties, and the award and its courier record shall be recorded in the local competent court.[②]

Overall, the Draft emphasizes the importance of party autonomy, drawing experience from international legislation, such as the New York Convention and the UNCITRAL Model Law. This reaffirms the positive stance of Chinese authorities towards arbitration. The goal of the Draft is to modernize Chinese arbitration practices in alignment with established international practices and strengthen the faith of business operators and international arbitrators to conduct arbitration in China. Last but not least, this will also raise the awareness of the Chinese public in alternative and non-judicial dispute settlement," boosting the high-guality development of China's economy and society".

---

① Article 92, the Draft.
② Article 93, the Draft.

第十九章

结语——山洪冲不走的，雨后观澜坚如磐石

本书基于读者阅读《公约》而感受到的法律文化共通性来解读《公约》。《纽约公约》制定于二战结束后世界经济复苏的十多年间。《公约》制定人看到并展望战后和平期间跨境贸易和经济活动会更加昌盛。由于《公约》制定人主要为西方法律人士和学术专家，因此，经过深思熟虑考量制定的《公约》体现出的价值观来源于西方主流学派的自由市场经济和勤奋理念。另外，当时，众多民族国家正在自身寻求国家独立，由此，《公约》条文体现了当事人意思自治和承认独立国家的主要价值观。

从东方至西方国家，对《纽约公约》的实践比较，呈现以下一些共同特色：仲裁合意及和谐精神，当事人意思自治和自强不息理念，各方有陈述案情机会和兼听则明思维，限制法庭干预和仲裁自治意识，爱邻如己和天助自助者精神。

一、仲裁合意及和谐精神

仲裁合意是指协商一致和达成同一意思。在仲裁中，最初的一致合意是当事人之间的仲裁协议。当事人对是否仲裁、争议解决方式和仲裁如何进行必须达成一致。是否通过临时仲裁或机构仲裁？仲裁管辖法律是当地

所在国的法律还是比如《联合国国际销售合同公约》的国际条约？仲裁员如何任命？一名仲裁员还是三名仲裁员？仲裁在哪里进行？这些问题是仲裁协议要解决的问题。

当事人以合同中的仲裁条款或提交仲裁的书面协议方式达成双方之间争议事项的仲裁协议。一旦达成仲裁协议，当事人需要执行仲裁协议。因此，制定《纽约公约》的主要目的之一是承认和强制执行仲裁协议。《公约》第2条第3款规定：全体缔约国的法院在处理当事人之间含有仲裁协议的争议时，法院应命当事者将争议提交至仲裁庭仲裁解决，除非该仲裁协议无效、不可操作或不能履行。

商事仲裁具有保密性。既然当事人之间的仲裁是保密的，提交仲裁解决争议的协议也令争议当事人保密（俗语"低调"）处理争议。该保密性要求实质上符合东方哲学的和谐精神。即使当事人之间有不同意见或争议，凭公众观感，当事人之间的关系仍呈现和平景象，并非出现"战争"弥漫。前述持续发展的仲裁合意及和谐共处思想意味着东西方文明深层次中都青睐和平、和谐的争议解决方式。

二、当事人意思自治和自强不息的理念

众所周知，当事人意思自治是仲裁裁决的基本原则。在确保当事人意思自治的前提下，当事人可以自由表示同意选择仲裁、聘选仲裁员、仲裁地点、仲裁实体适用法律，等等；当事人也可以共同合意或限制仲裁庭采取临时措施、同意或限制仲裁员资格、管辖权决定和裁决。

中国法律文化下，人们常常鼓励自强不息的思想。这是个体事务自我负责精神的体现。未来有关中国文化的研究和改进在中国势必将持续展开。因此，有关仲裁，当事人可以自由约定，达成一致同意选择仲裁、仲裁语言、仲裁机构等。在仲裁程序中，当事人可以再度合意专家证人、开庭日期、

开庭方式和程序中使用的语言。仲裁程序事项也可以通过一致协议或再次合意。

仲裁程序中应用的调解同样表达出自强不息的理念。许多案例中，因为现实因素和其他原因，当事人一方并不了解争议缘由的全部事实情节。通过包括提交仲裁、抗辩和证据反驳的仲裁程序，当事人可以拥有更好的机会审视有关案件争议的全貌、诱发争议发生的背景事项和案件中自身争议的优势和弱势。那时，当事人可能同意通过调解的方式改善他们的关系，以达成合适的解决方案。当事人可以同意仲裁员兼任调解员听审，帮助当事人达成全面的最终争议解决方案。自强不息原则的效用在于当事人自己推动当事人之间达成友好的争议解决方案，主动权握在自己手中，尤其是在相关长期进行的项目中，和解对双方的合作关系至关重要。

在仲裁与调解相结合的程序中，当事人才是真正的程序专家。当事人达成促进他们之间关系的和解协议。和解协议意味着当事人之间就新的事项／业务能达成新的协议。新的协议打开了当事人之间螺旋交织的共同利益的门户。

三、各方陈述案情的机会和兼听则明思维

《纽约公约》中有条款表述：若证据显示，一方当事人未被给予合理机会出庭陈述案情，仲裁裁决可能不会被法院承认和执行。这个规则在全球商业贸易中对理解如何适用正当程序保护时尤为重要。仲裁案件出庭中，仲裁员未遵循正当程序，比如未给予当事人出庭陈述案情的机会，仲裁程序结束时，仲裁裁决将会受到质疑和挑战。

"出庭陈述案情的机会"就是说任何方当事人有权并有机会在仲裁庭审时出庭陈述案情。中国传统文化中的谚语说："兼听则明。"唐太宗曾言："以铜为镜，可以正衣冠；以史为镜，可以知兴替；以人为镜，可以明得失。"

唐太宗治理朝政时运用"兼听则明"。太宗鼓励自由表达意见，决策时，主动听取当事方的意见。

再看《纽约公约》，《公约》第 5 条第 1 款第（b）项条文要求当事人有机会陈述案情，没人会想到这是中国文化中"兼听则明"谚语的另一面（从陈述者角度有机会陈述情况）的规则。这是文化共通之魅力。尽管上述规则发展的历史阶段不同，可见人类的理性思维有共通点，存在于不同法律文化中。

抛开《纽约公约》在世界其他国家是否成功，中国比预期更成功地接受了《纽约公约》，原因是《公约》的主要规则与中国文化根植的原则匹配吻合。

四、法院有限干预和仲裁自治性意识

根据《纽约公约》，仲裁和法院的关系是并行不悖的关系，在当事人同意选择仲裁后，在有必要时，法院方可有限干预仲裁。转而言之，选择仲裁即排除法院的管辖。除非当事人之间的仲裁协议无效、不能操作或不能履行时，法院不得受理包含仲裁协议的争议案件。

在承认和执行仲裁裁决程序中，只有在证据显示是主要关于[《纽约公约》第 5 条第 1 款第（a）项至第（e）项]仲裁程序方面有瑕疵时，法院方可拒绝承认和执行外国仲裁裁决。公约第 5 条不允许法院复审仲裁案件实体问题，仲裁案件实体问题由仲裁员最终裁定（涉及有关"公共政策"的问题不在此限）。

法院依职权复核仲裁裁决，范围涵盖可仲裁性至公共政策[第 5 条第 2 款第（a）项至第（b）项]，但是法院主动依职权审核只限于上述两个理由，且第二个理由适用狭义解释的原则。

法院和仲裁司法工作的划分充分表明仲裁员在国际仲裁中的准司法工

作备受尊重。当事人之间若有仲裁协议，法院应命当事人提交仲裁，法院在当事人的需要范围内应支持仲裁而不得干预仲裁。

在中国，主要的、系统性的仲裁是机构仲裁，故仲裁制度设置中仲裁机构有相对的自治性。仲裁机构在案件中始终主管仲裁程序，需要法院支持的地方相对较少。法律规定临时措施由法院实施。仲裁案件中，一方当事人请求采取临时措施，比如财产保全或证据保全，仲裁机构将该请求转送至法院处理。对于任命仲裁员，当有仲裁员受到质疑或挑战时，且今为止法院实际上不介入更换仲裁员的事情，更换仲裁员并任命新的仲裁员的权利由仲裁机构主任行使。

我们希望出台的新仲裁法会允许法院切实支持仲裁程序事项的具体实施，包括在需要指定替代性仲裁员时，可以代为指定仲裁员。这在临时仲裁制度中有必要的制度设置需求。

五、爱邻如己与天助自助者精神

《圣经》有谚语云：爱邻如己，在寻求永生的情景下，耶和华回答门徒："不许杀戮""不许奸污""不许偷盗""不许伪证""尊敬你的父母""爱你的邻居就像爱你自己"（马修 19：19）。

《纽约公约》的富有哲理的地方是"让爱给予你的邻国"。《公约》规定，外国仲裁裁决原则上应当在缔约国被承认和执行，只有很少例外的前提下方可拒绝承认和执行。该前提是基于对前述《圣经》中的基督教宗教文化的理解。同理，在中国传统文化价值中，有谚语云：天助自助者。夫仁者，己欲立而立人，己欲达而达人。（《论语·雍也》）慈爱之人应得助。该谚语推崇发扬利他的精神，助人者最终自助。

毋庸置疑，通过承认和执行外国仲裁裁决作为公约一项原则，《纽约公约》提供了一个所有本国的仲裁裁决只要符合公约的规则应由公约其他成员国承认和执行的世界性广阔平台。

　　现在《纽约公约》已有 172 个成员国。可以想象每天都有可能达成商业贸易上的仲裁裁决。所有的裁决只要符合公约的规则现在都可以在《纽约公约》成员国得到承认和执行。可见当时公约制定人在发展国际贸易和人类命运共同体中作出了多么巨大的贡献！

　　上述观察彰显我们热爱《纽约公约》的原因是该公约向各国商业界和世界展示出人类慈爱的理念和人文价值观。我们相信，《纽约公约》经历过中国象形文字所组成文明的内化程序的跌宕起伏洗礼后，将会在中国本土文化中备受接纳，因为公约中耀射出了中国传统法律文化的价值观的光芒。山洪冲不走的，雨后观澜坚如磐石。

Chapter 19

Concluding Remarks—What Stays in the Mountain Torrents Becomes Rock Solid after the Rain

This book looks at *the New York Convention* from the cultural commonalities that the readers may feel when reading the provisions of *the New York Convention*. *The New York Convention* was drafted more than a decade after the World War II just ended and the world economy was recovering from the warring time. The drafters expected more trade and economic activities across borders in the peaceful time.

As the drafters were primarily legal professionals and academic elite in the West, the value imbedded in the deep thought of the Convention was the resulting school of thoughts from the free economy and industriousness concept. On the other hand, many nations were seeking state independence among nation states. Noticeably party autonomy and state recognition are the key values underlying the provisions of *the New York Convention*.

From the West to the East, comparatively speaking, the following commonalities can be discerned from the practice of *the New York Convention*: consensus and harmony; party autonomy and self-improvement; opportunity to present its case and hearing both sides; limited court intervention and arbitral autonomy.

1. Consensus and Harmony

Consensus means agreement or accord. In arbitration, the first consensus is the arbitration agreement of the parties. The parties must reach consensus on whether arbitration is to be chosen method for dispute resolution, and how arbitration is to be conducted. Is it by way of an *ad hoc* arbitration or an institutional arbitration? Will the arbitration be governed under a local law or under international convention such as the CISG? How will arbitrators be appointed? Will there be one arbitrator or three arbitrators? Where should the arbitration take place?

The parties reach agreement on these matters when they enter into the arbitration clause contained in the contract or the submission agreement for the arbitration. Once such agreement is made between the parties, consensus of the parties means that arbitration agreement needs to be enforced. Therefore, one of the objectives of the New York Convention is to recognize the validity and enforce the arbitration agreement. Article II (3) requires the courts of all member states to refer the parties to arbitration when they are seized of a matter in respect of which an arbitration agreement is made between the parties, unless the arbitration agreement is null and void, inoperative or incapable of being performed.

Confidentiality is the basis of commercial arbitration. Since arbitration is confidential between the parties, the agreement to resolve the disputes by way of arbitration will maintain the disputing parties in confidentiality (or in "low-key" manner). This, in essence, accords with the spirit of harmony in oriental philosophy. Even there are differences or disputes, the parties are at peace with their relationship and do not appear to be "fighting" with each other, in the eyes of the general public. The constant-growing consensus to arbitration and the thinking of co-existential harmony illustrates the in-depth preference for peaceful and harmonious means of dispute resolution in both the West and the East in cultural aspects.

2. Party Autonomy and Self-Improvement

As we all know, party autonomy is the fundamental principle for the method of arbitration. By party autonomy, the parties are free to agree on the choice of arbitration, the appointment of arbitrators, the place of arbitration, the law applicable to the substance of the disputes, etc. They may also by mutual agreement, grant or limit the powers of the arbitral tribunal as to the interim measures, the qualification of the arbitrators, the making of jurisdictional decisions and the award.

In the Chinese legal culture, there is a strong concept of encouraging a person to strive for self-improvement (自强不息). This is essentially based on the spirit of he who should be responsible for his own affairs. Further learning and improvement is a constant thing for one's life in Chinese culture. Therefore, in arbitration, the parties are free to agree on the choice of arbitration, choice of language and the choice of arbitration institution etc. In the arbitration process, the parties may improve the process by further agreeing on expert witnesses, hearing dates, and method of hearing, language to be used in the proceedings etc. These procedural aspects may be improved by way of consensual agreement as well.

The use of mediation in the process of arbitration is also illustrative of the concept of self-improvement. In many cases, the parties do not know the whole story of why the dispute occurred, for practical reasons or otherwise. Through the proceedings in the arbitration, including the submissions of arbitration, defense and rebuttal with evidence, and through exchange of views at the hearing, the parties may have better opportunity to have a panoramic view of the disputes, the background events that led to the disputes, including the strengths and weaknesses of their own case. At that time, they may agree to improve the relationship of the parties by consenting to mediate the case for a proper settlement. They may give consent for the arbitrators to sit as mediators who help them to seek a full and final settlement between the parties. Self-improvement principle works to promote the parties to have a friendly settlement of the disputes in such situations where mutual relationship really counts in the project.

In such Med-Arb proceeding, the parties are really the masters of the proceedings. They enter into a settlement agreement to improve their mutual relationship in business. The settlement agreement is a new agreement for their new business relationship. This new agreement opens the door for a spiral improvement of the common good between the parties.

3. Opportunity to Present its Case and Hearing Both Sides

Under *the New York Convention*, there is a provision to the effect that if evidence shows that a party is not given proper opportunity to present its case, the arbitral award may risk being not recognized and enforced. This rule is so important in protecting the due process of arbitration in the global business community. Where the arbitrators fail to give due process to the parties in the arbitration proceedings, including failure to give reasonable opportunity to a party to present its case, there will be challenges against the arbitral award at the end of the arbitration process.

"Opportunity to present its case" means that a party has the right and the opportunity to present its case before the arbitrators. From Chinese traditional culture, there is a saying: Hearing both sides, one will be wise (兼听则明). Emperor Taizhong of the Tang Dynasty once said: "With copper as a mirror, you can correct your clothes; with antiquity as a mirror, you can know the rise and fall; with people as a mirror, you can know the gain and loss." He applied this rule of hearing both sides to the governance of the country. He encouraged the free expression of views and actively listened to the opinions from all parties before making decisions.

From the perspective of *the New York Convention*, it would never have been thought the provision in Article V 1 (b) would mirror the rule in Chinese culture on "hearing both sides". This is the beauty of cultural exploration to understand that despite the different stages of development, in terms of human rational thinking, there is a strong commonality that existed in different cultures. Whether New York Convention succeeded in other parts of the world, it is expected *that New York Convention* will be more successfully accepted in the land in China, because the principal rules accord with the culturally and deeply self-rooted principles in Chinese.

4. Limited Court Intervention and Arbitral Autonomy

Under *the New York Convention*, the relationship between the court and arbitration is built on the parallel basis that the court supports arbitration to the extent where needed, once the parties agree on the method of arbitration. In other words, the choice of arbitration excludes the jurisdiction of the court. Court will take a hands-off approach unless the parties requests and unless the arbitration agreement is null and void, inoperative and incapable of being performed.

Even in the application for recognition and enforcement of arbitral awards, the court may refuse to recognize and enforce a foreign arbitral award only when proofs in evidence shows that there are defects, primarily with regard to the procedure aspects of the arbitration [Article V 1 (a) to (e) NYC]. Article V does not allow the court to re-visit the merits of the arbitration case (except in matters relevant to public policy). The merits are to be decided finally by the arbitrators.

The court may *ex officio* review the arbitral award from arbitrability and public policy aspects [Article V 2 (a) and (b)]. However, the review is only limited to these two grounds, and the latter ground is to be interpreted on rather narrow basis.

This division of judicial work between the court and arbitration effectively means that the arbitrators are fully respected in international arbitration as far as their judicial work is concerned. The court refers the parties to arbitration where there is a valid arbitration agreement and provides support but not intervention in arbitration to the extent as needed from the parties.

In China, as the system is primarily an institutional arbitration system, the arbitration institutions are relatively autonomous in the system. They manage the arbitration process from birth to end, with little support from the court. The law grants the interim measures to the courts. In case where a party requests for interim relief such as preservation of property or preservation of evidence, the arbitration institution will pass the request to the people's court for handling.

In terms of appointment of arbitrators, the court is not made available for the replacement of arbitrator when there is a challenge of arbitrator. The function of appointing a replacement arbitrator rests with the director of the arbitration institution.

It is hoped that the new Arbitration Law will address these functions to permit the court to be actually supportive in these procedural matters in the future. There is need for such basic rules for the court to function its support in *ad hoc* arbitration.

5. Loving One's Neighbor Like Loving Oneself v. He Who Helps Others Helps.

Under the Bible, there is a famous saying: Love your neighbor as yourself. In the context of enquiring about eternal life, Jesus answered the disciples in the following words: Do not murder, do not commit adultery, do not steal, do not give false testimony, honor your father and mother, and love your neighbors as yourself (Matthew 19:19).

One of the underlying philosophies of *the New York Convention* is the "love to be granted to your neighboring country". The premise of the Convention is that the arbitral awards from a foreign country shall be recognized and enforced as a matter of principle, with a few exceptions. This premise is based on the understanding from the Christian value as shown in the Bible above.

Coincidentally, in Chinese traditional Confucius value, there is a saying: He who helps others helps. 夫仁者，己欲立而立人，己欲达而达人。(Confucius, Analects.《论语 雍也》) A benevolent person who helps others will be helped. The adage promotes the altruistic spirit of he who helps others finally helps himself.

Needless to say, by way of recognizing and enforcing foreign arbitral awards as a principle, *the Convention provides* a vast platform where all the arbitral awards from its own country will also be recognized and enforced in member states of the New York Convention, when they comply with the rules of the New York Convention.

Now there are 172 member states to *the New York Convention*. Imagine that every day there is likely an award rendered somewhere in the planet in the commercial world. All these awards can now be recognized and enforced in the member states of the New York Convention, when they comply with the rules of the New York Convention. What a contribution the "then" drafters of the New York Convention have made to the development of international trade and to the human community with shared future!

The above examination shows that we love *the New York Convention* because it provides loving philosophies and humanistic spirits for the people in the commerce around the world. We are confident that *the New York Convention*, having experienced the internalization procedural ups and downs in the pictorial language space and civilization in China, will generate more waves of acceptance in the local culture because the values from the New York Convention shine and mirror those values in the traditional cultural space in China. What stays in the mountain torrents becomes rock solid after the rain!

附件三

生产销售协议（中文）^①

生产销售协议

本协议由如下双方于2019年＿＿＿月＿＿＿日签订：

(A) 泰平服装实业公司（"生产商"），一家在中华人民共和国（"中国"）广东省成立的公司，注册地址为：【　　】；以及

(B) MERINGE Holdings (Pte) Ltd. ("Meringe")，一家注册于新加坡的公司，注册地址为【　】。

鉴于：

(A) 生产商从事包括牛仔裤在内的服装的生产。

(B) Meringe 从事牛仔裤（"产品"）及其他产品的销售，并希望利用生产商的生产设施。

(C) 生产商愿意按照本协议的条款为 Meringe 生产并提供产品。

(D) 根据 Meringe 和生产商之间的一份购买订单（"订单"），生产商已同意生产三万零三百一十六（30316）件产品并以每件20美元的价格销售；Meringe 亦已同意购买这些产品。

双方在此达成如下协议：

———————————————

① 本文件仅是一个供参考的协议初稿文本，请勿对号入座。

1. 解释

1.1 除非上下文另有规定，下列术语在本协议中含义如下：

"协议" 指销售和购买产品的本协议；

"Meringe" 指 MERINGE Holding (Pte) Ltd.，一家承担有限责任的公司，注册于新加坡，其注册地址为【 】；

"交付地址"指中山美霖服饰有限公司的地址或者定单中确定的任何其他地址；

"知识产权"指任何专利、版权、经注册或未经注册的设计权利、对上述权利的应用、有关保密信息的权利以及任何其他知识产权；

"订单" 指 Meringe 购买 30316 件牛仔裤的附有本协议条款的定单，牛仔裤单价为 0 美元 / 件，订单副本见本协议附件【 】；

"包装材料" 指 Meringe 不时提供的适于包装产品的所有物件，包括但不限于塑料材料和包装盒；

"价格" 指产品价格；

"产品" 指清单 1 所列的产品；

"服务" 指定单中所指的服务 (如有)；

"规格"包括清单 2 所列的由 Meringe 向生产商提供的任何样品、计划、制图、数据或与产品有关的其他信息，以及根据第【 】条对其所做的不时修改；

"条款" 是指本协议的标准购买条款，并且除非上下文另有规定，包括 Meringe 和生产商以书面方式达成任何特别条款；

"商标" 是指 Meringe 的注册商标。

1.2 "书面" 以及任何类似表述，包括传真以及其他类似通信方式，但不包括电子服饰邮件。

1.3 本条款中任何提及法令或法令规定应当解释为提及在相应时候修订、重新制定或续展的该法令或规定。

1.4 本条款的标题仅为方便目的而设立，不应影响其解释。

2. 购买的基础

2.1 生产商同意按照定单的条款（定单副本见本协议附件【 】）生产三万零三百十六（30316）件产品并以每件 20 美元的价格销售；Meringe 亦同意按此条款购买这些产品。

2.2 定单构成 Meringe 根据本协议条款购买产品的要约。

2.3 生产商只有在定单日期后 7 天以书面方式无条件接受订单，订单才有效。

2.4 除非 Meringe 和生产商的授权代表以书面方式达成一致，订单和本协议条款不得更改。

3. 授予许可

3.1 仅为本协议之目的并为使生产商履行定单条款，Meringe 特此授予生产商非排他性地使用规格来生产和包装产品以仅向 Meringe（或 Meringe 直接在订单中书面通知生产商的任何其他方）供应的许可。

3.2 生产商不应对规格做任何变更，并应根据 Meringe 不时修订的规格来生产产品。

3.3 Meringe 在考虑执行成本以及已知的生产商能力之后，可对规格做合理的变更和调整，但是应当将该等变更向生产商做合理的事先通知。

3.4 Meringe 授予生产商非排他性的、不可分割的权力，生产商据此可以在 Meringe 提供的包装材料或产品上，使用和提供 Meringe 的商标，但该授权无论自愿或依照法律，均不可转让或设定权力障碍。

3.5 根据第 3.3 条的规定，生产商不应享有有关 Meringe 任何知识产权或商标的权利，并且除根据本协议外不得使用任何知识产权。

3.6 生产商应按 Meringe 在本协议附件【 】（即本书附件四）授权书中规定的形式和方式在产品上或与产品有关的地方使用商标，不得有其他使用。

3.7 Meringe 不时提供的用于与产品有关用途的艺术品或其标签和包装，以及与之有关的所有知识产权应单独为 Meringe 所有。

3.8 经 Meringe 要求，生产商应采取 Meringe 合理要求的所有措施，以协助 Meringe 保持知识产权和商标的有效性和可执行性，并为此目的签订 Meringe 合理要求的任何正式许可。生产商不得声明其对商标拥有所有权，也不得从事或促使任何他人从事任何损害 Meringe 商标权的行为，或使商标注册的有效性产生争议。

3.9 如果生产商获知任何对知识产权或商标实际的或潜在的侵权，或怀疑该等侵权已经发生或即将发生，其应立即详细通知 Meringe。

4. 产品的生产

4.1 生产商应当严格按照规格、Meringe 发出的订单以及任何其他合理的书面指示或者 Meringe 不时对规格做出的修订的要求生产和包装产品。

4.2 生产商应当根据 Meringe 指示，为生产产品提供所有必要的厂房和设施，包括下列要求(但无损于上述一般性要求)：提供令中国的保险公司满意的干净、安全的存储设施，并能相应地防盗、防火；为按照规格和根据第 8.1 条规定的交货进度生产产品提供充足的劳动力；以及为履行其义务提供必要的、处于良好工作状态的、充足的设备。

4.3 生产商应当将任何缺陷、停机或其他事项或可能干扰其履行义务的事件及时通知 Meringe。

4.4 生产商应当运用合理的谨慎和技巧生产产品。

4.5 生产商应当负责替换任何有缺陷的产品并承担费用，以确保根据第

5.4 条规定符合本协议。

4.6 生产商应当：

4.6.1 保留全部、真实、准确的下列记录：

(i) 生产的产品数量；

(ii) 收到的和库存的包装材料数量；

(iii) 已经使用的包装材料数量；以及

(iv) 已经交付的或者发货的产品数量。

并允许 Meringe 在所有合理的时间检查该等记录，并在 Meringe 书面要求时 3 个工作日内向 Meringe 提交该等记录。

4.6.2 遵守与产品生产并向 Meringe 供应该等产品有关的所有有效的法律、法规，包括但不限于管辖中国境内生产产品、环保和劳动以及海关、税务等任何法律、法规。

4.6.3 除非根据 Meringe 的书面指示，不应交付或发送产品。

4.6.4 没有 Meringe 的书面授权，生产商不应使用产品，或者让其他人使用、生产或直接推销或作为任何其他产品的零件。

5. 规格

5.1 本条款中规定的产品的数量、质量和描述应在定单和 / 或任何 Meringe 向生产商提供的适用的规格中明确，或经 Meringe 书面同意。

5.2 Meringe 向生产商提供的或生产商为 Meringe 特别制定的与协议有关的规格，以及规格涉及的版权、设计权利或任何其他知识产权，都是 Meringe 独占的财产，并且除支付价格以外，生产商应向 Meringe 转让所有这些版权、设计权利和其他知识产权无须任何对价。生产商不得向任何第三方透露或使用任何这些规格，除非这些规格非因生产商的过错或是出于本协议之目的成为了公共知识。

5.3 Meringe 有权在产品的生产、加工过程中或产品发运之前在生产商或任何第三方场所存储期间对产品进行检验和测试。生产商应在营业时间内的所有时候，或者事先由生产商为了检验设备、产品、包装材料以及产品生产的所有方面之目的而安排的其他时间，向 Meringe 提供检验或测试合理所需的所有设施。

5.4 Meringe 应在收到生产商交付的每批产品后 7 日内，对该批产品进行检验和测试（检验标准：【 】）。

5.5 如果经检验或测试，Meringe 认为产品不完全符合本协议、规格及样品，Meringe 可在检验或测试后 7 日内通知生产商，生产商应采取必要措施，以使产品与本协议、规格及样品相符，包括但不限于更换和维修。

5.6 产品应按照 Meringe 的指示以及承运人的任何适用的规定或要求进行标识，并进行妥善包装，确保产品在通常条件下能被完整无损地运抵目的地。

6.产品价格

6.1 产品的价格为定单规定的 20 美元，除非另有约定：

6.1.1 不包括任何适用的增值税（由 Meringe 在收到增值税发票后支付的部分）；以及

6.1.2 包括所有的包装费、打包费、运费、保险费、产品交付至交货地址的费用以及任何增值税以外的关税和除增值税以外的其他税费。

6.2 未经 Meringe 事先书面同意，不得涨价（无论是因为原材料、劳动力、运输的费用增长，还是因为汇率波动或其他原因）。

6.3 无论生产商和 Meringe 之间的销售条款是否约定，Meringe 均有权享受生产商通常为立即付款、大批或大量购买所提供的折扣。

7. 支付条款

7.1 生产商可以根据情况而定，在交付产品时或者其后的任何时间向 Meringe 开出发票，每一份发票应当标明定单的编号。

7.2 除非定单中另有说明，Meringe 应当在其收到正确的发票当月月底起 30 日内，或者 Meringe 接受有关产品起 30 日内支付产品价款，以较迟者为准。

7.3 Meringe 可以用生产商欠 Meringe 的任何款项抵消价格。

7.4 就第 8.1 条规定的首批交货而言，Meringe 应当在收到生产商发票时预付该产品价值的三分之一。该批产品价值的三分之二的余款，应当在收到生产商发票之日起 30 日内支付。

7.5 Meringe 将以即期信用证的形式支付所有货款。

8. 交货

8.1 除非定单另有规定，交货进度如下：

时间	数量	小计
2019 年 6 月 30 日	× ×	× ×
2019 年 7 月 31 日	× ×	× ×
2019 年 8 月 31 日	× ×	× ×
2019 年 9 月 30 日	× ×	× ×
2019 年 10 月 31 日	× ×	× ×
2019 年 11 月 30 日	× ×	30316

除非定单另有要求，产品应在本条规定的日期或期限内发至交货地址，交货应在 Meringe 的营业时间内进行。

8.2 交货时间是本协议的重要条款。

8.3 每次交货都应有标明定单号的装箱记录，并应置于显著位置。

8.4 尽管产品将分批交付，本协议应被视为是不可分割的单一合同，如果任何一批产品迟延交付，那么：

8.4.1 Meringe 保留解除整个协议或本协议的一部分的权利；和 / 或

8.4.2 生产商应承担运回拒收产品的运费；和 / 或

8.4.3 如果 Meringe 接受了迟延交付的产品时，本协议任何部分因为迟延交货而被终止，则 Meringe 保留仅对接受的产品付款的权利，并且有权按照第 7.3 和 8.8 款做出扣除。

8.5 Meringe 有权拒收任何未按照本协议交付的产品，并且，直到 Meringe 在交货后有合理时间检验产品或者其在发现任何产品的潜在瑕疵之后 14 天内（以两者中晚者为准），不应认为 Meringe 已经接受了产品。

8.6 生产商应在交货之前或交货时向 Meringe 提供指导或其他必需的信息，以使 Meringe 能够接受产品。

8.7 无论 Meringe 是否接受产品，Meringe 都无义务退还任何包装材料。

8.8 如果生产商不能按时交货，Meringe 有权按照产品价款 2.5%/ 星期的比例或中国法律允许的有关违约金的最高比例从价款中扣除迟延交货的违约金，或者在 Meringe 已经支付产品价款的情况下，按此等比例向生产商主张违约金，并且 Meringe 有权采取其他救济。双方同意该等违约金比例公平合理地估算了 Meringe 因生产商迟延交货而遭受的损失。

9. 风险和所有权

9.1 产品损坏或灭失的风险自产品按照本协议规定交付给 Meringe 之日起转移至 Meringe。

9.2 产品的所有权自产品交付之日起转移至 Meringe，但如果支付货款早于交货，那么产品所有权应自 Meringe 付款并且产品特定化至本协议项下之日起转移至 Meringe。

10. 担保和责任

10.1 Meringe 签订本协议，是基于对生产商在生产产品方面的专门技术的信赖，因此生产商向 Meringe 担保，产品：

10.1.1 具有令人满意的质量；

10.1.2 符合与产品有关的所有国际标准和可适用的法规；

10.1.3 适用于生产商设定的或其在收到订单时书面获知的用途；

10.1.4 产品在设计，材料和工艺方面无瑕疵；

10.1.5 产品符合有关规格和样品；

10.1.6 产品符合所有与产品销售有关的法定要求和规定。

10.2 生产商向 Meringe 担保所述服务将由合格并经训练的人员完成，谨慎勤勉，并以 Meringe 在任何情况下合理期待的高质量标准提供服务。

10.3 如果任何产品未按照本协议交付，Meringe 除可以采取其他救济外：

10.3.1 有权要求生产商根据本协议在 7 天内提供更换的产品；

10.3.2 不管 Meringe 是否已经要求生产商维修或更换产品，Meringe 有权选择按生产商违约解除本协议并要求退还已经支付的价款。

10.4 生产商应对 Meringe 因如下原因导致或与如下原因有关的遭受或支付的所有责任、损失、损害、成本和支出（包括法律支出）提供完全的补偿：

10.4.1 违反生产商所作的任何与产品有关的担保；

10.4.2 有关产品或其进口，使用或转售侵害任何他人的专利、版权、设计权利、商标或其他知识产权的任何主张，除非该等主张是因为遵守由 Meringe 提供的规格而引起的。

10.4.3 《消费者权益保护法》规定的有关产品的任何责任；

10.4.4 生产商或其职员、代理商、分包商在提供和交付产品时的任何行为或疏忽；

10.4.5 任何生产商的人员有关履行服务方面的作为或疏忽。

11. 合同终止

11.1 Meringe 有权在不迟于发货前 48 小时通知生产商取消全部或部分产品的订单，而无须承担任何责任。

11.2 如果有如下情况，Meringe 可随时通知生产商终止本协议而无须承担责任：

11.2.1 生产商破产或清算（为合并或重组而进行的清算除外）或受行政处罚；

11.2.2 他项权人获得生产商财产或资产的所有权，或已为生产商的财产或资产指定了接受者；

11.2.3 生产商停止经营或威胁停止经营；

11.2.4 Meringe 合理获知任何上述事件即将发生并通知了生产商。

12. 其他条款

12.1 Meringe 是一个公司集团的成员，Meringe 可以自行履行本协议项下的义务，行使本协议项下的权利，也可以通过集团的其他成员履行和行使这些义务和权利，在后一种情况下，这些成员的任何行为或疏忽应被视为 Meringe 的行为或疏忽。

12.2 订单是专为生产商发出的，生产商不得向任何人转让或宣称转让其任何权利，或转包其在本协议项下的任何义务。

12.3 本协议条款要求或允许的由一方发给另一方的通知应以书面方式发至另一方的注册地址或主要营业地，或通知方在当时按照本条规定被告知的其他地址。

12.4 Meringe 对生产商的任何违约的放弃均不应被认为是对以后的任何相同违约或其他违约的放弃。

12.5 如果本协议任何条款被任何法院或其他有权部门认为全部或部分无效或不可执行，其他条款和该条款的剩余部分的效力不受影响。

12.6 本协议或产品销售产生的或与本协议或产品销售有关的任何争议应按照联合国国际贸易法委员会即时有效的仲裁规则在中国仲裁。仲裁由独任仲裁员进行。独任仲裁员由双方共同指定或在双方未共同指定时由中国国际经济贸易仲裁委员会按其规则指定。仲裁裁决是终局的。仲裁费用由败诉方承担，除非仲裁庭另有决定。

12.7 本协议受中华人民共和国颁布的和公众所知悉的法律管辖。

12.8 双方同意由中山美霖服饰有限公司代表 Meringe 签署本协议。

12.9 本协议正本一式三份，Meringe 持两份，生产商持一份。

在此见证，双方在本协议文首所志日期签署本协议。

泰平服装实业公司　　　　　　中山美霖服饰有限公司

姓名：　　　　　　　　　　　姓名：

职务：　　　　　　　　　　　职务：

代表 MERINGE Holdings (Pte) Ltd. 签署

附件四

授权书

【日期】

敬启者：

事由：生产商授权书

我方——MERINGE Holding (Pte) Ltd.，一家在新加坡注册的有限公司，注册地址【 】——在此委托泰平服装实业公司，一家按照中华人民共和国法律组建的公司，主要营业地【 　】，作为我方有效的授权生产商和供应商，开展如下活动：

生产我方随时以书面方式指定的产品，使用我方商标【 　】和/或我方版权作品或其他知识产权。

我方在此授予上述制造商采取和实施如同我方出于自己的目的和意图所采取和实施的所有必需的、必要的和适当的行动，以完全满足生产和供应上述产品的要求。并且经授权的生产商应拥有按照我方随时做出的书面指示使用我方的版权作品和商标的权利。

我方在此承认并确认上述生产商或其授权代表可以按照本授权书合法地处理与生产和供应产品有关的所有事项。

本协议一直有效，直至我方书面撤销。

接受日期：

泰平服装实业公司   MERINGE Holdings (Pte) Ltd.

姓名：   姓名：

职务：   职务：

Index

Ad hoc arbitration: 14、29、102–107、235、236、327

Arbitration Law of the People's Republic of China: 102、119、273、290

Arbitrators' Liability System: 187、190、193

Arb–Med: 74、81、172

CISG: 21、22、31–33、335

Competence–Competence Principle: 289

Disclosure: 91、92、93、175

Foreign related awards: 227

Future of Chinese Arbitration Law: 325

Good faith principle: 251

Hearing both sides: 337

HKSAR: 248、249、258、324

Incapacity: 135、144、255

Invalid arbitration agreement: 135、255

Key Commonalities: 287

Legally exempt: 187

Loving One's Neighbor: 339

Maintenance of Cooperative Relations: 175

Metaverse Business: 203、204

Minimum Court Intervention: 289

Party autonomy: 49、59、62、76、80、137、141、335

Procedural irregularities: 251

Pro-enforcement approach: 248、250、255

Proper law of the arbitration agreement: 272

Public policy: 140、208、230、256、257、275、301、325

Reasons for non-enforcement: 229

Seat of arbitration: 211、269、270、272、326

Setting aside: 190、275、286、291

Singapore Mediation Convention: 173、178、180

Taiwan Arbitration Legislation: 299、302

The composition of the arbitral authority: 77、145、233

The Singapore court: 271、275、276

UNCITRAL Model Law: 48、51、78、82、93、117、268、275、289、291

中华人民共和国仲裁法: 7、8、110、264、265、267、282、311

仲裁员责任制度: 181、184

元宇宙业务: 194、195

台湾仲裁立法: 293、295、296

新加坡法院: 263、266、267

调解制度: 164、165、169、170

香港特区: 185、247、260、282